The Secret Connexion

The Secret Connexion

Causation, Realism, and David Hume

REVISED EDITION
Galen Strawson

I am not such a sceptic as you may, perhaps, imagine.
(Hume, letter to Stewart, February 1754)

OXFORD
UNIVERSITY PRESS

OXFORD
UNIVERSITY PRESS

Great Clarendon Street, Oxford, OX2 6DP,
United Kingdom

Oxford University Press is a department of the University of Oxford.
It furthers the University's objective of excellence in research, scholarship,
and education by publishing worldwide. Oxford is a registered trade mark of
Oxford University Press in the UK and in certain other countries

First published 1989
First issued in paperback with corrections 1992
This edition published 2014

Impression: 1

Published in the United States of America by Oxford University Press
198 Madison Avenue, New York, NY 10016, United States of America

British Library Cataloguing in Publication Data
Data available

Library of Congress Control Number: 2014933805

ISBN 978-0-19-960584-2 (Hbk.)
      978-0-19-960585-9 (Pbk.)

As printed and bound by
CPI Group (UK) Ltd, Croydon, CR0 4YY

[N]ature has kept us at a great distance from all her secrets, and has afforded us only the knowledge of a few superficial qualities of objects; while she conceals from us those powers and principles on which the influence of these objects entirely depends.

[W]e are ignorant of those powers and forces, on which [the] regular course and succession of objects totally depends.

[E]xperience only teaches us, how one event constantly follows another; without instructing us in the secret connexion, which binds them together, and renders them inseparable.

(Enquiry 32–3/4.16, 55/5.22, 66/7.13)

Preface to the First Edition

Does Hume endorse a regularity theory of causation? The view that he does is very widely held—it seems that it is still the standard view. But there seems to be no evidence for it in the first *Enquiry*—whatever one thinks about the *Treatise*.

My doubts began when I started teaching the first *Enquiry* at an elementary level at Oxford in 1980. This discussion of Hume grew directly from that teaching. I finished the first draft convinced that I was heroically alone in my doubts, but I was quite wrong. Three works deserve particular mention. Craig's *The Mind of God and the Works of Man* (1987) refutes the commonly accepted conception of Hume's philosophical position. Wright, in *The Sceptical Realism of David Hume* (1983), and Livingston, in *Hume's Philosophy of Common Life* (1984), also argue powerfully against it. As far as the question of causation is concerned, they argue not only that Hume is not a regularity theorist, but also, as here, that he believes in the existence of something like natural necessity—in the existence of *causal power* conceived of in some essentially non-regularity-theory way.[1]

The fact remains: the view that Hume held a regularity theory of causation is still the standard view.[2] It is still worth arguing against. As Beauchamp and Rosenberg say, '[al]most all recent writers on causation believe that Hume holds a pure regularity theory of causation' (1981: 31). As Blackburn remarks, Hume has 'been shamefully abused by many commentators and their victims' (1984: 211).

This is not just a book about Hume. It also argues directly against the regularity theory of causation, which has taken on a life of its own. Chapters 5, 8, and 22.2 form a discussion of the regularity theory of causation which is independent of the material on Hume. Chapter 23, on the meaning of 'cause', is independent both of this discussion of the regularity theory of causation and of the main discussion of Hume. Chapter 7 on the notion of the ultimate nature of reality, together with its Appendix, can also be read independently of the discussion of Hume.

---

[1] Throughout this book I use the expression 'causal power' to mean 'causal power conceived of in some essentially non-regularity-theory way'.

[2] For recent expressions of the view, see e.g. Woolhouse: 'Hume's conclusion [is] that so far as the external objects which are causes and effects are concerned there is only constant conjunction' (1988: 149); so far as the 'operations of natural bodies' are concerned, 'regularity and constant conjunction are all that exist' (p. 150). See also O'Hear: Humeans hold that there is not 'any more to causality than 'regularity of succession'' (1985: 60). 'The Humean attitude to causality is...that there is nothing in the cause...that mean[s] the effect has to follow' (p. 61). See also Kripke: 'If Hume is right,...even if God were to look at [two causally related] events, he would discern nothing relating them other than that that one succeeds the other' (1982: 67). Hamlyn, by contrast, scrupulously avoids this error, in his *History of Western Philosophy* (1987). So does Schacht (who restricts his discussion to the *Enquiry*) in his *Classical Modern Philosophers: Descartes to Kant* (1984).

I also discuss a number of other questions about meaning, understanding, knowledge, and existence. These are questions which are naturally and vividly raised by the study of Hume—questions about the relations between semantics, epistemology, and ontology and metaphysics. I defend—where I do not assume—a straightforwardly realist position on these issues (see especially Chapters 7 and 12). Virtually all the worthwhile features of the current debate about them are present in the seventeenth- and eighteenth-century debate.[3]

Someone who believed that the regularity theory of causation was true, and came to the conclusion that Hume never held it, would probably not much enjoy writing a book that tried to show that this was so. But if one thinks that the regularity theory of causation is (in its standard version) metaphysically fantastic one sees things differently. One's task is to clear a great philosopher of a damaging charge, and to show that his attitude to the question of causation is in most respects right. This is how I see it.

The foundations of the case for saying that Hume believes in causal power or natural necessity can be established without any close consideration of what he says about causation, and I try to do this (among other things) in Part 1. One problem with this approach is that the more detailed analyses of Hume's discussion of causation in Parts 2 and 3 (which consider the *Treatise* and the *Enquiry* respectively) may then come as an anticlimax. I have accordingly signalled short cuts at various points throughout the book for those who want to get on to Part 2 or Part 3 quickly.

A period of illness in the spring of 1984 gave me time to reread Hume and organize the quotations used in this book. The main text was written up in the spring and summer of 1987, and for comments on what I wrongly took to be the final version I am most grateful to John Cottingham, Edward Craig, William Jordan, Paul Snowdon, and P. F. Strawson. For some helpful conversations, and for contributions to a class I gave on Hume at Oxford in the Hilary Term of 1988, I would like to thank Thomas Baldwin, Bob Hargrave, Dan Isaacson, Martha Klein, John Roe, Helen Steward, Luigi Turco, and David Womersley. For comments of a non-philosophical kind I am grateful to Angela Blackburn, Redmond O'Hanlon, Andrew Rosenheim, and finally to José Strawson.

---

[3] This book contains relatively little discussion of the intellectual context in which Hume wrote (Kant, rather than any of Hume's contemporaries or immediate predecessors, provides the other main source of historical reference). For a good account of Malebranche's influence on Hume's thought about causation, see McCracken 1983: 257–69.

Preface to the Paperback Edition

I wrote this book very fast. The speed of writing shows in the tone and in the excessively numerous and sometimes intrusive footnotes. I have not, however, done any major rewriting for this paperback edition. Instead I have made a few corrections, a few small cuts, and a few small additions. The most substantial changes occur in the paragraph on pp. 56-7, on page 201 in note 5, on page 203 which has a new note 8, and on page 210 which has a new note 8. (These page references are to the first edition.)

As remarked in the original Preface, Chapters 5, 8, and 22.2 of this book present an attack on the 'regularity' theory of causation which is independent of the discussion of Hume. One objection to the attack is so common that it is worth mentioning here. Briefly, it claims that one must in the end admit that the regularity of the world's behaviour is a 'brute' fact, and hence admit that the regularity theory of causation is true. For if one tries to deny that the regularity of the world is a brute fact, and proposes that there is something x which is other than the regularity of the world, and is the reason for the regularity of the world, then one will need an account of why x is itself regular in its underwriting of the regularity of the world. And either one will have to say that x's regularity of operation is itself a brute fact, or one will have to embark on a regress which can be stopped only by saying that there is *something* whose regularity of operation is a brute fact. Hence the regularity theory of causation—or something like it—must be true.

I tried to answer this sort of objection on pp. 91-2 of this book. I'm not sure what 'brute' means, but I'm not worried by the brutishness of the regularity of the world so long as it does not have the consequence that the regularity of the world is, as it continues from moment to moment, and from year to year, a continuous fluke or chance matter. With hindsight, I think that the best statement of the correct alternative to the regularity theory that the book contains is on pp. 225-6 below). I made a third brief attempt to say what is wrong with the regularity theory in a paper called 'The Contingent Reality of Natural Necessity' [1991; included here as an Appendix to Chapter 22].

The 1996 and 2003 paperback impressions incorporate a few minor corrections, a more substantial change to note 30 on page 50, and a new Index of Passages from Hume.

Preface to the Revised Edition

In this new edition of *The Secret Connexion* I've made almost no substantive alterations to the book's original content, because I haven't read anything that has given me reason to doubt its main arguments and conclusions. I have, however, thinned the text throughout, reworked Chapters 14 and 15 on the *Treatise*, and added quite a number of further thoughts and quotations. The original Appendix A is now an appendix to Chapter 6. Appendix B is now an appendix to Chapter 7 (reproduced essentially unchanged, although it later grew into a separate paper (Strawson 2002)). The original Appendix C, a summary of the overall position, has been dropped. It was superseded in 2000 by a paper, 'David Hume: Objects and Power', from which I've here incorporated some considerations about the relative importance of the *Treatise* and the *Enquiry* in assessing Hume's considered view (pp. 10–13). I've also included as an appendix to Chapter 22 a reply to a helpful objection to *The Secret Connexion* raised by Nicholas Everitt in 1991.

Many now talk of 'Old Hume' as opposed to 'New Hume'.[1] According to the supporters of Old Hume, Hume holds that 'even if God were to look at [two causally related] events, he would discern nothing relating them other than that one succeeds the other'.[2] On this view, Hume holds a metaphysical regularity theory of causation, according to which things in reality succeed each other in a regular fashion, but *nothing ever really causally influences anything else in any way at all*. All supporters of New Hume deny that he holds this view. Some go further and follow John Wright, as I do, in holding that Hume is a 'sceptical realist'.

The question of what it means to say that Hume is a realist about causal power is part of the subject of this book, but one thing that is clear is that to be a realist about causal power is to hold that there really is such a thing as causal influence. That is, there is something more in reality, causally speaking, than one thing's just following another, even if all we can ever actually empirically detect, strictly speaking, is one thing regularly following another.

According to the sceptical realist view of Hume, he's not only a sceptical realist about causal power, but also about physical objects like tables and chairs. He's not concerned to deny categorically that things that we ordinarily suppose to exist don't exist. Real sceptics don't do that. His general, sceptical, empiricist, philosophical

---

[1] The terms derive from Kenneth Winkler's paper 'The New Hume' (1991).

[2] This is Kripke's accurate report (1982: 67) of the view of Hume that prevailed thirty years ago. Jackson in 1977 invites us to 'consider...the possible world where every particular fact is as it is in our world, but there are no causes or effects at all. Every regular conjunction is an accidental one, not a causal one. Call it, for obvious reasons, the Hume world' (1977: 5). See also p. vii n.2, p. 13 n.8, and p. 22 n.2. Some who take themselves to be supporters of 'old Hume' now deny that this used to be the standard view.

point is simply that we can form no empirically respectable, clear, and distinct conception of the 'real nature' of concrete reality (other than the concrete reality that consists in the existence of our experiences). We can't hope to have insight into its 'real nature and operations' (63, 638/1.2.5.25, 1.2.5.26), its 'ultimate original qualities' (xvii/Int§8), its 'ultimate principles' (xviii/Int§10). We can't hope to have insight into the 'internal structure or operating principle of objects' (169/1.3.14.29), 'the nature of bodies' (64/1.2.5.26), 'the essence and construction of bodies' (660/Abs§32). And 'the essence of the mind [is] equally unknown to us with that of external bodies' (xvii/Int§8).

The terms 'Old' and 'New' are unfortunate, for 'New Hume' is simply Hume—but also because the 'New Hume' interpretation isn't new. As Helen Beebee observes, Norman Kemp Smith classifies as a supporter of 'New Hume' in his 1941 book *The Philosophy of David Hume* (Beebee 2006: 173). Kant was equally clear in 1783 that Hume didn't deny the existence of causal power (Kant 1783: Preface).

Even if this were not so, the terms would be obsolescent. Don Garrett has recently argued that so far as the textual evidence is concerned, there's nothing to favour one of the views decisively over the other (Garrett 2009). It may be that supporters of the old Hume are now in the minority (at least outside Canada). It's hard to be sure, for many who take themselves to support 'Old Hume' have shifted their ground considerably over the last thirty years.

One of the ironies of the debate has been that some 'Old Hume' supporters have suggested that 'New Hume' supporters, being themselves realists about things like objects and causation, have been motivated to interpret Hume in such a way that he agrees with them. The irony is that almost all those who have argued in this way have tended to be 'anti-realists' of some stripe or other, determined to maintain an interpretation of Hume that agrees with their anti-realism.

'Old Humeans' have also charged that 'New Humeans' (like myself) rely on isolated quotations to support their view. Again this seems back to front, although it's true that the three quotations on p. v that form the epigraph to this book suffice, in effect, to establish the 'New Hume' case. The 'Old Hume' interpretation relies principally on overliteral readings of a relatively small number of passages from the *Treatise*, whose publication Hume later regretted (see p. 10); the deep drift of Hume's epistemology and metaphysics is 'New Humean' to the core.

I'm very grateful to Peter Momtchiloff for encouraging me to produce this new edition, and to Keith Turausky for reading through the whole text with care and insight.

Contents

Abbreviations and Conventions

When I cite a work by someone other than Hume I give the first publication date or estimated date of composition, while the page reference is to the published version listed in the bibliography. For Hume's *Treatise* I give a page reference to the Selby-Bigge and Nidditch edition followed by the paragraph reference in the Norton and Norton edition: a typical *Treatise* reference is '233/1.4.5.5'. For the first *Enquiry* I give the Selby-Bigge page reference followed by paragraph reference in the Beauchamp edition: a typical *Enquiry* reference is '163/12.34'. In the case of the Abstract, the Appendix, and the Introduction to the *Treatise*, I refer to their seventh paragraphs (e.g.) as 'Abs§7' and 'App§7' and 'Int§7' respectively. In the case of Hume's *Dialogues Concerning Natural Religion* I give two page references. The first is to the second edition, published in 1779; the second is to the Kemp Smith edition. I use 'L' to refer to Hume's anonymously published *Letter From A Gentleman To His Friend In Edinburgh*, which he published anonymously in 1745. 'C1', 'C2', and 'C3' refer respectively to the three volumes of correspondence published by Oxford University Press: *The Letters of David Hume* volumes 1 and 2 (1932), and *New Letters of David Hume* (1978).

I refer to Locke's *Essay Concerning Human Understanding* as 'Essay', to Berkeley's *Treatise Concerning the Principles of Human Knowledge* as 'Principles', and to Kant's *Critique of Pure Reason* as 'Critique'.

Within quotations I mark my emphases by *italics*, and the author's by **bold italics**. Bold italics are also used to emphasize terms that are italicized for other reasons. Simple number references are to chapters of this book.

PART 1

Meaning, Scepticism, and Reality

1

Introduction

One response to the claim that Hume believes in causal power is that it's obviously true and entirely uncontroversial. 'Of course he does. The fact that he does is a principal consequence of his central doctrine of "natural belief"[1]—his doctrine about the sorts of things we can't help believing in "common" or everyday life, irrespective of our philosophical conclusions. He has no doubt that we can't help believing in causal power, just as we can't help believing in truly external physical objects.'

This point is important, because the force of Hume's doctrine of natural belief is often underestimated. But I hope to show that Hume takes the existence of something like natural necessity or causal power for granted not only in common life but also as a philosopher.

This too may be said to be obvious: 'Of course he does. One of his deepest and most characteristic philosophical claims is that true sceptics must be sceptical of their own sceptical conclusions, and that a philosophy which abandons the fundamental tenets of ordinary, instinctive, common-sense, natural belief in favour of some supposedly superior set of tenets—moving upward and outward (or downward and inward) in a complication of negatively sceptical or positively metaphysical refinements—is likely to remain merely "extravagant" (214/1.4.2.50), incredible, and superficial.'

This too may be granted. For even if it's true—it will surprise many—there's still something important left to say. In what follows it will be argued that the claim that Hume believes in real causal power—not only in common life but also as a philosopher—is not deducible only in some merely general fashion, as above. It's not deducible just from his general endorsement of the view that we ought as philosophers to accept the deliverances of natural belief (or at least some suitably qualified version of them). Rather, the truth of the claim that Hume believes in causal power is deducible from the details of his discussion of causation considered independently of his doctrine of natural belief: the most direct evidence for the view that Hume believes in causal power is that he standardly takes its existence for granted in his discussions of causation in the *Treatise* and in the *Enquiry*, making essential

---

[1] In Kemp Smith's terms (1941: ch. 21).

appeal to the idea that it exists in contexts that contain no relevant trace of irony and no explicit appeal to the notion of natural belief.[2]

Some will grant that it follows from Hume's doctrine of 'natural belief' that there's a sense in which he believes in causal power, while insisting that there remains a crucial sense in which he holds (as a philosopher) that causation in nature is definitely just regular succession, and that therefore there is no sort of causal power or force in nature. Against this, I'll argue that Hume believes in causal power independently of natural belief. It never occurs to him to question the existence of causal power—i.e. to question the idea that there must be and is something about reality given which it is ordered and regular in the way that it is—even in his most extravagantly sceptical (or Pyrrhonian) mode.

Perhaps it ought to have occurred to him; but he never got round to such a thought. He was, in his discussion of causation, principally concerned to refute contemporary philosophers who believed in the *intelligibility* of causal power. They believed we could somehow grasp or understand its true or essential nature considered as a concretely existing phenomenon: many of them believed that we could know for sure that all causal power is ultimately mental in character. Given such opponents, Hume was concerned to argue that we know nothing about the true nature of causal power and have no genuinely contentful conception of its nature, and with explaining how it is that we are so very strongly and so very naturally inclined to suppose that we do. He was not—never—concerned to argue that it didn't exist.

At the end of his famous discussion of objects, in section 1.4.2 of the *Treatise*, Hume concludes that although there are no good rational grounds for believing in external objects distinct from perceptions,[3] nevertheless we ought to do so. He continues as follows: 'but to be ingenuous, I feel myself *at present* of a quite contrary sentiment.' He has at this point managed to disrupt the power of his natural belief in external objects by hard sceptical philosophical reflection, at least temporarily; and, having done so, he is temporarily 'inclin'd to repose no faith at all' in the existence of external objects (217/1.4.2.56). The present suggestion is that he never considers the parallel move with respect to causal power. He never considers the suggestion that one may after hard sceptical philosophical reflection interrupt one's natural belief in the existence of something in reality given which reality is regular in the way that it is, and so come (at least temporarily) to have no belief at all in the

---

[2] Cf. e.g. Part 2, quotations (1)–(7), (9), (23), Part 3, quotations (1)–(4), (6)–(11), (13)–(18), (23), (24), (26)–(28), (30), (38)–(40).

[3] 'Perception' is Hume's general word for a mental content. Perceptions subdivide into *impressions* and *ideas*, i.e., roughly, into sensory experiences and other feelings on the one hand, and concepts and thoughts on the other hand. Impressions are in turn subdivided into impressions of *sensation*—sensory experiences—and impressions of *reflexion*—e.g. emotions, feelings of love or disgust, etc. All three words ('perception', 'impression', 'idea') can be used to refer both to concretely occurring mental contents (actual sensations, actual deployments of concepts) and to sensations and concepts considered as types, i.e. independently of any actual occurrence.

existence of any such thing. He always takes it for granted that there is such a thing, and insists only that we have no real grasp of its nature, despite our conviction to the contrary.[4]

This difference of attitude—with regard to objects on the one hand and causal power on the other—might be thought to be an oversight on his part. But it's eminently defensible. For belief in something like natural necessity—i.e. belief in there being *something about reality in virtue of which it is regular in the way that it is*—is far less open to serious sceptical doubt than belief in external physical objects. For even if one abandons belief in external physical objects and adopts some kind of idealist view of objects, holding that all reality is mental in some sense, one still has as much reason as ever to suppose that there is something about reality in virtue of which it is regular in the way that it is; something in what one calls 'objects' which is the reason why they behave regularly in the way they do.

Even if this natural view is questionable in some way (see e.g. pp. 24, 205 below), I think that there is little doubt that Hume would have conceded its force.[5]

It's an extraordinary fact that so many philosophers have seen fit to doubt the existence of some sort of natural necessity in reality while not doubting the reality of external objects, conceived of in something like the ordinary everyday way. This gets things exactly the wrong way round. The nature of objects may be very unlike what we suppose it to be, but the belief that there is something about reality in virtue of which it is regular in the way that it is remains plausible *whatever* the nature of objects, so long as we retain any sort of conventional understanding of time.

'So long as we retain any sort of conventional understanding of time': there's a real question about what force is left to the idea of natural necessity if one adopts a four-dimensionalist or 'block universe' conception of reality, according to which everything in reality, throughout all time, is (as it were) already laid out in full in one great block—so that there is, in some solid if difficult sense, just a great big given pattern. These matters extend beyond my competence, and they are I take it irrelevant to the discussion of Hume. But I think we can characterize a four-dimensionalist notion of natural necessity without too much difficulty. Consider all the different arrangements of the stuff of the world that would result from different *initial* arrangements of the stuff of the world (I'm assuming we can make sense of the idea of an initial state of the world given a four-dimensionalist conception of reality). For natural necessity to exist in the four-dimensionalists' world is simply for it to be true that a certain pattern of structural invariance holds across all these different arrangements. The

---

[4] It may be said that, so far as natural belief in causation is concerned, the most fundamental description of what we can't help, for Hume, is one that speaks of our natural, non-rational habits of expectation, our instinctive reactions to the world as if it were governed by natural necessity—these being things which we can be said to share with languageless animals. But we are fully linguistically equipped creatures, concept-exercising creatures in the strongest sense, and in our case natural belief also (and distinctively) takes the form of fully linguistically expressible belief in causal power or forces.

[5] This will perhaps be obvious to anyone familiar with his *Dialogues Concerning Natural Religion*.

existence of natural necessity is revealed in a certain structural invariance that characterizes the temporal dimension of reality in particular. Natural necessity in the four-dimensionalists' world, then, is that feature of reality that would be revealed in the structural similarity that all these worlds would have in this particular respect.[6]

Before beginning on the main business, let me say that this book is not restricted to an examination of Hume's metaphysics and philosophy of mind, and is selective in its discussion of them. It's principally concerned to examine his realist presuppositions, and pays little attention to some of the matters that most concerned him, such as his analysis of the nature of belief. It bypasses the standard discussion of his views on objects, and the notorious discussion of the precise content of his famous two definitions of cause. And before continuing I would like to mention four other aspects of Hume's philosophy about which I will say little.

The first of these is his 'projectivism'—his account of the mind's propensity to 'spread itself upon external objects' (167/1.3.14.25), and so to believe that it is reacting to objective features in the world when it is in fact reacting to features it has itself 'projected' onto the world in such a way that they appear to it as mind-independent, objective features.[7] This is an important aspect of Hume's philosophy, and is duly mentioned in the discussion (in 10) of how Hume applies his theory of ideas to the particular case of the idea of causation, but it has no major part to play in the present argument.

The second is Hume's denial that the proposition *every event must have a cause* is either self-evident or provable a priori; the denial, in his terms, that '*whatever begins to exist, must have a cause of existence*' is either 'intuitively or demonstratively certain' (78–9/1.3.3.1–3). I won't discuss this, but it's worth quoting from a letter which Hume wrote to John Stewart in 1754:

But allow me to tell you, that I never asserted so absurd a Proposition as *that anything might arise without a Cause*: I only maintained, that our Certainty of the Falshood of that Proposition proceeded neither from Intuition nor Demonstration; but from another Source.[8]

---

[6] Philip Goff (in correspondence) has made the simpler suggestion that there is nothing incoherent about a four-dimensionalist holding that certain events 'timelessly' happen *because* certain other events 'timelessly' happen.

[7] 'Projectivism' is of course also central to Hume's moral philosophy. It's sometimes said that Hume's metaphysics is posterior to, and must be understood in the light of, his projectivist moral philosophy, but Hume's metaphysical writings must be judged in their own right.

[8] 1754: 187. Kemp Smith, Livingston and Wright, op. cit., all quote this revealing passage (Kemp Smith quotes the whole letter on pp. 412–13). On the question of what Hume thought this source was, it may be suggested that he had no certain view, or that he took it to be 'natural belief'. One objection to this last suggestion is that natural belief isn't a source of genuine certainty, even if it involves subjective conviction. The letter to Stewart continues: '*That Caesar existed, that there is such an Island as Sicily*; for these Propositions, I affirm, we have no demonstrative nor intuitive Proof. Woud you infer that I deny their Truth, or even their Certainty? There are many different kinds of Certainty . . .'. Cf. Descartes's discussion of 'moral certainty', *Principles* 4.205 (1644: 289–90).

It may be objected that this isn't strictly speaking true of the *Treatise* as it stands, given that Hume repeatedly claims that whatever is imaginable is possible, and that 'a beginning of existence [without a cause] is plainly possible for the imagination' (80/1.3.3.3). Two points may be made in reply.

The first and weaker point is that even if this 1754 comment isn't true of Hume's earlier work (the *Treatise* was published in 1739–40, and the first edition of the first *Enquiry* in 1748), it is his considered position. It's a position which is particularly striking to any student of Kant, given Kant's view that one of the fundamental tasks of philosophy, made vivid by Hume, is precisely to provide an adequate account of the source of certainty of this kind.[9]

The second and stronger point is that there is no reason to think that this 1754 comment isn't true of Hume's earlier work. When he says that whatever is imaginable is possible, his point is simply that so far as *reason* goes there's no *logical* (or indeed metaphysical) contradiction in the idea that something might arise without a cause. It doesn't follow that he thinks that such a thing is in fact possible, physically possible, as things are—now that the world has begun, as it were. And he doesn't think this. He thinks, as does Philo in the *Dialogues Concerning Natural Religion*, that 'Every thing is surely governed by steady, inviolable laws' (*Dialogues* 125/174). His claim, again, is just that we can't appeal either to reason or to 'intuition' in the attempt to justify our conviction—certainty—that nothing can arise without a cause. Kant clearly understands Hume's meaning, and sympathizes with him for having been misunderstood: 'The question was not whether the concept of cause is correct . . . , for this Hume had never held in doubt; but whether it is thought a priori by reason' (1783: Preface).

It would be a great mistake to think that the stress Hume lays on this claim confirms the view that he adopts a regularity theory of causation, as this is ordinarily understood. Irritated as he was by the suggestion that he asserted 'so absurd a Proposition as *that anything might [in fact, and as things are] arise without a Cause*', he would have been equally irritated by the allegation that he asserted that regularity is definitely all there is to causation in reality, i.e. that there is definitely nothing about the nature of reality in virtue of which it is regular in the way that it is. His comments on his two definitions of cause suffice to make this clear (see 21).

The third thing about which I will say little is this: whatever one thinks about the claim that Hume believes in the existence of causal power in 'the world', where 'the world' is conceived of as independent of or external to the mind, it seems that he is committed to belief in the existence of something like natural necessity as governing the operations of the mind.[10]

The fourth thing about which I will say little is Hume's famous discussion of induction. He argues that reason cannot justify reliance on inductive argument. This

---

[9] In Kant's terms, the general task is to show how synthetic a priori truths are possible.
[10] See e.g. Strawson 2011.

fact, however, provides no grounds for supposing that he adopts a regularity theory of causation. Conviction that the world is governed by causal powers or natural necessity is fully compatible with the correct view that *reason* cannot prove this fact, or guarantee the trustworthiness of inductive argument. To think that Hume's discussion of induction supports the view that he held a regularity theory of causation is an elementary error, but it is perhaps not uncommon, and the question is touched on in an aside in 9, and more directly in 17.

2

The 'Humean' view of causation; and an exegetical principle

What is it to be a 'Humean' about causation? I'll give a widely accepted answer to this question, and argue that Hume wasn't a 'Humean'. That is, I'll argue that the standard account of Hume's views on causation is incorrect. The 'Humean' account of causation is a classic example of that magnificent contradiction in terms, positivist metaphysics, and it seems worth trying to rebut its attribution to Hume in detail, quotation by quotation. Perhaps the best reason for not attributing it to Hume is that he is too good a philosopher to hold such an implausible view: I'll argue against the 'Humean' account of causation as well as its attribution to Hume.[1]

The argument will have a fairly narrow focus, and the central points will be repeated in a variety of ways. One way to defend the inclusion of so much illustrative detail might be to endorse Kant's approval of Abbot Terrasson's remark that 'if the size of a volume be measured not by the number of its pages but by the time required for mastering it, it can be said of many a book *that it would be much shorter if it were not so short*'. But Kant's position is more complex: aids to clarity are sometimes counterproductive, and 'we can say with equal justice *that many a book would have been much clearer if it had not made such an effort to be clear*'.[2] Perhaps only love of the text can justify the quantity of quotations offered in support of the main claim of this book, and the repetitions they occasion. It explains them even if it can't justify them.

---

[1] Are 'Humeans' about causation really Brownians? Brown writes that 'the invariableness of antecedence and consequence, which is represented as only the *sign* of causation, is itself the *only essential circumstance* of causation', and that '*cause* . . . simply and truly is, only another name for the immediate invariable antecedent of an event' (1805–1818: xii–xiii, 196–7). Kemp Smith claims that 'Thomas Brown is the first, and outstanding, exponent of the uniformity view of causation' (1941: 91 n.), and Psillos concurs: 'we might say that [Brown] was the first defender of a pure and simple regularity theory of causation' (2011: 221). At crucial points, however, Brown qualifies claims of the kind just quoted with remarks to the effect that this is all causation can be to us—allowing that there may be something more. He's concerned with the notion of 'a cause, in the fullest definition which it philosophically admits' (1818: 17), and his criterion of philosophical admissibility appears to be the same as Hume's: clarity and distinctness of content of the sort conferred by proper empirical grounding in experience. There is no decisive reason to suppose that Brown thinks that reality doesn't and can't extend further than properly empirically grounded human conception. (On Brown see also Wright 2005, Harris 2005b, Dixon 2010: 11–16.)

[2] *Critique* Axix. *Exemplum docet, exempla obscurant*, to quote an older adage.

The discussion presupposes some knowledge of Hume. I don't think it's more than what is expected of a second-year undergraduate, and I hope the argument will interest more professional readers. The main case rests on the *Enquiry*, as it should, given the 'Advertisement' Hume prefixed to the 1777 edition:

Most of the principles, and reasonings, contained in this volume, were published in a work in three volumes, called *A Treatise of Human Nature*: a work which the author projected before he left college, and which he wrote and published not long after. But not finding it successful, he was sensible of his error in going to the press too early, and he cast the whole anew in the following pieces, where some negligences in his former reasoning and more in the expression, are, he hopes, corrected. Yet several writers, who have honoured the author's philosophy with answers, have taken care to direct all their batteries against the juvenile work, which the author never acknowledged, and have affected to triumph in any advantages, which, they imagined, they had obtained over it: *a practice very contrary to all rules of candour and fair-dealing, and a strong instance of those polemical artifices, which a bigotted zeal thinks itself authorized to employ.* Henceforth, the author desires, that the following pieces *may alone be regarded as containing his philosophical sentiments and principles* (2/Advertisement).

These are strong words for Hume, and they express hurt. Responding anonymously in 1745 to an early attack on the *Treatise*, he described the quotations from the *Treatise* given by his 'accuser'—which read like a summary of what many for most of the twentieth century regarded as Hume's essential views—as 'maimed excerpts' (L3) selected with 'a degree of unfairness which appears to me altogether astonishing' (L20). The accuser (probably William Wishart) used Hume's words, but 'pervert[ed] them and misrepresent[ed] them in the grossest way in the world' (C3: 15). Hume's public response was to write the *Enquiry* (1748). He wrote it to counteract the misinterpretation of the *Treatise*, and to correct certain mistakes:

The philosophical principles are the same in both: but I was carried away by the heat of youth and invention to publish too precipitately....I have repented my haste a hundred, and a hundred times' (C1: 158)....I...acknowledge...a very great mistake in conduct, viz my publishing at all the Treatise of Human Nature....Above all, the positive air, which prevails in that book, and which may be imputed to the ardor of youth, so much displeases me, that I have not patience to review it (C1: 187).

He expected a happier reception for the *Enquiry*, in which 'the same doctrines [are] better illustrated and expressed'—a striking remark when one is trying to establish Hume's views about causation, given that the main *prima facie* support for the view that Hume was an outright regularity theorist derives from the *Treatise* and vanishes in the *Enquiry*.

In asking that the *Enquiry* alone should 'be regarded as containing his philosophical sentiments and principles', Hume lays a clear exegetical obligation on us. We may—must—read the *Enquiry* back into the *Treatise*, when trying to understand his considered view; we can't go the other way. Everything in the *Treatise* that is or appears incompatible with the *Enquiry* must be discarded. Nothing in the *Treatise* can legitimately be used to throw light on any passage in the *Enquiry* unless two conditions are fulfilled: the passage in the *Enquiry* must be unclear (this is not often the case), and the passage from the *Treatise* must not be incompatible with anything in the *Enquiry* that is not in dispute. Even when a passage from the *Treatise* is called in evidence, its claim to make a contribution to interpretation must be weak when compared with competing claims from passages in the *Enquiry* other than the passage under consideration. We need not, perhaps, apply these rules rigidly, but Thomas Brown's attitude to the question—

As the [*Treatise*] was not sanctioned by the later judgment of its Author, who, in the advertisement to his Essays, has "desired that they alone should be regarded as containing his philosophical sentiments and principles," I must request my readers to make the same distinction and reservation, as to any quotations which I may venture to introduce from the earlier Treatise, and to consider them rather as illustrative of Mr. Hume's sentiments, than as exhibiting a faithful view of the results of his mature reflection (1818: 371n).

—seems exemplary. If we also respect Hume's insistence that 'the philosophical principles are the same in both' the *Treatise* and the *Enquiry*, we have a further crucial obligation. In order to understand the *Treatise*—in order, in particular, to avoid being misled by the dramatic and polemical exaggerations of the 'ardor of youth'—we must read the *Enquiry* back into the *Treatise* wherever possible, and give it priority. For it was written to correct the misunderstanding of the *Treatise*.

Many commentators have ignored this obligation (the situation has considerably improved in the last thirty years).[3] They've had their exegetical principles the wrong way round. Hume deserves our sympathy. It's bad to be attacked for views one never held, worse to be praised and famous for holding them.[4] Many love the *Treatise* because they love argument, and this is understandable; many philosophers (consciously or not) are more attached to cleverness and argument than truth. But Hume is not among them, and no one can avoid the obligations just described. It can't be plausibly argued that there is early Hume and late Hume, that they're importantly different,[5] and that each deserves study in his own right. Hume was at work on the *Treatise*-clarifying *Enquiry* within five years of the publication of the *Treatise*, and probably earlier, and (again) was insistent that the philosophical principles are the same in both. We have no reason to judge him to be self-deceived on this matter.[6]

Some may say the *Enquiry* is of less philosophical importance than the earlier *Treatise*. There is, however, every reason to take the *Enquiry* as more representative of Hume's considered views, even if one thinks that one can ignore Hume's repudiation of the *Treatise* in the Advertisement—and even if, as Russell says, Hume in the

---

[3] See in particular Buckle 2001; see also Beebee 2006, Kail 2007a, 2007b.

[4] It is bad to be praised for holding views one never held even when they are right, but worse when they are absurd.

[5] Here I disagree with the interpretative trend discussed by Hill 2012.

[6] See Flew 1961: ch. 1, Buckle 1999a and 1999b.

Enquiry leaves out most of his reasons and arguments for his views. Hume was at the height of his powers when he wrote the *Enquiry*. He had had more time to think. He was trying to make his position as clear as possible. He meant what he said and said it beautifully.

That said, his views about causation in the *Treatise* aren't different from his views in the *Enquiry*, as he says; although it's less obvious what they are in the *Treatise*. In the *Treatise*, inflamed with the 'ardor of Youth', he's inclined to dramatic overstatement in his polemic against the deluded pretensions to metaphysical knowledge which were unchecked in his time. In the *Enquiry* his vision is clearer and calmer, but fundamentally unchanged.[7] So although Mary Shepherd is considerably less accommodating than Thomas Brown, when it comes to the comparison of the *Treatise* and the *Enquiry*, in a way that some will approve—

Mr. Hume cannot fairly avail himself of the higher esteem he has called upon us to grant to his *Essays* above his juvenile *Treatise*; for, as the conclusions are the same in the Essays as in the Treatise, and as the *medium* arguments used in the Essays are the *conclusions drawn in consequence of great detail of previous discussion in the Treatise*, it is both fair and necessary to examine these details.

It may be, as is hinted in the Advertisement to the Essays,—'that *these details* contain some of those *negligent reasonings that he could have wished not to acknowledge in after life*'.

I shall not, however, readily allow of the advantage of such an excuse; for, as long as the premises that support his matured opinions are only to be found regularly deduced in this unacknowledged work, it is incumbent upon one attempting an Answer to expose them; for, there is no little art, in refusing to adopt the 'negligent reasonings of youth', in a state of advanced judgment, yet covertly making use of a material proposition (that might pass as true, even in many an acute mind, in reading these popular and elegant Essays), which is only supported by the sophistical reasonings of the youthful Treatise, and is evidently adopted in consequence of them. It is also possible, that Mr. Hume might not intend to deny his opinions, in every particular that regarded these points, as he continued to hold the consequential doctrine deduced from them. (1824: 2–3)

—Hume has nothing to fear from any sensitive interpreter of the *Treatise* who also knows the *Enquiry*.

So much for exegetical obligation. Now for the standard 'Humean' view of causation. On this view, causation considered as something existing in 'the objects' or in 'the world', i.e. in nature, or concrete reality, is nothing but regularity of succession. That is, one particular object or object-involving event of type A—call it A1—is truly said

---

[7]   At various points I'll quote from the *Dialogues Concerning Natural Religion*, which provide powerful and illuminating support for the present view (Hume was working on them in the years 1749–51, immediately after the publication of the first edition of the *Enquiry* in 1748). Some think that the dialogue form means that the *Dialogues* can't really be appealed to as evidence of Hume's views, so I'll rest nothing essentially on them, but this attitude to the *Dialogues* isn't really defensible. See e.g. p. 185n below, and Strawson 2000a.

to be the cause of another particular object or object-involving event of type B—call it B1—just in case A1 is prior to and spatio-temporally contiguous to B1, and all objects or object-involving events of type A are prior to and spatio-temporally contiguous to objects or object-involving events of type B. I'll call this the 'regularity theory of causation', taking it in the apparently straightforwardly ontological way just set out.[8]

It would seem that there can be no real question that Hume adopted a regularity theory of causation 'in the objects' (166/1.3.14.24) in some sense. But in what sense, exactly?[9]

This last question can be put as follows. What did Hume mean by 'the objects'? The first part of the discussion of the question whether Hume was a 'Humean' (or Brownian) can be organized around an answer to this question. In 6.2–6.3 I'll argue that, insofar as he adopted a straightforward regularity theory of causation at all, he adopted it only about 'objects' understood in a sense remote from our current sense.

But before beginning on the discussion of objects I'll give a brief statement of the main present line of argument against the standard view of Hume's theory of causation. And, in order to do this, I will understand the word 'object' in an ordinary, straightforwardly realist way.[10]

---

[8] See e.g. A. J. Ayer: 'in nature one thing just happens after another' (1963: 183), and this is all there is to causation, so far as it is anything in the world, considered independently of our thought about it. See also Hume's first or 'philosophical' definition of causation: 'A cause is an object precedent and contiguous to another, and where all the objects resembling the former are plac'd in like relations of precedency and contiguity to those objects, that resemble the latter' (170/1.3.14.31, 172/1.3.14.35).

Many questions of detail arise concerning this first definition, and its relation to Hume's second definition of cause, which aren't of present concern. For example, it seems that regularity theorists who take themselves to be following Hume should hold that if A1 causes B1, then the relation between A-type events and B-type events is not only such that if A, then B, but also such that if B, then A (cf. 173/1.3.15.6, and—if it is not just a slip on Hume's part—the second statement of the first definition of cause in the *Enquiry* (76/7.29), which is notoriously not equivalent to the first statement, both insofar as it claims that a cause is a necessary rather than a sufficient condition of its effect, and insofar as it has an explicitly counterfactual character). For a discussion of the natural view that 'pure' regularity versions of the 'Humean' view unacceptably leave out Hume's second definition of cause, see Beauchamp and Rosenberg 1981; see also Craig 1987: §2.4.

[9] One thing worth noting is that Hume drops the spatial contiguity requirement in the *Enquiry*. I'll register this fact by speaking sometimes of the precedency ± *contiguity* condition on causation. Hill (2012) argues that Hume does this because he is by this time more prepared to embrace the idea of causal action at a distance, an idea that seemed to many to be implied by Newton's theory of gravity.

[10] The view that I am calling the 'standard' view is by no means universally held, as remarked in the Preface. Among recent writers, Wright (1983: ch. 4), Livingston (1984: ch. 6), and Craig (1987: ch. 2) reject it forcefully and effectively: Wright suggests (ibid. p. 128) that Ernst Mach's *Science of Mechanics* was a particularly influential source of the misinterpretation (although it did not begin with him), and that H. H. Price may also have a lot to answer for.

3

A summary of the argument

The central objection to the 'standard' view is that it fails to distinguish clearly between two quite different notions, one ontological (O), the other epistemological (E). It fails to distinguish sufficiently between

(O)   causation *as it is* in the world,

the real world, and

(E)   causation *so far as we know about it* in the world.

This distinction is crucial, on the present view. For, in the end, Hume's regularity theory of causation is only a theory about (E), not about (O). As far as (O) is concerned, Hume believes firmly, and with overwhelmingly good reasons (noted in 5), in something like natural necessity. So it will be argued.[1]

Of course the standard view can claim textual support, as well as support deriving from wider considerations about Hume's overall theoretical position.[2] For one thing, it's not clear that Hume can legitimately (or at least without considerable theoretical strain) distinguish between (O) and (E), given his theory of ideas. It seems, furthermore, that he doesn't always distinguish clearly between them; especially in the *Treatise*. Usually, however, he does. In the *Enquiry* he is scrupulous in his respect for the distinction, in spite of the fact that his theory of ideas may be thought to make it problematic for him.

The present suggestion, then, is that the standard view confuses an epistemological claim with an ontological claim. More specifically, it confuses Hume's epistemological claim that

(E1)   all we can ever *know* of causation, in the world, is regular succession

with the positive ontological claim that

(O1)   all that causation actually *is*, in the world, is regular succession.

---

[1] J. L. Mackie states the distinction between (O) and (E) clearly in ch. 1 of *The Cement of the Universe* (pp. 20–1), but he is wrong (on the present view) to claim that 'Hume usually says that [causation as it is in the objects] is regular succession and nothing more'.

[2] There would be something seriously wrong with the present account if it failed to acknowledge any passages that appeared to support the standard view.

It moves, catastrophically, from the former to the latter. The former is arguably true. The latter is wildly implausible.

As just remarked, the elision of the distinction between (E1) and (O1) appears to be true to something in Hume's thought, something that derives from his theory of ideas or meaning. On this view, the passage from (E1) to (O1) is thought to be effected via Hume's semantical claim that

> (S1) all we can possibly *manage to mean* by the idea or concept CAUSATION or the term 'causation', when thinking or speaking of the real world, is regular succession.

The transition is made as follows:

(1) (E1) is true.
(2) If (E1) is true, (S1) is true (that's strict empiricism for you).
(3) If (S1) is true, (O1) is true.
So
(4) (O1) is true.

Why does (O1) follow from (S1)? Because, given (S1), when the idea or concept CAUSATION occurs in our thought (when the term 'causation' occurs in our talk), it inevitably just means regular succession. So (O1) causation in the objects—here is the concept or word in use, meaning regular succession—just is regular succession. After all, regular succession is regular succession.[3]

This initially plausible view of Hume's theory of ideas or meaningfulness will be rejected below (first in 6.5, then in 12). It's worth noting straight away that even if there were good grounds for thinking that his theory of ideas, strictly interpreted, did license the move from (E1) to (O1) via (S1), it would still have to be granted that (O1), which makes a positive assertion that something definitely does not exist, is profoundly at odds with Hume's strictly non-committal scepticism with regard to knowledge claims about the nature of reality—his strictly non-committal attitude to questions about what we can know to exist *or know not to exist*, in reality.

The word 'sceptic' is often used loosely. It's often thought that to be a sceptic with respect to the existence of an 'external' (or 'mind-independent') world is to hold that it doesn't exist. But this is obviously not a strictly sceptical position, because it involves a positive claim about the ultimate nature of reality: the claim that an external (or mind-independent) world doesn't exist. Genuine or strictly non-committal scepticism never makes such a claim. In general, it simply claims that

---

[3] Mill says that Hume maintains 'not merely that the only causes of phenomena which can be *known* are other phenomena, but that there *is* no other kind of causes: cause as he interprets it, *means* [just] the invariable antecedent' (Mill 1865: 266). Mill's colon shows, I think, that he takes it that, for Hume, (O1) follows from (S1).

Note that the same type of invalid argument can be made if one replaces 'causation' ('causation') and 'regular succession' with 'external objects' ('external objects') and 'perceptions' respectively, or with 'self' ('self') and 'a series of perceptions' respectively.

we know far less than we think. In the case of the external world, it claims that we don't and can't know whether or not there is such a thing. Strictly sceptical claims have the form 'We do not (and cannot) know that *p* (or that not *p*).' They never have the form 'It is definitely (knowably) not the case that *p*' or 'It is definitely (knowably) the case that not *p*.'

Hume's scepticism is of this strictly non-committal kind, and the fact that this is so furnishes a very powerful argument against the claim that Hume could have wished to assert that causation in the world was definitely (knowably) nothing but regular succession (it's decisive, once the misunderstanding about Hume's notion of mean-ingfulness has been cleared up): his strictly non-committal scepticism rules out such an assertion. Insofar as Hume takes up a sceptical position, he's obviously not concerned to make positive claims about what definitely does exist (apart from mental occurrences or 'perceptions', whose existence he takes as certain). So insofar as he writes as a sceptic, he's not concerned to assert that there is definitely (knowably) an external world of non-mental, physical objects—even when he says that this is something 'we must take for granted in all our reasonings' (187/1.4.2.1). But, equally, he's not concerned to make positive claims about what definitely (knowably) does *not* exist. For these claims are equally unwarranted, from the strictly non-committal sceptical point of view.

Some doubt this. They think that Hume's theory of meaning does permit him and indeed oblige him to make inferences which conform to the pattern set out above in the case of causation (from (E1) to (O1) via (S1)). This is a mistake. Hume holds, correctly, that we can 'suppose' and indeed firmly believe something to exist, and have what he calls a 'relative' idea of it, on account of some relation which we take it to stand in to us, and hence refer to it, although we have no sort of positive, empirically contentful conception of its nature.

We can locate the fault in (S1) and correct it to

(S1*)   all we can manage to mean by the idea or concept CAUSATION or the term 'causation', insofar as it has any *empirically warranted positive descriptive* content, and therefore has a *fully legitimate use in philosophy when thinking or speaking of the real world*, is regular succession.

The conclusion (S1*) permits is no longer (O1), an outright ontological conclusion, but (OE1), a qualified, *ontological/epistemological* conclusion:

(OE1)   regular succession is all that causation is or involves *so far as we have any empirically warranted positively descriptively contentful conception of causation*.

This is Hume's position, the position of a consistent, moderate sceptic.[4]

---

[4] Once again one can substitute the case of external objects or bodies for the case of causation, or the case of the mind or self. See Strawson 2011.

I hope to show this in detail later. Until then, and in order to consider an objection to the present position, let it be granted that appeal to Hume's scepticism does furnish a very strong argument against the claim that he could have wished to make the definite, positive, patently metaphysical assertion that we can know for certain (1) that causation, in the objects, or reality, is definitely nothing more than regularity of succession, and (2) that there is definitely no such thing as power or force in the objects.[5]

The objection will no doubt already have occurred to many. 'If this argument is accepted, it backfires spectacularly against the claim that Hume believes that there's something like natural necessity or causal power. Clearly, as a strict sceptic with respect to knowledge claims, Hume isn't going to claim that we can know that there is definitely nothing like natural necessity or causal power in reality. But, equally clearly, he isn't going to claim that there definitely *is* something like natural necessity or causal power in reality.'

This is a reasonable objection. It fails because it ignores the distinction between knowledge and belief, and Hume's understanding of it.[6] Those who think that Hume is a straightforward regularity theorist with respect to causation standardly suppose that he makes a *knowledge claim* on the question, arguing that there is definitely nothing like natural necessity or causal power in the world. Such a claim is definitely ruled out by strictly non-committal scepticism of the Humean kind. The *belief* that there is such a thing as natural necessity or causal power is not ruled out, however. Strictly non-committal scepticism can acknowledge the naturalness and overall theoretical plausibility of this belief, and grant that it may be true (or something like the truth); it will merely insist that we cannot know it to be true.

Some may doubt whether Hume can suppose such a belief to have content in such a way that it can be intelligibly supposed to be true, or even something like the truth. I will argue that this doubt is *prima facie* reasonable but misplaced—but not until 6.5 and 7.

It may now be objected that Hume's scepticism precludes him from even admitting to *believing* in the existence of anything like causal power or natural necessity. Some tend to think that true scepticism not only precludes knowledge claims, but requires suspension of belief in the 'Pyrrhonian' style—refusal to accept any positive belief-claim at all, so long as it is uncertain. But Hume has little regard for such 'extravagant' scepticism,[7] and the objection fails to take account of his doctrine of 'natural belief'. We have certain natural beliefs (e.g. in the existence of external

---

[5] One line of interpretation of Hume takes it that (1) doesn't entail (2), and that Hume asserts (1) but not (2). This suggestion may seem surprising, but I think it expresses something of the truth. It's brought out by Beauchamp and Rosenberg (1981), and I discuss it in 8 and 15.5 below. (From this perspective, it's arguable that one of the principal sources of misinterpretation of Hume is the belief that if he asserts (1) in any sense, then he must also be committed to (2).)

[6] For the importance of this distinction, see e.g. Kemp Smith 1941: 62–8.

[7] Cf. e.g. 214/1.4.2.50, 155/12.16 n.

objects) which we find it practically impossible to give up. Strictly non-committal scepticism does *not* say that these beliefs are definitely not true (or unintelligible in our current sense of the word). *Belief* in the existence of something *x* is entirely compatible with strictly non-committal, Humean scepticism with regard to *knowledge* claims about the existence of *x* or indeed about anything else.[8]

As it is, Hume never really questions the idea that there is something like causal power in reality, i.e. *something about reality in virtue of which reality is regular in the way it is*.[9] He certainly insists on the epistemological claim that nature 'conceals from us those *powers and principles on which the influence of... objects entirely depends....*' (33/4.16), but he never seriously doubts that these powers and principles *exist*. He's clear on the epistemological point that 'we are ignorant of *those powers and forces*, on which [the] regular course and succession of objects *totally depends*' (55/5.22), but he's equally clear on the point that the regular course and succession of objects does indeed *totally depend* on these powers and forces of whose nature we are so utterly ignorant. It would be very odd if he also thought that they didn't exist. It would be very odd if he thought that the 'power or force' which on his view 'actuates the whole machine... of the universe' (63/7.8) did not exist.

Some may think that Hume can't on his own principles speak of powers and forces in this apparently straightforwardly referring way, so let me briefly anticipate a central point of the following discussion. Hume's essential claim about words like 'power' and 'force' is not that they have no acceptable use at all, as applied to the world. He uses them too often himself for this view to be plausible. His point is rather that their use is risky and potentially extremely misleading, for it strongly encourages philosophers to think, quite wrongly, that they can arrive at substantive conclusions about the true *nature* of power or force.

This is a prelude to themes that will recur repeatedly. Some may find them hard to credit at first; I hope they will be patient. Note in conclusion that one can distinguish here between a weaker and a stronger objection to the standard view of Hume. The weaker objection is negative: it's just that Hume didn't hold that causation is definitely (knowably) nothing but regular succession. The stronger claim is positive: it's that Hume believed in the existence of something like causal power or 'natural necessity'. Clearly one can grant the weaker objection and reject the stronger. In due course I'll argue for the stronger, which entails the weaker, but I want now to return to the question raised in 2. What exactly does Hume have in mind when he talks of objects?

---

[8] Some will again be thinking that Hume cannot allow that these beliefs—in an external world, or in causal power—are meaningful in any way. This is perhaps the key error about Hume, and I will come to it in due course.

[9] 'Something about reality in virtue of which reality is regular in the way it is' is the minimal version of what Kail usefully calls 'the Bare Thought' (Kail 2007*b*: 83–98): the thought of causal power, or simply of the nature of things, that is available to us (and Hume) in spite of the restrictions imposed by the theory of ideas. The other component of the Bare Thought involves the 'AP property' of causal power discussed in 11, invoked by Hume to explain why we can never be acquainted with causal power.

4

'Objects': preliminaries

An 'object', in Hume's texts, is as likely to denote a perception considered specifically as such, a mental occurrence with whatever content it has, as it is to denote a table or a chair. Among the things he took to be covered by 'object' are the taste of a fig, a passion, a moral reflection, and a flame.[1] The immediate question, though, is what he meant by the word 'object' when he had things like tables and chairs—hats, shoes, stones (202/1.4.2.31), figs, and billiard balls and their interactions principally in mind? Certainly he meant hats and shoes and stones—figs and billiard balls. But what are these things—objects? What did Hume think they are?

This is an absorbing question; Hume's appreciation of the philosophically possible answers is sophisticated. His discussion ranges over the Lockean, Berkeleian, and direct realist options without positively endorsing any of them, and leaves a place for something like the Kantian option.

A first reply is that he undoubtedly means the 'objects of our senses' (188/1.4.2.2), things like tables and chairs. This doesn't solve anything, however. For are the 'objects of our senses' to be understood in a familiar way as

    (1)   'realist' objects: tables and chairs more or less as ordinarily conceived, as constituents of a fully mind-independent, external world[2]

or are they to be understood as

    (2)   'idealist' objects: tables and chairs conceived of as constituted out of 'perceptions', or sets of 'perceptions'

—and thereby thought of in something like the way Berkeley originally (or at least at one point) thought of them? Or, thirdly, are they to be understood in some seemingly more refined idealist fashion as

---

[1] 235–7/1.4.5.8–11, 87/1.3.6.2. See also 5/1.1.1.8: 'to give a child an idea of scarlet or orange, of sweet or bitter, I present the objects, or in other words, convey to him these impressions'.

[2] Locke gives one philosophically influential account of objects as 'realist' objects. Descartes gives another. The ordinary, 'common-sense' view of objects is a conception of objects as realist objects, as is the scientific account of objects. The term 'realist object' classifies these positions together, despite their differences.

(3)   'strict-idealist' objects: tables and chairs which are in some sense constituted merely by features of the *content* of perceptions?[3]

These seem to be the main options. (2) and (3) are obviously closely connected, and the distinction between them will for the most part be unimportant (it will matter in 6.2–6.3).

Actually, Hume very often means an event, an *object-involving event* (an event that involves objects in our everyday sense) when he speaks of 'objects'; but this only complicates the present question without either answering it or changing its basic import as a question about what general conception of the nature of reality, if any, may be supposed to correspond to Hume's use of the word 'object'.[4] Sometimes he means type of event by 'object', as when he speaks of objects being constantly conjoined (e.g. 93/1.3.6.15). Again this merely complicates the present question without altering the main options.

I'll call (1) the *realist* option: realist objects (or, as Hume often says, 'bodies') are entirely non-mental, physical objects, 'external objects' or 'external bodies',[5] 'objects independent of the mind'.[6] This is the first option he considers when he asks

by what argument can it be proved, that the perceptions of the mind must be caused by external objects, entirely different from them, though resembling them (if that be possible) and could not arise either from the energy of the mind itself, or from the suggestion of some invisible and unknown spirit, or from some other cause still more unknown to us? (152–3/12.11)

His answer unequivocally acknowledges the possibility that this answer may be correct, although we can never know whether it is or not:

It is a question of fact, whether the perceptions of the senses be produced by external objects, resembling them: how shall this question be determined? By experience surely; as all other questions of a like nature. But here experience is, and must be entirely silent. (153/12.12)

(2) and (3) are two versions of the *idealist* option: idealist objects are objects-taken-as-being-constituted-of-perceptions, or *perception-constituted objects*. Or, more narrowly,

---

[3]   In particular, impressions of sensation which have the character of being sensations of external objects conceived in the ordinary realist way. Hume's view is that it is only after our custom-influenced faculty of 'imagination' has worked on the impressions of sensation that we naturally construe them as experiences of external objects conceived in the ordinary realist way. The character of being experiences of an external reality is not part of their content just *qua* impressions of sensation.

[4]   The question becomes 'Did Hume intend the word "objects" to refer to objects *and object-involving events* construed in the ordinary realist way, or did he intend it to refer to objects *and object-involving events* construed in some sort of idealist way?'

[5]   Cf. *Treatise* and *Enquiry passim*, e.g. 66–8/1.2.6, 241/1.4.5.20, 366/2.2.6.2, 13/1.13, 63/7.6, 153/12.11.

[6]   193/1.4.2.14. Some may wonder whether Hume's use of the word 'external' necessarily implies some kind of realist construal of the word 'object' or 'body', rather than some idealist or phenomenalistic construal (as in Kant's talk of 'outer' objects). I think it does, but there's no need to insist on the point.

they're objects-taken-as-being-constituted-of-contents-of-perceptions: they're not just perception-constituted objects, they are perception-*content*-constituted objects.

Clearly, this subdivision of idealist perception-constituted objects into those which are thought of as perception-*content*-constituted objects and those which aren't is significant only if perceptions can be distinguished from their content. This possibility will be discussed further in 6.2. The basic idea is that perceptions may be thought of as real mental events or mental states which *have* content but are in some way more than just their content, ontologically speaking; just as pictures on a wall have pictorial content, but are at the same time something more than their content, ontologically speaking.[7]

Most generally characterized, an idealist position is one that understands thought and talk about objects to be ultimately a matter of thought and talk just about experiences or 'impressions of sensation' or perceptions, or about aspects of the content of experiences or 'impressions of sensation' or perceptions.

I'll return to this question in 6. First, though, I wish to state the principal objection to the ordinary, realist form of the regularity theory of causation. It will be useful to have this to hand when discussing the idealist conceptions of objects.

---

[7] Given the current focus on the sense in which reference to particular physical objects, and to that extent particular physical objects themselves, may enter essentially into the specification of the content of mental episodes like perceptual experiences and thoughts (see e.g. McGinn, 1996: ch. 5), it's worth stressing that the notion of content in question here is a notion of *purely mental* content. There may be difficulties in this notion, but it's a notion which is familiar in the history of philosophy, and the 'brain in a vat' thought-experiment sufficiently dramatizes the essential idea behind it: there's an important and obvious sense in which a being which was a 'brain in a vat' could have experiences which were, as regards their content, just like one's own, even though it was not in fact in experiential contact with any of the objects one was in contact with, or indeed with any object other than the computer which fed it with electrical impulses. One can put the point by saying that according to the present conception of content all content is phenomenological content—while bearing in mind the point that there is cognitive-phenomenological content as well as sense/feeling content (see e.g. Bayne and Montague 2011). Even if one dislikes this crucially important way of conceiving of mental content, it is of course wholly appropriate for the discussion of Hume.

5

The untenability of the realist regularity theory of causation

The regularity theory of causation, in its ordinary, straightforwardly realist version, is the theory that asserts, bizarrely and dramatically, that (1) there is indeed an external world of fully mind-independent realist objects, and that (2) all that causation is, in that world, is regularity of succession, so far as it is anything at all. It is the view that 'in nature one thing just happens after another',[1] and that this is absolutely all that causation is or consists in or involves, so far as it is anything 'in the objects' (166/ 1.3.14.24, 167/1.3.14.25). The claim is not just the epistemological claim that regularity of succession is all we can strictly speaking perceive, so far as causation is concerned; it's the claim that this is all that causation is.

On the regularity realist view, then, our natural belief that causation in the objects involves something more than just regularity is false. It forms part of our natural 'imaginative arrangements and extensions' of the 'primary facts' about what causation is. Considered in themselves, these primary facts (definitely) consist of nothing more than the facts of regular succession, of one thing's 'just happening' after another.[2]

Whether or not anyone really holds this strong, straightforwardly realist version of the regularity theory of causation (many apparently do), it seems to be open to a simple and devastating objection, which I will state briefly. First, the theory realistically asserts that there is an external world (of physical objects) which is highly regular in its behaviour. Then it insists that there is, quite definitely, *absolutely*

---

[1] Ayer 1963: 183.

[2] Ayer, ibid. Ayer might not want to use the word 'cause' at all in talking about nature considered independently of our thought about it, for he says that (the notions of) cause and effect themselves 'have their place only in our imaginative arrangements and extensions' of the primary facts of regular succession. But this doesn't affect the main point.

Compare David Lewis's espousal of the doctrine he calls 'Humean supervenience', 'named in honour of the great…denier of necessary connections. It is the doctrine that all there is to the world is a vast mosaic of local matters of particular fact, just one little thing and then another' (1986: ix). As a realist about 'possible worlds', a Lewisian arguably has better grounds than most for being some sort of regularity theorist (see n. 11), although Lewis himself did not accept a regularity analysis of causation. For Lewis's second thoughts about his use of the term 'Humean', see Strawson 2013.

nothing at all about the nature of the world given which it is regular in its behaviour: there is *just* the regularity; that is all that causation in the world amounts to.

According to the realist regularity theory of causation, then, the regularity of the world's behaviour is, in a clear sense, a complete and continuous fluke. It is not just that we don't know whether or not there is any reason for it in the nature of things. According to the regularity theory of causation, there is definitely no reason for it in the nature of things. It is, certainly, an *objective* regularity, a real regularity in the world. But it is also an objective fluke, in the simple sense that there is, objectively or in the nature of things, absolutely no reason at all why regularity rather than chaos occurs from moment to moment. Or alternatively—if we call the particular regularity exemplified by our world 'R-regularity'—there is no reason why R-regularity occurs from moment to moment, rather than S-regularity or T-regularity or any other regularity.[3]

The objection to the realist regularity theory of causation is accordingly very simple. It is that the theory is utterly implausible in asserting categorically that there is no reason in the nature of things for the regularity of the world. The objection is not that the regularity theory is logically inconsistent in any way. There is (we may grant) no *logical* inconsistency in asserting that the regularity of the world is an objective fluke, in the sense given above.[4] It's just that it is absurd, given the regularity of the world, to say—to insist—that there is definitely no reason in the nature of things why regularity rather than chaos (or R-regularity rather than S- or T- or Z-regularity) occurs from moment to moment. Such a view is a typical dogmatically anti-realist overshoot: a strict empiricist epistemological claim about what we can

---

[3] I assume that holders of the strong regularity theory don't invoke any *super*natural agency—some agency conceived of as external to the world which the regularity theory is a theory about—in order to account for the regularity; although the Occasionalists did exactly this (with respect to realist objects—cf. 20 below), as also did Berkeley (although not with respect to realist objects—cf. 6.3).

[4] For an argument that the realist regularity theory of causation is incoherent, given our ordinary notion of an object, see Strawson 1987: §4.

One bad objection to the notion of global fluke is (roughly) that the notion of fluke or coincidence makes sense only given a background of regularity relative to which certain unusual or irregular events are counted as flukish. On this view, one can't intelligibly suppose that the whole phenomenon of perceivable regularity is a fluke. But this objection appears to confuse (1) an epistemological point about concept acquisition with (2) a point about metaphysics. As for (1), it's plausible to suppose that one can acquire the concept of a fluke only in a context in which one counts certain (many) things as non-flukish, but it doesn't follow (2) that the supposition that the whole regularity of the world might possibly be a fluke is incoherent. (Compare the unimpressive but once popular argument against scepticism with regard to the external world, according to which it can't possibly be true that all our apparently genuinely external-world-concerning perceptions are illusory or non-veridical, because the notion of illusion makes sense only if some of our perceptions are not illusory. Here too it's true (1) that one can acquire the notion of perceptual illusion only given a grasp of the correlative notion of a perception's being veridical. But once one has grasped the concept one can go on to accept a natural view of what has to be true if one's apparently genuinely external-world-concerning perceptions are veridical (i.e. a 'real world out there') relative to which it makes sense to suppose (2) that all one's apparently genuinely external-world-concerning perceptions may possibly be non-veridical.)

observe flowers into a vast and spectacular metaphysical claim about the nature of things.[5]

The objection to the regularity theory needn't be merely negative. It needn't be just that (1) it is absurd, given a regular world, to insist that there is definitely nothing about the nature of the world given which it is regular rather than chaotic. It may also be positive: it may also be that (2) it is reasonable (in some perhaps irreducibly vague but profoundly unshakeable sense), given a regular world, to suppose, positively, that there definitely is something about the nature of the world given which it is regular, something which is therefore not itself just the fact of its regularity.

Some may be chary of (2), the positive claim, which may be held to do no more than express a fundamental and not further justifiable metaphysical assumption or prejudice; but (1), the negative claim—the central objection to the regularity theory— is independent of this assumption. Someone who wished to reserve judgement on (2), the positive claim, might well still endorse (1), the negative claim, saying that we are indeed rationally obliged not to insist on the definite *absence* of any reason for the regularity, even if, in the final analysis, we have no more reason to suppose that there is some reason in the nature of things for the regularity than that there is not.

In the final analysis, we return to the fact of the world. And either (i) there is something about it (something about the nature of matter) in virtue of which it is regular in the way it is, or (ii) there is not. To refuse to endorse (2), the positive claim, is to say that there is nothing to choose between claims (i) and (ii). But who would actually endorse (ii), in some strange situation in which their life depended on giving a correct answer, and say that there is definitely nothing about the causal nature of the world *in virtue of which* the world is (and is going to go on being) regular in character, since, so far as causal process goes, there is quite literally nothing but the fact of the regularity?

Some may challenge the intelligibility of the idea that there is a correct answer, since the issue is undecidable. I respond to this challenge in 7.

Has anyone ever really held the regularity theory, as here described? It seems hard to believe. Perhaps many who are supposed to hold it really only hold the following view: that while there is of course (or at least extremely probably) something about the world in virtue of which it's regular, that's not what *causation* is; it's not what our word 'causation' is a word for. Later on I'll consider the suggestion that this is

---

[5] I argue further for this claim in Strawson 1987. Compare phenomenalism, behaviourism, and all reductionist versions of functionalism in the philosophy of mind. In each case the move is from an arguably defensible epistemological claim to an obviously unacceptable ontological claim. Positivist methodology turns into *positivist metaphysics*—a contradiction in terms. Note that even if one attempts the hypothesis that the universe is composed of a series of entirely discrete flashes of being, a hundred or a hundred billion a second, say, interspersed with moments of total non-existence, it's still overwhelmingly reasonable (although still not logically obligatory) to suppose that there is something other than those flashes of being in virtue of which it is the case that flash $n + 1$ resembles flash n as closely as it does.

Hume's view.[6] I think it is at least part of the truth about Hume. For now, though, I'll continue with some further remarks about the implausibility of the regularity theory of causation. I think that the central, simple point can be extremely difficult for present-day philosophers to take in, and that it is therefore worth trying to express it in a number of ways.

Perhaps one way to get a sense of the true force of the regularity theory is to look hard at the world and reflectively apply the regularity theory as one looks, rather than thinking about the theory in that curiously abstract way that philosophy encourages. Consider any large scale natural phenomenon—yourself sitting in a chair in a room in a building—and the massive complexity of regularity of succession involved in this phenomenon from moment to moment. According to the (basic, ontologically outright) realist regularity theory of causation, there is *absolutely nothing* about the nature of reality that makes this so, as it continues from instant to instant. From instant to instant it is pure chance—nothing 'underwrites' or 'sustains' (unashamed metaphors) the regularity constituted by the persistence and continuous development of things, shapes, and processes. In fact the regularity of the sequence of events in the world as a whole is just like the regularity of the sequence of natural numbers 0, 1, 2, 3, 4, 5..., in the extraordinary but obviously logically possible case in which the sequence is being generated by a true random number generator. Nothing at all underwrites the causal regularity of the world, on the pure regularity view. There is just the regularity. That is the whole truth about the causal nature of the world.

The present claim is that this is not true (for some purposes, the point is best expressed in this entirely negative manner): that there is something about the nature of reality which is the reason why it is regular in character. Call this 'X'. Every time one's (epistemological) sense of the perceptual or observational inaccessibility of X grows acute, and threatens to flip over into an ontological conclusion that there's no such thing as X, one should simply remind oneself that if X doesn't exist, then the regularity of the world really is, from moment to moment, a complete fluke, exactly like the fluke involved in the sequence of natural numbers being produced by a random number generator. (It's more like billions of perfect random number generators all producing the sequence of natural numbers in unison.)

Here is another analogy. Imagine a true randomizing device determines the colour value of each pixel on a 1200×800 pixel computer screen, running on a ten-times-a-second cycle—so that each pixel can take any colour value for each 1/10th second period. On the screen it appears that there is a film showing. A woman enters a house, walks over to a stove, and puts on a kettle. Life—a world, as it were—goes on

---

[6] In 8 and 15.5. Among the many philosophers who have recently [1989] raised serious doubts about or rejected the regularity theory of causation are Armstrong (1983) Foster (1982–3), Harré and Madden (1975), Kneale (1949: 70–103), Levine (1986–7), Mackie (1974), Molnar (1969), and Tooley (1987); after 1989 the list explodes. Most philosophers take a non-regularity-theory conception of cause for granted when discussing philosophical issues other than causation itself. So too, almost all philosophers are straightforward realists about consciousness outside the philosophy of mind.

in an ordered, regular fashion, exactly as regularly as in our own world. But the image is being generated by the true randomizing device. It's pure fluke that what happens on the screen appears to tell a coherent story of a regular, ordered world, rather than filling up with—or suddenly switching to—a fizz of points of colour. At each 1/10th second moment, what occurs on the screen is one of many millions of objectively equally probable alternatives. To say that the analogy is inadequate at this point, because physical particles are not totally and instantaneously alterable as are the pixels with respect to colour value, is in effect to concede the present point: i.e. that there is something about the nature of matter (or rather, more generally, something about the stuff of reality whatever it is) which is the reason why it is regular in the way that it is (something about As, Cs, and Es, which is the reason why they are followed by Bs, Ds, and Fs respectively), *something which is therefore not just the regularity itself.*[7]

The screen world is a simple example of a highly regular 'world'—or a certain regular sequence of events—in which there is nothing to the regularity (nothing to it ontologically, one might say) but itself. This regularity is pure regularity. It is not 'backed' by anything. It does not 'flow' from anything. It is not an expression of the nature of anything. There is, objectively, no reason at all for the particular regularity displayed on the screen. It's an objective fact about the envisaged system that any colour could be displayed at any pixel point at any 1/10th second period of time. The analogy is an attempt to convey some idea of the true (and astonishing) nature of the regularity theory of causation as applied to our own world.[8]

To get closer to a real-world equivalent, replace the pixels with 'pixel-particles' in a 'Universe', one pixel-particle for each of the particles in our universe, and tell the same story. The behavioural properties of the particles of this Universe are alterable from instant to instant[9] in a way which is strongly analogous to the alterability of the colour values of the pixels. But this Universe, we may suppose, is (by objective fluke) perfectly regular in a certain way: it is, let us say, R-regular. In fact, in respect of its perfect regularity, it is *just like* our universe, which is also R-regular (rather than S-regular or T-regular). And so, according to the regularity-theory account of causation, it is, in respect of *causation*, just like our universe.

In fact, if the (straightforward ontological) regularity theory account of our universe is correct, this Universe is identical to our universe in all respects—once one subtracts the randomizing device that determines the behavioural properties of the pixel-particles from instant to instant.[10] For, on the regularity-theory account of

---

[7] I say something further about this last clause—which some may find particularly dubious—in 8, p. 94.

[8] Of course the reason why we interpret what happens on the screen as involving a certain extremely rich kind of regularity (and not just certain kinds of colour-patch-evolution regularity) is that it tells a story we can naturally understand. Does this suggest that regularity is in the eye of the beholder? I will shortly consider the suggestion that every sequence is in principle interpretable as a regularity.

[9] What instants are I leave vague.

[10] This subtraction is easily done. In place of the randomizing device, as the thing which determines the behavioural properties of the particles of our universe, one leaves Nothing At All. This is equivalent to the randomizing device, for if there is nothing at all which determines the behavioural properties of the

our universe, particles cannot be said to have a nature which is such that they have to behave regularly as they do, or even which is such that they do behave regularly as they do. For there is *simply nothing* which is the reason for the regularity, according to the regularity theory of causation. For if there were something, X, which was the reason for the regularity, then that something X would have to be granted to be part of what causation is, or involves. And to grant that would be to abandon the regularity theory of causation (a point taken up again in 8).[11]

The basic objection to the regularity theory of causation is that it's absurd to insist that reality is definitely like this—a vast and continuous fluke. This is the old 'outrageous run of luck' objection, taken one step further: the objection is not only that the regularity theory of causation would have to count an outrageous run of luck as a causal regularity, but that it asserts that all causal regularity actually is is an outrageous run of luck.

Another more difficult way of trying to express the problem is as follows.[12] The trouble derives from the endorsement of a bad, separatist picture of the relation between matter and the forces which determine its behaviour. According to this picture, matter (objects, particles) is something which is in its nature somehow quite distinct from the forces—the so-called 'fundamental forces'—which determine its behaviour. Once this picture has been adopted, it can make it seem easy to think of matter in some robustly realist way while doubting whether there are any such forces.

The objection to the picture is that it's hopelessly superficial. Matter—particles, objects—has a certain *nature*. And it is (to say the least) natural to suppose that its behavioural properties, and hence its regularity properties, are a function or expression or manifestation of its nature. But we've now allowed that the fundamental forces are responsible for the behavioural and regularity properties of matter. This is

---

particles from instant to instant, then every possibility is equally probable at each instant—exactly what the randomizing device is invoked to achieve.

[11] It's arguable that some variety of outright realism about possible worlds can provide grounds for being a regularity theorist. Briefly: if all possible worlds are real, then every possible sequence of events is realized; in which case there is (arguably) nothing in need of explanation in the fact that the actual world contains the particular—in fact regular—sequence of events that it does. It's just one sequence of events among all the other sequences. All sequences are realized in whatever sense it is that all possible worlds are real. It just happens to be this sequence that is the sequence of the actual world.

One way of expressing the intuition that there is in this case nothing in need of explanation in the fact that our world is regular in the way that it is is perhaps this: the space of possible worlds, like the space of logical possibility, is automatically full—full of all possible possibilities. So the explanation (or anti-explanation) of why our world goes as it does is just that all possible sequence-possibilities are real, and this is just one of them, and that's that. Note, though, that even if this realism about possible worlds were acceptable, it wouldn't and couldn't *rule out* realism with respect to a strong notion of causation, or the possibility that this world is a world in which there is such causation. So realists about possible worlds shouldn't positively endorse a regularity theory of causation, even if they can make better sense of it than most. The same goes for any 'many-worlds' theorists who think that all possible sequences of events are actual.

[12] I develop it at more length in Strawson 1987: §4.

not, so far, a problem. It does, however, require us to grant what is surely true: that what it is for the fundamental forces to exist isn't anything over and above what it is for matter to exist with the nature that it has. The existence of matter cannot come apart from the existence of the fundamental forces—contrary to the bad, separatist picture. (Note that one can replace 'fundamental forces' with 'laws of nature' conceived of as non-linguistic, objective principles of operation rather than human linguistic creations.)

Suppose that the regularity theorists do deny the existence of objective fundamental forces, while continuing to think in terms of the existence of matter or physical objects. They will still surely concede that physical objects have a certain *nature*. But now they appear to be in trouble. For, given that objects have a certain nature, it is as remarked natural (not to say obligatory) to suppose that their behavioural and regularity properties are an expression or manifestation of their nature. But regularity theorists who have granted that objects have a certain nature will presumably have to deny that their regularity of behaviour is a function or manifestation or expression of their nature, because there is on the regularity view nothing about the world which is the reason why it's regular in its behaviour. In so doing they will embrace a weird picture of matter as a stuff with a nature given which the question of how it behaves in and through time is still *completely open*. The only alternative seems to be to deny that matter has a nature at all, for it seems that the ordinary notion of the nature of matter (the nature of concrete reality) is an essentially non-regularity-theory notion; this, it seems, is what the regularity theory self-defeatingly leads to, when strictly interpreted. Matter is essentially matter-in-time. Perhaps we should always call matter 'matter-in-time', so that we never forget this (Strawson 1987: 394). For it to have a nature just is for it to have a nature-in-time, not just at an instant, a time-freezing theoretical abstraction. It just is for it to be stable in its dispositions across time, hence regular in its behaviour.

Objection. 'In effect, the account of things just given—call it *T*—simply builds objects' regularity into their nature (since their regularity is said to be an expression of their nature). *T* is fine, but it constitutes no objection to the regularity theory. For now, according to *T*, to say that the nature of objects is the (ultimate) reason for their regularity is to concede after all that regularity is itself an ultimate fact—since it is in effect *part* of what *T* proposes as the ultimate reason for regularity, to wit, the nature of objects. So the regularity theory is vindicated after all. It's vindicated in the sense that the ultimate reason that is given for the existence of regularity is just regularity. In other words no further reason for regularity—something other than regularity—is given.'

This objection is understandable, but it mistakes the point at issue. For what is crucial in *T* is simply that it has the consequence that the continuing regularity of things is not at each moment a completely chance matter—a fluke. According to *T*, a world whose regularity is a function of the nature of its matter is a causally ordered world, whereas an *ex hypothesi* objectively random world which is in fact qualitatively identical to our world in respect of its regularity properties (like the pixel-particle universe discussed above) is not a causally ordered world at all. The regularity theory must deny the existence of this difference between the two worlds, since it holds that all there is to causation is regularity. It must hold that the objectively random world is causally ordered in every sense in which our world is.

This is the crux. One postulates two worlds which are apparently qualitatively identical, behaviourally speaking; one in which it is, in fact, in the nature of things to be regular, and one in which it is *ex hypothesi* a complete fluke from instant to instant. The regularity theory says that these worlds are equally causally ordered, for causal order is just this regularity.

Regularity theorists may claim to be able to accept this consequence. 'Even if the regularity of our world is a function or expression or aspect of the nature of matter, so that there is a reason for the regularity of the world, something which is therefore not just the regularity itself, still what is correctly called "causation" in our world is just the regularity of what happens. So that a regularity theory of causation is correct in any case.'

To this it may be replied, again, that if this is so then the randomizer-generated world must also be said to be a causally ordered world, which it is not. If the assertion that the randomizer-generated world is not a causally ordered world is rejected as simply begging the question, it may be replied that to grant that there is a reason in the nature of things for the regularity, but to hold that this is no part of what causation is or involves, seems a hopeless move, a concession of defeat, although it can't of course be ruled out as a linguistic manœuvre. (The suggestion that this was at least part of what Hume was saying will be considered below, initially in 8.)

It may now be objected that chaos and regularity are essentially relative terms, and that every possible (finite) sequence of events can be seen to instantiate a regularity, given a sufficiently complicated theory of the nature of the regularity in question. And that, this being so, the distinction invoked above between a world which is regular and a world which is chaotic is spurious. If any world is regular, all worlds are regular.

I think we can ignore, by allowing, this curious point. We can grant that there may be a sense in which all worlds are regular.[13] For the distinction that matters here is not the (supposedly discredited) distinction between a regular world and a chaotic world. It is, rather, and again, the distinction between a world in which there is something in the nature of things which is the reason why things happen in the way

---

[13] It certainly doesn't follow that none are, any more than it follows from the fact that any sequence of numbers can be seen as the exemplification of a rule-governed series that none can be so seen. In fact this provides a good analogy for the point at issue. Consider two identical sequences, one constructed by someone applying an algorism, the other generated by a true random number generator. There is of course a sense in which both 'instantiate' some regularity or 'exemplify' some pattern, but in only one case is there a reason for the regularity, a reason why the next number conforms to the pattern (I'm putting aside the point that some sequences of numbers are 'incompressible').

they do, and a world in which this isn't so. Getting back to the (actual, only) world, which both sides agree is regular in character, the distinction that matters is the distinction between (1) an account of what happens in the world according to which there is something about the world's nature *given* which it is regular in the way it is, and (2) an account of what happens in the world according to which this isn't so.[14]

All one needs for the present argument to proceed is something which is not in dispute—the claim that the world is indeed highly regular in character. As soon as this is granted, the objection to the regularity theory of causation applies: the objection that, given such regularity, it is absurd (even if not incoherent) to insist (ontologically) that there is definitely nothing about the nature of the world given which it is regular in the way that it is; rather than insisting (merely epistemologically) that there is a sense in which regularity is all we can ever observe.

It is, I suggest (and argue in 22) absurd to insist on this *whatever* one's view of the nature of reality—even if one holds some extreme idealist view. But there is something particularly wonderfully absurd about the regularity theory of causation when it is conjoined with a solidly realist conception of the world. One is presented with all these massy physical objects, out there in space-time, behaving in perfectly regular ways, and then one is told that there is, quite definitely, no reason at all for this regularity; absolutely nothing about the nature of reality which is the reason why it *continues* to be regular in the particular way in which it is regular, moment after moment, aeon after aeon. It is, in that clear sense, a pure fluke. It is, at every instant, and as a matter of objective fact, a pure fluke that state n of the world bears precisely the relation to the previous state of the world that one would expect, in line with the previous pattern of regularity.[15] For all there is to causation and causal process is just the fact of this regularity. There is no reason for it in the nature of things.

Am I attacking a straw man? it doesn't seem so. Hume is often thought to hold just this view. This just is the 'Humean' view, in the eyes of many. But Hume never held it.

But if he didn't hold this view and yet did argue for a regularity theory of causation in *some* sense, as he most surely did, then there seem to be only two other possibilities. Either (1) he didn't hold the regularity theory of causation with respect to realist objects, but only with respect to objects conceived of in some other, idealist way as mental contents, 'immediate' mental objects of mental attention. Or (2) he did hold it with respect to something like realist physical objects, but held it only about causation *so far as we know about it* in realist objects (or equivalently, only as a theory about the content of our positive conception of causation in the objects).

---

[14] Suppose that the world is such that there is apparent chaos by our lights. Suppose some claim that this apparent chaos is in fact a manifestation of some superlatively complicated but non-flukish regularity. It is then just as implausible for them to adopt the regularity theory of causation about this world—the theory which asserts that there is no reason for its regularity—as it is for us to adopt it in our actual, patently highly ordered world.

[15] Note that even if there is some objective indeterminism there is still massive regularity: the mistake of thinking that the postulation of such objective indeterminism makes this view defensible is discussed in 8.

I'm going to argue that there is truth in both these alternatives, but that the second is closer to the overall truth: not only because Hume was in general firmly committed to talking in terms of realist objects,[16] but also because of something he says about his two definitions of 'cause' (both in the *Treatise* and in the *Enquiry*), which I'll discuss in 21.

The claim that Hume was firmly committed to talking in terms of realist objects of some sort will be substantiated in various ways in what follows. His commitment leaps to the eye in the *Enquiry*, and at many places in the *Treatise*, but some will doubt it, believing that Hume was, *de facto* at least, some sort of idealist about objects, forced to be so by a theory of meaning which entailed that talk of realist objects was utterly unintelligible. For this reason I will now return to the question of what 'objects' may be supposed to mean. The main reply to the doubt just mentioned will be given in 6.5.

The first three sections of 6 are relatively complicated, and although I think they consider some interesting questions, nothing in the main discussion of Hume depends essentially on them. Those who want to jump straight to 6.4 should however note certain definitions of terms which are used later on. These occur as follows: 'strict idealism' p. 34; 'pure-content idealism' p. 36; 'perception-constituted objects' ('*pc* objects') and 'perception-content-constituted objects' ('*pcc* objects') p. 37; 'ontologically moderate' and 'ontologically outright' 'pure-content idealism' p. 38.

Only sections, 6.4, 6.5, and 6.8 of the next chapter are directly concerned with Hume, and anyone who is primarily interested in Hume can omit all the others, after adding the definition of basic realism on p. 52 to those which need to be noted on the way.

The radical short cut continues as follows. After 6.8, note the definition of 'Causation' with a capital 'C' in 8 (p. 37), the definition of the 'Meaning Tension' in 12 (pp. 117–18), then go on to 17, 20, 21, and possibly 22.1, then stop.

---

[16] Or at least—to anticipate the terms of 6.6—firmly committed to the idea that some 'basic-realist' construal of the term 'the objects' must be correct, even if we cannot know which.

6

'Objects': complications

6.1 Strict idealism

I wish now to consider certain idealist aspects of the speculative metaphysical background against which Hume wrote about external objects or 'bodies'. I won't, however, say much about the details of his famously difficult discussion of objects in section 1.4.2 of the *Treatise*, 'Of scepticism with regard to the senses'. One reason for looking at these idealist conceptions of objects is the following: perhaps the claim Hume adopted some sort of ontological regularity theory of causation is defensible only on the assumption that he had in mind one rather special idealist way of conceiving of objects.

I'll discuss the various idealist positions in a straightforwardly ontological idiom. Once a position has been stated in the ontological idiom, one can go on to raise epistemological or semantic questions about whether one could know it to be true, or whether one can intelligibly deny its truth, or whether it is really meaningful in the way that it appears to be.

The idealist position introduced in 4 (pp. 19–20), according to which objects (tables and chairs, etc.) are perception-constituted objects, or, more narrowly, perception-*content*-constituted objects, needn't be any sort of standard, Berkeleian idealist position. And the position that is of principal present concern is not a standard, Berkeleian position.[1] It's more radical. Its key idea is that in thinking of objects as perception-constituted, or as perception-content-constituted, one doesn't 'go beyond' perceptions in any way at all, ontologically speaking, in one's account of what is involved in the objects' existence: either causally, or with respect to 'substantial ground', or in any other way.[2] The epistemological motive for restricting oneself in this way in one's account of objects, given a Humean epistemology, is that it's the only way of guaranteeing that one doesn't in any way go beyond the kind of thing one can know about, or know for certain to exist, or have direct experience of. For, given a Humean epistemology, perceptions are the only kind of thing one can know about or know for certain to exist, or have direct experience of, so far as real existents are concerned.[3]

---

[1] Although it may once have tempted Berkeley; see n. 5.

[2] The phrase 'involved in the existence of' is intentionally imprecise.

[3] Perceptions are called 'ideas' in Berkeley's writings, but I'll use Hume's term 'perception' even when discussing Berkeleian views.

Whether this epistemological motive for not 'going beyond' perceptions should be allowed to determine one's ontological views is highly dubious; but here I'm concerned only to describe a certain radical idealist option, not to justify it. When it's more fully described, it may sound arcane and uninteresting to some; but it can't be uninteresting to those who are interested in Hume, and its theoretical significance should become apparent in the next two sections, where it will be suggested that it— or something like it—is the only account of the nature of objects which is plausibly cotenable with a regularity theory of causation in those objects. (The implausibility of the *realist* regularity theory of causation was noted in 5.)

Suppose, then, that one is determined not to go beyond perceptions in any way, ontologically, in one's overall account of the nature and being of objects. One thing is immediately clear. One can't think of perceptions (in particular impressions of sensation, but I'll talk simply of perceptions) as caused by anything like realist objects. Equally, one can't think of them as directly caused by some (divine) mind—so long as one thinks of that divine mind as ontologically distinct from its perceptions, in the sense of not being wholly constituted out of its perceptions in the way proposed by the infamous 'bundle' theory of mind.[4] For, given a Humean epistemology (of the kind which motivates the present attempt to give an account of the nature and being of objects just in terms of perceptions), a mind conceived of as something other than a series or 'bundle' of perceptions is as 'perfectly inexplicable' (84/1.3.5.2) as a realist object.

So one can't even think of objects as Berkeley arguably sometimes does—i.e. as perception-constituted objects which are (sets of) perceptions caused by the direct mental action of some god ('God') upon our minds.[5] For to do this is to go beyond perceptions in at least two ways, ontologically speaking, in one's overall account of what the existence of objects involves. First, it's to think of God as directly causally involved in the existence of objects, and himself 'ontologically perception-transcendent': neither a perception nor a series of perceptions. Secondly, even when one puts the question of their cause completely to one side, objects are still thought of as things whose existence involves the existence of something ontologically perception-transcendent. For they're still thought of as having some essential ontic grounding in something ontologically

---

[4] The ontological idealist 'bundle' theory of mind is very strange, and was never endorsed by Hume (see Craig 1987: §2.5; also 12.3 below and Strawson 2011 *passim*), but it has a role to play in the argument: the motives for adopting it are from a certain perspective highly understandable. Like Hume, Berkeley explicitly (and almost inevitably—cf. 6.7) considered a bundle theory of mind in his *Philosophical Commentaries* §§ 577–81 ('Mind is a congeries of Perceptions. Take away Perceptions & you take away the Mind'), but he didn't of course adopt it. Hylas raises the issue in the 'Third Dialogue', telling Philonous that 'in consequence of your own principles, it should follow that you are only a system of floating ideas, without any substance to support them' (1713: 198). Philonous replies, 'How often must I repeat, that I know or am conscious of my own being; and that I myself am not my ideas, but somewhat else, a thinking active principle...'.

[5] Here I'm concerned with what is perhaps the most well known version of Berkeley's views (cf. n. 8). On the whole I use Berkeley as a familiar idealist reference point, without taking account of all the various subtleties of his position(s).

distinct from all perceptions, i.e. one's own non-bundle-theory, non-perception-constituted mind (they're presumably states or modes or modifications of this mind). And one cannot think of them in this way either, on the present radical idealist view.

I'll call this radical idealist view the *strict-idealist* account of objects. It's strict insofar as it supposes that the existence of objects involves nothing more than the existence of perceptions in any way or at any stage. Berkeley's position is often taken as the paradigm of an idealist account of objects, but it's not strict-idealist on the present view, because it supposes that things other than perceptions—minds which are not constituted out of perceptions—are essentially involved in the existence of objects. One may say that Berkeley is a strict *mentalist* (nothing non-mental exists) but he's not a strict idealist. He is an idealist *with respect to* objects, or the external world, but he's not an all-out ontological idealist, who holds that ideas are all that exist.[6]

Strict idealism, then, is committed to the existence of only one type of existent—perceptions ('ideas'). It quite rightly observes that the existence of perceptions is undeniable, but refuses to commit itself to the existence of anything else. It seems clear that those who are strict idealists about everything must endorse that strange thing, the bundle theory of mind. For perceptions are, quite simply, all that exist; they're the ultimate constituents of reality, and they are therefore all that anything could be made of, including minds.

It seems that one could reasonably be said to be a strict idealist about what one thought of as objects (the whole world of physical objects and events, tables and chairs and storms) while not being a strict idealist about absolutely everything (not in one's overall metaphysic). It seems that one could think of *minds* as ontologically perception-transcendent, ontologically distinct from and over and above perceptions, but still be said to think of *objects* in a strict-idealist way as nothing more than perceptions.[7] It's arguable, though, that those who are strict idealists about objects must also accept a bundle theory of mind. For a perception is by definition a mental occurrence; and a mental occurrence is necessarily a state or part of or event in a mind (anyone who claims that mental occurrences exist while minds don't can be classified straight away as a bundle theorist of mind). So a perception is necessarily a state or part of or event in a mind—which is to say that some mind is necessarily involved in the existence of any perception. So some mind is necessarily involved in

---

[6] Berkeley's view has several variants (see in particular Foster 1982: ch. 2, 1985). But even when he adopts a kind of representational theory of perception—presenting our perceptions as resembling representations of 'archetype' perceptions in God's minds—his account is still one in which minds (both ours and God's) not constituted out of perceptions are (both causally and as 'substantial ground') involved in the existence of perceptions.

[7] There are of course indefinitely many other strange metaphysical possibilities: one could for example postulate some strange, non-mental and non-physical substance that was quite unlike what one thought of as objects.

the existence of any object, since objects are ontically nothing over and above perceptions, according to strict idealism. But to say that objects are ontically nothing over and above perceptions is to say that nothing other than perceptions is involved in their existence. So it seems that one can't after all be a strict idealist about what is involved in the existence of objects, and not also be a strict idealist about minds—which means accepting a bundle theory of mind (insofar as one holds that there are minds at all).

This argument seems valid, but there remains an interesting sense in which even someone like Berkeley can be said to be giving a strict-idealist account *of objects*, even though he's clearly not a strict idealist *tout court* (he's not a strict idealist about minds). I'll consider this version of the strict-idealist account of objects in the next section. Then I'll connect it with the regularity theory of causation. It may be thought to be far from Hume's concerns, but it's arguable that Hume adopted a straightforward regularity theory about causation in the objects only insofar as he sometimes thought of objects in the way about to be described.

6.2 Perception-constituted objects and perception-content-constituted objects

In order to evaluate the suggestion that 'the objects' are just perceptions, I'll consider perceptions 'just as such', i.e. entirely independently of any speculation about their causal origin (God, in Berkeley's view). On these terms, one can distinguish at least three idealist conceptions of the nature of objects. Two of them are strict-idealist; one will turn out to be of particular importance.

According to the first, rich, *non*-strict-idealist, arguably fully Berkeleian conception of perceptions

p1   perceptions are, in themselves, real states, 'modes', or 'modifications' of minds, which are themselves something over and above perceptions, ontologically speaking (they're not bundle-theory minds).

The existence of perceptions essentially involves the existence of something other than perceptions. It involves the existence of ontically perception-transcendent things—minds. One could call these *non-self-subsistent* perceptions.[8]

According to the second, non-Berkeleian, strict-idealist conception of perceptions

p2   the existence of perceptions doesn't involve the existence of any ontically perception-transcendent thing like a Berkeleian mind. Perceptions don't require the existence of anything other than perceptions in order to exist.

---

[8] Perceptions are also non-self-subsistent on the materialist account of the mind.

One could call perceptions so conceived *entirely self-subsistent* perceptions.[9] Clearly, if one adopts this second conception of perceptions, and grants that (1) minds are essentially involved in the existence of perceptions, one must adopt a bundle theory of mind according to which (2) minds are entirely constituted out of perceptions.[10]

The third conception of perceptions is also strict-idealist, and arises from a subdivision of the second. For there are at least two ways of interpreting the conception of perceptions as entirely self-subsistent entities. According to the first, although perceptions are entirely self-subsistent, they are nevertheless *something more than their content*, ontically speaking, where by 'content', I mean something entirely concrete, concretely occurring experiential qualitative content. That is, they have some ontic aspect or mode of being which is over and above their having the content they have. They're not just contents, they're content-possessing *vehicles* of content; they have some *content-transcending* nature, ontologically speaking (compare pictures and their pictorial content). Perhaps each involves the existence of some kind of content-carrying, ontologically speaking content-transcending 'immaterial stuff', or indeed material stuff.

I'll restrict the label 'p2 perceptions' to perceptions conceived of in this way. p2 perceptions, then, are entirely self-subsistent entities—they're not essentially based in Berkeleian minds—but they are nevertheless something more than just their (occurrent experiential) content, ontologically speaking.[11]

According to the second way of interpreting the conception of perceptions as entirely self-subsistent entities

p3   perceptions have no content-transcending nature or mode of being whatever.

This is the purest form of idealism. It's not only strict idealism (all that exist are perceptions), but what one might call *pure-content idealism*: perceptions are pure contents; all there is, ontologically speaking, is content. Contents don't require non-content-constituted vehicles of some sort in order to exist. They are entirely self-subsistent in their pure contenthood, occurring and existing, the ultimate *realia*. On the p3 view, the existence of perceptions not only involves nothing *perception*-transcendent (as p1 perceptions do by contrast with p2 perceptions); it also involves nothing *content*-transcendent (as p2 perceptions do by contrast with p3 perceptions).

There's no need to spend much time assessing the relative merits and demerits (let alone the coherence or incoherence) of these three idealist conceptions of perceptions. All three have their place, either explicitly, or implicitly and confusedly, in the history of philosophy. The p1 and p3 conceptions are no doubt more important than

---

[9] Hume adverts to the possibility of such a view at several points in the *Treatise*; cf. 233/1.4.5.5, 634/App§12.

[10] Hume may be thought to deny (1) in the *Treatise* (206/1.4.2.37), but his reference there to 1.4.6 shows that things are not so simple (for a discussion of this point see Strawson 2011: 2.14).

[11] p1 perceptions are also 'vehicles' of content: they too have some non-content-constituted nature, and may thus be thought of as vehicles of content.

the **p2** conception. What matters here is that to these three conceptions of perceptions there obviously correspond three different idealist conceptions of objects (tables and chairs, etc.). For idealists think of objects as constituted out of perceptions.

According to the first (non-strict) idealist conception of objects

> **o1** objects are constituted out of (Berkeleian idealist) non-self-subsistent perceptions.

The ultimate ontological truth about them is that they're real states of immaterial, non-bundle-theory minds, ontologically speaking perception-transcendent minds. They're grounded in some ontologically perception-transcendent substance.

According to the second and third (strict-idealist) conceptions, objects are constituted out of entirely self-subsistent perceptions. As such they're either

> **o2** things which do (like **o1** objects) have some content-transcendent ontic aspect or mode of being

or

> **o3** things which have no content-transcendent ontic aspect or mode of being whatever

According to the second conception, objects are constituted out of perceptions conceived of as entirely self-subsistent but ontologically content-transcendent things. According to the third conception, objects are entirely constituted out of perceptions conceived of not only as entirely self-subsistent things, but also as entirely content-constituted things.

We have, then, three idealist accounts of the ultimate ontological nature of perceptions, and, hence, of objects. All three take objects (the things we call tables and chairs—perhaps this reminder is never superfluous) to be entirely constituted out of perceptions, to be entirely *perception-constituted objec*ts or as I will say *pc objects*. The third, **p3**, supposes this simply because it supposes that there is nothing more to perceptions than their content. Of the three, it alone gives a *pure-content-idealist* account of objects—**o3**. It gives what one may call an ontologically outright pure-content-idealist account of objects. Objects are entirely *perception-content-constituted objects* or as I will say *pcc objects*.

There is, however, a different and more moderate way of interpreting the idea that objects are entirely perception-content-constituted entities, and of thereby giving a pure-content-idealist account of objects. This more moderate version of pure-content idealism is more important for present purposes than **o3**, the ontologically outright version, because it casts more light on the respect in which an idealist conception of the nature of objects is the point of origin (and true home) of the regularity theory of causation. I'll describe it in the rest of this section. In the next section I'll link it to the issue of causation.

We need to go back to the suggestion at the end of 6.1, the suggestion that there's a sense in which even those with a broadly speaking Berkeleian outlook can be said to give a strict-idealist account of *objects*, even though they're not strict idealists *tout court*, because they take minds to be more than just ideas: to be ontically perception-transcendent things.

As it stands, the Berkeleian position on objects isn't strict-idealist at all. Objects are constituted out of perceptions, but perceptions are **p1** perceptions, real states or modifications of ontically perception-transcendent minds. Such minds are therefore 'involved in the existence of' objects. The perceptions which constitute objects are, furthermore, caused by an ontically perception-transcendent entity (God).

One can, however, consider perceptions independently of their cause. In fact one can go further. Even if one takes it (with Berkeley) that perceptions have some content-transcending nature, one can still consider them *just in respect of their content*, i.e. not only independently of their cause but also independently of any non-content-constituted substantial ground or realization which they may have.[12] That is, one can, when considering perceptions just in respect of their content, abstract from all sorts of questions about their ultimate ontical nature as perceptions (questions to which **p1**, **p2** and **p3** above give different answers). One can then go on to conceive of *objects* (tables and chairs, the things we talk and think about) as in some sense entirely constituted of the content of perceptions, while continuing to abstract from all further questions about these perceptions' ultimate ontical nature.

These are aery regions. I'll try to be clear. As remarked, the **p1**, **p2**, and **p3** accounts of the nature of perceptions all give different answers to these questions. (So too, of course, does the materialist account of the nature of perceptions; but that is not of present concern.) We're not concerned with the **p3** account, since we're not concerned with ontologically outright pure-content idealism, but only with ontologically moderate pure-content idealism, which allows that perceptions may and indeed do have some non-content-constituted nature. That leaves the **p1** and **p2** accounts.

To conceive of objects in the *moderate* pure-content-idealist way, within the scope of a **p1** or **p2** account of perceptions, is not to conceive of objects as simply identical with (sets of) perceptions. Only a **p3**-type account of perceptions allows a pure-content-idealist account of objects to *identify* objects with perceptions, since it conceives of perceptions as pure contents. Both **p1**-type perceptions and **p2**-type perceptions, by contrast, have some content-transcendent ontic aspect or mode of being—something one has to abstract from if one is going to claim to be giving some

---

[12] It's not only when one considers them as **p1** or **p2** perceptions that one can do this; one can also consider them just in respect of their content on a materialist account according to which the realizing grounds of perceptions are physical states of the brain; or on some other account according to which the true and unknowable substantial nature of the world may be neither physical nor mental. (Some properly sceptical versions of phenomenalism are of this form.)

sort of pure-content-idealist account of objects. So one must consider **p1** or **p2** perceptions just in respect of their content, and not in all respects.

One may then be reasonably said to be giving a pure-content-idealist account of *objects*. But one isn't giving a pure-content-idealist account of reality considered as a whole, because one allows that there are non-content-constituted aspects of reality. One allows that the contents out of which objects are constituted have some sort of content-transcendent (non-content-constituted) *vehicle*; one simply leaves the vehicle out of account. One distinguishes the perceptions taken as a whole, and considered as content-carrying vehicles of content, from their content considered in isolation, and one refers only to this content considered in isolation, in giving one's account of objects.

This is moderate pure-content idealism. It gives an account of objects according to which they are in themselves purely content-constituted, even though (if full onto-logical truth be told) they're constituted out of perceptions which have some content-transcendent nature, being *vehicles* of content, and not just pure contents. This seems an accurate description of one of Berkeley's accounts of the physical world, and it is in any case historically important: there is I think a deep connection between moderate pure-content idealism about objects and the regularity theory of causation. In putting the case for this view I'll begin by considering a pure-content-idealist version of Berkeley ('Berkeley^Pci', whose relation to the historical figure is friendly but unclear), and then go on to Hume.

Consider in conclusion a person called Louis who is a 'brain in a vat'. A materialist might suggest that the best account of the world of objects Louis believes himself to inhabit is an idealist account according to which the objects in his world are *pc* objects, or, more particularly, *pcc* objects. The point of classifying the objects that exist in Louis's world in this way is immediately apparent, and it's clearly fully compatible with the materialist thought that the perceptions out of which the objects in question are constituted are, ultimately, physical states of his (computer-affected) brain. This case provides a clear example of the more moderate version of pure-content idealism about objects; it makes it vivid that the pure-content-idealist account of objects abstracts completely from questions about the ultimate (ontic) nature of the perceptions.

It also illustrates the epistemological point of adopting the moderate pure-content-idealist account of objects if one is a sceptic like Hume. To the extent that one admits that one can't refute the suggestion that one might be something like a brain in a vat (or something much stranger than a brain, in something much stranger than a vat), one grants that the moderate pure-content-idealist account of the world of objects one takes oneself to inhabit, which seemed appropriate for the brain in a vat, expresses all one can know for certain about objects, although there may well be something more to them in fact.

6.3 A viable regularity theory of causation

Berkeley is a pure-content idealist about objects only in the second, more moderate sense. Insofar as he can be said to think of objects as *pcc* objects, he still thinks of them as ultimately vehicle-based. They're vehicle-based if full ontological truth be told, constituted by the content of **p1**-type perceptions which are themselves real states or modifications of ontically perception-transcendent, non-bundle-theory immaterial minds.

Consider the Berkeley^{Pci} world of objects. What if anything can *causation* be, in this world? On this question, Berkeley^{Pci} agrees completely with historical Berkeley: there is no causation. In a world of objects literally constituted of perceptions considered just in respect of their content (and so considered completely independently both of their ultimate cause—God—and of their basis in non-bundle-theory immaterial minds) there are only and at most regular-succession relations between objects and object-involving events, without any real causal relations between them whereby one thing actually brings about or derives from another. Both Berkeley^{Pci} and historical Berkeley say this, and so they should, given their other commitments. The sense in which there are causal relations between objects and object-involving events in the pure-content-idealist world is exactly the same as the sense in which there are causal relations between objects and events in a story depicted in successive frames of a cartoon film.[13]

There's still a reason for the regularity of the world of (content-constituted) objects, on this Berkeleian account, i.e. God; the Berkeleian account does not court absurdity (see 5) in the way that the realist regularity theory of causation does. But, crucially, the reason for the regularity lies entirely outside world of objects. It's God, conceived of as external to the world in question, who gives rise to the (*pcc*) objects and their regularity.[14]

What about Hume? *To the extent that* he sometimes uses the expression 'the objects' in something close to the present moderate pure-content-idealist way, when

---

[13] For an expansion of the cartoon analogy, see the appendix on pp. 60–4 below.

[14] Historical Berkeley doesn't have to endorse the explicit complications of moderate pure-content idealism in order to reach the conclusion that causation in the objects is at most regular succession. The basic idea behind moderate pure-content idealism is latent in his theory, and when he talks of perceptions ('ideas') as being entirely 'passive', i.e. causally inefficacious entities, this may very well be because he is in effect thinking of them just in respect of their content, like a moderate pure-content idealist. But even if he is thinking of perceptions as real states of immaterial non-bundle-theory minds, his position is that they are entirely 'passive' entities. It follows immediately that there can't be real causal relations between objects *qua* perceptions. Whatever the differences between Berkeley^{Pci} and historical Berkeley, the sense in which the regularity theory of causation is the right theory to adopt about causation in the objects is the same in both cases. Was Berkeley the secret father of the regularity theory of causation (he considers it in the *Philosophical Commentaries*, e.g. sects. 850, 855–6)? Then Malebranche was the unwitting *grand-père* (see C. J. McCracken, *Malebranche and British Philosophy*, pp. 96–9, 257–61). Both he and Berkeley stressed the idea that regularity is all we ever strictly speaking perceive in objects; but Descartes and Locke—and no doubt others—must also be taken into account.

talking about causation, he agrees with Berkeley completely. He just puts it rather differently. Instead of holding that there is only regular succession in this world of objects, and that therefore there isn't any real causation in the world of objects, he allows that there is causation in the world of objects, but that all it is (and can be), in this world so conceived, is regular succession.[15]

It's to just and only this extent that Hume is ever any sort of outright or ontological regularity theorist about causation in 'the objects'. Rightly so, for in this case the 'causation' isn't real causation; it's mere regular succession; cartoon-film-content causation. In the cartoon world, there is a clear and instructive sense in which it really is true to say, with Ayer, that nothing ever really brings anything else about, and that 'one thing just happens after another'.

But even when Hume is conceiving of 'the objects' in this way he can't be supposed to be a regularity theorist *tout court* and with respect to everything (any more than Berkeley is a regularity theorist *tout court* in his overall account of reality). It can't be supposed that he is a regularity theorist with respect to the operations of the 'perfectly inexplicable...ultimate cause' of perceptions, for example. In fact it is only because the moderate pure-content-idealist account of objects allows that objects do in the final analysis have some further content-transcendent nature and cause (in being the contents of perceptions which have some ontically content-transcendent nature and cause) that it can confidently go ahead and give a pure or mere regularity-theory account of causation in the objects. It can do this because it abstracts from a part or aspect of what it thinks of as reality-as-a-whole, in giving its official account of the world of objects, thereby leaving somewhere where the reason for the regularity in the world of objects can be located. In this way it avoids the absurdity of the realist regularity theory of causation, which leaves no place in which a reason for the regularity can be located, and thereby commits itself to the view that there is definitely no reason at all in the nature of things why objects are regular in the way that they are.

6.4 Hume uncommitted

But what does Hume mean by 'the objects'? One suggestion about what he may sometimes have meant has just been considered, but the general question is still unanswered.

The root question is this: Was Hume's use of the word 'object' realist or idealist? The first answer is that he is (especially in the *Treatise*) not entirely consistent in his

[15] In thus comparing Hume with Berkeley I am taking it that Hume did think that perceptions have some perception-transcendent cause or ground, although its nature is unknowable (see 84/1.3.5.2, 152–3/ 12.11). This will be supported in various ways in what follows, starting in the next section. His strict sceptical position is that perceptions may have some such unknowable cause or ground, but that whether they do or not is unknowable. He certainly considers the suggestion that 'for aught we can know a priori' there might exist nothing but perceptions (on e.g. 233/1.4.5.5, 634/App§12).

intentions with regard to the force of the word. Sometimes it seems that he clearly intends to give it some sort of realist force (objects are genuinely 'external objects'). Sometimes it seems that he supposes it to have some merely idealist force (objects are the 'immediate' objects of mental attention).

This is perhaps not surprising. As a sceptic, Hume holds that we can never establish which general theory of reality, realist or idealist, is right. He holds that such metaphysical questions are fruitless; not meaningless, but fruitless. Berkeley's idealist theory, for example, cannot be refuted (155/12.15 n.). So rather than uselessly asking whether our natural realist beliefs about objects are true, we should ask a new question, a question about our psychological nature: 'What is it about us which makes it the case that these beliefs arise in us, given the nature of our sensory experience?'

This move of Hume's was profound; it's justly celebrated. But it may now be objected—perhaps with some irritation on the part of some Hume scholars—that a more definite answer can be given to the question of what he means by 'the objects'. 'Look, it can never be right to attribute any sort of realist use to Hume, because, on his own principles (in particular his strict empiricist theory of ideas), the realist notion of a physical object is "unintelligible", "fiction"-involving, "absurd" (188/ 1.4.2.2). Our ideas and words cannot in their content or meaning or reference in any way "go beyond" what we have access to in our experience, and since all we ever really have access to in our experience are perceptions and their contents, all that objects can *be* are idealist objects—"*pc*" objects or "*pcc*" objects in the terms of 6.3. We never have access to anything like realist objects, and cannot properly suppose that we can talk of such things in any way at all.'[16]

Suppose that this general account of Hume's 'strict empiricism' were right (it's certainly arguable that this is what he ought to have said, given his theory of ideas). It would appear to have the following consequences. When he writes about objects

(1)   he is only ever concerned with some idealist interpretation of 'the objects' to mean *pc* objects or more particularly *pcc* objects.

[16] 'What's more, Hume can have no use for the distinction between *pc* objects and *pcc* objects. He can only be talking of the latter, because he can't admit *pc* objects which are not also *pcc* objects. For (i) he can't allow that objects have *any* aspect which is inaccessible in experience (they can have no hidden ontic backside). But then (ii) they must just amount to *pcc* objects. For (iii) only the content of experience is strictly speaking accessible in experience (the content of experience is all there is to experience). But (iv) to suggest that objects are *pc* objects, but possibly not just *pcc* objects, is to suggest that they're constituted out of perceptions which are in some respect ontically more than their content. But then (v) this respect in which they're more then their content is necessarily inaccessible in experience. Hence (vi) it can't be part of what we mean by "objects". The conclusion that Hume can only ever really mean *pcc* objects by "objects" is inescapable given premises (i) and (iii).' Reply: Yes; the fault lies in (i).

Hence

(2)   he is only ever concerned to propound the regularity theory of causation with respect to some variety of idealist objects (6.3)

—simply because he is only ever concerned with idealist objects when he talks about 'the objects'. And

(3)   he's not at all concerned to propound the regularity theory of causation as a theory about causation in realist objects.

Can this be right? I think it's partly right. (3) is true: Hume never adopted the 'Humean' view, the regularity theory of causation as a theory about realist objects. And (2) is close to the truth: it's plausible to say that if and insofar as he ever propounded the regularity theory of causation as a positive ontological theory of causation in the objects, rather than of causation so far as we can know about it or distinctly conceive it in the objects, Hume was only concerned with objects conceived as *pc* objects, perception-constituted objects.[17] But (2) as just restated contains an important 'if', and (1) is false. It's false that Hume is never concerned with objects conceived of in some sort of realist way. For one thing, he holds that 'the perceptions of the mind are perfectly known', while 'the essence and composition of external bodies are so obscure, that we must necessarily, in our reasonings, or rather conjectures concerning them, involve ourselves in contradictions and absurdities' (366/2.2.6.2). Plainly, then, such bodies can't be perceptions, or constituted out of perceptions.

So (1) is certainly false. *A fortiori*, it's false that (2) and (3) are true (or more or less true) *because* (1) is true. That is, it's wrong to say that Hume is never concerned to assert the regularity theory of causation about realist objects of some sort *because* he never really talks about realist objects at all. It's quite clear, overwhelmingly so in the *Enquiry*, and no less so at many points in the *Treatise*, that Hume very often intends to be understood to be talking about something like realist objects (at the very least, perception-transcendent objects) both in general and when writing about causation in particular. In the *Treatise* he remarks that rejecting the view

that there is such a thing in nature as a continu'd existence [i.e. of external objects] . . . has been peculiar to a few extravagant sceptics; who after all maintain'd that opinion in words only, and were never able to bring themselves sincerely to believe it.[18]

---

[17]   The doubt about (2) stems from doubt about whether he ever propounded the regularity theory at all, as a positive ontological theory of what causation is in the objects. I think it may be just about acceptable to allow a sense in which he did (as noted in 6.3). It would, however, be quite wrong to take the 'first definition' of cause (quoted on p. 9, n. 7/000) as evidence that he did, for reasons given in 21 below.
[18]   214/1.4.2.50. Some may think it significant that Hume here says that rejection of the belief in 'the independence and continuance of our sensible perceptions' has, '*in a manner*, [as a] necessary consequence', the rejection of 'the opinion of [the] continu'd existence [of objects]'. But note 'in a manner'; this is not Hume's own considered view, as will emerge in the next section. Here Hume is simply describing a

Clearly, Hume does not himself reject the opinion of a continued existence of external objects.

6.5 Supposing and conceiving

This may be doubted. What happens when he explicitly considers the thought that such talk of realist objects is illegitimate or 'unintelligible', given his theory of ideas? Speaking generally of the notion of external objects, he says that it is 'impossible for us so much as to conceive or form an idea of any thing specifically different from ideas and impressions' (67/1.2.6.8). By 'specifically different' he means 'of a different species or kind of thing', and his claim is that it's impossible for us to form any idea of anything that is thought of as being of an entirely different species or kind of thing from ideas and impressions. But a realist object—an object conceived of as an entirely non-mental thing, a mind-independent external physical object—is plainly of an entirely different species or kind of thing from a mental thing like an impression or idea (though see the comment on Locke in note 19). So Hume seems to be saying that we can never conceive of or form any idea of such a thing as a realist object. For 'we never really advance a step beyond ourselves, nor can conceive any kind of existence', except for that of impressions and ideas (67/1.2.6.8; cf. also 218/1.4.2.56).

But Hume then grants that we can after all form some sort of conception of external objects. It's just that

the farthest we can go towards a conception of external objects, when *suppos'd* **specifically** different from our perceptions, is to form a *relative* idea of them, without pretending to *comprehend* the related objects. (68/1.2.6.9)

This is the farthest we can go. But a relative idea is not no idea at all. True, we can't 'comprehend' external objects in any way on the terms of the theory of ideas. We can't in any way positively grasp or encompass (consider the etymology of 'comprehend') their real nature in thought. We can't form any *positively descriptively contentful conception* of their nature. We can't form any positively descriptively contentful conception of their nature of a sort that could count as a genuine comprehending or taking hold (or *Begriff*) of them in thought, because according to the theory of ideas

(1) we can form a positively contentful conception of something only out of impressions-and-ideas material,

i.e. impressions material—for all ideas are in turn formed only by a kind of copying and combining of impressions material. But we've just supposed that

---

natural train of thought on the part of the imagination, and pointing out a consequence of a strict interpretation of the claim that 'our perceptions are our only objects'.

(2)   external objects are entirely different in *species* or *kind* from impressions and ideas,

and Hume takes it that it follows from (2) that

(3)   any impressions-and-ideas material we have is useless, in the attempt to form a positively descriptively contentful conception of the nature of external objects,

where these are supposed to be specifically different from perceptions. One might as well try to get a congenitally blind person to form a positively contentful conception of particular colours by giving them shapes to feel.[19]

But although we can't form any idea of external objects that counts as positively contentful on the terms of the theory of ideas, we can still form a *relative* idea of such objects. It's a merely relative idea because we can't in any way conceive of or positively descriptively represent the nature of an external object (when it's supposed specifically different from perceptions). We can conceive it only indirectly. We may for example conceive it as something that stands in a certain relation (the relation of cause) to our perceptions (cf. 84/1.3.5.2).

So we can conceive it only as something that stands in certain relations, or holds a place in a system of relations,[20] while having no positive conception of its nature considered on its own. But a merely relative idea of something X is not no idea of X at all. A merely 'relative' idea of X is merely 'relationally of' X, in Quine's idiom, and not in any way 'notionally of' X (Quine 1956). Nevertheless—to use a different form of the Latin word from which 'relative' and 'relational' derive—it may and does *refer* to X. It hits X referentially, although it doesn't constitute any sort of substantive positive descriptive characterization of X.

---

[19] Note that the idea that we can form no sort of positive conception of external objects depends, for Hume, on the view that no version of Locke's claim about the resemblance between the primary qualities of objects and our ideas of these primary qualities is defensible. For if Locke's resemblance claim is defensible, then our ideas of primary qualities can indeed contentfully capture the nature of realist objects to some degree. So we can after all 'comprehend' external realist objects to some degree through the medium of our ideas of primary qualities (although we can never know that we do). In the *Treatise* Hume follows Berkeley in being highly sceptical of Locke's resemblance claim, but in the *Enquiry* he says that it is a straightforward but undecidable 'question of fact' whether or not it or something like it is true (153/12.12).

Note also that 'X is specifically different from Y' means something stronger, in Hume's use, than what we mean when we say that cats, elephants and roses are of different species. The idea is that X and Y are of entirely different metaphysical kinds in such a way that they can't be supposed to have properties in common; so that we can't form any sort of positive conception of Xs on the basis of experience of Ys. Hume takes external objects and perceptions to be of entirely different kinds in this sense, but if some form of Lockean representative realism is after all defensible, and perceptions of primary qualities can be held to resemble and thus in some way truly represent primary qualities as they are in objects, then there's a respect in which external objects and perceptions are not after all of entirely different kinds in this sense. (This issue will be taken up again in 13.2.)

[20] Compare our relation to the referent of a variable in a theory expressed by a 'Ramsey sentence' (Ramsey 1929, Lewis 1972).

This line of thought will be developed in 12. For the moment, consider the idea one has of something when one can refer to it only as 'whatever it was that caused this appalling mess'. In this case one may have no positive conception of the nature of X. (Except, perhaps, the thought that it is a physical phenomenon. But then, who knows? It may not even be a physical phenomenon.) Here one has a referentially efficacious but in a sense contentless and hence 'merely relative' idea of X.

Similarly—and to anticipate—the merely relative idea of causal power or force in nature is: *whatever it is in reality which is that in virtue of which reality is regular in the way that it is*; or, in Hume's terms, 'those powers and forces [unknown and "unintelligible" as they are], on which [the] regular... succession of objects *totally depends*' (55/5.22); whatever unknown thing is in fact the 'reason of the conjunction' of any two objects' (93/1.3.6.15). This description suffices to pick causal power out, given that it exists, in such a way that we can *refer* to it while having no positive conception of its nature on the terms of the theory of ideas.

It may be objected that when Hume refers back to the passage quoted at the beginning of this section, in which he distinguishes supposing from conceiving (67–8/1.2.6.7–9), he says that the notion of external objects specifically different from perceptions is 'absurd' (188/1.4.2.2). But he doesn't mean what we mean by 'absurd', if by saying that something is absurd we mean that it can't possibly exist.[21] He means that the idea of external objects specifically different from perceptions is empty or void in the sense of having no positive, directly experience-based, sensory-experience-like content. He doesn't take this to imply that there are no external objects. His concern is with the question of what sort of contentful *idea* we may reasonably or legitimately suppose ourselves to have of external objects. *Some* version of the idea that there are such things is something 'which we must take for granted in all our reasonings' (187/1.4.2.1). We must take it for granted in all our reasonings although 'the essence and composition of external bodies are so obscure, that we must necessarily, in our reasonings, or rather conjectures concerning them, involve ourselves in contradictions and *absurdities*' (366/2.2.6.2).[22]

When philosophers today say that something X is unintelligible, they imply that a term 'X', which is being used as if it referred to something, isn't really a term for anything that does or could exist. When Hume says that something X is unintelligible he means the same as Locke. He means that we can't form any idea of or term for X which has any positive content, in the special restricted sense of content specified by the theory of ideas. He doesn't mean that the term 'X' can't be supposed to refer to X, or that the notion of X is an *incoherent* one—any more than Locke supposed that the notion of the unknown real essence of gold was an entirely incoherent one, or that the word 'gold' could not 'carry reference' to the real essence of gold, despite the

---

[21] Absurd: 'against or without reason or propriety; incongruous, unreasonable, illogical' (*OED*).

[22] The meaning of 1.4.2. is endlessly disputed, and I wish to avoid the dispute as far as possible (for an outstanding discussion, see Wright 1983: ch. 2).

fact that he thought that this real essence might be forever undiscoverable by us.[23] As a sceptic, Hume continually stresses the point that there may exist aspects of reality which are not only unknown by us but also unknowable by us, beyond our powers of comprehension, and in that sense entirely unintelligible to us: not *understandable*.

In fact he assumes that there are such aspects, and he is by his overall philosophical theory committed to their existence in various ways. 'The perceptions of the mind are perfectly known', but 'the essence of the mind' is unknown to us, 'equally unknown to us with that of external bodies' (Int§8/xvii).[24] The mind's capacity for reason is 'a wonderful and unintelligible instinct in our souls' (179/1.3.16.9), but it is certainly something real. 'The imagination', so central to Hume's philosophy, 'is a kind of magical faculty in the soul', which is 'inexplicable by the utmost efforts of human understanding' (24/1.1.7.15), but it is certainly something real. (Roughly speaking, Hume uses 'the imagination' to refer to certain very basic features of our cognitive apparatus, those, in particular, in virtue of which we automatically come to conceptualize the world in certain fundamental ways—e.g. as a world of objects subject to Causation—on the basis of our sensory experience. From now on I'll mark Hume's special use of the notion of the imagination with a capital letter—'the Imagination'.)

As for external bodies, 'the essence and composition of external bodies are so obscure, that we must necessarily, in our reasonings, or rather conjectures concerning them, involve ourselves in contradictions and absurdities' (366/2.2.6.2). But this is not to say that there no such things. It is, once again, 'in vain to ask, Whether there be *body* or not? That is a point, which we must take for granted in all our reasonings' (187/1.4.2.1).

The question of the status of our idea of external objects is of fundamental importance to anyone who, like Hume, hopes to combine some kind of strict empiricism with a sceptically open mind on questions about what may or may not exist, and he returns again to the distinction between supposing and conceiving when he closes his discussion of this question at the end of 1.4.2. 'We may well *suppose* in general' that objects are specifically different from perceptions, he says, but '"tis impossible for us distinctly to *conceive*' this.[25] The supposition isn't unintelligible or absurd in our present-day sense; it has genuine content, as a supposition. Nor is an indistinct conception absurd, in our sense of the word; still less is it no conception at all. Hume's point is the same as before: if external objects are indeed

---

[23] See e.g. Locke 1689–1700: 3.10.17–19, and Mackie 1976: §3.7, 'Locke's Anticipation of Kripke'.

[24] Note that this refutes the view that Hume endorsed the outright ontological version of the 'bundle theory of mind'. See further 12.3 below, Strawson 2011 *passim*.

[25] 218/1.4.2.56. When we try to do so, Hume says, what happens at best is that we come up with a 'new set of perceptions', not with mind-independent objects, because all we can ever form a distinct conception of are perceptions. This looks like a clear rejection of the Lockean view that genuinely external objects are at least partly conceivable (because perceptions may genuinely resemble and hence contentfully represent intrinsic properties of things that are not perceptions), in favour of the Berkeleian view that 'an idea [perception] can be like nothing but an idea [perception]' (1710: §8). But Hume was, on the whole, uncertain on this last question—despite the discussion in 1.4.4.

specifically different from our perceptions, then we can only form a 'relative' idea of them: e.g. as 'that which gives rise to our perceptions'.[26]

He returns to the topic in 1.4.5, having decided

to take anew into consideration the question concerning the substance of the soul; and tho' I have condemn'd that question as utterly unintelligible, yet I cannot forbear proposing some farther reflections concerning it' (240/1.4.5.17).

There follow ten pages of entirely intelligible (and brilliant) discussion of the 'utterly unintelligible... question': sufficient proof, if further proof be needed that Hume doesn't mean what we now standardly mean by 'unintelligible'.

Whatever difference we may *suppose* betwixt... [a perception and an external object taken to be specifically different from a perception], 'tis still incomprehensible to us; and we are oblig'd either to *conceive* an external object merely as a relation without a relative, or to make it the very same [as] a perception or impression. (241/1.4.5.19)

Five lines later:

we may *suppose*, but never can *conceive* a specific difference betwixt an object and an impression. (241/1.4.5.20)

Anything that is to count as a genuine conception of something must be descriptively contentful on the terms of the theory of ideas: it must have directly impression-based, impression-copy content. By contrast, a supposition that something is the case can be a genuine supposition, genuinely about something and hence intelligible in our present-day sense, without being contentful (meaningful, intelligible) on the terms of the theory of ideas. We're obliged to 'conceive an external object merely as a relation without a relative' in the sense that nothing can occupy the place where the idea of the external object should be when we attempt a theory-of-ideas-contentful conception of an external object.[27] But it's still an intelligible supposition in our sense of 'intelligible'. Hume respects the principles of his scepticism, which rules out any claim to the effect that we can know that there isn't anything to which the 'relative' or 'suppositional' idea of an external object might relate or refer. He grants that there might be such external objects, explicitly assumes that there are (cf. 218/1.4.2.57), and insists only that if there are, there will always remain a sense in which they are (84/1.3.5.2) 'perfectly inexplicable' by us.[28]

---

[26] We can't even know if external reality is (if 'the objects' are) plural or singular in its (their) ultimate nature. Kant faced the same problems with his 'noumenal reality'.

[27] Earlier, in a passage just quoted (218/1.4.2.56), he says only that we can't conceive this 'distinctly'.

[28] Kant's position on the question of our ability to have something 'specifically different from perceptions' in mind is arguably close to Hume's, if one supposes this something to be 'noumenal reality'—although he distinguishes between the *thinkable* and the *knowable*, rather than between what we may intelligibly suppose and descriptively-contentfully conceive, and appears to make some ill-advisedly definite claims about the non-spatial and non-temporal nature of the noumenal. Locke touches on closely related issues (see 12), and the same question is in various guises the subject of much present-day debate.

Consider how the passage from 241/1.4.5.20 continues:

Since we may suppose, but never can conceive a specific difference betwixt an object and impression; any conclusion we form concerning the connexion and repugnance of impressions, will not be known certainly to be applicable to objects.

Here Hume states that the relations we discover on the basis of our impressions cannot be known to apply to real objects. His closing use of the word 'objects' is straightforwardly realist, and the clause 'will not be known certainly' adds the scepticism to the realism. He goes on to say that although we cannot have certainty, we can 'by an irregular kind of reasoning from experience, discover a connexion betwixt objects, which extends not to impressions' (242/1.4.5.20). No one who acknowledges no distinction between objects and perceptions can say this.[29]

The general issue about meaning will be considered further in 12. For the moment it seems clear that Hume grants the intelligibility-in-our-sense of the supposition that there are realist external objects, even if they're unintelligible on the terms of the theory of ideas, in being 'specifically different from perceptions'.

A stronger claim can be made: Hume regularly writes as some sort of realist. That is, he standardly takes himself to be talking about genuinely external objects, both in general and when writing about causation—certainly in the *Enquiry*, but also in the *Treatise*. The conclusion of 1.4.2, the main discussion of objects in the *Treatise*, is not that there are no external objects, or that the notion of such things is unintelligible in our sense. In the penultimate paragraph, Hume remarks that he began his discussion of objects by 'premising, that we ought to have an implicit faith' in our natural, sense-and-Imagination-based belief in external objects (217/1.4.2.56). He concludes by reaffirming this position, announcing that he will henceforth take as read the 'supposition [that] there is both an external and internal world' (218/1.4.2.57), in spite of the fact that we can't supply any decent rational foundation or justification for our natural belief that there are external objects.

There is, certainly, something seriously inadequate—incomplete, misleading, defective—about any concept of external objects that we can claim to have, on his view, and the question he faces is this: '*What exactly is the content of a natural belief containing a defective concept?*'—whether it be a belief about external objects or causal power. The answer is that it's more or less what we take it to be before we do philosophy, but that it is from the point of view of philosophy fundamentally defective, not distinct, not empirically warranted. When it comes to the question of empirical warrant, the most we can have is a merely 'relative' notion of these things—unless something like Locke's resemblance claim can be made out.

---

[29] Craig (1987: 124–5) and Wright (2000) have good discussions of this passage. Blackburn (1990) claims that little weight can be placed on the fact that Hume makes a distinction between what we can suppose and what we can conceive, in spite of the fact that it features centrally in the ways just illustrated. For a reply see Strawson 2000b: 425–7. Alternatively, and decisively, enter the search term 'suppos' in an electronic copy of Hume's texts.

Shortly before he claims that it's a question of fact whether or not there are Lockean objects (153/12.12), Hume has a parenthesis noting Berkeley's doubt about whether the notion of non-mental objects resembling perceptions even makes sense. But he goes on to grant that it's a possibility: it's a question of fact; an undecidable question of fact, no doubt, but a question of fact nonetheless. Even if we suppose that Hume rejected any version of Locke's resemblance claim, the essential point remains: Hume accepts the intelligibility of, and furthermore endorses, some sort of realist conception of objects.

'Hume says that external objects are "fictions". How can you say that he writes as a realist about objects?'

The word 'fiction', like the verb 'feign', is derived from the Latin *fingo*, which features famously in Newton's remark '*Hypotheses non fingo*' (1713: 547). A 'fiction' is a posit or supposition or hypothesis which goes beyond the evidence in some way; that's all. Some fictions are better and more useful than others; some, like the fiction of external objects, are practically speaking indispensable. They're not necessarily delusive. They may represent how things are—however inadequately. They're partly or wholly 'unintelligible' or 'incomprehensible' on the terms of the theory of ideas, lacking directly impression-based content, but they're not meaningless or unintelligible in our sense. Hume not only grants that the fiction of external objects distinct from perceptions is a genuine supposition, and hence intelligible in our sense; he's also quite sure that it's true, except for an hour or so after he has been concentrating on sceptical arguments (217/1.4.2.56). His principal concern with regard to the question of external objects is his usual concern: he wishes to show that we are, in our belief in external objects, as in so many other matters, (a) *far less rational* and (b) *far more ignorant* than we think, even though we are no doubt right to believe in them. As for (a): the actual *causes* of our belief in such objects don't in fact constitute good rational *grounds* for the belief. As for (b): philosophers shouldn't suppose that they can know anything for sure about the nature of external objects.

Arguments about Hume's views on objects will never cease, but one useful thought for those who doubt that he generally writes as some sort of realist is as follows: whenever he allows any distinction between the 'sensible qualities' of objects or bodies, and the objects or bodies themselves and their 'secret' or unknown nature or internal structure, as he so often does,[30] he is *ipso facto* thinking of objects or bodies as something more than perceptions (more than pc objects or more particularly pcc objects). For he holds that there is nothing hidden or unknown in perceptions. They have no unobservable ontic backsides or innards, unlike genuine external bodies. 'The perceptions of the mind are perfectly known', but 'the essence and composition of external bodies are...obscure' (366/2.2.6.2). So bodies are not perceptions. 'Sound

---

[30] Cf. e.g. quotations (2), (3), (6), (8), (13), (15), (22), in Part 3. Sometimes it seems that 'unknown' means 'merely (contingently) unknown'; sometimes it seems that it means 'unknown because unknowable, at least by us'. This fact is of some importance, and is discussed in 18.

reason convinces us that there are bodies *vastly* more minute, than those which appear to the senses' (48/1.2.4.24), and our senses are defective because 'they give us dis-proportion'd images of things, and represent as minute and uncompounded what is really great and compos'd of a vast number of parts' (28/1.2.1.5).

At the very least, the *Treatise* grants the intelligibility of the thought that objects— the things that we human beings talk about when we talk about 'objects', limited as we are—are something more than strict-idealist objects (*pc* objects or more particu-larly *pcc* objects). The distinction between (a) what we can contentfully conceive, given the strict-theory-of-ideas-based account of contentfulness, and (b) what we can coherently suppose, must be added to the theory of ideas, strictly or narrowly understood, to get Hume's overall theory of meaning or intelligibility. The highly restricted strict-theory-of-ideas-based notion of intelligibility is complemented by the notion of what is intelligible in the sense of being coherently supposable. Hume is, in Wright's term, a 'sceptical realist' about external objects, just as he is about causation. In this respect he follows Locke, although he is considerably more sceptical than Locke insofar as he questions the idea that our ideas of the primary qualities of objects can be said to resemble any of the intrinsic properties of objects. I return to this issue in 12.

The wrangles about 'objects' in the *Treatise* seem unimportant when one comes to the *Enquiry*, given that Hume there takes it to be a straightforward 'question of fact, whether the perceptions of the senses be produced by external objects, resembling them' (153/12.12)—i.e. a question of fact, albeit an entirely undecidable one, whether some kind of realist account of objects is true. In the *Enquiry*, he takes it that some sort of realist account of objects is true.

Some think that he shouldn't have done so, even though he did. This is simply to refuse to accept the full dynamic of Hume's position. It's a common move among philosophers who favour some sort of 'anti-realist' position in their own philosophy. Some of them charge that defenders of the sceptical realist interpretation of Hume espouse this interpretation because they are themselves realists about objects and causation and want Hume to be like themselves. This may be so in certain cases (there's no necessary harm in it), but exactly the same is true, *mutatis mutandis*, of the anti-realists.

Note finally that when Hume says that ordinary people ordinarily 'suppose the very images, presented by the senses, to be the external objects, and never entertain any suspicion, that the one are nothing but representations of the other' (151/12.8), he doesn't mean that ordinary people are Berkeleians, or that phenomenalism is vulgar common sense. For as he says in the preceding paragraph, 'we always suppose an external universe, which depends not on our perception, but would exist, though we and every other sensible creature were absent or annihilated' (151/12.7). If what he says is misleading, it's because he presents the 'direct realism' of common sense, according to which we 'directly perceive' objects, in the context of the philosophical dogma that perceptions are the only immediate or direct objects of perception.

One last bad objection appeals to the passage in which Hume says that 'no man, who reflects, ever doubted, that the existences, which we consider, when we say, **this house** and **that tree**, are nothing but perceptions in the mind' (152/12.9). Here again Hume is in mid-dialectic, contrasting the ordinary person's belief that the things we 'immediately perceive' are external objects with the philosophical (reflective) view that all we immediately perceive are mental things. Even if he were endorsing the philosophical view outright (he isn't) he would certainly not be endorsing idealism; for the sentence goes on to say that these perceptions are taken to be 'fleeting copies of other existences, which remain uniform and independent'.

6.6 Basic realism

I've argued that Hume standardly writes as some sort of realist about objects, but there's a further complication. Behind his apparently straightforwardly realist talk of objects there always lies a wider and more basic-realist position. I'll call this *basic realism*: it involves an interestingly less committed construal of 'the objects' than an ordinary realist position, while—crucially—still taking objects as something essentially more than (strict-) idealist objects.[31]

The argument of this section is slightly exotic, and you don't need to follow it in order to understand the main argument about causation. The point of focusing on basic realism is that it seems that Hume rejects the regularity theory of causation not only insofar as he writes as some sort of realist about objects, but also insofar as he accepts any sort of basic-realist theory of objects at all. His general awareness of the basic-realist position and of its consequences will be brought out at various points below, e.g. in 14 and 18, in the discussion of passages about causation (such as 93/1.3.6.15, 159/1.3.14.7–8, and 54–5/5.21–2). In defence of the complications that follow, it may be said that they would immediately have seemed familiar to Hume, even if barbarously expressed.

When we ask what objects are, we're considering them as things we human beings have to do with, whatever their exact nature, or our exact nature, or the exact nature of our relation to them. Our question is about the nature of what we naturally call 'external reality'. A *basic-realist* theory of what objects are (what external reality is) is: any theory according to which the existence of objects involves the existence of *something other than our perceptions*—whatever the exact nature of our perceptions.[32] Ordinary everyday realism about objects is one variety of basic realism.

---

[31] Perception-constituted (*pc*) objects or perception-content-constituted (*pcc*) objects.

[32] Maximum caution would require that one write 'one's own perceptions' rather than 'our perceptions', but Hume, like Kant and Berkeley, pays little attention to the problem of other minds (Malebranche does better; cf. McCracken, op. cit. 81–2). On one strict-idealist approach to the question of what 'the objects' are, the reference of one's use of 'the objects' can only be supposed to be to (features of the content of) *one's own* perceptions; on another interpretation it can be supposed to be to (features of the content of) human perceptions in general. I'll ignore this issue, and speak of 'our' perceptions.

This definition of basic realism won't quite do,[33] but the fundamental idea is simple. It's not just (1) that there is something 'external' or 'out there' in the sense of being independent of, or something other than, our perceptions (more particularly, our impressions of sensation). To this is added the idea (2) that this something somehow *affects* us, and so gives rise to our perceptions, and is the reason why they are as they are (leaving aside any contribution we may also make to their character). Roughly, whatever it is that is 'out there' in this sense just is 'the objects' (strong version of basic realism); or is at least an *essential part* of what the existence of 'the objects' consists in (weak version). It's the thing (whatever its exact nature) which stands in relation to us (whatever our exact nature) as affecting object or thing encountered.

Unlike a strict-idealist theory, then, a basic-realist theory distinguishes essentially between our perceptions, on the one hand, and the objects or external reality, on the other hand. 'The objects' doesn't name just our perceptions (or their content), even if our perceptions are, somehow, *part* of what it names; it also names something which our perceptions are (fully relationally and not merely 'notionally') of, something which gives rise to them and is the reason why they are as they are.[34]

Our perceptions are not relationally of whatever is involved in the causal process of their arising (thus, on our ordinary realist view, our visual perceptions are not relationally of the rods and cones in our eyes, or of the light waves that give rise to the perceptions). But this raises no difficulty for the basic-realist claim that our perceptions are relationally of something which is what 'the objects' or 'external reality' names (or is at least part of what 'the objects' or 'external reality' names).

As remarked, basic realism comes in two versions. According to the 'strong' version, which is also the most natural version, the objects are *entirely* distinct from our perceptions. Our perceptions are not only not the objects; they're not even any part of what the existence of the objects consists in. 'The objects' simply names what our perceptions are perceptions of (relationally speaking). According to a weaker and more puzzling version, 'the objects' are certainly not to be *identified* with our perceptions or their content (as in strict idealism), because the existence of the objects essentially involves the existence of something more than our perceptions; nevertheless our perceptions are *part* of what the existence of the objects consists in.

---

[33] The initial definition takes one out beyond the strict-idealist world in which objects are entirely perception-constituted things (with an interesting qualification noted in n. 43), but it doesn't quite nail the key basic-realist idea that whatever our perceptions are, they're perceptions of something that concretely exists and is ontologically distinct from them and is what the expression 'the objects' or 'external reality' denotes. It seems to allow a peculiar position—*Unaffected Solipsism*—which it isn't natural to call a basic-realist position, according to which (1) 'objects' *are just* one's perceptions, but (2) they do nevertheless involve the existence of something other than one's perceptions, because (3) one's perceptions are real states of a mind which is (a) necessary for their existence, (b) not a bundle-theory mind, hence (c) at least partly ontically distinct from one's perceptions. In this case it may be said that our perceptions are not really relationally of any external reality distinct from them.

[34] Leaving aside our contribution to their character (I omit this qualification from now on).

The strong version of basic realism is very familiar; it includes all realist theories like Locke's. But it may also include theories that are usually thought of as completely idealist (but might be better called 'mentalist' or 'immaterialist'),[35] for basic realism doesn't require any sort of *mind-independent* reality. It simply requires an *external* reality, a reality that is external in the sense given in (1) above: something different from our perceptions, which affects us.[36] One example of a purely mentalist version of strong basic realism is provided by Berkeley, when we read him as taking 'the objects' to be 'archetype' perceptions in God's mind: our perceptions are then resembling representations of these (*pc*) objects, and are to that extent not to be counted as the objects themselves (or even as any part of them).[37]

The weak version of basic realism occupies far more controversial ground (it's the Alsace-Lorraine of metaphysical speculation about reality, essentially contestable and arguably uninhabitable). It's fundamentally less clear—an essentially tension-involving position—although it's always idealist in some sense, given that it holds that perceptions are at least part of what the expression 'the objects' names. One possible example of weak basic realism can again be derived from Berkeley.[38] On this view, our perceptions may themselves reasonably be called 'the objects'; nevertheless the objects' existence, considered in full (the existence of the tables and chairs we encounter and talk about, considered in full), essentially involves the existence of something other than our perceptions, something which affects us and so gives rise to our perceptions and is the reason why they are as they are—i.e. God. According to this theory, certain of God's manifestations and mental contents constitute the external affecting reality which is at least part of what the expression 'the objects' names. Thus the objects (tables and chairs) have a basic-realist backside, ontologically speaking; they're more than just our perceptions.

Kant's theory of the 'empirically real' world seems to be another example of weak basic realism. There is on his theory a respect in which 'the objects'—the 'empirically real' spatio-temporal objects we deal with from day to day—are nothing but 'appearances', a 'species of representations'. But they're also, crucially, appearances of (relationally of) 'noumenal reality', which is to that extent part of what their existence consists in. This may be too simple—but Kant makes vivid the difficulties to which weak basic-realist theories are an eminently understandable philosophical response.[39]

---

[35] See Strawson 1994: ch. 5 ('Mentalism, Idealism, and Immaterialism').

[36] 'Mind-independent' and 'external' are to be distinguished insofar as 'external' suggests simply that there is some reality external to one's own mind or perceptions (or our human minds or perceptions), while 'mind-independent' suggests further that there is some non-mental reality. 'Mind-independent' entails 'external', but the converse is not true.

[37] Cf. Foster, *The Case for Idealism*, ch 2.

[38] Although this attribution is even more disputable than the preceding one.

[39] Cf. e.g. *Critique*, A181/B223, A370, and *passim*. Significantly, Kant uses more than twenty different expressions in his attempt to characterize the relation between our perceptions or representations and their noumenal 'ground'.

Clearly basic realism extends very far.[40] Unsurprisingly, most theories of objects or external reality that have actually been proposed are basic-realist. An example of an account of objects which is not basic-realist is the pure-content-idealist account given in 6.2, according to which objects are '*pcc*' objects, constituted out of perceptions, and indeed out of nothing more than the content of perceptions.[41] This strict, pure-content-idealist position is not a basic-realist position about objects at all. However strange it is, it claims that 'objects' are just pure contents, and so involve nothing other than our perceptions, and indeed nothing other than their contents. Perhaps it only succeeds in avoiding being a basic-realist theory by simply avoiding pressing ontological questions. (Can these contents just float about without any sort of content-transcending ontic aspect or mode of being?) But it is as it stands an example of a theory of what the objects are that is not a basic-realist theory at all.[42]

In what follows I'll treat basic realism and strict idealism as opposites. It's arguable that they overlap, if a certain variety of panpsychism is true, but one can safely ignore this for the purposes of the present discussion, and take 'strict idealism' as a name for that conception of 'the objects' or 'external reality' which is not basic-realist in any way, because it considers objects as just our perceptions, or as the content of our perceptions.[43]

Clearly, any theory that involves the denial of basic realism is likely to be very odd, as a theory of the nature of the universe, insofar as it's asserted as an account of how

---

[40] There's even a basic-realist version of *Solipsism*, according to which there's an unknown part of one's mind which (1) is ontically distinct from one's perceptions, (2) gives rise to one's perceptions, and (3) is the reason why one's perceptions are as they are ((2) and (3) guarantee that the part of one's mind in question isn't just the supposed substantial basis or 'realization' of one's perceptions, as in the Unaffected Solipsism mentioned in n. 33). In this case one can no longer talk of something distinct from one that affects one; one must talk simply of something giving rise to one's perceptions. But there is still a kind of basic-realist affection relation, even if it just involves one part of the mind affecting another. (Perhaps the limiting case of basic realism is the arguably Hegelian view that all there is, in the end, is the self-affection of Absolute Spirit.)

[41] On the **p3** conception of objects described in 6.2, perceptions can't be distinguished from their contents. On the **p1** and **p2** conceptions they do have some content-transcendent (non-content-constituted) ontic aspect.

[42] The 'ontologically moderate pure-content-idealist' account of objects described in 6.2 is arguably a third version of a Berkeleian view. A fourth version is as follows: (1) the objects are just our perceptions, (2) these perceptions are caused by God, (3) they're based in immaterial, non-bundle-theory minds as real states or modifications of such minds, so they're not floating about without any content-transcending substantial basis or causal history. Nevertheless (4) the expression 'the objects' *just names our perceptions*.

[43] According to *Panpsychist Basic-Realist Mentalism*, (1) only perceptions exist, so objects are of course just perceptions (the theory is strict-idealist in this sense). But (2) the existence of our perceptions does involve something other than our perceptions, for our perceptions are caused to arise by something other than our perceptions: an affecting something which is the reason why they are as they are (the theory is basic-realist). But (3) this affecting something is itself just a perception or collection of perceptions (in accordance with strict idealism). Thus those things which we call 'the objects' have a basic-realist backside, ontologically speaking: the story of what their existence involves is more than just the story of *our* perceptions or their content, and our perceptions can be said to be perceptions (relationally) *of* something. But all the story mentions, in addition to our perceptions, are just more perceptions—and not, for example, realist objects, or God's mind considered as an active, immaterial substance ontically distinct from perceptions, or something 'still more unknown' (153/12.11).

things actually are in the universe, rather than as an account of what we can know about, or know about for certain.[44] This doesn't mean that it couldn't be something like the truth;[45] one constant lesson of science is that the nature of the world as it appears to us on scientific investigation is, by our ordinary lights, extremely strange. Nevertheless it does increase the significance of the claim (made at the beginning of this section, and to be developed later) that Hume rejects the regularity theory of causation not only insofar as he adopts some sort of realist stance about objects, but also insofar as he accepts, more non-committally, that *some version or other* of basic realism about objects is true (while insisting that we could never know which one). For it really is very implausible to reject the claim that some version of basic realism is true, and to claim instead that there does not in fact exist anything which (1) is other than our perceptions and (2) affects us and (3) is the reason why our perceptions are as they are—even if it's important to insist that we could never know which version is true (and that we can never even prove the truth of basic realism). This Hume knows. He standardly accepts that there *is* some unknown 'ultimate cause' of our perceptions (84/1.3.5.2), which has some unknown or unknowable nature or other, even while maintaining his perfectly agnostic scepticism with regard to claims about what does or does not exist, other than perceptions, as his official background position.[46]

The highly unspecific basic-realist conception of 'the objects' is far wider than the ordinary realist conception of objects. One could introduce a new term—'the objects*'—to stand for it. Thus, to suppose as an ordinary realist that there are external and indeed mind-independent physical objects is first to suppose that 'the objects' are objects* (and are therefore not just strict-idealist objects), and then to adopt just one possible basic-realist view of the specific nature of the objects*.[47] In what follows, I will usually approach questions about how to take 'the objects' in terms of the distinction between the straightforwardly realist conception of external objects on the one hand, and the strict-idealist conception of objects on the other hand, returning

---

[44] Fully (and partly redundantly) specified, the opposite of basic realism about objects (as adopted by one of us) is something like *Atheistic Solipsistic Bundle-Theory-of-Mind Non-Self-Affecting Strict Idealism* about objects. ASBTMNSA strict idealism is not just a weird sport, if by 'weird' one means that it's far removed from the realities of actual philosophical debate. By inclination at least, twentieth-century phenomenalism is a version of ASBTMNSA strict idealism—insofar as it is ever presented in an ontological style. Nor would eighteenth- or nineteenth–century metaphysicians have found it hard to understand.

[45] The expression 'something like the truth' is not just cautious. The problematic character of the idea that any theory of the nature of reality could be 'the' truth is discussed briefly in 7 and its Appendix. For Hume's views on the question, see e.g. 272–3/1.4.7.14, and Wright 1983: §2.

[46] In 22 I argue that Hume would have rejected the ontological regularity theory of causation even if he had rejected the idea that some version of basic realism was true and had opted instead for some sort of strict idealism, so that he would have rejected the regularity theory of causation in every possible case. For the moment it's useful to focus on the more moderate claim that he rejected it insofar as he granted that some version of basic realism was true.

[47] Kant is trying to express some such entirely unspecific basic-realist notion of the objects in his *Critique of Pure Reason* with some at least of his references to the 'transcendental object = x' (A109), or the object which 'must be thought only as something in general = x' (A104).

as far as possible to the original terminological simplicity of 4, and understanding the word 'object' in the ordinary, unspecific realist way, unless the contrary is explicitly stated. It will often be possible to replace 'realist' by 'basic-realist', and I'll regularly signal this, but I'll let the standard realist theory of objects function as the general representative of all other basic-realist theories. It's the most familiar example of a basic-realist theory, and it's the one that Hume is most often concerned with.

6.7 Bundles and fiction

Clearly anyone who accepts a basically Humean (or more generally strict classical empiricist) epistemology is going to be led or forced (as were Berkeley and Hume) to consider the possibility of a merely 'bundle' theory of mind, according to which a mind is just 'a system of floating ideas, without any substance to support them' (Berkeley 1713: 198). More generally, they're going to be led to consider the possibility of giving a strict-idealist account of everything: an account according to which all that ultimately exist are perceptions. For however dubious such a strict-idealist theory is, it is (given a Humean epistemology) the *only way* not to go beyond the kind of thing one can know to exist, and know the nature of, or have direct experience of, in giving an account (an 'ontologically outright' account) of the nature of whatever one is trying to give an account of. It's the only way not to get involved in '*fiction*'.[48]

In fact it's the only way to avoid committing oneself to the view that some 'fiction' or other is actually true. Any (basic-realist) theory that rejects a strict-idealist or bundle theory of mind, or a strict-idealist theory of the nature of reality as a whole, must accept that some 'fiction' is actually true (given a Humean epistemology). To accept this is not merely to accept that there *may* be something that we cannot know about or 'comprehend', on the terms of the theory of ideas. It is to accept that there actually *is* something that we cannot know about or 'comprehend', on the terms of the theory of ideas. Clearly, it's going to be very difficult not to accept this, given a classical empiricist epistemology. The alternatives are very unattractive.[49]

I have as far as possible treated these issues in a straightforwardly ontological idiom because it keeps things simple. The ontological idiom doesn't obscure the fact that philosophers' ontologies and metaphysics are often motivated—partly or sometimes almost wholly—by their epistemologies (and accompanying theories of meaning).[50] Such a motivation is usually disastrous, as Hume was well aware—he castigates the Occasionalists on just this point (see pp. 183–5 below). Yet current misinterpretation—travesty—of Hume as some sort of prototypical logical positivist

---

[48] Cf. p. 50. To postulate a mind that is not a mere bundle of perceptions, as Berkeley does, is already to be involved in 'fiction', according to Hume.

[49] Twentieth-century phenomenalism duly worked them out, proceeding in accord with a classical empiricist epistemology.

[50] Consider Berkeley, Kant, the wilder phenomenalists.

rests almost entirely on supposing that he restricts his view of what could exist to what his epistemology admits as knowable or directly experienceable. So it is that the great sceptical expositor of the extent of human ignorance is held to believe that there is definitely nothing we cannot know about (or is at least considered as a heroic foreshadower of this view). I can think of no greater irony in the history of philosophy.

6.8 Hume in metaphysical space

After this excursion into early eighteenth-century metaphysical space, it seems important to repeat the point that behind any realist (or basic-realist) stance that Hume may adopt for the purpose of argument there always lies his non-committal sceptical position on all ontological or metaphysical questions. As a sceptic, Hume doesn't claim to know the correctness of any basic-realist position about the nature of objects. One can't know for sure what gives rise to one's perceptions, for

by what argument can it be proved, that the perceptions of the mind must be caused by [*Lockean*] external objects, entirely different from them, though resembling them (if that be possible) and could not arise either from the energy of the mind itself [as in *Solipsism*], or from the suggestion of some invisible and unknown spirit [as in *Berkeley's* view], or from some other cause still more unknown to us [as in *Kant's* view, for example]?[51]

Hume is clear: we can never decide between these various basic-realist options.[52] At the same time he takes it for granted that there does exist an external reality, i.e. something other than our perceptions, something which affects us and gives rise to our perceptions; and in this sense he does positively, and crucially, adopt a basic-realist position of some sort with regard to 'the objects'.

In fact—to return to the point that originally prompted the present excursion—he regularly writes as some sort of fully fledged realist, adopting a straightforwardly realist way of talking about an external and indeed mind-independent world of physical objects or bodies. Certainly he concedes the irrefutability of an idealist version of basic realism: he agrees that Berkeley can't be refuted, for example. But he doesn't really take Berkeley's arguments seriously: '*they admit of no answer*'; but they '*produce no conviction*' (155/12.15n.).

---

[51] 152–3/12.11. Compare the corresponding passage in the *Treatise* (84/1.3.5.2): the 'ultimate cause [of impressions of sensation] is perfectly inexplicable by human reason, and 'twill always be impossible to decide with certainty, whether they arise immediately from the object, or are produc'd by the creative power of the mind, or are deriv'd from the author of our being'. See also Philo in the *Dialogues*: 'Our experience, so imperfect in itself, and so limited both in extent and duration, can afford us no probable conjecture concerning the whole of things' (133/178). The fundamental basic-realist thought remains: there must be something other than our perceptions. (Note in this connection that the quotations from the *Treatise* and first *Enquiry* both appeal to a non-bundle view of the mind when they consider the solipsist option: perceptions are 'produced by' or 'arise from the energy of' the mind, which is not itself just perceptions.)

[52] The sense in which solipsism qualifies as a minimalist basic-realist position was noted in n. 40 above.

6.9 Writing as a realist

It's the fact that Hume standardly adopts some sort of straightforwardly realist position on objects, together with the fact that he obviously endorses a regularity theory of causation in *some* sense, that obliges one to consider the suggestion that he was after all a crude 'Humean', and really did adopt the regularity theory of causation with regard to realist objects—despite the wild implausibility of such a view, and the *prima facie* plausibility of the claim that on his own (strict theory-of-ideas) principles he could only ever legitimately suppose himself to be talking about strict-idealist objects (*pc* objects or more particularly *pcc* objects), and so could only ever have adopted the regularity theory of causation with regard to such strict-idealist objects.

Strictly speaking, Hume is a *basic* realist about objects, insofar as he's a realist about objects at all. He's clear on the point that even after we've made the fundamental basic-realist assumption (that there is something other than our perceptions which affects us and gives rise to our perceptions) we must grant that we can know nothing for sure about its nature independently of the effects it has on us. And this fact needs always to be borne in mind. Nevertheless, it remains accurate to say that Hume standardly writes as some sort of fully fledged realist.

So: *given* that Hume standardly writes as a realist, and *given* that he espoused a regularity theory of causation in some sense, he's open to the charge that he adopts the strong or realist regularity theory of causation (since this just consists of realism with respect to objects plus a regularity theory of what causation is in those objects). On the present view, however, he can be completely cleared of the charge. His position can be summarized as follows.

Insofar as Hume adopts any sort of outright regularity theory of causation in the objects

(1)   he adopts it only with respect to objects understood in an idealist way as perception-constituted or *pc* objects (more specifically, perception-content-constituted or *pcc* objects) and so considered in abstraction from their 'ultimate cause' (84/1.3.5.2) or any 'substantial ground' they may have. He assumes that objects have some such further ultimate cause or substantial ground, while insisting that we can never know what it is (84/1.3.5.2, 153/12.12).

Insofar as Hume writes as a realist (or indeed as any sort of basic-realist)

(2)   he is a firm believer in something like natural necessity or causal power in the objects, and rejects the regularity theory of causation in the objects.[53]

---

[53] Or rather, he would have rejected it *if* it had ever occurred to him that anybody might adopt the regularity theory of causation (in its currently standard atheist version) as a theory about causation in realist objects. Perhaps the closest he gets to such an idea (although see 20 n. 8) is when he criticizes the Occasionalists, who—roughly—think of the world as lacking any intrinsic causal powers or principles of working (159–60/1.3.14.8–10; 70–3/7.21–25; see also 247–8/1.4.5.30). The Occasionalists, however, take it that the world's regularity is directly brought about by God's intervention, and Hume (who was

Finally, insofar as Hume adopts the regularity theory of causation about causation in the objects *construed as realist objects*,[54]

(3)   he adopts the regularity theory of causation only about causation so far as we can *know* about it or *contentfully conceive of* it in the objects, and not about causation as it is in the objects.

The 'standard' view about what it is to be a 'Humean' about causation involves rejecting all of (1), (2), and (3). That is, it involves adopting the ontologically outright regularity theory about causation in the objects, where these are understood in the ordinary way as realist objects.

So there are two main (and connected) aspects to the present claim that Hume isn't a 'Humean'. First, he never espoused the strong regularity theory—the realist regularity theory. Secondly, insofar as he did adopt a realist (or any basic-realist) view of objects, he took the existence of something like natural necessity for granted (this has yet to be shown), and didn't hold any sort of mere regularity theory about causation as it is in the objects.

I need to say more about what I mean by 'something like natural necessity'. I'll do this in 8. Before that I'll end the discussion of objects with some remarks of a fairly programmatic kind about the notion of the ultimate nature of reality. These deserve a chapter to themselves.

Appendix Cartoon-film causation: idealism and the regularity theory of causation

1. In order to get a better idea of the pure-content-idealist conception of the world of objects (p. 37), and of what causation may be supposed to be in that world, it's worth pursuing the analogy of the cartoon film mentioned in 6.3. Many of the points apply equally to phenomenalistic conceptions of objects.

Consider a traditional cartoon film like a Walt Disney cartoon, except that it's much more realistic. It tells the story of a world of objects. It can be described in many ways, but in one crucial description it consists of a series of separate frames, each with a certain (pictorial) content. In order to consider it just as a series of separate frames—or indeed just as a series of contents—one abstracts from the conditions of its production. One abstracts, for example, from the fact that the production of each frame has involved the photographing of a prepared scene, and indeed from the fact that the production of successive frames may have involved photographing the same model or drawing—of a duck, say—several times, moved slightly to the left or right of the prepared scene in order to give an impression of motion. (Clearly the

---

a profoundly sensible man) would have found it hard to believe that anyone could adopt a theory—allegedly his own!—which not only adopted the Occasionalist view of the lack of any real causes in nature, but also dispensed with any kind of *super*natural agency to keep things running regularly.

[54]   Or as basic-realist objects of some sort—e.g. Berkeleian God-based objects.

drawing of a duck, considered as something the photographic image of which recurs in several frames, unacceptably mimics many aspects of the role of a realist physical object in the production of our experience.)

Next, one abstracts from the fact that the cartoon has a creator (or team of creators), someone who has so organized it that the successive frames should tell a coherent story about a regular world. (If one is thinking of Berkeley, one needn't abstract from this feature for all purposes of discussion; but so long as one is considering any atheistic or agnostic pure-content-idealist account of objects, one should do so.)

How far should one go? Perhaps one should abstract from the fact that the cartoon is a continuous celluloid physical object, and from the fact that it is, as such, running through a light-emitting projector, and so causing certain wavelengths of light to hit a screen; and so on. Perhaps one should abstract from all this—even the screen—until one can consider the cartoon, as far as possible, just as *a series of frames occurring*, a series of frames with a certain content (a certain concretely occurring 'phenomenal' content).

If the cartoon analogy is being offered as an analogy for ontologically outright pure-content idealism (p. 37), this is what one should do. The process of abstraction must to continue until one is thinking of the cartoon as just a series of contents with (ontologically speaking) no content-transcending nature at all. But it's the more moderate (and I believe historically more important) version of pure-content idealism which is best illustrated by the cartoon analogy. And if one is trying to illustrate ontologically moderate pure-content idealism, one can continue to think in terms of *frames with* content, and not just in terms of contents. One can grant that the frames have some ontic aspect or mode of being other than their contents— that the contents are vehicle-based in the frames. The point is that even while one grants that the frames have some content-transcending nature, one will, in giving one's account of the cartoon world of objects, consider the frames just in respect of their content. One will consider only their content in giving one's account of what constitutes the existence of the cartoon world of objects.

I propose that the cartoon frames are strongly analogous to the experiences from which, strict idealists suppose, objects and object-involving events, and everything which we ordinarily call the world, are constituted. It's true that the notion of the frame having fully table-and-chair-like content in and by itself is artificial, for we normally think of the content of a visual experience as being the resultant of at the very least two components, a basic light-wave-array input to our eyes which is then automatically and unconsciously transfigured into table-and-chair experience by us as interpreting subjects. The present artificial—but for the purposes of the analogy acceptable—supposition is that this fully interpreted content is somehow already all there in the frame. (This point does, however, raise a serious problem for ontically outright pure-content-idealists. Intuitively, if there is just content, how can there be anyone or anything for whom it has meaning? Content can't have meaning for content.)

Suppose the cartoon is about a kitchen. Someone picks up a saucepan and hits another saucepan with it. The second saucepan shoots off the table, flies across the room, and knocks over a vegetable rack. Onions scatter. A large pot is boiling on the stove. There are a lot of dramatic causal relations here in this cartoon world, not to mention a large number of persisting objects.

Now according to the ordinary, essentially non-regularity-theory notion of causation, causal relations essentially involve more than mere regular succession, 'one thing just happening after another'. Indeed they essentially involve one thing producing another or bringing the other about; one thing deriving from another, in Anscombe's terms; relations of true existential dependence, in Hume's terms (Anscombe 1971: 136; Hume 212/1.4.2.47) Can one suppose such causal relations to hold between the objects that feature in a cartoon film (the person, the saucepan, the onions, etc.)? Obviously not. 'Of course, if water boils in a pot, steam comes out of the pot and also pictured steam comes out of the pictured pot [pictured in the cartoon]. But what if one insisted on saying that there must be something boiling [i.e. real causal goings-on] in the picture [or cartoon] of the pot?' (Wittgenstein 1953: §297).

Clearly, then, there can't be causal relations among cartoon-film objects, when causal relations are understood in the ordinary way. And the same goes for (ontologically moderate) pure-content-idealist objects. Even if there could be causal relations between cartoon-frames, considered in themselves as physical objects with some content-transcending nature, there couldn't be supposed to be causal relations between their contents, considered in themselves. Berkeley was very clear on this point—see e.g. *Principles* §§65–6: nothing ever really caused anything else, in his world of objects. The most one could say was that events of type A were reliable signs, marks, or 'prognostics' of events of type B. But there is of course *regularity* in the cartoon world or pure-content-idealist world. In respect of regularity, we may suppose that it's just like our own world (it *is* our own world, according to pure-content-idealists). Thus car impacts, say, are always followed by car crumplings, in the pure-content-idealist world. They stand in a regular-succession relation. It's just that the former don't really cause the latter in any sense—any more than the content of the car impact frame of the cartoon *in itself* causes the content of the next few car-crumpling frames of the cartoon. (In being considered in themselves as physical objects with some content-transcendent nature, the frames are considered independently of their creators: the fact that their creators are influenced by the content of frame *n* in constructing the content of frame *n* + 1 is thus irrelevant.)

Suppose, then, that we have for whatever reason opted for a pure-content-idealist—or as one might say 'Cartoonist'—account of the 'physical world' of objects. We now wish to go on to characterize a notion of causation that can be correctly applied to that world. It has become clear that the ordinary notion of causation can't apply to the 'physical world' in question. So the question arises as to what is the best we can do, in the way of a notion of causation? And the answer seems clear. The regular-succession or constant-conjunction relation is plainly the best or strongest possible available analogue of the causal relation as ordinarily understood: given that we are concerned with a Cartoonist or pure-content-idealist world, it is the most that causation can be.

This, then, is the sense in which pure-content-idealists should accept the regularity theory of causation: one can't go beyond the constant-conjunction relation, in the direction of something like bringing-about relations, if one's objects or events stand to each other in something like the relations in which objects and events that feature in cartoon films stand to each other. Regular succession is the most that 'causation' can be, in the Cartoon or pure-content-idealist world. But it is of course also true that, for all the purposes of *appearance*, it is enough: all cartoon creators have to do, in order to give an impression of a regularly causally ordered world just like our own, is simply to observe appropriate regular-succession rules in the construction of their film. (The fact that fantastic things happen—boys turn into fish—in cartoon films doesn't affect the present point.)

In offering this analogy, I'm not claiming that one can rule out a priori the idea that pure contents—or alternatively experiences conceived of in some non-materialist way as things that may have some non-physical ontic aspect over and above their content—might be the ultimate *realia*, and might even have real (non-regularity-theory) causal relations among themselves. Outright ontological pure-content-idealists may indeed ask why pure contents can't be supposed to have causal powers, and although this is an extremely bizarre idea, there's no need to claim that one can rule it out a priori (in 22.2 below I argue that ontically outright pure-content-idealists can no more be regularity theorists than outright realists). I'm simply offering an analogy which many may be prepared to accept as capturing an important feature of the idealist (strict-idealist, pure-content-idealist) conception of the 'physical world', in order to try to bring out the sense in which the regularity theory of causation can be said to be the right—the only possible—theory for certain idealists to adopt about causal relations, considered as things that hold in what they think of as the 'physical world'. I think that the regularity theory of causation, considered as making an ontological claim about the nature of causation in the physical world, belongs not only historically but also naturally with a certain specific idealist conception of the 'physical world'. In the context of this conception of the physical world, it's not only entirely reasonable; it's effectively unavoidable. In any other context—e.g. some realist context—it's deeply bizarre, even if neither incoherent nor provably false (5 and 8). What is truly extraordinary is the way in which some philosophers have abandoned phenomenalism for realism about objects while retaining an outright regularity theory of causation.

Idealists about objects who adopt some sort of regularity theory about causation in the objects still face the question about *why* there is regularity in their world of objects. Berkeley had an answer of a relatively speaking robust kind, for he wasn't a strict idealist, and gave an answer in terms of something—God—that existed outside the world of objects. Strict idealists who believe that perceptions have some mode of being other than their content (i.e. they are **p2** perceptions, 6.2) can do something similar. They can say that (1) the regularity in the perception-content-constituted 'world of objects' obtains in virtue of (2) real (non-regularity-theory) causal relations holding between perceptions in virtue of their content-transcendent nature, these real causal relations being the reason why the regularities which hold in the 'world of objects' hold as they do. Saying this—invoking (2) as the reason why there is (1) regularity in the world—it's still reasonable for them to adopt the regularity theory about causation in what they think of as the 'world of objects', considered in and by itself. It's reasonable in just the sense in which it's reasonable to say that causation, in the world of a cartoon film, *really* consists entirely in the relations of succession of various images, there being no sense in which anything *really* causes anything else, or *really* brings anything else about, in the cartoon world.

2. A lot more could be said on this subject. Note in conclusion that it's arguable that Kant can't have genuine non-regularity-theory causation in what he calls the 'empirically real' spatio-temporal world. The objects (tables and chairs) that make up the 'empirically real' world are in some sense just a 'species of representations' (see e.g. *Critique* A181/B223, A370, A385–6, and *passim*) and can as such only have cartoon-film or regular-succession causation, not true bringing-about or producing causation.

On this view, then, what Kant adds to regular-succession causation in the empirically real world is not true causal power but rather *certainty* about the existence of regularity and order and its continuance, in that world. (Roughly, he argues that we can be certain that (perfect) causal order will hold in the empirically real world, the world we experience, because its having perfect causal order is a condition of the possibility of our experiencing it at all.) Clearly the same question arises for him as for all others: what is the reason for this regularity? It can't be located in the empirically real world itself, considered just as a species of representations, so it must be located outside the empirically real world. And so it is: not in the doings of a Berkeleian God, but in the nature of the noumenon. The reason for the causal regularity of the empirically real world lies in the nature of the noumenon both (1) insofar as our category-and-form-of-intuition-imposing minds are part of the noumenon, and also (2) insofar as something else—that which noumenally (non-temporally) affects us—is part of the noumenon. (Here there's a respect in which Kant's position is close to Hume's: Hume also thinks that the reason for the overall character of the world-as-we-experience-it lies in something unknowable, both in the unknown ultimate nature and structure of our minds, and also in the 'perfectly inexplicable' nature of something other than our minds which affects us, the 'ultimate cause' of our perceptions (84/1.3.5.2).)

It may be said that Kant can allow that there is non-regularity-theory causation in the empirically real world of objects: he allows it inasmuch as he holds that our empirically-real-world-constituting experiences are experiences which are relationally of something else—to wit, the noumenal 'ground' of appearances in which the reason for their regularity really does lie (see 13 n. 1). Against this, it may be said that Kant can't on his own principles suppose that there is causation in the noumenal world, because our concept of causation has no legitimate employment outside the empirically real world. To this it may be replied that Kant can on his own principles suppose or intelligibly think that there may be causation in the noumenal world, so long as he bears in mind that this supposition is not a supposition about causation as we know it in the empirically real and specifically spatio-temporal world, and in a clear sense lacks any positive descriptive content, since it is only the unschematized category of causation that features in the supposition (see further 7).

7

The notion of the ultimate nature of reality

In 6.6 I suggested that some basic-realist theory of the nature of things could be 'something like the truth', although we could never be sure whether it was or not. The 'something like' isn't just an apotropaic gesture of philosophical caution. There's a fundamental problem with respect to the whole notion of 'the' truth of any account of the nature of reality 'as it is in itself'.

For present purposes, however, the most important thing about the problem is what it's not. It's not that there is any deep difficulty in the supposition

(1)   that something is real—reality, no less—and that reality does ('in truth') *have* some 'intrinsic' or 'ultimate' nature.

Of course something is real. And of course it has some ('intrinsic', 'ultimate') nature. Nor is there any deep difficulty in the supposition

(2)   that there may be aspects of reality which are completely inaccessible to and completely unintelligible by us.[1]

Barest common sense—not to mention a minimum degree of modesty—requires us to grant the truth of (2).

Hume would be the first to agree. One of his principal philosophical concerns was to show precisely and in detail that far more aspects of reality are unintelligible to us (or at the very least not yet understood) than many previous philosophers had believed.

If there is a difficulty, then, it's not with (1) or (2). It is, rather, with the idea

(3)   that there could ever be an *account* or *representation* of the general nature of reality given by some particular being or race of beings—necessarily in the particular terms of some particular descriptive or more generally representational system—which expressed *the* truth about the general nature of reality; the truth *tout court*.

---

[1] I sometimes say 'unintelligible by' rather than 'unintelligible to' because I take 'unintelligible' as 'ununderstandable'.

One has to separate the notion (1) that there is a way things are from the notion (3) that it is possible to give some definitively true account of how things are. (3) doesn't follow from (1)—not so long as we're concerned with finite sensory-intellectual beings like ourselves, at least. (Perhaps it follows for God.)

The fact that (3) doesn't follow from (1) may seem surprising at first, but not I think for long. I'm going to relegate discussion of (3) to the appendix to this chapter, since the questions it raises are difficult, and not of central importance in the discussion of Hume. Here I'll say something more about (1) and (2).

(1)—the supposition that reality is in fact a certain way, whatever we can manage to know or say about it—is as remarked obviously true. Some have denied it, of course. Every absurd position has its defendants, and the mystical (apophatic) *Schwärmerei* of some overexcited quantum theorists and other anti-realist extremists should never be underestimated.[2] But not all positions are worth arguing with. (1) is obviously true. Nothing can exist or be real without being a certain way (at any given moment).[3] If this is metaphysics, thank heavens for metaphysics. To be is to be somehow or other.

I will accordingly talk without reservation of the 'intrinsic' or 'ultimate' nature of reality, or of 'reality as it is in itself'. The propriety of such talk derives entirely and sufficiently from the thought that, if a thing exists, it is a certain way. 'As it is in itself' is a phrase that we've been taught to treat with special suspicion. But anyone who doubts its honesty should consider the modest account of it that has just been given. We all agree that something (reality, no less) exists. And all that is added here is that, if something exists, then it is a certain way. And the way it is just is *how it is in itself.* How it is—and it certainly is somehow—is how it is in itself. That is all that is meant. (The 'as it is in itself' is in fact redundant.)[4]

This brief justification of the notion of the ultimate or intrinsic nature of reality is all that is needed for the following discussion of Hume, who never doubted the intelligibility of the notion of the ultimate nature of reality. He had no doubt that it

---

[2] Note that the irresistible truth of (1) is not threatened in any way by such facts as the fact that our best (human) models of the behaviour of things like photons credit them with properties that seem incompatible to us—e.g. wave-like properties and particle-like properties. What we learn from this is just that this is how photons affects us, given their intrinsic nature. We acquire no reason to think that photons do not have some intrinsic nature at any given moment. Whatever claim anyone makes about the nature of reality—including the claim that it has apparently incompatible properties—just is a claim about the way it is (this applies as much to the Everett 'many-worlds' account of the nature of reality as to any other). Some think that what we learn from quantum theory is precisely that there is, objectively, no particular way that an electron is, at a given moment. They confuse an epistemological point about undecidability with a metaphysical claim about the ultimate nature of things. The problem is not so much that such a claim is unverifiable as that it's incoherent. Whatever the electron's strangeness (in a non-technical sense) at any moment, its being thus strange just is the way it is, at that moment.

[3] If one is worried by the notion of time, one can drop the last four words.

[4] It may be thought that there are special problems with the idea that conscious mental reality is a certain way, for any given conscious being *b*, at any given moment. But the case is the same: *whatever* happens mentally, at any given time, in the case of *b*, things will just be a certain way, mentally, with it at that time, even though—as will usually be the case—no one can give a definitive account of how things are, mentally, not even (sometimes least of all) *b*. It's very strange—the philosophical habit of supposing that there is no fact of the matter about how things are if we cannot (possibly) say how they are.

was in many respects unknown and (by us) unknowable. As remarked, his principal sceptical concern was to insist that we know far less about the nature of reality than we (and in particular many seventeenth-century philosophers) are inclined to think we do. He believed that we know even less than Locke, for example, thought. For Locke thought that we had some true grasp of the nature of power, given our experience of mental activity.

I now propose to try to go a little further with the notion of reality as it is in itself. In the hope of achieving clarity and comparative brevity I may sometimes sound less tentative than I am on certain issues, so let me repeat that nothing in the following discussion of Hume depends essentially on the rest of this chapter.

The first point is that the fundamental realist idea just set out ((1) and (2) above) is fully compatible with any reasonable interpretation of the 'anti-realist' or broadly speaking positivist or 'Protagorean' or *Unintelligibilist* claim

(4) that our ('human') concepts, have their whole origin, life, being, and legit-imate and intelligible employment utterly and entirely within the bounds of human experience, in such a way that we cannot even talk about reality, or intelligibly apply any concept to it at all, so far as we are thinking of it specifically as something which may transcend possible human experience.

We can distinguish two versions of the Unintelligibilist thesis about the 'Boundaries of our Thoughts', the 'bounds of sense', the 'limits of intelligibility'[5]: the Extreme or 'Mad' version and the Moderate or 'Sane' version.[6] Like 'anti-realism' in Dummett's use, Unintelligibilism is always a position taken up with respect to a particular statement or class of statements. The class of statements in question here is the class S of statements about reality considered specifically insofar as it is or may be something which transcends possible human experience in certain respects.

Mad Unintelligibilism accepts (4) unreservedly. So it rejects all members of S as unintelligible: all statements about reality considered specifically insofar as it is something which transcends possible human experience in certain respects are literally meaningless. Indeed the very notion of reality considered specifically insofar as it is something which transcends possible human experience in certain respects is an unintelligible one.

Sane Unintelligibilism, by contrast, accepts (4) with the crucial exception of two maximally general concepts: the concept of *reality* or *existence* itself, and the concept of *being somehow* or *having a property*. This allows it to grant the intelligibility of (1) and (2), which together express the fundamental realist thought. Let 'x' denote (more

---

[5] 'It seems probable to me, that the simple *Ideas* we receive from Sensation and Reflection, are the Boundaries of our Thoughts; beyond which, the Mind, whatever efforts it may make, is not able to advance one jot', Locke, *Essay* 2.23.20. On the 'bounds of sense', see Kant *Critique* Bxxv, P. F. Strawson 1966; on the 'limits of intelligibility', see Peacocke 1988.

[6] I've coined the name 'Unintelligibilist' in an attempt to put aside the diverse theoretical commitments of all the 'isms' that have been proposed as names for this sort of position.

cautiously, let 'x' be provisionally admitted as a term purporting to denote) those aspects of reality which transcend possible human experience and whose existence and indeed intelligibility are disputed. Using the two concepts excepted from the ban on experience-transcending use, Sane Unintelligibilism grants that the proposition

It is intelligible that x (a) exists and (b) is a certain way

is itself intelligible. That is, it grants that (2) is intelligible—the claim that there may be features of how reality is that are unknowable by us, and indeed unintelligible and inexplicable by us.

Clearly the concepts ('our' human concepts) of *existing* and *being somehow* must be allowed to be meaningfully applicable beyond human experience, if the proposition that reality may be something whose nature transcends possible human experience is to be meaningful at all. But this concession with respect to these two concepts is not unprincipled. It is in any case necessary, if the avoidance of absurdity is one of one's philosophical aims. It's necessary: the Mad Unintelligibilist claim that it isn't intelligible to suppose that there should be things which are unintelligible by us is one of the most ridiculous general theoretical claims ever made by a philosopher (the competition for this honour is intense). The most exotic metaphysical systems pale into banality beside it.[7]

It's not unprincipled: indeed it is arguably a consequence of the Unintelligibilist (or positivist) claim, properly understood (and clearly expounded both by Hume and Kant and indeed by Locke, and no doubt by many others). For the fundamental thought behind the (Sane) Unintelligibilist claim is surely, and simply, that our *descriptive powers* cannot be supposed to extend in any way beyond those with which our experience has equipped us, given our nature and our situation: words which have genuine descriptive force for us given the character of our experience cannot describe or characterize things, or aspects of things, of which we could not possibly have any experience (even if eternal and indestructible). So we cannot suppose ourselves to be able to make any properly meaningful, *positively descriptive* claim about aspects of reality that transcend possible human experience.[8] But the validity of this thought about the limits of our descriptive powers is in no way impugned by the merely existential and completely non-descriptive realist claim (1) that reality is real, and is some way or other, and (2) that it's intelligible to suppose that there are aspects of how it is that are unintelligible by us.

Even when (1) and (2) have been conceded, Sane Unintelligibilism still retains a great deal of force, in claiming that one cannot, using our actual empirical

---

[7] Thomas Nagel argues simply and powerfully against the ridiculous claim in *The View from Nowhere* (pp. 95–8). So does Locke in 4.3.23 of his *Essay*. (There is a more ridiculous claim: the claim that consciousness as we ordinarily understand it doesn't exist, or is an illusion.)

[8] Any claim which is 'intelligible' or 'comprehensible', or which involves something (positively-contentfully) 'conceivable', in Hume's terms (cf. 6.5). There are of course many views about what genuinely contentful concepts our experience does in fact equip us with or involve.

experience-embedded concepts, intelligibly say or suppose or think anything at all, however speculative, about the nature of reality conceived of as something putatively experience-transcending, over and above granting that it may exist and be a certain way. If we take this claim as the claim that any such statements are literally meaningless in our ordinary strong sense of the term, then Sane Unintelligibilism certainly goes further than Hume and Kant. For although both said that there was a sense in which such statements were 'without meaning' or 'unintelligible', both meant this in a weaker sense than the current sense of these words. Both were clear that such statements could not possibly be *verified* (cf. e.g. *Critique* B302n.), but neither held that such statements were really, literally and without qualification, meaningless. Hume held that we could coherently (and hence meaningfully) suppose and believe that *relatively specific* experience-transcending states of affairs might be the case, although we couldn't contentfully (or positively descriptively) conceive of them on the terms of the theory of ideas: e.g. that there might be external objects 'specifically different from perceptions', or that there was some kind of causal power whose nature was completely 'unintelligible' by us (on the terms of the theory of ideas). Kant held that it was possible to think (and so of course think intelligibly) about noumenal reality although it was inaccessible in experience: it was for example possible to think about it in terms of the categories, so long as these were taken in their 'unschematized' forms. 'The categories' he said, 'extend further [in their possible application] than sensible intuition, since they think objects in general, without regard to the special mode (the sensibility) in which they may be given' (B309). One can for example think (and one is within Kant's overall scheme of things effectively obliged to think) that something akin to the relation of cause as we know it in spatio-temporal reality—i.e. the 'because something is, something else must be' relation, to give it its most general specification in Kant's own words (B288)—obtains in the noumenal reality, while granting that one has no sort of positive conception of it as it obtains in the noumenal reality.[9]

I think even the Sane Unintelligibilist claim goes too far. Simply in order to make the traditional grounds for such a view clear, and not because I hope to convert anyone, I'll give two familiar examples of cases in which I think that speculations about the ultimate nature of reality—speculations which (of course) employ our human concepts—have clear sense although *ex hypothesi* they transcend our

---

[9] Kant held this view despite repeated claims that the categories (for example) 'allow only of empirical employment, and have no meaning whatsoever when not applied to objects of possible experience, that is, to the world of sense' (B724). What this shows is not that he was inconsistent, but that by 'meaningless' he didn't mean utterly unintelligible in our present-day sense. One clue to what he meant by 'meaning' occurs on B300: when the categories are applied in such a way that they are not applied to sensible intuition, he says, 'all meaning, *that is, all relation to the object*, falls away'. See also B166n.: '*for thought* the categories are not limited by the conditions of our sensible intuition, but have an unlimited field. It is only the *knowledge* of that which we think, the determining of the object, that requires intuition.'

capacities to decide whether or not they are true.[10] The first convinces many,[11] but the second is arguably more secure, and may be felt to have force even by those who are convinced that the apparent meaningfulness of the first is really illusory.

1. As for the first. Suppose three rival hypotheses are put forward about the overall nature of reality: first, a very broadly speaking Lockean or more generally realist hypothesis (e.g. an atheistic, explicitly monist, materialist version of realism); secondly, a Berkeleian hypothesis (alternatively, an atheistic but still immaterialist hypothesis); thirdly, some other (e.g. Kantian or 'neutral monist') hypothesis according to which reality is in its ultimate nature neither mental nor physical, as we understand these terms, but is, somehow, quite Other. Assume for the purposes of discussion that the second of the three is at least as coherent as the first.

Note that the first two make *positive descriptive* claims about the ultimate nature of reality, in claiming, respectively, that one of our two (actual, human, experience-related-and-grounded) notions of the mental and the physical 'latches on to' the ultimate nature of reality in a way in which the other does not, and indeed to the exclusion of the other. The third, by contrast, makes no positive descriptive claim at all—unless to say that reality is neither mental nor physical, as we understand these things, is to make a 'negatively positive' descriptive claim.

It's a familiar point that we can't decisively favour one of these hypotheses over the others on empirical grounds, as an account of the ultimate nature of reality. For they all have exactly the same empirical or experiential or evidential consequences. 'Here experience is, and must be entirely silent', as Hume says, discussing exactly this point (153/12.12) But they are, ostensibly, dramatically different hypotheses about the ultimate nature of reality (most philosophers really do favour one of them—the first—over the others), and it surely makes sense to suppose that one of them could be a better representation of the ultimate nature of reality than the others. It would be unwise to argue that the present state of science makes these old questions intellectually disgraceful; if they are to be shown to be disgraceful, the reasons given for this claim must be distinctively philosophical. As far as science is concerned, the contrary view seems nearer the truth: fundamental physics repeatedly suggests that reality is far, far stranger than we think. It seems imaginable that reasons might emerge—that pressure might build up—within science favouring one overall metaphysical view over the other. Consider the apparent intractability, for materialists, of the problem

---

[10] In other areas of anti-realist endeavour, the line that matters is not the line that separates the intelligible and the unintelligible, but the line that separates propositions that can be held to be true or false from those that can't. Thus the proposition that every even number is the sum of two prime numbers, and the proposition that Caesar thought fleetingly of peaches when he crossed the Rubicon, are allowed to be fully meaningful; the claim is only that one can't say or suppose that they are either true or false. I can't imagine the intellectual state of mind that makes such a position seem possible (but I don't infer its non-existence from its unintelligibility-to-me).

[11] But not Carnap; see e.g. Carnap 1928: 334.

of how it is possible that conscious experience should be based in or 'realized' by physical substance. It's such a big problem that panpsychism, judged by many to be absurd, appears to be one of the most respectable hypotheses in the field. (One hasn't really engaged with the mind-body problem until one sees that this is so.)[12]

A useful partial analogy of our situation is provided by the case of Louis, the person who is a 'brain in a vat'. Suppose that Louis favours a materialist, realist account of the ultimate nature of reality. He is, in a sense, profoundly wrong about his situation. He thinks that the tables and chairs he perceives are real physical objects, and they're not.[13] And yet, we may suppose, he has, on the basis of his experience of tables and chairs, etc., acquired a conception of the physical which really does reach out to what are, for him, inaccessible aspects of reality as it really is.[14]

The idea that we are right to think that reality as it is in itself is physical in nature amounts at least to this: our most general concepts of the nature of the physical—extended stuff in space and time—are, in some vague but solid sense, really on the right lines as an account of the nature of reality—even if we cannot in the end make good sense of the idea that any physics elaborated by finite sensory beings could ever be *the* truth of the matter. Whereas if the idealist or mentalist hypothesis is right, then this is not so at all. For there is really no such thing as space or extended stuff. The two theories have very different consequences. If the physicalist hypothesis is correct, then all mind could die out in the universe, and there could still be space, matter, stars, and rusty cars. If the idealist or Mentalist hypothesis is correct, then if mind ceased to be, nothing would exist.

Note that the present line of thought doesn't involve any picture of *two realms*—the realm of appearance and the realm of reality as it is in itself. We are in our everyday life, which is of course part of reality (as it is in itself), in direct contact with reality (as it is in itself). The idea is just that aspects of how it is may be unknown and—by us—unknowable.

---

[12] See e.g. Nagel 1979, Skrbina 2005, Strawson 2006. A better way of putting the point might be this: if conscious experience is indeed 'realized' in or by the physical as conceived by physics, then there *must* be physical properties of which we have as yet absolutely no sort of conception—not a glimmering. I return briefly to this idea in the main text below.

[13] They are, in the terms of 6.2, moderate pure-content-idealist perception-content-constituted objects.

[14] Compare the case in which one reads a purely fictional account of a fictional town which happens to correspond exactly to a real town. Clearly one might acquire, on this basis, a genuine 'working knowledge' of how to get about in the real town. Some may say that this example proves the opposite point. Louis's conception of 'the physical', they will say, necessarily has application only to 'the physical' as it features in his private world. To suppose that he has on this basis acquired a genuine concept of the physical is a bit like supposing that someone could acquire the concept 'horse' from acquaintance with what were, unknown to him, merely perfect mechanical models. But even if one thinks this last thing impossible, the case is not the same, because in Louis's case the reality with which he is in causal interaction—albeit not in the way he supposes—really is physical in nature. So even if 'the physical' is a natural-kind concept (it is the ultimate natural-kind concept), and is on that account such that grasp of it requires causal contact with the natural kind in question, this is not necessarily an objection, because Louis fulfils the causal condition.

Part of the present idea is that our concepts of the 'mental' and the 'physical' can be supposed to be genuine concepts of (concepts genuinely of) phenomena which surpass our understanding. Thus they are, so far as their positive descriptive force goes, only partially adequate to aspects of reality which they fail to encompass fully, so far as their positive descriptive force is concerned. Nevertheless, they are genuinely relationally *of* those aspects of reality, and they are so at least partly in virtue of their positive descriptive force (they're not genuinely relationally of aspects of reality just in the way that proper names are). Given their positive descriptive force, they can be supposed to 'latch on to' particular aspects of reality that they fail to encompass fully (given their positive descriptive force). On this view, our concepts of the mental and the physical, latching on to reality in the way just characterized, can intelligibly be supposed to reach out beyond what they encompass given the descriptive force which they have as employed by us now, to aspects of reality inaccessible to us; in such a way that it makes sense to suppose that one or other of the three hypotheses may be better as a representation of the nature of reality than the others, and indeed may be something like the truth.

Thoughtful materialists who accept the claim that the mental is 'realized' in or by the physical see that it follows that our conception of the physical ('C') must be radically incomplete. Why? Because, despite its richness, C contains nothing that offers any hope of solving the deep part of the problem of how physical events can 'realize' (or even 'be the basis of') experience. However complete the physical (neurophysiological) story of sensation, it fails to provide any genuine explanation of the possibility of something undeniably real: my sensations' having the phenomenal character they do as I watch the stormy sea. The physical (electrochemical, computational, photons-and-retina-and-rods-and-cones-involving) story leaves all the phenomenal properties out; it fails to explain them; it fails to explain even how they are possible. It is the existence of phenomenal experience that is the hard part of the mind-body problem. C must be hopelessly incomplete (given that materialism is true) until it contains a specification of some physical property which makes it unproblematic that the physical can 'realize' or 'be the basis of' such experiential goings on.[15] Nevertheless, despite this incompleteness, it seems reasonable to suppose that C may be accurate about aspects of the nature of the reality that gives rise to it, in virtue of its descriptive content, in a way in which it would simply fail to be

---

[15] See McGinn 1989. Note that the stronger one's belief that the nature of the physical is essentially well understood, the more acute one should find the mind–body problem. Hume didn't think the physical was well understood, and in his powerful response to the problem (246–50/1.4.5.29–33) argued that the nature of causal connection is no more intelligible to us in the case of body–body interaction than in the case of mind–body interaction. For in both cases we can detect no more than constant conjunction. But then we really have *no* good grounds for thinking that there is an intrinsically greater problem about mind–body interaction than there is about body–body interaction. (Idealists and 'neutral monists' have another solution; see Kant, *Critique* A385–6.)

accurate about reality if idealism (or the third theory) were true, even though our experience would be exactly the same in each case.

The notion of one of the three theories being in some sense a 'better representation of the nature of reality' than the others is of course extremely vague. But it doesn't involve any commitment to the idea that it must in principle be possible to give an account of the nature of reality which is *the* truth. Perhaps it has no more solid foundation than the (solid) intuition that certain essentially *comparative* judgements may be (unknowably) true—i.e. that one human account (realist or idealist) of the general nature of reality may be somehow superior, as a representation, to another. But this is enough for present purposes (which is not to say that it does not involve considerable problems, indicated in the appendix). It already brings with it the crucial idea that some of our slightly less general concepts (e.g. our concepts of the mental and the physical), and not just our maximally general concepts of existence, and being a certain way, are in some way meaningfully applicable, in some metaphysically speculative way, to reality as it is in itself.

This may be useless and fruitless from all sorts of points of view. This is not denied. The argument here is about intelligibility, not about usefulness or practical point. Its target is the specifically philosophical claim that these speculations are actually unintelligible. All that is being claimed is that the idea that one such speculation may be in some good sense nearer the mark than the other is legitimate, especially given the dramatically different character of the speculations. It's intelligible to suppose that some of our more particular concepts, evolved in the human experiential context, may be *in some way* meaningfully applicable beyond the bounds of experience.

There is no doubt that Kant held such a view, as already remarked—in spite of his various endorsements of a version of the (Sane) Unintelligibilist claim about the limits of our descriptive powers. While he claimed that we couldn't *know* anything at all about the nature of reality, or the 'noumenal',[16] he insisted that the nature of the noumenal was coherently *thinkable* about, and found it impossible not to suppose that there was something analogous to causation in the noumenal world whereby one thing somehow affected or 'determined' or 'conditioned' another.[17] Certainly the concept of causation we actually possess and employ is specifically and in some way constitutively geared to a spatio-temporal world. (It is 'schematized', in Kant's terminology, particularized or concretized in such a way as to be applicable to the deliverances of a particular—specifically spatio-temporal—mode of 'intuition'.) It doesn't follow that we have not, in acquiring the particular concept of

---

[16] It is, however, arguable that he did claim that we could know certain things about the nature of the noumenal—i.e. that it was, in itself, definitely *not* temporal or spatial in character, and, apparently, that it was diverse in character, containing, for example, a plurality of different moral subjects.

[17] A simple analogy of a non-temporal affection relation might be this: elements in a painting may determine or 'condition' the character of other elements. (But perhaps this idea depends on the idea of some—necessarily temporally extended—inspection of the picture.)

causation we have acquired, acquired a certain very general conception of causation ('because something is, something else must be', B288) which is intelligibly applicable in speculation independently of the actual general conditions of its empirical application.

These are difficult questions, and deserve fuller treatment. It may be argued that the third hypothesis—that reality is in its ultimate nature really nothing like what we think of as mental or physical (God, as it were, would not think much of these descriptive categories)—is in some way better off than the other two, insofar as it doesn't seek to apply one of our human-experience-grounded, positively descriptive categories to inaccessible aspects of reality. But I don't think this can be so as far as mental reality is concerned (see Strawson 1994: 50–1).

So much for the first example of speculation about the ultimate nature of reality. Nothing in the following discussion of Hume rests on accepting its cogency. I'll now consider another example. It's more immediately relevant to the present discussion of Hume, since it concerns the application of the concept of causation.

2. Suppose that two rival hypotheses are put forward about the nature of reality: according to the first, causation in reality is just regular succession. According to the second, there is something about the nature of reality which is the reason why it is regular in the way that it is, something which is therefore not just the regularity itself; and to talk about causation is to talk about this something, and not just about regular succession.

Here it seems clear that it *makes sense* to suppose that one hypothesis is a better representation of reality than the other (albeit unknowably), and is indeed something like the truth. Indeed, given the extreme generality of the specification of the content of the two hypotheses, it seems obvious that it makes sense to suppose that one is simply true and the other false, even if we can never know which is which. Either there is something about the nature of the world which is the reason why it is regular in its behaviour, something which is therefore not just the regularity itself, or there isn't. It's hard to believe that the two highly abstract and to that extent descriptively non-committal concepts deployed here—(i) regular succession, (ii) something or other which is not itself just regular succession but which is that about reality which is the reason why there is regular succession—are not in any way meaningfully employed in this speculation about the ultimate nature of reality.

Useless to speculate, some say. But many—most—philosophers think that one or other of the hypotheses is actually true. My present purpose is to support those philosophers in their belief that it *makes sense* to suppose that there is a truth of the matter here. For, to recur finally to (1), the realist thought with which this chapter started, reality is indeed real, and it does indeed have a certain nature, whatever we can or cannot know about it.

I return to some of these issues of meaning in 12. In the Appendix to this chapter I discuss some problems with the idea that any particular account of the nature of reality might be 'the' truth about reality.

Appendix Reality and truth

1. There seems to be a deep difficulty in the idea that any general account or representation or theory of the nature of concrete reality given by finite, sensory-intellectual creatures like ourselves could ever be *the* (single, final) truth—or, as I shall say, the Truth—about that reality. And some would say that the problem extends equally to the idea that any such account or representation could even be said to be 'something like' the Truth. I'll try to state the difficulty, and argue that it may be overestimated. As in 7, I'll sometimes write as if I were less tentative than I am. The subject is very difficult, and this brief consideration of it very inadequate. The point of restricting consideration to 'finite' and 'sensory' beings is that there's no need to rule out the (admittedly obscure) idea that some divine, non-sensory, purely 'intellectual intuition' of the sort hypothesized by Kant could count as a mode of knowledge of reality which did indeed yield—or involve—a true, full representation of the nature of reality 'as it is in itself'. I'll return to this idea shortly.

Given the restriction to finite beings, it's important to note that it's knowledge of the *general* nature of concrete reality which is in question. The present problem doesn't concern the uninteresting point that no finite being could grasp all facts about all things. It concerns the much more interesting idea that no *general* theoretical account of the basic nature of concrete reality offered by a finite being—general in the way that fundamental physics paradigmatically is—could ever be supposed to be the Truth about concrete reality (I'll omit 'concrete' from now on).

The overall form of the problem raised by the notion of the Truth of any account or representation of the nature of reality is familiar enough. In order to discuss it I'll assume that there is indeed a mind-independent, physical universe. In fact this assumption is itself problematic from the present perspective, as I'll try to show. But most of those who think about this question believe that the problem arises with its full force even given this assumption.

One way to try to bring it out is as follows.

(1) It seems that one can have *knowledge* of the essential nature of the reality one is trying to give an account of (call it 'X') only if one is *affected* by it, somehow or other. More generally, and more usefully for present purposes, it seems clear enough that one can form a *correct representation* of something only if one is affected by it. One must be in some sort of *contact* with it.[18]

(2) It's arguable, however, that one can have knowledge of the *essential nature* of X, or form a fully correct representation of the essential nature of X, only if one is *not* affected by X. Or rather—less paradoxically—it's arguable that one can attain knowledge of, or at least some correct representation of, the essential nature of X, only if the representation one forms of X, and which constitutes one's putative knowledge or correct

---

[18] The present point is not about knowledge as opposed to true belief or correct representation, because it's equally true that one can (as a finite, sensory–intellectual creature) have beliefs (true or false) *about*, or form representations (good or bad, correct or incorrect) *of*, some reality one is trying to give an account of only if one is affected by it. (A painting could be just like a photorealistically perfect portrait of a person the artist had never been in contact with—e.g. by meeting, picture, description. Obviously it wouldn't be a portrait of that person.)

representation of its essential nature, doesn't involve elements that depend essentially on the particular way in which one is (sensorily) affected by it.

(3) For the following is a general truth:

(a)   if an experiencing being B is affected by a thing X in any way, then how B is affected by X is necessarily a function not only of how X is, in itself, but also of how B is, in itself.

But

(b)   it is always logically possible that there should exist two experiencing beings B and C who differ in their natures in such a way that they differ significantly, even when they're functioning normally, given the kinds of being they are, in the way they are affected by X. ('Significantly' is vague, but it will do for present purposes.)

Hence

(c)   it seems that there can be no such thing as 'the right way' of being affected by X, the single, universally correct way. Instead one can talk only of how Bs are (normally) affected by X, how Cs are affected by X, how Ds are affected by X, and so on. One can't say that B1 is just right in the way it is affected, and C1 or D1 wrong. There's no such thing as the *right* way of being affected. Nor is one way of being affected closer to being right than another. The comparative notion is no more appropriate than the absolute notion of the right way of being affected. Nor can one speak of roughly the right way of being affected.

Kant's notion of 'intellectual intuition' is sometimes dismissed as a foolish obscurity, but it seems in the present context to be of great philosophical interest and importance.[19] For it is, precisely, an attempt to characterize a kind of knowledge-engendering or knowledge-involving *contact* or (most neutrally) *relation* with X which does *not* involve being affected by X. Kant's characterization of intellectual intuition appears to be motivated precisely by an awareness of the force of the thought that if one's potentially knowledge-engendering relation to X essentially involves one's being (sensorily) *affected* by X then there's an immovable sense in which one can only ever hope to attain to knowledge of an *appearance* of X, and hence (so the thought goes) never to knowledge of X 'as it is in itself'.

Kant suggests that intellectual intuition is the knowledge-engendering or knowledge-involving relation that a divine creator subject stands in to its works—call them X—in creating or originating them: X is somehow fully specified and grasped in its intellect, and therefore completely known, without the knowledge resulting in any way from X's being a thing that 'stands over against' the subject as something which affects it in some particular way. 'Awareness of things as they are in themselves', the result of intellectual intuition, is 'a *creative awareness* which produce[s] its own object' (Strawson 1966: 41). There is accordingly no sort of indirectness or mediatedness of apprehension of a kind which is arguably necessarily involved in any merely sensory intuition or experience of something. There's no *partiality of*

---

[19]   See e.g. *Critique*: B72, B307–12. No doubt the notion has, in various forms, a long history prior to Kant.

perspective of the sort which is apparently necessarily involved in any sort of sensory experience of something, and which seems to exclude the possibility of knowledge of the Truth about X. One has access to the 'absolute conception of reality', in Williams's phrase (1978: 65–8, 245–9), the 'view from nowhere'—the view from no particular perspective—in Nagel's phrase (1986). Although we 'cannot comprehend even the possibility' of such intellectual intuition, Kant says, the idea is free from contradiction (*Critique* B307; A254/B310).

It's arguable, then, that Kant is trying to describe precisely what genuine or perfect knowledge—'Knowledge'—of the nature of X (of reality) would have to be like. A *necessary* condition of such Knowledge, for any being B, is this: the Knowledge has to be contained in B's being *in relation with* X without B's being affected by X in such a way that B can be said to have access only to an appearance of X.[20]

It's an interesting question whether there is any model of the Knowledge-engendering relation other than the relation of divine creator to its works; but I'll now return to the main line of argument set out in (3) (a)–(c): there can be no such thing as the right way of being affected by X (by reality as it is in itself); nor is any one way of being affected by X, just as such, *closer* to being right than any other; one might as well claim that the decimal system was closer to being the right way of representing the nature of numbers than the binary system, or that English colour words were closer to being right than French ones.

To say this is not of course to deny that a being B, endowed with one characteristic way or set of ways of being sensorily affected by reality, might not be in a far better position to elaborate a practically speaking useful theoretical account of the nature of reality than another being C, endowed with a different characteristic way or set of ways of being affected by reality. This could be so even if B and C were equal with respect to *intellectual* capacities—assuming for purposes of argument that their intellectual capacities could be considered and compared independently of their sensory equipment. It would remain true that there can be no such thing as 'the right way' of being affected by reality.

Given (a), (b), and (c), the following conditional may seem plausible:

(d) *if* any (positive descriptive) account or representation of any aspect X of the nature of reality which can be given by any finite sensory being—say B—*necessarily involves, as an essential part of its content*, features of how B is sensorily affected by X which could be significantly different for other possible experiencing beings affected by the same aspect of reality X, then there can be no such thing as a (true or) correct positively descriptive account or representation of X, so far as any finite sensory being is concerned.

(d) needs to be restricted in certain ways, but it may be noted immediately that it helps, in this connection, to think not just of the possibility of creatures having greater or lesser discriminatory sensitivity in respect of a given sensory modality, but also of the possibility of colour-spectrum-inversion-type differences, and of the possibility of creatures possessing entirely

---

[20] 'Nothing which emerges from *any* affecting relation can count as knowledge or awareness of the affecting thing as it is in itself. Therefore there can be no knowledge or awareness of things which exist *independently* of that knowledge or awareness and of which that knowledge or awareness is consequently an effect. More exactly, there can be no knowledge of such things as they are in themselves, but only as they appear—only of their appearances'. Strawson, op. cit., pp. 238–9. Cf. also pp. 249–56, 264–5.

different sensory modalities.[21] Most importantly, perhaps, one should consider the possibility of radical differences between us and other highly evolved alien creatures, rather than just considering differences between species on earth.

Some philosophers would perhaps wish to accept the antecedent of (d): they would wish to accept that any (positively descriptive) account or representation of any aspect X of the nature of reality which can be given by a finite sensory being B does necessarily involve or incorporate, as an essential part of its content, features of how B is sensorily affected by X (which could be significantly different for other possible experiencing beings). These philosophers would detach the consequent of (d): there can be no such thing as a (or the) correct positively descriptive account or representation of X, so far as any finite sensory being is concerned. And some might go on to claim that the point can be extended to show that one cannot even talk of a finite being's account or representation or theory of the nature of reality being even as much as 'something like' the truth (Truth)—just as one cannot talk in absolute (or non-species-relative) terms of a way of being affected by something as being the right way of being affected, or even as being something like the right way of being affected by it.[22]

In either case it is important to note that the conclusion here is not just the unremarkable conclusion that one could never *know* that one had the Truth about X (or even something like the Truth). The conclusion is rather that it is demonstrably impossible for a finite, essentially sensory being to give or grasp any account or representation of the general nature of reality which could be said to be the Truth about X (or even something like the Truth). And this strong conclusion is reached despite a whole-hearted acceptance of the fundamental realist view that reality is ('in truth') some particular way, and does, in truth, have some particular 'ultimate' nature (sc. the thought summarized in (1) and (2) in 7 above).

This is fairly sketchy. The argument set out in (a)–(d) is too simple as it stands. (d) in particular raises several questions. The most important of them, I think, is the question of whether one might try to deny the antecedent of (d), at least in part. Perhaps a finite being's

---

[21]   On this see e.g. Kant *Critique* B43 and B72, Hume *Enquiry* 20/2.7. For an unbeatable discussion of the colour-spectrum case see Locke *Essay* 2.32.14–15; see also Shoemaker 1984, McGinn 1983: ch. 2, Strawson 1989.

[22]   As remarked, Kant considers the idea that there may be beings other than ourselves who have 'forms of intuition' completely different from ours—perhaps even non-spatial in character. These beings will experience reality as it is in itself (the noumenal) in a way quite unlike the way in which we experience it. In Kant's terms, their 'empirically real' world will be quite unlike ours. Just as we cannot free ourselves from our particular spatial form of intuition in forming any sort of positive representation of reality, so they cannot free themselves from their particular form of intuition. But, it may be said, neither they nor we can be said to have a more correct representation of reality. For we both experience everything in the particular framework of an *overall way of being affected*; and no way of being affected can, just as such, be said to be more correct than any other. (Note that a spatial 'form of intuition' is not itself a particular sensory modality. It is rather that some sensory modalities or ways of being affected—e.g. sight and touch—are essentially spatial in character.)

Put like this, the point may seem very doubtful. For if (e.g.) reality is really spatial, then beings with a spatial form of intuition will surely have a more correct view of reality (*ceteris paribus*) than those who have, say, an equally complicated view, but one which involves some entirely and unimaginably non-spatial mode of representation; certainly having a spatial form of intuition will be a necessary condition of attaining something like the truth, in this case. But although this seems right, one still can't say of one *way of being affected* that it is more correct than another, considered just as such. One way of being affected may lead one to form a better picture of the overall character of reality than another; but this doesn't make it more 'correct', specifically as a way of being affected.

representation of the nature of reality can in some way detach from its bases in sensory experience, even if those bases are genetically speaking indispensable to the being's achieving any representation of the nature of reality at all. I will devote the rest of this appendix to this suggestion; but from here on the argument becomes looser.

The following seems plausible in any case:

(e)   *if* we are going to give any good sense to the notion of B's achieving something like a *correct* representation or understanding of the essential nature of some range of aspects of reality—call this range 'X'—then we have to suppose that B's representation or understanding of the nature of X is—must be—intellectually *abstract* in some way: there must be some sense in which B can correctly be said to abstract, in its mode of representation of X, from all features of how it is sensorily affected by X which could be significantly different for other possible beings (C-type beings, D-type beings) who are also affected by X.

In thinking about this, it may help to suppose that these other beings have achieved an equally *practically speaking successful* representation of the nature of X. One thought behind (e) is that one needs to make room for the idea that two different races of beings with very different sensory equipment could possibly formulate theories with strong similarity of content—that they could possibly have essentially the same view of things, at some fundamental level— despite their differences of sensory equipment.

Doubts may be raised about the value of supposing that the B-type and C-type beings are equally successful in their practical applications of their theories or representations. It may be said that the successfulness from a practical point of view of a representation of reality certainly does not entail its truth; and that the equal practical successfulness of two such representations does not entail any strong similarity of content between them—even on some worthwhile, hospitable (non-scholastic, anti-incommensurabilist) account of similarity which admits similarity of content in e.g. the case of Newton's and Einstein's theories. The Copernican and Ptolemaic theories of planetary motion may perhaps be cited. They may be said to have been equally practically speaking successful (at least for a time), so far as their predictive power was concerned, while lacking any strong similarity of content.

I'm not competent to discuss the details of such examples, but whatever one makes of them it seems plausible to suppose that when one considers two sophisticated theories giving rise to equal practical success in something more than merely observational prediction—i.e. equal practical success in the complicated technical control and mechanical exploitation of certain fundamental aspects of reality—such success strongly suggests that there will be some interesting similarity of content between the theories at some crucial level of comparison.

It isn't necessary, for present purposes, to claim that equal success entails strong similarity of content; it's enough to claim that such similarity of content is very likely in the case of highly sophisticated and equally practically successful theories. All sorts of problems arise if one tries to make this similarity notion precise or watertight, and they may be insuperable, if the goal is to be precisely watertight.[23] But they're not of great concern at the moment, for the intuitive point is clear enough. Perhaps the naturally planet-bound Bs and Cs are equally capable of

---

[23] They have caused much subtle agony to philosophers of science.

space travel in machines they've constructed, and perhaps both species have achieved this on account of having formed theories about the *same* aspects of reality (the X-aspects). This parity of technical success in dealing with X strongly suggests that despite their fundamental differences of sensory–intellectual constitution they must have reached conclusions about X which are in some crucial sense similar or identical, and are so in respects which abstract from or transcend differences in the way they're sensorily affected by X.[24]

The distinction between primary and secondary qualities seems relevant here. It's true that we apply this distinction in the context of the supposition that the reality we're concerned with—X for short—is specifically physical and spatial in character. The distinction as we have it is embedded in a specific view of the nature of nature. But the fundamental idea behind the distinction is of quite general application, and it may provide a good and familiar framework in which to consider the present claim that a being B can possibly be said to form an *intellectual conception* of how X is, in itself, *on the basis of* how it is sensorily affected by X, in such a way that its conception of X is in some important sense fully independent of the particular quality of the sensory affection which is for it a condition of the possibility of its formation of the conception.

The old opposition between rationalism and empiricism is often not particularly helpful, but it provides a way of restating the present point. Part of the bad legacy of militant positivism has been an implausibly strict empiricist and, arguably, ultimately *sensualist* conception of the nature of human understanding and intellect,[25] and in particular of the possible content of those paradigmatic products of the understanding—our theories about the nature of reality. It seems we need an essentially more rationalist epistemology.[26] The mathematization of the physical sciences may be said to lend support to this claim, and no doubt it does. But the most basic point is better made, at least at first, not by appealing to anything like mathematical physics, but rather to the conception of the physical possessed, say, by a non-scientist with an amateur interest in science. This conception is already strongly (if only partially) abstract in the sense which is relevant at present: it's abstract in the sense that it abstracts from the particularities of our modes of sensory experience. It involves a general grasp of concepts like that of rest mass and electric charge which have no sort of direct correlate in sensory experience, even though their acquisition is essentially based on sensory-experience-involving episodes.

But perhaps the best way to make the fundamental point is to consider people who have no knowledge of theoretical physics at all, for it may be said that they have an understanding—a natural, unreflective 'theory', in some weak sense of that elastic word—of the nature of reality which is, in the relevant sense, abstract. It's abstract relative to the particularities of their sensory experience. There's a crucial sense in which it entirely *transcends* the phenomenal particularities of that experience, for it's a form of understanding which essentially involves the deployment of certain concepts which are, essentially, concepts of 'non-sensory properties'.

---

[24] Consider the more mundane comparison of birds and bats (or superbats) with respect to their representations of objects in space.

[25] Cf. Kant's remark that 'Locke... *sensualized* all concepts of the understanding' (*Critique* A271/ B327).

[26] McGinn makes the same suggestion (1983: 126).

Discussing those non-sensory properties which are traditionally called the primary properties (or qualities) of objects, as opposed to their secondary properties (or qualities)—those (concepts of) properties 'constitutive of the idea of material substance as *space-occupying stuff*'—Evans writes as follows:

These include properties of bodies immediately consequential upon the idea of space-occupation—position, shape, size, motion; properties applicable to a body in virtue of the primary properties of its spatial parts; and properties definable when these properties are combined with the idea of force (e.g. mass, weight, hardness). The way these [non-sensory] properties relate to experience is quite different from the way sensory properties relate to it. *To grasp these primary [or non-sensory] properties, one must master a set of interconnected principles which make up an elementary theory—of primitive mechanics—into which these properties fit, and which alone gives them sense.* One must grasp [implicitly, or more or less explicitly] the idea of a unitary spatial framework in which both oneself and the bodies of which one has experience have a place, and through which they move continuously. One must learn of the conservation of matter in different shapes, of the identity of matter perceived from different points of view and through different modalities, and of the persistence of matter through gaps in observation. One must learn how bodies compete for the occupancy of positions in space, and the resistance one body may afford to another. And so on.

To say that these primary properties of matter are theoretical is not to explain or to mystify, but to highlight an analogy between the way our grasp of them rests upon implicit knowledge of a set of interconnected principles in which they are employed, and the way our understanding of such a property as electric charge rests upon explicit knowledge of a set of propositions more familiarly regarded as a theory. Certainly, to deny that these primary properties are *sensory* is not at all to deny that they are *sensible* or *observable*, for we are obviously able, after the appropriate training, to perceive the shape, motion, and hardness of things. The point is rather that it is not possible to distil the concept of hardness solely out of the experiences produced by deformation of the skin which is brought into contact with a hard object, *for it is not possible to distil out of such an experience the theory into which the concept fits.* It is no more possible to have a purely sensory concept of hardness than it is possible to...master the concept of electricity solely by learning to recognize electric shocks. And, though this is less obvious, it does not appear to be possible to regard the concept of the shape of a material thing—with all the propositions about its characteristic behaviour and interaction with other bodies which that implies—as the same as whatever shape concepts might be grounded [only] in the colour mosaic thought to be given in immediate visual experience. This would certainly seem to be suggested if we can demonstrate, as I believe we can, that the blind are capable of a perfectly adequate mastery of shape concepts, and of spatial concepts generally, for no single *sensory* property can be defined in relation to different senses...

I do not take myself to be saying anything new in drawing the primary/secondary quality distinction in this way, since it is almost exactly the way Thomas Reid explains the distinction in his *Inquiry into the Human Mind* [pp. 55, 61]...In the words of a recent commentator, 'Reid tries to show that our concepts of certain primary qualities are bound up in an elementary theory of bodies, a natively [i.e. innately] given *primitive mechanics*'.[27]

---

[27] Evans 1980: 269–71. The commentator is Norman Daniels (1974: xiv). I quote part of this passage again in 23, where our ordinary, non-regularity-theory concept of causation is considered as a concept of a non-sensory property.

This general point seems to be of great importance.[28] One may concede that all our putatively sensory-element-transcending and essentially partly intellectual concepts of the nature of reality somehow involve sensory elements as a kind of vehicle or precondition, while insisting that the concepts may also reasonably be said to be, in some vital sense, independent of their sensory vehicle; or at least that they may reasonably be said to have certain key aspects which are, in a vital sense, independent of any sensory elements. Given the way we are, we somehow elaborate concepts of shape, or of physical objects, or of electricity, which radically transcend our sensory experience in certain respects. Accordingly, it makes sense to suppose that we may be said to share these concepts, given the key or core aspects in question, with other possible beings with radically different sensory equipment. And so in turn it makes sense to suppose that our concepts are or at least may be parts of a (the) correct representation of the nature of reality, despite all the particularities of the specifically human 'idiom' of reality-representation.

When one thinks of the concept of shape, it seems to be already fully independent of sensory elements in the vital sense.[29] It seems intelligible—natural—to suppose that different creatures may have acquired essentially the same concept of shape as we possess on the basis of very different sensory experiences; that superintelligent bats (e.g.) can on the basis of their 'sonar' experiences acquire the same general concept of shape (and size) as we acquire on the basis of visual and tactile experiences. In fact, it suffices to note that exactly the *same concept of shape* can plausibly be supposed to be fully masterable on the basis of sensory experiences in entirely different sensory modalities familiar to us—sight and touch—in order to illustrate the sense in which the concept of shape floats free of the different possible sensory bases of its acquisition.[30]

If this general idea is defensible—it seems indispensable—then it completely undercuts the argument in (1)–(3), which suggests that no account or representation of reality on the part of a finite sensory–intellectual creature can ever be supposed to be the truth or even something like the truth about the general nature of reality.

It may be worth adding that natural-kind terms are also essentially sensory-element-transcending notions. It is widely accepted that, even if we are in fact quite wrong about certain aspects of the nature of, say, mercury and electrons, we can nonetheless refer to them and talk about them. If so, then the statement that *mercury* has atomic number 80—that atoms of mercury have 80 *electrons*—may well be part of the Truth—the Truth *sans phrase*—about the nature of reality. The statement, although a statement of our human science formulated by

---

[28] In one way it is perhaps difficult to grasp it fully; in another way it's perhaps rather obvious. Note that Kant would reject the suggestion that the primary quality/secondary quality distinction corresponds in any useful way to the appearance-reality distinction—or rather, the distinction between the apprehension of (mere) appearance and the apprehension of some ultimate feature of reality. For on his view the primary-quality aspects of objects in the 'empirically real' world are as much a matter of 'mere appearance' as the secondary-quality aspects (See Kant 1783: §13 Remark 2; he grants the applicability of the primary quality/ secondary quality distinction within the 'empirically real' world, e.g. in the *Critique* A29–30/B45).

[29] Hume and Reid make the same point about the concept of solidity; see 228–31/1.4.4.9–14, and Reid 1764: §5.2 and §5.4. In accordance with his theory of ideas, Hume concludes that we have 'no just nor satisfactory idea of solidity', because our impressions of sensation can't represent solidity (231/1.4.4.9). He fails to acknowledge the sense in which—or at least the extent to which—many of our ideas or concepts are essentially non-sensory or intellectual in character, and this (as remarked in 23) is arguably his greatest philosophical failure.

[30] Here one may contrast the case of a congenitally blind person with that of a fully sighted person who is congenitally paralysed and devoid of tactile sensation.

us in our human terms, is true *sans phrase* even though we have an imperfect grasp of the Truth in question, given that we are wrong about or ignorant of certain aspects of the nature of mercury and electrons. Once one grants that our terms like 'mercury' and 'electron' ('tiger', 'DNA', and so on) can reach out to reality despite the particularities of our sensory–intellectual apparatus, one can say that millions of the accepted truths of human science and common knowledge are, without any qualification, Truths, parts of the Truth; as they most surely are. (That *cats* like *cream* is part of the Truth.) Even if other beings are sensorily affected by mercury and electrons in ways which are quite different from the way in which we are affected by them—even if their concepts of these things are embedded in more or less different theories—still we and they may talk about and refer to *the same things*.[31]

No doubt there are other objections to the present line of thought. But the fact that any finite, sensory–intellectual creature necessarily has one particular sensory nature among other possible sensory natures is no longer an insuperable problem. *Intellect* being what it is, different intelligent species with radically different sensory modalities can possibly converge upon what is, essentially, the same theory of the general nature of reality. *Reality* (as-it-is-in-itself) being what it is—the same for everybody who is in contact with it, whatever the differences in the way they *experience* it—the (irresistibly) best explanation of equal technical success in such ventures as space travel or the development of nuclear power on the part of radically different beings is that they have in some way or sense or other cottoned on to the same facts—the same truths. Indeed one would expect their theories to be representationally congruent in certain respects—to be in principle intertranslatable. It would be natural to suppose that there must be highly significant isomorphisms between the theoretical structures of their respective sciences.

It may be suggested that there could be radically different *intellectual* styles in something like the way in which there may be radically different ways of being sensorily affected. But the basic fact, rightly prized by realists, that both groups are dealing with what is in fact the same reality (as-it-is-in-itself) gives one strong reason to suppose that if they achieve similar solutions to problems whose solution presupposes a practically speaking successful theory of some *very fundamental* aspect of reality, then whatever the differences between their modes of sensory access to that aspect of reality, and whatever their differences of intellectual style, their theories must from some point of view be intelligibly similar in crucial respects.

Suppose that God exists, and has some absolute scale from one to ten on which he can rank the theories of finite beings with regard to their grasp of the general structure of reality (or some particular aspect of the general structure of reality). Suppose we score eight on the scale, and that we have, in our way, achieved quite a good grasp of the general structure of reality (or at least of certain aspects of it). It is then very natural to suppose that if any other beings of some radically different sensory–intellectual type also score eight on the scale, there will have to be very significant similarity of structure between our theories and their theories—simply because both are good representations (in some absolute sense) of a *single structure*. And, clearly, insofar as we may suppose such theories to improve in their sensitivity to the details of the general structure of reality as time goes on, it is reasonable to suppose they will converge further in their similarity of overall structure, and display an increasing degree of

---

[31] To say this is of course to reject the relativist–incommensurabilist line of thought in the philosophy of science.

isomorphism. These other beings don't have to have the same concepts as us, and obviously they don't have to count in kilograms, coulombs, or metres; but, if we have got atomic structure roughly right, then they too will have to have some account of reality according to which there are aspects of reality corresponding in some intelligible way (intelligible at least to God— but it doesn't matter if God doesn't exist) to our account according to which there are e.g. *electrons* which have a *rest mass* of 9.109558×10^{-31} *kilograms*, a negative *electric charge* of 1.602192×10^{-19} *coulombs*, and a *radius* (1989 estimate) of 2.81777×10^{-15} *metres*. They must have cottoned on to whatever Planck's constant has cottoned on to. And so on.

2. In mathematics there are results with two apparently very different proofs—Rogers–Ramanujan identities, for example, or Euler's identity (see Hardy and Wright 1960: 282–7, 290 ff; Euler's identity is a special case of an identity which belongs to the theory of elliptic functions, and whose mathematical 'roots' are therefore essentially *analytic* and *transcendental*. But there's a short proof of it, given by Franklin in 1881, which is wholly *combinatorial*, and which proceeds by considering it as providing a formula for the difference between the number of partitions of a given integer into odd and even parts.) A third example is provided by Liouville's and Cantor's proofs of the existence of transcendental numbers: using an analysis which showed that an algebraic irrational number cannot be very well approximated by rationals, Liouville proved that certain particular numbers are transcendental. But the existence of transcendental numbers is also deducible in a quite different way, because it is an immediate corollary of Cantor's later proof of the non-enumerability of the continuum. This example is perhaps less useful, because it is only under the rather general description 'proof of the existence of transcendental numbers' that these two proofs are proofs of the same thing—and the expression 'transcendental numbers' is also wide in its application.

I mention such examples because (given a moderate degree of mathematical realism) they might possibly be thought to provide grounds for an objection to the idea that different theoretical representations of the nature of the same fact must at some level display a significant degree of isomorphism. I'm ill-qualified to speak of these matters, but I'll venture three main points. On the one hand I'll propose some disanalogies between the mathematical case and the case of theories of reality, which seem to make the former dubiously appropriate as a basis for an objection to the present view of the latter. On the other hand I'll suggest that where there are resemblances or analogies, it's natural to take the same sort of line about the mathematical case as about the case of theories of reality.

(1) There seems to be an enormous difference between a proof of some particular pure mathematical formula M and a theoretical representation P of some particular aspect of the nature of physical reality P. For even given a form of mathematical realism according to which M is indeed a *representation* of some particular part M of mathematical reality, one needn't think of the steps of a proof of M as depicting the structure of M—of that part of mathematical reality represented by M *taken on its own*. One needn't think of the two proofs as constituting, *in their detail*, two good representations of a *single structure* (i.e. M taken on its own), whereas there is this pressure in the case of two rival representations P_1 and P_2 of some aspect of physical reality P. The two mathematical proofs do not, in their details, stand in the relation of *representation* to M taken on its own in the way that theories of the nature of physical reality purport to stand in the relation of representation to that which they are a theory of. It's true

that many mathematicians are inclined to see the proofs as themselves possessing a kind of representational content. They're inclined to see the proofs as explorations of—and hence in some sense representations of—the 'territory' surrounding M. But with this realist inclination there goes an equal inclination to suppose that in such cases of double proof it should (must) be possible in principle to see, from some standpoint, how there can be two ostensibly very different routes to the same result (except perhaps when they differ in the sort of way in which Liouville's and Cantor's proofs of the existence of transcendental numbers do). And in this respect the mathematical case matches, and does not provide grounds for an objection to, the present suggestion about the correct way to view rival theories of the nature of reality.

(2) A further element of disanalogy between the two cases is that in the case of mathematical proofs, unlike the case of theories of the nature of the universe, there's no reason at all to suppose that, because there are two apparently very different and equally good proofs of some result, neither can be simply true (part of the Truth). On the contrary, both are True.

(3) Finally—to bring mathematics and theories of the universe together—it might be suggested that precisely because of the essential abstractness of mathematics as a medium for the representation of non-mathematical reality, there is in fact no need to rule out the idea that it could perhaps be true both (a) that there were deep and perhaps irreducible differences between two apparently equally good (say equally practically speaking successful) mathematical accounts of some aspect of non-mathematical reality and (b) that they could, nevertheless, both be said to arrive at the Truth of the matter in question. Deep differences of representational form or medium might not in this case be a bar to the ultimate identity of what was represented—any more than they are in the case of a pie chart and a column graph representing the same distribution of some quantity.

In accepting this highly speculative suggestion, one doesn't have to give up one's conviction that there could not in fact be any such irreducible differences. Quantum theory supplies a classic case in which two apparently quite distinct mathematical accounts of some phenomenon—Heisenberg matrix mechanics and the Schrödinger wave equation—turned out to be essentially the same.

3. We live in a scholastic age, and philosophers (of science) spend a lot of time dismissing suggestions as worthless because they fall short of certain extremely exigent standards of precision. I think the story of the two intelligent species in 2. may be of use despite its vagueness. The fundamental idea is that it makes sense to think of certain key aspects of our representation of reality as entirely abstract or intellectual in character, in the sense that they abstract from the particularities of our particular mode of sensory representation. If this is so, then the idea that finite, sensory–intellectual creatures may be supposed to achieve something like a correct (even if partial) representation of the general nature of reality is a live option.

Those who think that this isn't so, and who wish to maintain the strong sceptical conclusion (that it's demonstrably impossible for a finite, essentially sensory being to give or grasp any account or representation of the general nature of reality which could be said to be the Truth about reality, or even something like the Truth), believe that the strong conclusion can be reached despite the assumption, explicitly made at the beginning of the discussion, that reality consists of a single, mind-independent universe. But there seems to be a serious tension between the strong conclusion and this assumption. For to make the assumption is to face the objection that Berkeley's theory of reality is irrefutable. Many admit this, but (naturally enough) don't consider Berkeley's theory to be worth serious attention. To do this, however, is apparently to accept that if we compare Berkeley's account of reality with some realist account, it makes sense to suppose that one of them is *nearer the truth*—more like something like the Truth—than the other. Contrary to the strong conclusion. It was argued in 7 that it's intelligible—not to say natural—to suppose that our common-sense account of things according to which there (really, ultimately) are mind-independent things is closer to the Truth than Berkeley's account of things. But those who accept the strong conclusion cannot do this.

4. Consider in conclusion suggestion about how things may possibly be that makes the strong conclusion seem appropriate. It is Kantian in inspiration.

Perhaps reality is far, far stranger than we suppose. And perhaps an appropriate analogy for the overall experiential relation in which we and other very different beings (of types B and C) stand to reality is provided by the case of three possible physical creatures who have exactly the same patterns of electrical impulses transmitted to their brains (these impulses play the role of the reality that affects us), but react to them in very different ways. In the first the impulses produce colour experience, in the second they produce auditory experience, in the third they produce smell and taste experience. Perhaps the differences between our *overall* (not merely sensory) sensory–intellectual apprehension of reality and those of the B-type and C-type beings are as great as the differences between these three modes of sensory experience. Perhaps we really do inhabit utterly different universes, experientially speaking, on account of the way we're affected by the same 'ultimate' reality. (Perhaps we are minds constituted of some unintelligible substance receiving the same input from one common thing, but experiencing things in inconceivably and utterly incommensurably different ways.) Here there seems to be no significant scope for the sort of qualified optimism about the possibility of achieving 'something like the truth' endorsed above. If the analogy is in fact appropriate to our actual situation, then 'ultimate' reality is as inaccessible for us and the B-type and C-type beings as any conception of the nature of electrical impulse is for beings whose only possible mental states are just uninterpreted colour experiences or sound experiences or smell and taste experiences.

We can't know that the analogy is not appropriate. Hence even if we have or can have something like the truth about reality, we can never know that we do. And this conclusion is correct: acknowledgement of the irrefutability of scepticism, so far as our knowledge of the ultimate nature of things is concerned, is an essential part of a genuinely realist attitude to the world.[32]

---

[32] See ch. 12 n. 4. It's arguable that Kant's principal philosophical mistake in the *Critique of Pure Reason* is to suppose that we can know for sure that we can't attain to 'something like the truth' about the ultimate nature of reality (the 'noumenal').

8

'Causation'

At various points I've used the expression 'something like natural necessity'. But what do I mean by it? It's not clear why anyone should ask, for its meaning is manifest: 'natural necessity' is a perfect expression for what it most clearly denotes. But one might also say of it, more heavily, that it stands for the ordinary, strong, essentially non-regularity-theory idea or conception of causation. It's intended to represent what Hume has in mind when he speaks of the 'power', 'energy', 'force', 'tie', or 'necessary connexion' in objects, or of the 'ultimate principles' that we naturally take to govern the course of nature. Hume holds that we can't really give any legitimate, 'distinct', 'clear', 'determinate', 'comprehensible', empirically warranted, positively descriptively contentful meaning to these terms, when we think of them as applying to objects (see e.g. 162/1.3.14.14). At one point he says that such words 'seem to be . . . absolutely without any meaning' (74/7.26). But he doesn't think of them as entirely contentless in all applications (see 10). He doesn't think of them as having no reference in our use of them (see 12 and 14–21).

In what follows I won't use the expression 'natural necessity'. Instead I'll capitalize the word 'causation'—'Causation'. 'Causation' will function as a completely general term that can be substituted for any of the other words ('power', 'energy', etc.) that Hume uses as terms that purport to refer to causation conceived of in some essentially non-regularity-theory way. I'll call these 'Causation terms'. I'll often use them when it's natural to do so in discussion of particular passages from Hume's work, but I'll mostly replace them by the term 'Causation'. They're all meant to be attempts to express the same sort of thing (even if they are attempts—in Hume's view—to express the inexpressible) and using a single term like 'Causation' may help to unify the discussion in a useful way.

For present purposes, then, 'Causation' may be negatively defined: it covers any essentially *non-regularity-theory* conception of causation. More positively (if essentially unspecifically): to believe that causation is in fact Causation is simply to believe (A) that there is something about the fundamental nature of the world in virtue of which the world is regular in its behaviour; and (B) that that something is what causation is, or rather is at least an essential part of what causation is or involves.[1]

---

[1] It may be added, by way of positive characterization of Causation, that the notion of Causation essentially involves the notion of one thing *deriving from* another. But nothing in the present argument

To *deny* that causation is Causation is to hold (C) that causation is just regular succession. It is therefore to hold (¬A) that there is *nothing* about the nature of the world in virtue of which the world is regular in its behaviour; for it would be wonderfully implausible to try to avoid this corollary (¬A) of (C) by saying that although (A) there *is* something about the nature of the world in virtue of which it is regular in its behaviour, still (¬B) that something is no part of what causation is.

This said, I think it's important to note that one possible interpretation of Hume's discussion of causation holds that (A) + (¬B) does indeed represent his position. On this view, Hume isn't concerned to deny that there is something about the nature of reality ('power', etc.) in virtue of which it is regular in character. He claims only that this isn't what *causation* is.

I think that Beauchamp and Rosenberg have this in mind at certain points, for example where they distinguish between the operations of nature and causal relations: 'Hume does say ... that "As to what may be said, that the operations of nature are independent of our thought and reasoning, I allow it" ...; but he does not here say that *causal* relations are independent of thought' (1981: 17, quoting *Treatise* 168/ 1.3.14.28). Such a distinction between the operations of nature and causal relations may seem very puzzling to us, since it's natural to identify the two; but it does have a foundation in Hume, especially in his line of thought according to which 'the nature of the [causal] relation depends so much on'—is in some sense a function of—human habits of inference (169/1.3.14.30), and is to that extent a 'thought-dependent' human creation to be distinguished from the real operations of nature.

I'll cite a further passage in support of this line of interpretation in 15.5 (p. 157). One good (conclusive) reason for holding it to be ultimately inadequate is provided by what Hume says about his two definitions of cause (see 21 below). Then there is his claim (see 19.1) that 'experience and observation' do not furnish us with 'any acquaintance with the nature of cause and effect' (68/7.18). This could hardly be so if cause and effect were just a matter of regular succession (of a sort that gives rise to a certain feeling of determination in the mind). For we experience and observe such regular succession, as well as the feeling of determination in the mind to which it gives rise.

The crucial point is this: even if the interpretation according to which Hume holds (A) and (¬B) is accepted, the claim that he is not a 'Humean' remains. If the interpretation is accepted, it may be possible to say that Hume really is a regularity theorist about causation in the objects in one sense. For on this interpretation, by 'the relation of cause and effect as it is in the objects' Hume simply means 'whatever it is,

depends essentially on this point. Nor will I explicitly consider whether the word 'necessity' is necessary in the description of Causation (for a doubt see Anscombe 1971, discussed in 23). But I will later in the chapter introduce the idea that the world *has* to be regular in the general way that it is, given its nature.

in the objects, which is *observable*, and hence capturable in the content of our positively contentful conception of causation in the objects'; i.e. regular succession. It does not, however, follow from this—given what is now meant by 'the relation of cause and effect as it is in the objects'—that Hume denied that Causation existed in the objects.[2]

The claim about what is involved in accepting that there is Causation can be put in other terms, independently of explicit mention of regularity: to deny that causation is Causation is to say that there is, definitely, *no 'because' in nature*. That is, no statement of the form 'X happened because Y happened' is ever literally true, given our ordinary understanding of its meaning. Such 'because' statements are just our (human) reactions to certain sorts of sequence.[3] Correspondingly, to assert that causation is Causation is to say that 'becauseness' is really part of nature, independently of human (or any) mental reactions; that statements of the form 'X happened because Y happened' can be literally true given our ordinary (realist, objectivist) understanding of their meaning.

It may seem extraordinary that anyone should ever have held the view that there is definitely no 'because' in nature—that there is definitely nothing about the world in virtue of which it is regular. It is, as remarked in 5, one of the most baroque metaphysical suggestions ever put forward—principally by people who pride themselves on dispensing with metaphysical extravagance.[4] But its truth is not actually logically ruled out (see 5), and it seems that many have held it—and have even attributed it to Hume.[5]

If this were not so, the present typographical distinction between 'Causation' and 'causation' would be unnecessary. For any philosophically sane version of realism requires the acknowledgement that causation is Causation; although the denial of the contrary view is not logically inconsistent. The typographical distinction between 'causation' and 'Causation' is necessary only because some have held the regularity

---

[2] I'll return to this initially somewhat puzzling thought. It may be noted that Beauchamp and Rosenberg's main concern is rather different from mine, in the passage from which the quotation is taken. They are concerned to defend Hume's 'second definition' from those who dismiss it as unimportant or aberrant.

[3] Ayer (1973: 183) is clear about this consequence of the regularity theory. See also van Fraassen's striking discussion of explanation (1980: ch. 5).

[4] 'Many of them don't commit themselves to the positive claim that regular succession is definitely all there is to causation.' So be it; it remains true that to entertain the supposition that regular succession might be all there is to causation is to entertain a wildly extravagant metaphysical position. Note that only those who admit the intelligibility of the supposition that there might be something other than regularity which is the reason why there is regularity can be absolved from the charge of full commitment to the vast metaphysical extravagance.

[5] Perhaps it appeals particularly to the young in philosophy (the intoxication of iconoclasm); or, more generally, to anyone who gets stuck at the 'Oedipal' stage of philosophical education, at which one feels a powerful desire to prove one's independence from Ordinary Opinion (*sc.* the authority of the Father), or at least from some (negatively cathected) aspect of it, and so simply abstracts from thought about the nature of things like stubbing one's toe, and indeed from anything else that gets in the way of one's revolt. A generally positivistic approach to things may also be presented as admirably modest and clean-limbed in its self-denying austerity, while simultaneously fulfilling a deep and unacknowledged psychological need, insofar as it renders everything safe, tidy, inspectable, masterable, encompassable, and relieves anxiety or unease about the unknown or unknowable.

theory of causation, so that (in philosophy at least) the word 'causation' can no longer be freely used in the natural way to mean Causation (i.e. to mean what it means).

Some interpretations of quantum theory involve the claim that there is objective indeterminism in nature, and it's worth observing that dispute about this claim has no bearing on the present issue. For whether the claim is true or false—suppose for the sake of argument that it's true—there is still (massive) regularity in the behaviour of things. And, this being so, the same choice remains. One can either claim (1) that there is something about the nature of the universe (or matter) which is the reason why there is such regularity, and which is not just the fact of the regularity itself (thereby claiming that there is Causation). Or one can claim (2) that there is nothing about the nature of the universe which is the reason why there is such regularity. The choice arises in exactly the same way for regularities which are correctly captured only by statistical or probabilistic formulae of the form '99 per cent (or indeed 29 per cent) of Xs which become Y become Z', as it does for regularities which are captured by exceptionless universalistic formulae of the form 'All Xs which become Y become Z.'[6]

There are, to rephrase, two possible views about statistical laws. One is that they're just the best we can do in certain areas, given our sensory–intellectual limitations, in giving an account of a reality which is in fact deterministic, and works according to exceptionless laws. The other is that nature does not work according to exceptionless laws—that (roughly) even the ultimate, perfect account of things would contain irreducible statistical laws. The present point is that even if the second suggestion is true it doesn't threaten the claim that it's reasonable to postulate Causation. For it's still the case that the world as a whole behaves in a certain characteristic and highly regular way. And it's still reasonable to suppose that there is something about it *given which* it is (cannot but be) regular in this way.

It may now be said that the debate about whether or not there is Causation is of no importance to science, which can get along just as well with mere regular succession. But this may be granted here (although it may also be disputed), because the philosophical importance of the issue remains untouched. It may be said that the issue is a ghostly one, since Causation is principally defined in a negative way as essentially non-regularity-theory causation, and has no positive characterization. In fact it does have a positive characterization, in terms of the intuitive notion of one thing bringing about another, or deriving from another.[7] But one may put aside this point, or discount it as unclear, and even grant that the issue is in a sense a ghostly one, while still insisting that it's an issue of enormous philosophical importance.

---

[6] If it is indeed a persistent fact that 99 per cent (or 29 per cent) of Xs which become Y become Z, then this persistent fact is *exactly* as much of a regularity manifested in the world as the fact that 100 per cent of Ts which become V become W.

[7] It can be hard to recover a proper grasp of the importance and legitimacy of this simple point, after a typical philosophical education in analytical philosophy (and despite one's everyday experience). It's discussed further in 23.

This is implicitly recognized precisely by those who are perhaps most inclined to deny it. For if the issue were unimportant, there would be no need for passionate insistence that causation is nothing but regular succession. To show such passion is to imply that the distinction between regularity-theory causation and Causation is real and important.

Some may offer an instrumentalist or pragmatist defence of the regularity theory. 'We're only concerned with what is empirically observable; we don't want to get into any metaphysics.' Fine, but don't then deny the existence of Causation. For this is to get into metaphysics in precisely the way that was to be avoided. Nor can realists give this instrumentalist reason for adhering to the regularity theory, because to be a realist is already to be involved in metaphysics, from the instrumentalist point of view (a point which is distinct from the point that a commitment to realism seems in any case to bring with it the need to accept the existence of Causation).

The worst motivation for such a denial of the existence of Causation is the view, wrongly if understandably attributed to Hume, and discussed further below, that Causation terms are completely meaningless in our sense of the term 'meaningless'. Whatever one makes of the claim that there is something about the nature of the world in virtue of which the world is regular in the way that it is, it's not meaningless. And Hume for one never doubted that it was true.

In a way, to say that there isn't just regular succession, and that there is something (the nature of matter) which is the reason why there is regularity, is to take a very small because extremely—maximally—unspecific step. In a way, it's to take a very delicate philosophical step. In another way, however, it's to take an enormous step—about as big as the step between a realist (or basic-realist) account of the nature of matter and some radically idealist (non-basic-realist) account. The two steps resemble each other in other ways. Each is a step from one strictly speaking unverifiable and unfalsifiable view to another (assuming that some such idealist view is at least not incoherent). And each is a step between a view of something X (matter or causation) according to which all aspects of X are in principle fully apprehensible in experience and a view of X according to which this isn't so. This second point classes belief in Causation with realism (or basic realism), and belief in the regularity theory with a radical idealist (and non-basic-realist) approach to the nature of matter. This is highly appropriate, both because this pairing of theories reflects their true theoretical affinities,[8] and because the regularity theory is certainly no more plausible than most people think the strict-idealist account of the universe is.[9]

---

[8] In 6 it was argued that objects have no 'ontic backside', on a strict-idealist account of their nature. Similarly, the regularity theory of causation supposes that causation has no ontic backside, in being nothing more than observable regularity.

[9] This is unfair to strict idealism, which is far more plausible than the regularity theory of causation. As already noted, it will in 22 be argued that a regularity theory of causation is utterly implausible even if one rejects basic realism in favour of some form of strict idealism.

The argument for allowing that there is something about reality in virtue of which it is regular doesn't depend on some tacit invocation of the Principle of Sufficient Reason, according to which there must be a reason for everything. Suppose we call the reason for the world's regularity *the nature of matter*. The answer to the question 'Why is the world regular (and regular in the particular way that it is)?' is then 'Because of the nature of matter.' But if someone then asks 'Why is the nature of matter the particular way it is?', the best reply may very well be to reject the request for a reason, and say 'That's just the way things are.'[10] For this question may be unanswerable in the same way as the question 'Why is there something rather than nothing?'

One shouldn't think that there is any conflict between using the name 'Causation' to denote *that about reality in virtue of which it is regular, and which is therefore not just the fact of its regularity* and the idea that the best simple answer to the question 'Why is reality regular in the way that it is?' is 'Because of the nature of matter.' The fact that Causation exists is not some further fact over and above the fact that matter has the nature it has.

Nor is there any tension between the claim that Causation exists and the idea that the question about why the nature of matter is as it is may be unanswerable. For even when its unanswerability is granted, there remains a fundamental difference between the present position and a regularity account of things. According to the regularity account the regularity of the world is objectively a complete fluke from moment to moment. The whole truth about it is that the world *just is* regular. There is nothing about it in virtue of which it is regular in the way that it is, nothing about it in virtue of which it *has*, given its nature, to be regular in the way that it is.

According to the present view this is not so, for there are, to change idiom, objective 'fundamental forces' governing the behaviour of the world. These forces are features of—essentially constitutive of—the nature of matter; in no way add-itional to it.[11] According to the regularity account, matter has no such features.[12]

---

[10] I'm putting aside considerations about the 'fine-tuning' of physical constants.

[11] The word 'forces' is taken to latch on to real, mind-independent, observable-regularity-transcendent facts about reality; it is not just to be positivistically understood.

[12] It may be that there is unclarity at the heart of the regularity theory of causation; and that many who profess to accept it are not fully aware of what is involved in accepting it. Michael Levine suggests ('Mackie's Account of Necessity in Causation', p. 83) that regularity theorists are standardly quite open-minded about the existence of Causation, allowing (1) 'that...there may be a reason for the regularities' despite holding (2) that 'an account of causation that is empirically based must be considered complete without it, since empirically speaking there are nothing but regularities'. I don't know how far this is true (this is part of the unclarity): many regularity theorists seem committed to a form of positivism which balks at (1). And those who aren't so committed, and who accept (1), still favour the (logically consistent but) magical thinking which can take seriously the idea that there may be nothing at all about reality in virtue of which it is regular in the way that it is. Further, (1) and (2) coupled with the thesis that an account of causation must be empirically based yield the wonderfully implausible (¬B): the thesis that even if there is something about reality in virtue of which it is regular in the way it is, this something is no part of what causation is.

—But now you must say why these *forces* are regular in their operation. You must suppose that there's a *reason*, R, for their regularity of operation. Otherwise you'll be back with a regularity account according to which the forces 'just are' regular in their operation, this being, in your terms, a 'complete fluke'.

This is a familiar line of thought, but the difference just presented—between the present account and the regularity account—remains untouched. It is, to repeat it once more, just this: the present account postulates the existence, as a fundamental aspect of reality, of something—fundamental objective forces—constitutive of the nature of matter, or physical reality, and given which it is in fact the case that it can't but behave as it does. The regularity account asserts positively that there is nothing about the nature of matter given which it can't but behave as it does, and that there is thus definitely no reason why it is regular as it is. This is a vast difference, even if it's an unobservable one.[13] It's a measure of the deep intellectual disarray induced by decades of over-aggressive positivism that we may find it hard to grasp.

Those who are attracted by the objection just voiced should note that it threatens to provide an a priori proof that the regularity account is correct. For it continues as follows: suppose the supporters of fundamental forces do postulate a reason, R_1, for the regularity of the operation of the fundamental forces. Then it seems that if they are to avoid a regularity account of R_1, they must postulate a reason, R_2, for the regularity of the operation of R_1 in grounding the regularity of the operation of the fundamental forces. Infinite regress ensues. And so it appears that a regularity account of things must be true.

I take it that this consequence of the objection—that it makes it an a priori truth that the regularity account of things must be true—refutes it. It's one thing to suppose that the coming into existence of the world, at a single instant, might have been a fluke. It's another thing to suppose that its regularity of behaviour ever since has been and is a complete fluke, from moment to moment to moment, right now and now again and now again. It's a trivial point that explanations must come to an end; it would be odd if it followed that the regularity theory of causation must be true. Ultimately we must stop and say 'This is just how things are', but this doesn't commit us to the fluke hypothesis. What we take to be 'just how things are' can be: matter (concrete reality, whatever it is) with a nature given which it cannot but behave as it does.

One more repetition of the point will do no harm, and may do some good.[14] The difference between the present view that causation is Causation and the regularity theory of causation is this. According to the outright regularity theory of causation

---

[13] Unobservable: 'experience only teaches us that a thing is so and so, but not that it cannot be otherwise'—Kant 1781–7: B3.

[14] This is questionable. One of the ironies of this topic is that attempts to argue for the existence of Causation can be counter-productive, arousing resistance even in those who don't normally doubt the existence of Causation, and making it seem that something that shouldn't be in question needs defence.

it's a metaphysical fact that the regularity of the world is a complete fluke—where the word 'fluke' simply expresses the idea that the regularity of things is not constitutive of the nature of things. According to the present view it's a metaphysical fact that it isn't a complete fluke. It's a metaphysical fact that it is *in the nature of things* to be regular. (This is as good an expression as any of the belief in Causation.) Thus it is true to say that there is something about reality given which it is regular in the way that it is, something which is (therefore) not just the bare fact of regularity itself. So causation is Causation. It is true that this is, in a way, a rather delicate point. But it is nonetheless fundamental.

Let me in conclusion try to be very clear about the force of the expression 'something which is not just the bare fact of regularity itself'. I don't mean to suggest that there's some mysterious extra thing or stuff in nature which the regularity theorists are ignoring. The situation is rather this. The regularity theorists hold that the world *just is* a regular world; that all there is to causation is regularity; that there's nothing about the world given which it is or has to be regular (otherwise there would be more to causation than regularity); that it just is regular in fact, and that's all there is to it; that one thing 'just happens after another'; that it's never literally true that one thing happens because another happened (their adherence to this claim may seem particularly astonishing when one thinks of their experience of action).

Those who believe in Causation, by contrast, standardly hold that the world *can't but* be regular in the general way that it is, *given* its nature.[15] It's this view—the view that it happens as a matter of fact to be true of the world that it can't but be regular in the general way that it is, given its nature—that we may take to be expressed by the claim that there is 'something about the nature of the world in virtue of which it is regular, something which is (therefore) not just the fact of regularity itself'.

Does anyone really believe that causation is just regularity—that it's not true of matter that there is something about it given which it can't but be regular in the way that it is, given its nature? Weakening the 'can't but be' to 'is', does anyone really believe that there's definitely nothing about the nature of matter or reality in virtue of which it is regular in the way that it is? It's a very fantastic view—in a distinctively philosophical way. (It's the hard-nosed positivists who turn out to be the most passionate believers in miracles, as their epistemology hardens into a metaphysics.) Perhaps the best thing to do, if one doubts this, is to go for a walk in order to exercise the idea that Causation doesn't exist—in order to exercise the idea that there is nothing about the reality that surrounds one in virtue of which it is regular from moment to moment, from century to century.

---

[15] The *'can't but'* corresponds to 'natural *necessity*'; 'general' responds to the point that even if there is objective indeterminism, there is still massive regularity.

9

Hume's strict scepticism

This seems an appropriate point to summarize the present account of Hume and review the objection raised in 3. I've argued that Hume can't wish to assert that there's definitely no such thing as Causation (nothing about reality in virtue of which it's regular in the way it is), given his strictly non-committal scepticism with respect to knowledge claims. But I've also claimed that he believes that there is Causation in reality (something about reality in virtue of which it is regular in the way it is), and this, it may be said, looks like a belief that a non-committal sceptic can't allow himself.

The first reply, given in 3, is that there's a crucial difference between knowledge and belief. The standard view of Hume is that he takes himself to have shown (to have established as a known fact) that causation in the objects is nothing but regular succession.[1] This can't be right: any such claim to definite knowledge of the true nature of reality is ruled out by strictly non-committal scepticism. Firm *belief* that there is such a thing as Causation is not ruled out, however—so long as it can be shown to be intelligible in the present-day sense of the word (see pp. 46–8 above, and, further, 117–18 below). Strictly non-committal scepticism can accept the naturalness of such a belief, and grant that it may very well be true (allowing that it is intelligible), insisting only that we cannot know it to be true.

Practically speaking, Hume treats this belief as something we can know to be true (this has yet to be shown in detail). For this reason, it's worth making a second, stronger reply to the objection. Grant for the sake of argument that Hume takes it that there is definitely such a thing as Causation. Clearly such a claim contravenes strictly non-committal scepticism as much as the claim that there definitely isn't such a thing as Causation. So how can Hume assert the one if he can't assert the other? Leaving aside the point that the former claim is put forward only as a belief, not as a knowledge claim, I suggest that the relevant difference between the two claims—it suffices to explain Hume's different attitude to them—lies in the fact that the first claim (according to which the world's regularity is a fluke from instant to instant) is intrinsically vastly implausible, while the second claim (according to which the

---

[1] It isn't normally supposed that Hume put forward the claim that causation in the objects is nothing but regular succession merely as something he believed but didn't claim to have shown.

regularity isn't a fluke, but an inevitable consequence of the fundamental nature of things) is as plausible as the first is implausible.

This notion of plausibility or reasonableness has been subjected to all sorts of sophisticated doubts. Some will think that it is, in the end, just a great big metaphysical prejudice. Most, however, will grant its force. And what matters here is that even if sophisticated present-day empiricists find it unconvincing, Hume didn't. He never thought to question it. I hesitate to quote the *Dialogues*,[2] but here I will do so, for the general question of what reason or experience can reveal about the source of regularity and order in the universe is the central question of the *Dialogues Concerning Natural Religion*, as Wright remarks (1983: 169–70), and it's a question with which Hume was preoccupied from an early age. The idea that there might be no source or ground of order and regularity at all in reality—that there might be *just* regularity—is never considered. The main objection to the religious hypothesis in the *Dialogues*, according to which some god is the source of order, is that matter itself might contain the principle of order (and that things might have got into their present complicated state by some process of evolution). As Philo (Hume's main representative in the *Dialogues*) says

> For aught we can know *a priori*, matter may contain the source or spring of order originally, within itself... there is no more difficulty in conceiving, that the several elements, from an internal unknown cause, may fall into the most exquisite arrangement, than to conceive that their ideas, in the great, universal mind, from a like internal unknown cause, may fall into that arrangement. The equal possibility of both these suppositions is allowed. (55–6/146)

We can't decide between these two possibilities. But one thing which is clear is that there must be some source of order. As Philo says,

> How could things have been as they are, were there not an original, inherent principle of order somewhere, in thought or in matter? (125/174)

When Hume talks of order in the *Dialogues* he's often principally concerned with the order displayed in the complexity of plants and animals and their adaptation to their environment, and not just with order as causal regularity, but the former necessarily involves the latter, and can be bracketed with it for present purposes.

(1), (2), and (3) in 6.9 represent the central claims of this book.

(1) If Hume is any sort of regularity theorist about causation in the objects, then he is a regularity theorist only about objects *qua* perceptions, 'immediate', purely mental objects of mental attention, considered independently of their ultimate causes.

---

[2] Some think that the *Dialogues* somehow don't count when considering Hume's views on causation. Although they're wrong, it's preferable not to appeal to the *Dialogues* for this reason.

(2) Insofar as he is any sort of basic realist (52ff.) about objects or reality, Hume believes in Causation, i.e. something about reality in virtue of which it is regular in the way that it is.

(3) Hume propounds the regularity theory of causation only as a theory about causation so far as we can know about it in the objects—or (equivalently) so far as we can form some positively (descriptively) contentful conception of it on the terms of the theory of ideas.

In Parts 2 and 3 these claims will be supported by direct quotation from the *Treatise* and the *Enquiry*, but there is still some preparatory work to do. Chapter 10 puts forward a more detailed account of how Hume applies his general theory of ideas in the particular case of the idea of Causation. Chapter 11 discusses his assumption that genuine knowledge of causation as it is in the objects would have to give one the ability to make causal inferences with a priori certainty. Chapter 12 returns to the problem of meaning deferred in 6.5, and to the suggestion that he has to classify all Causation terms as meaningless. Chapter 13 considers some analogies and disanalogies between Hume's treatment of the notion of external objects and his treatment of the notion of causation. In the rest of this chapter I say something further about Hume's strictly non-committal philosophical scepticism.

The dialectical complexity of Hume's position can (with some redundancy) be set out as follows. Consider the realist regularity theory of causation. It's anything but non-committal. It makes a highly dramatic positive ontological claim about the nature of the world conceived in the realist way. It not only assumes, positively, that there's a realist world (of objects). It goes on to make a further positive assertion about the particular nature of the world, in asserting that causation in that world is definitely (knowably) nothing but regular succession.[3] As a strictly non-committal sceptic with respect to knowledge claims, Hume can't make any such claim about causation, as already remarked. He's simply not concerned with any such claim. As he says, 'our ignorance [is not] a good reason for denying the existence of any thing' (72–3/7.25). As a sceptic he holds not only that

(1) one can't know either that there is or that there is not some external (basic-realist) reality

but also that

(2) even if one simply assumes that there is for purposes of argument or general plausibility (as he standardly does), one can't claim to know anything for sure about its nature

---

[3] Regular succession which has—to add Hume's second definition to the first—the property of affecting human minds in certain ways.

from which it follows that

(3)   one cannot know either that there is, *or that there is not*, some sort of Causation in it.

This seems clear. However things are not so clear. (3) isn't in fact accurate as a statement of Hume's position on causation in the objects. This is so for at least two reasons, which are strikingly in conflict with each other. This conflict will have to be discussed at length.[4]

The first reason concerns Hume's theory of ideas: according to one apparently natural interpretation of the theory of ideas, one cannot give any sense at all to Causation terms. More precisely: although one can give some sense to an expression like 'Causation' ('power', 'force'), one can't give any sense to it in the case in which one supposes that it denotes some quality 'in the objects'. One may try to mean something when one attributes Causation (power, force) to the objects, but in fact one simply fails to mean anything.

Clearly, if this is Hume's view, it must be wrong to attribute (3) to him. For (3) seems to presuppose that Causation terms are at least meaningful when applied to objects. I will return to this objection.

The second reason why (3) is too quick as a statement of Hume's position is quite different. It's not that (3) is unintelligible for him. It's rather that it isn't strong enough to represent his position, because he takes it for granted that there *is* Causation in the objects or external world.

The situation can (again with some redundancy) be redescribed as follows. Assume that

(4)   there is indeed an external world or reality

and consider three claims:

(5)   there is some sort of Causation in the external world or in reality (but we cannot know anything about its nature)
(6)   there is no sort of Causation in the external world or in reality; there's nothing but regular succession ('in nature one thing just happens after another')
(3)   (as before) we can't know either that there is, or that there is not, some sort of Causation in the external world or in reality.

(5) and (6) are positive, directly contradictory ontological claims. (3) is a negative epistemological claim. If one positively asserts either (5) or (6) one must deny (3), and if one asserts (3) one can't assert (5) or (6).[5]

---

[4] It's not a fault in a discussion of Hume that it should have a slightly exotic dialectical movement to it, given the apparent tension in his position.

[5] Although the assertion of (3) is compatible with the assertion of (5a) 'There may be something like Causation in the external world', or (6a) 'There may be nothing like Causation in the external world', and although (5) and (3) or (6) and (3) can both be *true* together.

(6) is standardly taken to be the 'Humean' view. According to the present view, it's not only wrong to attribute (6) to Hume, it's also right to attribute (5) to him. It is, however, arguable that there's also a sense in which it is right to attribute (3) to him. But one can't consistently assert both (5) and (3), despite the fact that (5) and (3) can be true together; so (first main problem) I appear to be accusing Hume of inconsistency. Furthermore, if (5) is put forward as a knowledge claim about the nature of the world, it's a claim of the sort that is ruled out by Hume's strictly non-committal scepticism. What's more, the unintelligibility objection applies to (5) just as it does to (3). It's arguable that Hume denies the very *intelligibility* of (5), because of the occurrence of the term 'Causation' (replaceable by 'necessary connexion', 'power', etc.) in it.[6] So (second main problem) it seems that I'm not only accusing Hume of inconsistency, but also attributing to him views which he rules out as unintelligible.[7]

The solution to the first problem can be stated as follows: (3), the view that we can't know whether or not there is Causation in reality, together with (1), the view that we can't (even) know that there is or is not an external world, may be supposed to represent Hume's strictly sceptical position with respect to knowledge claims (although he never actually asserts (3), only (1)). (4) and (5), by contrast, the view that there is indeed an external reality, and that there is such a thing as Causation in reality, represent Hume's actual belief about how things are. Clearly, his firm *belief* that there is an external reality, and that there is Causation in that reality, is compatible with his strictly non-committal scepticism with respect to knowledge claims, which simply tells him that these beliefs cannot be known to be true. To believe something is to believe it to be true, but it is not to know that it's true, or to claim to know that it's true.

The point deserves to be restated in terms of basic realism. It's not only when writing as a realist about objects, and thus accepting (4), that Hume accepts (5) that there is some sort of Causation, although I'm focusing on this case for the sake of simplicity. For standard realism about objects is just one variety of basic realism, the view that the existence of objects involves the existence of something other than our perceptions, something which affects us and thereby gives rise to our perceptions and is the reason why they are as they are (leaving aside our contribution to their being the way they are). And in fact Hume takes it that there is Causation (this is still to be shown in detail) insofar as he accepts (4) for any reason—insofar as he accepts *any* basic-realist theory of the nature of the objects as possibly true. Thus (for example) he takes it that there is Causation even while granting as a sceptic that *Berkeley*'s story

---

[6] (6) also contains the expression 'Causation'; but the claim that the notion of Causation is unintelligible can form part of a position which is naturally expressed by saying 'There is no such thing as Causation.'

[7] It may be re-objected that he also rejects the notion of an external world 'specifically distinct from perceptions' as unintelligible. This objection was answered in 6.5.

about the nature of reality cannot be ruled out.[8] Indeed, and importantly, the fact that it is reasonable to posit some sort of Causation (some reason for the regularity of things) even while being unable to decide between solipsistic realism about one's own mind, Berkeleian realism about the mental in general, or essentially Lockean or 'common-sense' realism about physical objects, is itself one of the two principal reasons we have for being sure that we know nothing about the ultimate nature of Causation.[9]

So much (for the moment) for the first problem. Later on (in 22.2) it will be argued that Hume would have accepted (5) that there is Causation in reality even if he had positively *rejected* any and every basic-realist view of things (as he did not). It will be argued that he believes that there is such a thing as Causation—that he takes it entirely for granted—even at the furthest, formal limit of his scepticism, where all he is prepared to admit the certain existence of are perceptions.

More provocatively: in effect, Hume takes it that we can *know* that there is such a thing as Causation. In other words, his strictly non-committal scepticism extends to everything except two things: first, the existence of perceptions, secondly, the existence of Causation. These two things alone he never seriously questions the existence of. It's ironic that Hume is famous not just for doubting but for categorically denying the existence of one of the only two things whose existence he never seriously questioned, and about which his sceptical claim was simply that we could know nothing about its nature.

This merits an aside. One of the worst reasons for this mistake about Hume is the misinterpretation of his remarks to the effect that 'any thing may produce any thing' (see e.g. 173/1.3.15.1, 247/1.4.5.30, 164/12.29). The misinterpretation is possible only on a very superficial reading of Hume, but it is perhaps worth a mention. In saying 'any thing may produce any thing' Hume isn't saying or imagining that the regularity of the world actually is or could be somehow fortuitous—a fluke—from moment to moment. What he is saying is only that anything may produce anything *so far as reason alone is concerned.* 'If we reason *a priori*, anything may *appear* able to produce anything' (164/12.28). In other words

(7)   reason—logic—has absolutely nothing to say on the matter of *what goes with what* in nature or in reality:

This correct view is wholly compatible with the view that

(8)   given the way things actually are in nature or reality, independently of anything that reason has to say about them, nothing can possibly happen any differently from the way it does.

---

[8] Berkeley's theory certainly doesn't entail that there is no such thing as Causation in the universe, only that the nature of Causation is very different from what is normally supposed, being purely mental in character.

[9] Cf. the quotation from the *Dialogues* on p. 96. The other principal reason is discussed in 11.

Hume is one of many who hold both (7) and (8), although many today register reservations about (8) in the light of alleged but unprovable objective, subatomic indeterminacy.

Hume's basic position on this question, then, is the same as his position (discussed in 1) with respect to the proposition that something might arise without a cause. As Hume says, he 'never asserted so absurd a Proposition as *that anything might arise without a Cause*' (now that the world is up and running). He merely said that so far as reason goes there is no logical contradiction in the idea that something might arise without a cause. So too there is no *logical* contradiction, so far as any real thing in nature is concerned, in the idea that it might 'produce any thing'.

To return now to the main line of argument: the suggestion that Hume's belief in Causation was not even conditional on his basic realism will be considered in Part 4. For the moment, and throughout Parts 2 and 3, I'll continue to argue merely that Hume accepts that there is such a thing as Causation insofar as he writes as a realist, or as some sort of basic-realist, about objects.

The second problem remains—the problem about unintelligibility. It arises because Hume appears to holds that 'Causation' words ('power', 'energy', 'force', etc.) are simply unintelligible when applied to 'the objects'—this being a consequence of his theory of ideas. If this is right, how can he possibly assert something like (5)?

This problem is of central importance. The essentials of an answer were provided in 6.5, in the discussion of Hume's attitude to the question of whether the notion of external objects is an intelligible or conceivable one, and the discussion of Hume's distinction between what is intelligible in the sense of being 'positively contentfully conceivable' and what is intelligible in the sense of being coherently supposable. Even so, his treatment of the question as it arises in the case of the notion of Causation deserves a separate treatment, which I will now try to provide. (Here is another opportunity for those familiar with Hume's views to skip to 20 and 21, after picking up the definition of the 'Meaning Tension' in 12, pp. 117–18.)

10

Hume's theory of ideas as applied to the idea of causation

Hume's empiricist theory of ideas or concepts has many faults, but it's beautifully simple.[1] All one has to do, in order to find out what the content of an idea or concept or word is—and hence in order to find out *what one is (really) thinking about*, when employing the idea in thought, or equivalently *what one is (really) talking about*, when one uses the word—is to consider the impression(s) from which it is derived. All one has to do is consider its 'impression-source', because its content—its true content—is ultimately just the result of some process of copying (and perhaps combining) the contents of impressions, and is wholly derived from these impressions.

When it comes to the idea of causation conceived as something *in the objects*, Hume's basic position seems correspondingly clear.[2] He distinguishes, in effect, between the evidentially licensed and hence genuinely positively contentful idea of causation as it is in the objects (I'll call it 'X'), and the ordinary, illegitimately strong idea of causation in the objects ('Y'). X, the evidentially licensed idea of causation in the objects, is the idea of regular succession, and excludes the idea of necessary connection.[3] Y, by contrast, includes (or consists in) the idea of power or necessary connection.[4]

To ask about the exact *content* of X and Y is simply to ask what their impression-sources are. Hume's answer to this question can be diagrammed as in Figure 1, with the two ideas on the right, and their impression-sources on the left. The total impression-source for X, the evidentially licensed idea of causation as it is in the objects, consists of impressions P (precedency), C (contiguity), CC (constant conjunction). These give X its content, represented in the box for X. The dotted lines

---

[1] Its simplicity is one of its faults; it's perfunctory, as Craig remarks (1987: §2.1).

[2] The following is one way of putting it, at least—it ignores a number of complexities. Those who think it takes insufficient account of Hume's second definition of cause must be patient.

[3] In this chapter I will mostly use 'necessary connection' instead of 'Causation'.

[4] The claim that Y is on Hume's view illegitimately strong may be thought to be at odds with the principal claim of this book, to the effect that Hume firmly believed in Causation. But there is no inconsistency here. As will emerge, the point is that, although there is such a thing as Causation, Y fails to be a theory-of-ideas-acceptable, positively-contentful idea of it.

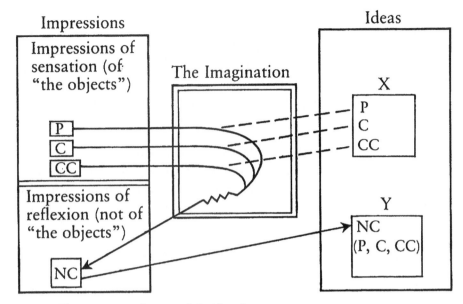

Figure 1 The experience of cause and the idea of cause

represent the way we might have formed nothing but this evidentially licensed idea of causation if the Imagination hadn't interfered, in the way represented by the curving lines, to give rise to the necessary-connection impression NC. It is experience of regular succession (P, C, and CC) which affects the Imagination in such a way that NC arises.[5]

As for the impression-source for Y, the strong, illegitimate idea of causation in the objects, one could say that it consists both of impressions of P, C, and CC (in the objects), and of the necessary-connection impression NC (in the mind). But its immediate impression-source, the impression-source from which it derives all its

---

[5] The diagram elides various issues. For example, P, C, and CC are treated as themselves impressions of sensation in the largest sense, but this cannot be strictly accurate. One might try saying that P and C are relations between individual impressions, and that CC is a relation between types of individual impression, but impressions can't really stand in spatial contiguity relations, even if they can stand in precedency relations, and it's better to say that C (and indeed P) is a relation between features of the *content* of impressions, rather than a relation between impressions of sensation themselves. Another obvious point is that CC experience always involves P and C experience, on Hume's view, as stated in the *Treatise*, or at the very least P experience, on his view as stated in the *Enquiry* (for the abandonment of the contiguity requirement, see p. 13 n. 9 above). The diagram is also unstable in a familiar Humean way so far as it (intentionally) avoids any clear ruling on whether 'the objects' are to be understood as truly external (realist or basic-realist) bodies, or as 'immediate' mental objects of experience, and therefore as themselves in a sense only 'in the mind'.

distinctive content as an idea, is just NC. So one may reasonably say that its impression-source is just NC.[6]

So much for the basic position. According to Hume's theory of ideas, what we mean, what we're thinking or talking about when we employ an idea or correspond-ing word, is a strict function of the idea's impression-source. Some consequences of this may now be noted. In particular, it may be noted that this leads to two rather different views about what happens when we purport to talk about causation in the objects.

The first view is this: (1) when we talk about causation in the objects, and intend to be talking about causation understood in the ordinary, strong, necessary-connection-involving sense Y, we simply don't succeed. Despite what we think, we're really talking only about P, C, and CC. When we look to the impression-sources of the idea of causation that actually lie *in the objects that we take ourselves to be talking about*, all we actually find are P, C, and CC.[7]

The second view subdivides into two: (2) when we talk about causation, and intend to be talking about necessary connection, (2a) we're really talking only about the mind, and not about the objects at all. We're really talking about the mind because that's where the immediate and vital impression-source for the necessary-connection idea we're using actually lies.[8] Or, at the very least, (2b) we're talking *partly* about the

---

[6] This may be supposed to correspond to Hume's claim that 'necessity...is nothing but an internal impression in the mind' (165/1.3.14.20), which sounds like support for the standard view (the discussion of Hume's 'global subjectivism about necessity' in 15.3 (p. 147) throws a strikingly different light on this remark). Presumably many of those whom Hume was attacking for thinking that their idea of NC was a genuine idea of causation in the world simply took it that NC entailed P, C, and CC—i.e., roughly, they took it that if a necessary causal connection holds between A and B then events of type A and type B are constantly conjoined in some spatio-temporal contiguity relation. Thus P, C, and CC may be allowed to feature in brackets in the NC idea-box in the diagram. (Many now would say that NC entails only CC, and neither P nor C.)

Note that Hume is forced to describe the source of our idea of necessary connection as an impression of reflexion by the Procrustean framework of his theory of ideas. Usually he calls it a feeling, or, better, a 'determination of the mind' to react in a certain way. More naturally put, his thought is that exposure to regularities in our experience leads us (given the way we are innately disposed) to come to believe in Causation or necessary connection in the objects, or, equivalently, to put our trust in certain habits of inference. For a discussion of some of the difficulties raised by this account of the source of the idea of necessary connection, see B. Stroud 1977: 80–7. Note also that Hume's account of the origin of the idea of necessary connection in an internal impression is arguably in tension with what he says when discussing the origin of the idea of space: 'our internal impressions are our passions, emotions, desires and aversions; none of which, I believe, will ever be asserted to be the model, from which the idea of space is deriv'd. There remains therefore nothing but the senses, which can convey to us this original impression' (33/1.2.3.3).

[7] It's natural here to understand 'objects' in the realist way, but it's important that Hume's general argument runs equally well if 'the objects' are taken as purely mental, as impressions of sensation or their contents (as perception-(content)-constituted objects; see 6.2). The point is then that all we find in the *impressions of sensation*, or in their content, are P, C, and CC. We do not find NC.

[8] Note that the impression-source for NC doesn't lie in 'the objects' even if the objects are taken not as (realist or basic-realist) external objects, but just as idealist (perception-constituted) objects which are themselves in a clear sense 'only in the mind'. If 'the objects' are so taken, Hume's point can be put by

mind, even if we're also talking about objects, because part at least of the impression-source of the necessary-connection idea lies only in the mind, and not in the objects.[9]

(1) and (2) aren't actually incompatible. (1) will be the more appropriate thing to say when one insists that one is, in talking about causation in the objects, definitely succeeding in talking about *objects*. For if it's given that one is talking about the objects, then one must look to the objects, and only to the objects, to find the impression-source that determines *what one really means*. And then one will find only P, C, and CC. (2), by contrast, will be more appropriate when one insists that one is, in talking about causation, definitely talking about *something that essentially involves necessary connection*; for then one must look for the location of the impression-source of the necessary-connection idea, wherever it is, in order to establish *what one is really talking about*; and then it turns out, according to Hume, that one is really talking (partly or only) about the mind, for that is where the relevant impression-source lies.

So it is that, when we purport to use the word 'cause' in the strong, non-regularity-theory, necessary-connection-involving sense to talk of objects, we don't know what we're talking about (literally, given Hume's theory); or else we're not talking about what we think we're talking about, given the source of our idea of cause. We think we're talking about a feature of objects, but we're really talking about a feature of the mind. We're talking about the mind because it's the locus of the immediate impression-source of the idea of necessary connection, the impression of reflexion in the mind. The mind is 'spread[ing] itself on external objects' (167/1.3.14.24), projecting the 'internal impression' of NC onto them, and then taking it—mistaking it—for a genuinely detected feature of external objects.

One importantly mild way in which Hume puts this point is to say that if we try to apply the ordinary, strong idea of causation to objects, we have no *distinct* idea or meaning, because there is no impression-source for the idea in the objects:

when we talk of any being … as endowed with a *power* or *force*, … when we speak of a *necessary connexion* betwixt objects, and suppose, that this connexion depends upon an *efficacy* or *energy*, with which any of these objects are endow'd; in all these expressions, *so apply'd*, we have really no *distinct* meaning…. (162/1.3.14.14)

Sometimes this claim is apparently strengthened, from the mild claim that one can give no *distinct* meaning to these expressions, and can form no *adequate* idea of what they purport to denote, to the claim that these notions or expressions are entirely

---

saying that the impression-source for NC idea lies only in the impressions of *reflexion* ('only in the mind'), not in the object-constituting impressions of *sensation* ('in the objects').

[9] Which of (a) and (b) one chooses—is one talking partly or wholly about the mind?—depends on whether one considers the question of what one is talking about to be determined (a) by the immediate impression-source, NC, or (b) by the total impression-source, P, C, CC, and NC. (b) seems to fit well with Hume's inclination to offer his famous two definitions of cause as somehow complementary. (a) arguably fits better with such remarks as the remark—to be discussed later—that the idea of necessary connection does not 'represent … any thing, that does or can belong to the objects' (164/1.3.4.19).

inconceivable or unintelligible. But, once again, Hume doesn't mean what we mean by 'unintelligible' (6.5, 12). He goes on to grant that

'tis more probable, that these expressions do here lose their true meaning by being *wrong apply'd*, than that they never have any meaning; (162/1.3.14.14)

and then gives the account depicted in the diagram of the impression-source—and hence meaning—of Causation expressions or ideas like 'necessary connexion': such an expression or idea is obviously not entirely meaningless; the point is rather that it doesn't 'represent...any thing, that does or can belong to the objects'.[10] But the reason this is so is simply that what the idea or expression contentfully represents is, necessarily, a strict function of its impression-source, and its impression-source is just a certain kind of feeling, a feeling of determination which lies wholly in the mind (it's certainly not because we can know for sure that there isn't anything like Causation in the objects). It's true that it's only the idea's (or expression's) immediate impression-source that lies in the mind; but it's only this immediate impression-source that gives the idea or expression its special content—its character of being, specifically, some kind of genuinely contentful idea of or expression for necessary connection. The idea's ultimate impression-sources in the objects (P, C, CC) must be referred to in the full causal account of its occurrence, but they do not *ipso facto* feature in the account of its content.[11]

To summarize. X—the revised, evidentially licensed idea of causation in the objects—is correct because it tells us all we really, positively-contentfully or descriptively mean, or really talk about, when we talk about causation in *the objects*. All we really talk about are P, C, and CC, because these constitute the whole impression-source of the idea in the objects. It's necessary to present an explicitly revised account of the concept of causation because we're ordinarily in error on the matter. We ordinarily take ourselves to be correctly applying Y, an idea of Causation, to the objects. But when we apply Y to the objects (or so we think) we're not really talking about the objects at all, but only about the mind. Or at least, we're talking partly and indeed centrally about the mind (insofar as we are talking about anything more than regular succession), and not just about some quality in the objects, as we thought. Y, the apparently meaningful Causation idea (necessary-connection idea) isn't literally meaningless or unintelligible, according to the theory of ideas. It's just that it's wrongly applied to *objects*, insofar as it's meaningful according to the theory of ideas. Hume sometimes puts the point by saying that it's meaningless or unintelligible as applied to objects, because we 'comprehend' nothing in the objects by it (where to 'comprehend' something is to take hold of or genuinely represent it in

---

[10]   164/1.3.14.19. I consider this quotation further in 15.4 (p. 150) because it may be wrongly thought to provide strong support for the standard view that Hume positively denies that there is anything like necessary connection or Causation in the objects.

[11]   In fact, though, they do feature in its content, insofar as they are taken to be entailed by NC; cf. n. 5.

virtue of the fact that one has some sort of directly impression-based, descriptively contentful conception of it). He doesn't, however, mean that it's meaningless *tout court*; only that, given its meaning-bestowing origins, it represents something in the mind, not in objects.

On the face of it, this account of Hume's theory of ideas supports the standard view of Hume. It says that given the Causation idea or terms we actually have, there neither is nor can be Causation in the objects. For when you use these terms, you will at best mean something only in the mind. The direct argument that this is an inadequate representation of Hume's position on meaning, prefigured in 6.5, begins in 12. But there is another matter which needs to be dealt with first.[12]

---

[12] The diagram and discussion of this chapter ignore many difficulties of exegetical detail raised by Hume's 'two definitions of cause' (170/1.3.14.31, 172/1.3.14.35, 76–7/7.29). But the substance of the first definition is I believe adequately represented here. And the same goes for the second definition—*if* the essential point of the second definition is that causal sequences have a further objective property in addition to having the property of involving P and C (individually considered) and CC (considered as types): i.e. the property of being such as to set up certain habits of inference (and necessary-connection-positing thoughts) in our minds, given appropriate conditions. (The phrase 'given appropriate conditions' qualifies Hume's account in a natural and arguably necessary way.)

11

The 'AP' property

11.1 The curious idea of a priori causal inference

The fundamental thesis behind Hume's discussion of our idea of causation is a thesis about the nature or content of our *experience* of causation: all we ever actually experience in objects, so far as causation is concerned, are regular-succession relations of P, C, and CC between objects or events or types of object or event.[1]

This thesis is widely accepted, even by those who are realists about objects, and it's important to see that it may be fully granted (taken specifically as a thesis about our *experience* of causation) even by those who don't believe that regular succession is all that causation actually is. That is, the epistemological thesis that there's a sense in which all we ever experience of causation is regular succession may be granted even by those who reject the ontological thesis that regular succession is all that causation actually is.

The epistemological thesis has also been directly questioned,[2] but I'm going to accept it here, because the present argument against the standard view of Hume (and the 'Humean' view) doesn't depend on rejecting it.[3] It is nevertheless worth mentioning one of the reasons why Hume was so sure that the epistemological thesis was true, for it has some relevance to later parts of the discussion.

Why is Hume so confident that we can never have any genuine impression or experience of Causation in the objects, and so can never have any genuine idea or conception of it? It's certainly not because he thinks there is no such thing as Causation. The principal reason for his confidence lies in the fact that his conception of what something would have to be like, in order to count as an idea or impression of Causation or power or necessary connection in the objects, is so demanding that it turns out to be obvious that nothing could ever count as such an idea, or such an impression.

---

[1] Of course Hume holds that we also experience a feeling of determination, on seeing certain things following certain other things; but this is not experience of causation, so far as causation is taken as something in the objects.

[2] e.g. by Anscombe (1971: 137f). See also 23.

[3] For general criticism of Hume's theory of ideas, see Stroud 1977: ch. 2. Even if one accepts that Hume's theory of ideas has some validity as a rudimentary and essentially partial theory of concept acquisition, it's hopeless as a general theory of meaning and as a theory of thought.

This conception of what an idea or impression of Causation in the objects would have to be like, and of what it would have to make possible, is not peculiar to Hume. He's simply accepting and developing a view widespread at the time, in order to criticize it.[4] Thus he takes it that the idea of Causation or necessary connection is the idea of something which has the following property: if we could really detect it holding between events, then we could get into a position in which we could make valid causal inferences a priori. Or at least, we could get into a position in which we could make causal inferences that had exactly the same degree of certainty as paradigmatically a priori mathematical or geometrical inferences. (This second way of putting it is the one to retain at first if one is puzzled by the idea of a priori causal inference.)

In the *Treatise* he expresses the point by saying that to possess a genuine idea of a necessary connection holding between some particular cause-and-effect pair C and E—or alternatively to possess a genuine idea of the causal powers possessed by the particular bodies involved in the causal interaction consisting of C followed by E—is, necessarily, to be in a position to be able to say with certainty, on seeing C alone, that it must be followed by E, or, on seeing E alone, that it must have been preceded by C, prior to *any* experience of seeing E-type events follow C-type events (161/1.3.14.13). It's to be able to say this with just the same sort of certainty as when one infers that there are four oranges from the information that there are two groups of two oranges.

In the *Enquiry* he puts it as follows: 'were the power or energy of any cause [C] discoverable by the mind', i.e. genuinely observable and understandable, 'we could foresee the effect [E], even without experience' of seeing E following C; 'and might...pronounce with certainty concerning it, by mere dint of thought and reasoning' (63/7.7). But we can't do this. For us, all particular causal knowledge is a posteriori. So we can't have any genuine impression of power or Causation in the objects. A genuine impression of power or Causation would have to make us capable of something of which we're incapable. So we cannot have any genuine idea of power or Causation in the objects either.[5]

I'll say that on Hume's view Causation has the 'a-priori-inference-licensing property', or 'AP property', for short. It has the property that genuine detection of it brings with it the possibility of making *a priori certain causal inferences*. So the AP property is defined in essentially epistemological terms, and Hume's idea is not just that the causal inference from C to E (or from E to C) would have to have the same

---

[4] For a brief account of this view and its prevalence, see e.g. Craig 1987: 37–40.

[5] See also 27–30/4.6–4.11, 37/4.21. Malebranche had rather special views about this matter, but it's worth noting his view that 'a true cause is...one such that the mind perceives a necessary connection between it and its effect' (1674–5: §6.2.3). The general rationalist position under attack involved 'the belief...that causal connections had to be "intelligible": there had to be something, in principle detectable by reason, which made *that* effect suited to *that, that* lawlike relationship between *those* two variables appropriate rather than any other. If it were not so, there would be facts about the course of events which were intrinsically inexplicable; and this thought...was in the seventeenth century widely felt to be intolerable' (Craig: 1987: 39–40).

degree of certainty as paradigmatically a priori inferences like mathematical inferences. It is that causal inference would itself be a priori inference, in the sense that it
would be possible to make it prior to any experience of events of type E following
events of type C.

11.2 An objection

I don't want to say much more about this feature of Hume's views.[6] The important
point is that it immediately explains his confidence that we can have no genuine
impression or idea of Causation. There is, however, an objection to the present
approach which may be based on this feature of Hume's views, and which needs to
be answered at some length.

It may be said that the following things are true:

(1) Hume certainly does take it that anything that could correctly be called 'Causation' ('power', 'energy', etc.) would have—would have to have—the AP property.
(2) Taking Causation to have the AP property in this way, Hume certainly does
deny that there is anything like Causation in the objects.
(3) If he does deny this, he is certainly right to do so.

The reply is that (1) may certainly be granted, but (2) is false. One initial point is this:
it's not obvious that Hume would wish to rule out the idea that if we did *per
impossibile* have angelic or divine knowledge of the workings of nature, we would
somehow find causal connections as 'intelligible' or graspable as a priori connections
between squareness and equiangularity. There's something deeply attractive—
plausible—about the idea that if one really knew the 'intrinsic' nature of matter
one would have to know, in advance of particular experiences, all about how it would
behave—so long as its intrinsic nature did not change, that is (a point that will be
taken up shortly). Consider Philo, who has a very strong claim to represent many of
Hume's views (see e.g. Strawson 2000a):

And were the inmost essence of things laid open to us, we should then discover a scene, of which,
at present, we can have no idea. Instead of admiring the order of natural beings, we should clearly
see, that it was absolutely impossible for them, in the smallest Article, ever to admit of any other
disposition' (125–6/201).

In Part 9 Philo makes essentially the same suggestion, in a striking passage:

It is observed by arithmeticians, that the products of 9 compose always either 9 or some lesser
product of 9; if you add together all the characters, of which any of the former products is
composed. Thus, of 18, 27, 36, which are products of 9, you make 9 by adding 1 to 8, 2 to 7, 3 to 6.

---

[6] J. L. Mackie has a good discussion of this in ch. 1 of *The Cement of the Universe*. He calls necessary
connection conceived of in this a-priori-inference-licensing way 'necessity$_2$', and argues convincingly that
this is only part of what Hume had in mind when he used Causation terms. See also Locke on 'necessary
Connexion', *Essay* 4.3.10–16, 22, 28–9.

Thus, of 369 is a Product also of 9; and if you add, 3, 6, and 9, you make 18, a lesser product of 9. To a superficial observer, so wonderful a regularity may be admired as the effect either of chance or design; but a skilful algebraist immediately concludes it to be the work of necessity; and demonstrates, that it *must for ever result from the nature of these numbers.* Is it not probable, I ask, that the whole oeconomy of the universe is conducted by a like necessity ... ? And instead of admiring the order of natural Beings, may it not happen, that, could we penetrate into the *intimate nature of bodies*, we should clearly see why it was absolutely impossible they could ever admit of any other disposition? (*Dialogues* 167–9/191).

This is, without doubt, Hume's own view. He is always principally concerned to deny that we could ever detect Causation in such a way as to be able to form a positively or descriptively contentful conception of its intrinsic nature. He's not concerned to deny that it exists. His target is the claim, common among philosophers of the time, to have knowledge of its nature. His position might be expressed as follows. It's not that Causation or power doesn't exist, and it's not that it doesn't have the AP property. It surely does exist—it is after all that 'on which [the] regular course and succession of objects totally depends' (55/5.22)—and it does (or at the very least may) have the AP property. It's just that no one can ever fulfil *the epistemological detection condition* laid down in the description of the AP property, the condition regarding what would count as genuine detection of Causation. It's just not possible to 'penetrate into the nature of bodies' in such a way that one could see, on first encountering C, that E just has to happen, given that C has happened (or in such a way that one could see, on first encountering E, that C must have happened, given that E has happened).

Perhaps this last point should not be immediately taken for granted. In many cases scientists can, given their overall theory of things, predict with complete confidence, and in advance of any experience of the particular type of event in question, that E will happen given C, or that reaction Y will occur in substance X if condition Z is realized, given the nature of X. Properties of hitherto undiscovered elements (e.g. germanium) were confidently and correctly predicted in advance of experiment, once the general principles of atomic organization were understood. Locke made this point clearly (*Essay* 4.3.25), and it's arguable that it removes one of Hume's reasons for saying that we can never predict a particular effect in advance of experiment. But his main reason for saying this (also noted by Locke, ibid.) remains untouched. For the certainty of all such predictions will always and for ever be conditional on the assumption that the fundamental nature of matter is not going to change. And Hume's unassailable central point is that no sort of penetration into the nature of matter could ever guarantee certain knowledge of the truth of *this* assumption; hence it could never really yield unconditional, a priori certain knowledge that E has to happen given C (or that Y has to happen to X given Z).[7] Certainly it could never yield

---

[7] This is exactly his point on 37–8/4.21, which is discussed in 17. It is after all just one way of expressing the 'problem of induction'. Kant put the point in a sentence in the *Critique of Pure Reason*: 'Experience teaches us that a thing is so and so, but not that it cannot be otherwise' (B3).

such knowledge to a finite, non-divine mind, even if it is intelligible to suppose that a divine mind might attain such certainty.

We may say that on this view Causation, understood as having the AP property, is utterly and forever undetectable (by us, by any finite being), because detection of it would have to bring with it a priori certain knowledge—that things will continue to behave in the same way in the future—of a kind that is evidently impossible. I suspect this is Hume's principal point. Here as always his main concern is to stress our ignorance of the nature of things, in the light of previous philosophers' claims to the contrary. He's not concerned to make categorical ontological claims about the non-existence of anything, such as Causation.

If this is really all Hume is saying, then it's of far less interest to us today than is ordinarily supposed. It isn't very interesting to say that something can't possibly be detected when it's defined in such a way—i.e. as having the AP property—that it's obvious (to us today) that it can't possibly be detected. His arguments were highly apposite and important given the philosophical debates of his time and the belief of some philosophers in the ultimate—and divinely underwritten—intelligibility of nature. But we have largely lost sight of his target, precisely because his attack on it was so effective.

This, perhaps, is why Hume's argument is now often conceived to be an argument against the possibility of detecting Causation even when Causation is *not* thought of as something which has the AP property: even when it's not thought of as something detection of which—or indeed the mere existence of which—would have to give rise to the possibility of impossible a priori certain causal inferences about the unobserved. Hume might well have accepted this extension of his argument: his other argument for the unknowability of the nature of causal power—i.e. that we cannot even decide between Lockean and Berkeleian accounts of the nature of things—would remain untouched and decisive. The fact remains that his actual argument is standardly taken in a way which is different from the way in which he intended it.

11.3 The objection varied

There's another natural and more explicitly ontological way of developing this point. It is, arguably, a better way, if one's aim is to undermine the belief that Hume is concerned to deny the existence of Causation, rather than to deny knowledge of it. But it's also arguably worse, because it's more complicated. Those who wish may skip to the next chapter.

Suppose the definition of the AP property is expanded as follows—

a thing X has the AP property if and only if X is (a) such that detection of X brings with it the possibility of making a priori certain causal inferences and (b) *in principle detectable*[8]

---

[8] Clause (b) is the addition to the original definition; it is of course Causation which is imagined to have the AP property.

—and call the proposition that a priori certain causal inferences are impossible '(P)'.

Now if (P) is true, as we believe, then clause (a) of the definition of the AP property entails the undetectability of X. But clause (b) explicitly affirms the in-principle detectability of X. So the AP property turns out to be contradictory, on this definition. Nothing can possibly have it. Hence Causation cannot possibly exist—for having the AP property is one of its defining properties, according to Hume. Hence—to return to the three claims considered at the beginning of 11.2—it seems that we do after all have reason to suppose (2) that Hume did assert that there is definitely no such thing as Causation, and (3) that he was right to do so. In which case the standard view is vindicated.

No. Even if Hume had wished to assert that there is no such thing as Causation, it's extremely doubtful that he would have wished to assert it on anything like these grounds (i.e. (P) together with the idea that Causation has the AP property as redefined in clauses (a) and (b)). For, first, it's most unclear that he would have wished to accept clause (b) of the expanded definition of the AP property, given his insistence on our perfect ignorance in this area. Second, and contrariwise, if we suppose that he would have wished to accept clause (b) in addition to clause (a), then it immediately becomes quite unclear that he would also have wished to accept (P), the absolute impossibility of a priori certain causal knowledge. For, given his certainty that Causation is undetectable by human beings, it seems that he could be motivated to accept clause (b) only by the thought that divine knowledge of the nature of nature might possibly attain the status of a priori certain causal knowledge.

If these two points are correct, Hume can't reach the conclusion that there's definitely no such thing as Causation on the present grounds. For (P) and the proposition that Causation has the AP property entail that there's no such thing as Causation only when the definition of the AP property includes clause (b) in addition to clause (a), and it has been argued that any reason that Hume may have for accepting clause (b) will be a reason for rejecting (P).

Nothing, however, depends on this argument. For suppose it's simply granted (implausibly, on the present view) that Hume would wish to accept clause (b) of the redefinition of the AP property, together with the ontological conclusion that it licenses in conjunction with (P)—the conclusion that there is definitely no such thing as Causation. The consequence of granting this is that this ontological conclusion is, once again, uninteresting (it's uninteresting to us, however important it was at the time). For Causation is now so defined that it's obvious (to us) that it cannot exist; and it's not very interesting to claim that something which is obviously impossible doesn't exist.

If this is right, Hume's alleged claim that there is no such thing as Causation in the objects is genuinely interesting (to us) only if the notion of Causation is understood in some weaker, AP-property-excluding but still essentially non-regularity-theory sense—e.g. as some kind of natural necessity which can be discovered only a posteriori, and which is to that extent nothing like logical necessity, which can be known a priori. Hume's alleged claim that there is no such thing as Causation is interesting only if the Causation it rejects is conceived of in such a way that it doesn't commit its supporters to the idea that a priori certain causal inference might be possible.

This is, indeed, how the 'Humean' view of causation is often taken, insofar as it's a view that has still wide currency outside commentaries on Hume. It's taken as a denial of the existence of any kind of natural necessity or Causation even when natural necessity or Causation is conceived of as something whose manifestations can be established in detail only a posteriori.

It's also true, of course, that the so-called 'Humean' view is taken as a rejection of any non-regularity-theory notion of causation whatever. But the impossibility of a priori certain causal inference—the idea that all knowledge of causal connections is necessarily a posteriori—is usually taken to be unquestioned common ground between defenders and opponents of the 'Humean' view. So present-day proponents of the 'Humean' view are only concerned to oppose defenders of the notion of Causation who grant that any knowledge of (particular) causal connections is necessarily a posteriori in character, and who probably never even imagine any other possibility.

The present-day debate is undoubtedly interesting (see e.g. Psillos 2009, 2011), but those who defend the 'Humean' view in this debate shouldn't suppose that it's Hume's view. This is particularly so given that they face the charge of absurdity considered in 5. Hume doesn't face it, given his entirely different concerns.

The principal aim of this chapter is to establish two points: (1) the idea that Causation has the AP property is one of Hume's main reasons for being sure that we could never detect or know the nature of Causation (the other is given on pp. 99–100): detection of it would have to give us an ability we couldn't have. But (2) it doesn't follow from the fact that Hume thinks that it's impossible for us to detect Causation that he thinks that Causation doesn't or couldn't *exist*, when conceived of as something that has the AP property as originally defined on p. 109. The objection introduced at the beginning of 11.2 is thus rejected.

Note finally that the 'Humean' view of causation is not only untrue to Hume in attributing to him the view that there's definitely no such thing as Causation (the case that he doesn't hold this view has yet to be made in detail). The 'Humean' view of causation is also untrue to Hume insofar as it doesn't conceive of the Causation whose existence it denies as something that essentially has the AP property. This means that it makes a far stronger claim than the claim Hume would have been making if he really had denied that there was any such thing as Causation (as he did not). For it doesn't just deny (with Hume) that there is any reason for the world's regularity whose nature is knowable in such a way that the future can be known with a priori certainty. It goes much further. It denies that there is any sort of reason at all for the world's regularity (as remarked in 5 and 8).

I'll now return to the main line of argument.

12

The problem of meaning

12.1 The 'Meaning Tension'

In 10 I gave an account of how Hume applies his theory of ideas in the case of causation. It may be thought that the account provides strong support for the 'standard' interpretation of Hume's views on causation. For it may seem that to say (1) that no Causation term can *manage to mean* anything in the objects (from now on I'll use 'term' to apply both to words and to ideas or concepts) is in effect to make the negative ontological claim (2) that there is nothing like Causation in the objects. In fact, to make such a move as this, from (1) to (2), is to slide down the great anti-realist (positivist, radical empiricist, phenomenalist, etc.) epistemologico-semantic slide into metaphysical confusion. It's to turn ontology and metaphysics into a ghostly, automatic by-blow of epistemology—and human epistemology at that. Or rather: it's to limit what there can be in the universe, and equally what there can intelligibly be supposed to be in the universe, to what our concepts can contentfully 'comprehend'; usually after making certain fairly narrow empiricist assumptions about their possible content.

Hume didn't make this mistake, even if the 'Ardor of Youth' and a certain rhetorical relish propelled him into some ostensibly ontological dramatizations of his strictly sceptical, merely epistemological conclusions about the limits on what we can claim to know. Barest common sense requires that members of the human race—including even philosophers—should grant that there may be things in the universe that are completely beyond their comprehension, and that it is intelligible to suppose that this is so (cf. 7). As a brilliant sceptic whose polemical energies were principally directed against his contemporaries' grandiose claims to metaphysical knowledge of the unknown or unknowable, Hume (following Locke, as so often) was vividly aware of this.[1]

In another idiom, and in its simplest form, the anti-realist error is to collapse the limits of *thought*, and of what is conceivable, into the limits of possible *knowledge*, as

---

[1] In *The View from Nowhere* (ch. 6) Nagel speculates on the *arrogance* (the lack of humility) that this radically 'Protagorean' and Procrustean (not to say cosmically Pickwickian) view seems to involve. It's equally arguable that the view involves a certain kind of excessive *humility*. It is in any case a view which has its modern origins in the *modesty* whose epistemological necessity was so forcefully argued for by Hume and Kant in their rejection of the pretensions of speculative metaphysics.

defined by empiricism, for example.[2] In the particular case of causation, it is to deny the validity of the distinction invoked in 3 between (O), causation as it is in the objects, and (E), causation so far as we know about it in the objects. It's to take the merely epistemological claim (E1) that causation so far as we know about it (or can know about it) in the objects is just regular succession to entail (in effect) the dogmatic and essentially non-sceptical claim (O1) that causation as it *is* in the objects is just regular succession—on the semantic ground (S1) that no idea of ours could ever really manage to mean or represent that it was anything else. No doubt Hume's theory of ideas creates some pressure on him to say something like this (this pressure is evident in the *Treatise* although not in the *Enquiry*). But his strictly non-committal scepticism with respect to knowledge claims about what does or doesn't exist in reality creates a much greater pressure on him to accept that we can intelligibly *suppose* that there may be something like Causation, and that this is so even though we can't really contentfully *conceive* it on the terms of the theory of ideas (see 6.5). Acceptance of the fundamental realist idea that it is intelligible to suppose that there may be realities which we cannot understand, and of which we may in some sense be unable to form any positively contentful conception, is built into the foundations of scepticism (and reappears as its keystone).

This is very clear in many places in Hume's text, for example in the passages discussed in 6.5 above, and in a clarificatory addition to Book 1 of the *Treatise* published in the Appendix marked for insertion into 1.2.5:

as long as we confine our speculations to *the appearances* of objects to our senses, without entering into disquisitions concerning their *real nature and operations*, we are safe from all difficulties, and can never be embarrass'd by any question. If we carry our enquiry beyond the appearances of objects to the senses, I am afraid, that most of our conclusions will be full of scepticism and uncertainty (638–9/1.2.5.26).

---

[2] But not only as defined by empiricism, for Kant was clearly drawn by a move of this sort, although he was no empiricist. He was drawn to accept some sort of 'principle of significance' according to which 'there can be no legitimate, or even meaningful, employment of ideas or concepts which does not relate them to empirical or experiential conditions of their application' (P. F. Strawson 1966: 16). And yet Kant clearly rejected any extreme version of this move, as remarked in 7. In the *Critique of Pure Reason* he matched Hume's distinction between the *supposable* and the *conceivable* with a distinction between the intelligibly *thinkable* (and hence the meaningful) and the empirically or experientially encounterable or *knowable*, and granted that the limits of the former were wider than the limits of the latter (see e.g. B 166 n.).

One respect in which Kant's treatment of these issues is arguably deeper than Hume's lies in the way in which he seeks to enlarge the scope of the experientially encounterable: he introduces the idea that certain things can properly be said to be encounterable in experience taken as a whole insofar as they can be shown to be necessary conditions of the possibility of experience of the kind we know ourselves to have. In many respects, though, Hume matches Kant in his insight into the general problem. The problem also has many sophisticated expressions in contemporary debate, in which it's presented in a different idiom (centred on language and propositional thought, and on whole propositions or sentences, rather than on individual ideas or concepts). Most of the sophistications are, however, unimportant (not to say a waste of time), and the change of idiom hasn't changed the basic problem.

THE PROBLEM OF MEANING 117

A year later, in the opening paragraph of his essay 'The Sceptic', he wrote that

philosophers...confine too much their principles, and make no account of that vast variety, which nature has so much affected in all her operations...Our own mind being narrow and contracted, we cannot extend our conception to the variety and extent of nature; but imagine, that she is as much bounded in her operations, as we are in our speculation (1742: 159–60).

Appeal to Hume's (Lockean) scepticism, then, provides one powerful source of support for the claim that he didn't make the great metaphysical, anti-realist mistake about Causation (or indeed anything else, e.g. the mind), whatever the pressures of his theory of ideas. The other main source of support lies simply in the fact that Hume repeatedly uses Causation terms in an apparently straightforwardly referring way (as I will try to show by quotation in Parts 2 and 3), although these terms are terms for something which counts as completely 'unintelligible' according to his theory of ideas. The view that all these uses are simply ironic or tongue-in-cheek is, I will suggest, incredible. Hume would have had a permanent deformity of the cheek—not to say a forked tongue—by the time he finished writing the *Enquiry*. The irony theory is vastly more incredible than the theory that, in the *Treatise*, Hume sometimes indulges in dramatic and polemical abbreviation of his epistemological conclusions in such a way that he sounds—especially when his remarks are taken out of context—as if he is making ontological knowledge claims of a sort ruled out by his scepticism.[3]

This said, it must be granted that there is an apparent tension in Hume's thought, on the present view—a tension already noted in the discussion of his attitude to the notion of external objects in 6.5. It arises from the opposition between (1) a certain interpretation of the strict empiricism of his theory of ideas or meaning, on the one hand, and two other things, on the other hand: (2) his strictly non-committal scepticism with respect to knowledge claims about what may or may not exist and (3) his strong, considered tendency towards realist forms of thought and expression. The theory of ideas rejects as 'unintelligible' or 'meaningless' certain ideas or expressions that both scepticism and realism allow as intelligible.[4]

---

[3] Mackie is cautious on this point. He first writes that 'Hume usually says that...causation as it is in the objects [as opposed to causation so far as we know about it in the objects]...is regular succession and nothing more'. He then adds that 'sometimes, indeed, [Hume] speaks of secret powers and connections of which we are ignorant', and comments that Hume 'may well have his tongue in his cheek here' (1974: 20–1), rather as if he thought (rightly on the present view) that the most natural interpretation of Hume's use of such expressions is that he doesn't have his tongue in his cheek.

[4] Scepticism and realism may be said to be in tension themselves, insofar as realism involves the positive claim that physical objects do exist more or less as we suppose them to (putting aside the strangenesses of physics), whereas scepticism is strictly non-committal on all ontological questions (apart from the existence of perceptions). This tension is not serious, however, for strictly non-committal scepticism precisely grants the possible truth of realism. As far as Hume is concerned there's no incompatibility between his realist *beliefs* and his scepticism with regard to *knowledge* claims. He doesn't claim to know whether realist objects exist: it's a 'question of fact' whether or not they do, but an undecidable one (153/ 12.12). Wright's book, *The sceptical realism of David Hume*, is well named.

There is, moreover, no deeper, general incompatibility between scepticism and realism (here I consider scepticism only about ontological questions, not about reason itself.) For on the one hand scepticism entails

I'll call this the 'Meaning Tension'. Take the case of causation. Hume uses Causation terms in a way that is arguably ruled out as illegitimate by his theory of ideas: although he officially holds that no Causation term can manage to (*descriptive-contentfully*) *mean* anything like Causation—which is what he ought to say given his theory of ideas—he clearly concedes, in his usage, that they may manage to mean something like Causation at least in the sense of genuinely *referring* to it—which is what he ought to do given his strictly non-committal scepticism with respect to claims about what may or may not exist (other than perceptions).

It may be said that to discern the Meaning Tension in Hume is to attribute a kind of inconsistency to him; that it is always a fault in discussion of a philosopher to attribute such a major, systematic inconsistency; that the best interpretation is always one that makes the best sense of the texts that is compatible with the supposition that there is no such inconsistency. I hope it will come to seem that attributing the Meaning Tension to Hume is (by far) the best way to reconcile the consequences of his theory of ideas with his strictly non-committal scepticism with regard to knowledge claims about what may or may not exist in reality, and with his (basic) realist beliefs. I call it a tension because it's something very much less than an inconsistency. I think, in fact, that there's no real tension in his position, although his treatment of a certain problem about meaning (explicitly faced by Locke and Berkeley among others) is perhaps inadequate. Any appearance of tension arises because our understanding of words like 'meaning' and 'unintelligible' is not the same as Hume's. There's no inconsistency or tension in the idea that we may refer to a thing of which we have no descriptively contentful conception—the idea that we may have a 'relative' idea of a thing, in Hume's terms, although we do not in any way 'comprehend' it.

This is Hume's position with respect to Causation. Causation is: that in reality in virtue of which reality is regular in the way that it is. In more Humean terms, it is that in reality, whatever its nature, on which the 'regular course and succession of objects totally depends' (55/5.22); it's that in reality which is in fact 'the reason of the conjunction' of any two objects (93/1.3.6.15), although we know nothing of its nature. Such an abstract description suffices to *pick out* causal power—it provides an 'identifying description'—in such a way that we can go on to refer to it while having absolutely no sort of positively contentful conception of its nature, on the terms of the theory of ideas.[5]

---

the possibility that any particular (non-contradictory) realism may be true. By its nature it rules out nothing non-contradictory; it just insists on the limits of our knowledge and understanding. On the other hand, there's a sense in which realism entails scepticism: any realism at all which holds reality to extend beyond one's own (conscious) experiences (e.g. to something which affects one and gives rise to one's experiences) entails scepticism. For any such realism postulates something which has the following properties: (1) if it exists, then it cannot be known for certain to exist, precisely because of the way in which it is thought of as radically independent of the enquirer's conscious mind or experiences; (2) even if it could somehow be known for certain to exist, still its *nature* could not be known for certain.

[5] It may be objected that the second of the 'abstract descriptions' of Causation is problematic because it contains the potentially causal-relation-implying word 'depends'; and the same might then be said about

I'll speak of the Meaning Tension, then. But there is—to repeat—no real tension. There is simply a familiar ambiguity in the word 'mean'. On the one hand, 'mean' means 'positively-contentfully' mean (this is how Hume standardly uses the word 'mean'): a term can positively-contentfully mean something, according to Hume, only insofar as it has descriptive content, impression-derived, impression-copy content. On the other hand 'mean' means 'refer to'. As long as we have a way of picking out something X by reference to some relation or relations in which it stands, and ultimately some relation to us, some detectable impact or effect on us, we can have a 'relative' idea of it, and so refer to it, and so mean it, even though there's a sense in which we don't have any conception of its nature, and may therefore be unable to 'positively-contentfully mean' it in any way at all.[6] We can successfully refer to and genuinely think and talk about something, as Hume acknowledges in his use of the notion of a 'relative' idea, even though there's a *sense* in which we don't know what we're thinking or talking about.[7]

The central observable effect that Causation has on us is the regular character of our experience (this includes our maintaining our normal human form from moment to moment). Causation's having this effect on us is itself a Causal matter, and Causation also governs the workings of our minds. But there's nothing problematic about the reference to a Causal effect in an account of how we can come to acquire a ('relative') idea of Causation.[8]

We can't of course prove that there is something X that we stand in this relation to.[9] We may nevertheless take ourselves to have overwhelmingly good reason to

'in virtue of ' and 'reason' in the first and third descriptions. But there's no difficulty or circularity here. Even if these words were causal-relation-implying in these contexts, none of them would be such that its legitimate use presupposed possession of some positively contentful conception of the nature of Causation, in Hume's sense. These phrases could still function to indicate what we were talking about in talking of Causation, compatibly with the idea that we have no positive conception of its nature insofar as it is more than regular succession. I return to this topic in 18. Compare Kail (2007*b*) on the 'Bare Thought' of Causation that is available to us, on Hume's view, in spite of our epistemic limitations.

[6] For a Humean use of this sort see 168/1.3.14.27, where he talks of our 'meaning . . . unknown qualities'. We may alternatively have some *completely* mistaken conception of what something is, which is nonetheless *about it*, given that it is indeed the thing that is affecting us. Robert Boyle makes the same general point: there are things (e.g. God or Causation) 'of which we can know but *that they are*, and *what they do* [witness observable regularity all around us], not *what they are* and *how they act* [i.e. their ultimate nature and mode of operation]'. Such things are 'incomprehensible', although we may be sure they exist (1681: 242; cf. also p. 211).

[7] I don't wish to claim that all this is explicit in Hume's use of the notion of a relative idea. Note that this remark about there being a sense in which we don't understand what we are saying corresponds closely to Hume's use of 'unintelligible'. Compare Evans's remarks on the possibility of a successful use of a name to refer which is in a clear sense not accompanied by understanding of what is said (1982: §§4.1, 11.5). It may be objected that Evans is discussing cases in which understanding of the relevant sort could possibly be acquired, whereas in the Humean case it is arguable (and argued by Hume) that such understanding may be forever unobtainable by human beings. The parallel may nevertheless be suggestive.

[8] It would be foolish to claim that one can't legitimately appeal to the notion of causation (i.e. Causation) in one's account of how we come to acquire causal notions, given that we have to appeal to the notion of causation in an account of how we come to acquire any notion.

[9] We can prove nothing about anything other than 'relations of ideas'.

suppose that there is, and, accordingly, take it for granted. This is what Hume does in the case of Causation. On the present view, his position is exactly right. It's exactly right because it's overwhelmingly reasonable to suppose that there is something about reality in virtue of which it is regular in the way that it is (i.e. that there is Causation), even if all we can ever observe are regularities of succession.

More generally: when one faces large-scale metaphysical issues of the sort that arise concerning causation and external objects, one can avoid the pressure of epistemological considerations that seem to make some kind of idealist, phenomenalist or anti-realist attitude unavoidable, simply by saying that when we think or talk about objects or causal goings on (tables and chairs, blows and explosions), we genuinely refer to whatever thing X it is that affects us and thereby gives rise to our experience.[10] One can say this even while granting that we can't know anything for sure about the nature of X.[11] Our thoughts and words can reach out, referentially, beyond the character of our experience. This is especially clear when 'experience' is defined, as in Hume, in such a way that its content is understood to be in principle fully characterizable in terms of purely mental contents, the 'immediate objects' of experience, and so without any reference to non-mental things.

12.2 Experience-transcendent reference: E-intelligibility and R-intelligibility

This is to move rapidly over a complex field of issues, but the fundamental idea is familiar. It's explicit in Locke, who observes (somewhat unwillingly on account of his official theory of ideas and of meaning) that the word 'gold' is not used merely as a name for whatever has the 'nominal essence' (roughly, the observable properties) of gold, but in such a way that it incorporates a 'tacit reference' to gold's unobserved and perhaps forever unobservable 'real essence'—even when we have no positively contentful conception of this real essence (*Essay* 3.10.19). Insofar as it is considered as incorporating 'this tacit reference to the real Essence . . . , the Word *Gold* . . . comes to have no signification at all, being put for somewhat whereof we have no *Idea* at all'.[12] At the same time, he allows that the word 'gold' does in our ordinary use undoubtedly carry this reference. Hume allows the same with regard to his frequent use of Causation terms.

---

[10] Its 'ultimate cause', in Hume's terms (84/1.3.5.2; compare Putnam 1981: ch. 3). Recall the variety of possible accounts of this ultimate cause discussed in 6.6—e.g. Berkeley's account, or the extreme suggestion that the affecting thing might be a part of one's own mind. There are of course further problems with this idea, noted in 6.6 (given our ordinary understanding of the world, we don't think we're talking about the photons that hit our retinas when we talk about tables and chairs).

[11] We can't know that our perceptions do not arise 'from the energy of the mind itself, or from the suggestion of some invisible and unknown spirit, or from some other cause still more unknown to us' (153/12.12).

[12] *Essay* 3.10.19. Hume must say the same: the real essence is 'unintelligible' and 'incomprehensible' according to the theory of ideas, being something of which we have no positive conception.

Berkeley supplements his general term for mental contents, i.e. 'idea', with the term 'notion', in order to give an account of the intelligibility or contentfulness of ideas (e.g. the idea of mind) which comes out as empty or 'unintelligible' according to his theory of ideas (see e.g. *Principles* §§27, 89, 140–2). He proposes that the term 'notion' be used as a 'term for things that cannot be understood' (1721: §23). It is, he says, 'absurd for any man to argue against the existence of [a] thing, from his having no direct and positive notion of it'. It is only where 'we have not even a relative notion of it' that we 'employ words to no manner of purpose, without any design or signification whatever'; 'many things, for anything I know, may exist, whereof neither I nor any other man has or can have any idea or notion whatsoever' (1713: 177, 184).

This line of thought has a long history. It has become familiar in contemporary discussion: there's a sense in which 'natural kind' words like 'gold' can (roughly) mean more than we know. The current proposal is that this idea can be legitimately taken out of everyday contexts and reapplied at the most general metaphysical level. Our words may not only mean more than we know, they may mean more than we can know.

This idea is arguably present in a strong form, and at the most general metaphysical level, in Kant's *Critique of Pure Reason*, as noted on p. 116. On the one hand, he says that the categories, which include the concept of cause, 'have only an empirical use, and have *no meaning whatever* when not applied to objects of possible experience' (A696/ B724). On the other hand, he says that 'in *thinking*', and a fortiori in intelligible— hence contentful, hence meaningful—thinking, 'the categories are not limited by the conditions of our sensible intuition, but have an unlimited field. It is only *knowledge* of what we think...that requires intuition' (B166 n.). Connectedly, the appearances which make up what Kant calls the 'empirically real world' must always be understood as appearances *of* (relationally of) something—noumenal reality—of which we can have no experience of a sort that would furnish us with any sort of positively contentful conception of its intrinsic nature; something, therefore, of whose nature we can have no knowledge. Nevertheless, when we talk of 'empirically real' objects, our words have genuine referential purchase beyond the empirically real world. They carry reference to something whose nature we know we cannot know.

The present claim is weaker: it's simply that it makes sense to suppose that a term or idea 'X' may have a proper use, and genuinely refer to a thing X, even if there are aspects of X's nature of which we have, and perhaps can have, no sort of positive conception. The acceptance of this claim is fundamental to realism in the widest sense.

Before returning to Hume, consider the suggestion that the term 'Causation' or 'power', or indeed our ordinary term 'causation', is itself a variety of natural-kind term. Thus it carries reference to the (unknown) 'real essence' of causation in the world—to whatever it is about the world (or matter) which is that in virtue of which it is regular in the way that it is. This is at best only half right. The idea that the term 'causation' carries such reference, even if all we can ever actually *experience* of causation is regular succession, is plausible. But 'causation' is not a true natural-kind term. It's more like the word 'temperature' than the word 'gold', because it could conceivably have different 'realizations' in different possible universes which had different basic natures, so that there were different reasons why the different universes were regular in the ways that they were.

So 'causation' is not a natural-kind term in the central sense, for a natural-kind term has the same reference in every possible world. Nevertheless, we can plausibly speak of the term 'causation' as referring to the 'real essence' of causal phenomena in the actual universe—i.e. to whatever it is about the universe (or matter) which is that in virtue of which it is regular—has to be regular—in the way that it is. It's odd that so much has been made of the potentially experience-transcending referential reach of terms like 'gold', while nothing similar has been said about the term 'causation'. Those today who deny that the term 'causation' can really or properly mean more than 'regular succession' seem like Locke when he claims that the word 'gold' has 'no signification at all' insofar as its use incorporates a reference to the real essence of gold—except that some of them go wrong in a way in which Locke doesn't go wrong in the case of 'gold'. For they proceed to infer that all there is to causation is regular succession; whereas Locke does not infer that all there is to gold is its nominal essence.

To return now to Hume. In his scepticism, in his notion of a 'relative' idea, in his closely connected distinction between what we may intelligibly *suppose* and what we may genuinely contentfully *conceive* (241/1.4.5.20), and in his realist (or basic-realist) linguistic practice, he acknowledges that words may have a proper use or meaning (a proper use and hence a meaning) beyond the use or meaning granted to them by the theory of ideas. This is the 'Meaning Tension': Hume knows that it is intelligible (mandatory, given strictly non-committal scepticism) to suppose that there may exist things or aspects of things that are unintelligible to us in the special, semi-technical sense that we can form no genuinely contentful conception of them on the terms of the (strict) theory of ideas. Here his attitude is close to Newton's attitude to our knowledge of physical laws and forces.

One could call this wider notion of intelligibility the 'realist' conception of intelligibility, or 'R-intelligibility' for short, as opposed to the strict empiricist conception of intelligibility as found in Hume—'E-intelligibility', for short. Thus the merely 'relative' idea that we may have of external objects 'specifically different from perceptions' (6.5) is an R-intelligible but E-unintelligible idea. It is E-unintelligible because by hypothesis it contains no impression-copy content (or at least goes essentially beyond all impression-copy content).

This distinction adds nothing new, because it corresponds exactly to Hume's distinction between what we may (contentfully) conceive and what we may (coherently) suppose. To be 'conceivable' is to be E-intelligible, contentfully representable with the impression-copy representation-resources available on the terms of the theory of ideas; but 'suppositions' (or 'fictions') may be R-intelligible, and possibly correct, despite being E-unintelligible. In fact Hume not only accepts that it is intelligible to suppose that there may exist things which are (E-)unintelligible to us. He also accepts that there actually are such things—that there is such a thing as the 'ultimate... perfectly inexplicable... cause' of our perceptions (84/1.3.5.2); that there are (utterly 'incomprehensible' and 'inconceivable') 'powers and forces, by which the [course of nature] is governed' (54/5.21). He accepts this not only in the case of the 'external world', and in the case of Causation, but also in the case of the mind, which provides some further useful illustrative quotations.

12.3 Example: Hume on the mind

'To me it seems evident that the essence of the mind [is] equally unknown to us with that of external bodies' (Int§8/xvii). Plainly, to say this is not to say or suggest that the unknown essence doesn't exist. In the case of both body and mind we face the 'impossibility of explaining [their] ultimate principles' (Int§8/xviii). Plainly, to say this is not to say there are no such principles. 'Reason is... a wonderful and unintelligible instinct in our souls' (179/1.3.16.9); the Imagination is a kind of 'magical faculty in the soul, which... is... inexplicable by the utmost efforts of human understanding' (24/1.1.7.15); 'the uniting principle among our internal perceptions is as unintelligible as that among external objects' (169/1.3.14.29). Plainly, to make these claims is not to claim that these things don't exist—definitely don't exist. When Hume writes 'that other beings may possess many senses of which we can have no conception' (20/2.7), he doesn't mean to say that these senses neither do nor can exist.

—No. Hume held a 'bundle' theory of mind, according to which the mind is just a 'heap' of 'perceptions', and is, as such, wholly E-intelligible.'

But this can't possibly be right. For how, in this case, can 'the essence of the mind [be] ... unknown' (Int§8/xvii)? For 'the perceptions of the mind are perfectly known' (366/2.2.6.2). And how, in any case, can Hume, a strictly non-committal sceptic, wish to make any such definite negative ontological claim—to the effect that the mind is definitely (knowably) nothing more than perceptions? As E. J. Craig (1987: §2.5) shows, when Hume makes the apparently ontological claim that the mind is nothing but a heap of perceptions (he does so a number of times), his main concern is with the epistemological claim that all we can know of mind are its perceptions. His main claim is that the mind so *far as we know about it* is nothing but a bundle of perceptions—'*that we have no notion of it, distinct from the particular perceptions*' (635/App§18). His target is those philosophers who hold that we have some sort of a priori or in any case certain knowledge of its essential nature specifically insofar as it is considered as something more than perceptions (knowledge that it is a simple, indivisible, perduring substance distinct from material substance).[13]

---

[13] Compare Kant: 'I know my mind only... by appearances which constitute an inner state [i.e. I know only my perceptions], and *the essence of it in itself which lies at the ground of these appearances* [or

'The comparison of the mind [to]...a kind of theatre...must not mislead us. They are the successive perceptions only, that constitute the mind [so far as it is in any way at all an object of human knowledge]; nor have we the most distant notion of *the place, where these scenes are represented,* or of *the materials, of which it is composed*' (253/1.4.6.4). 'The uniting principle among our internal perceptions is...unintelligible' (169/1.3.14.29). We have no notion of these things. Yet no doubt there *is* such a 'place', and such 'materials'; ignorance, not non-existence, is what is in question. And certainly there is some such 'uniting principle'. Yet we know nothing for certain about the ultimate nature of these things. All we know of the mind are perceptions: 'the essence of the mind [is]...unknown'. We are more ignorant than we suppose. The question of whether the mind is material or immaterial is 'utterly unintelligible'.[14]

The following point is also worth making: on Hume's view, an idea of X can arise in the mind only if there has been a preceding impression of X.[15] But if the mind is nothing but a stream of perceptions, ontologically speaking, then there can be *no possible mechanism* whereby the prior occurrence of an impression of X provides any sort of basis for any later idea of X (e.g. one which occurs after a period in which many other different impressions and ideas have occurred). It must be a complete fluke that impressions of X always precede ideas of X.

Given that this is unacceptable, there must be something more to the mind than just a series of occurrent perceptions, something which as it were serves to *preserve contents* through time in such a way that an impression of X at time t_1 can somehow be the basis of—and accordingly be the basis of an explanation of—the occurrence of an idea of X at a later time t_2. A similar point can be made about the operation of memory. The idea that Hume simply didn't think of this, or thought it didn't matter, and claimed dogmatically that the mind is just a series of perceptions ontologically speaking, rather than merely claiming that all we can ever *know* or *experience* of mind is a series of perceptions, is ludicrous.[16]

---

perceptions] is unknown to me' (*Prolegomena*, §49; cf. *Critique* B404). See also Locke: ''Tis plain then, that the *Idea* of corporeal *Substance* in Matter is as remote from our Conceptions, and Apprehensions, as that of Spiritual *Substance*; and therefore from our not having any notion of the *Substance* of Spirit, we can no more conclude its non-Existence, than we can, for the same reason, deny the Existence of Body' (*Essay* 2.23.5).

[14] 240/1.4.5.17. Hume goes on to discuss it nevertheless, in the rest of 1.4.5, and it's arguable that the meaning of 'unintelligible', as applied here to 'question', is close to 'undecidable'. The question is about aspects of reality which are real but utterly unencompassable by us. The second half of 1.4.5 contains some wonderful argument, and is in part fully anticipated in Locke, *Essay* 2.23.

[15] I'll stick to considering simple ideas. For a complex idea Y, composed of simple ideas Z, V, and W, the claim is that Y can't arise unless there have been preceding impressions of Z, V, and W.

[16] One might say insulting. Note that these points all gain purchase before one considers any of the consequences and commitments of his *moral* philosophy—his appeal to innate virtues, passions, and so on. Note also Hume's neurological speculations (see p. 140 n. 5). Note also that Hume's talk of the faculties of reason, sense, and imagination, which is as it stands incompatible with the bundle theory of the mind as ordinarily understood, does an enormous amount of work in his philosophy. Taken at face value, the

All this seems clear enough. It is, however, arguable that there is an ambiguity in Hume's use of the word 'mind', an ambiguity which may explain why he has been misunderstood. On this view, he uses 'mind' to mean, roughly, both (1) conscious mental phenomena considered just as such, just as mental contents, and (2) the mind considered as a whole, in all ontic aspects, and hence considered as something which may well have (certainly does have) some ontic nature over and above perceptions or conscious mental phenomena: some 'unknown...essence' given which it is, for example, appropriate to talk of it as containing or involving faculties of sense, reason, and Imagination, and so on.

With this distinction in hand, one can perhaps allow a respect in which Hume did assert a bundle theory in an ontological sense, even though he later doubted its viability (in his Appendix to the *Treatise*). On this view, what he asserted was a bundle theory of the mind in sense (1): all there are, *so far as mental contents are concerned*, are particular perceptions; there isn't something extra called the 'self' among the mental contents. But he did not assert a bundle theory of mind in sense (2).

Using 'mind' just in sense (2), one might restate the point as follows. What Hume asserted was a bundle theory of the *self*, not of the *mind*. Thus the *mind*, considered as a whole, presumably (surely) has some unknown, faculty-involving, ontically perception-transcendent nature; but there's no such thing as the *self*, considered as something which features among the mental contents of the mind over and above all the perceptions that make up the mental contents of the mind: so far as the basic mental *contents* of the mind are concerned, all there are are perceptions.[17]

These are questions about which it's difficult to be clear. Consider by way of analogy a *pointillé* painting of a face. According to the analogy the whole painting is the mind (sense (2)), the points of colour considered just in respect of their colour-content are the perceptions, and the face is the self. The face (self) is nothing ontically over and above the points of colour (perceptions), but the painting (the mind) is indeed something over and above the points of colour, being a physical object, frame, canvas, paint—the 'place' and 'materials' of the mind, in Hume's words.

12.4 Conclusion

I discuss this difficult question further in Strawson 2011. Here I want to return to the main issue. The central point, as always, is the simple sceptical point

---

bundle theory requires that these faculties be dismissed as definitely non-existent 'fictions' that we come to believe in (on introspection) on account of certain sorts of regularities and constancies in the sequence of perceptions. But then what about *this* coming to believe? To explain it in Humean terms one will again have to appeal to something like the effect of custom on the imagination. (For further powerful support for this view see Weissman 1965: 18–28, 50–1, 76–8.)

[17] This is the sense in which someone like Parfit, say, is an ontological 'bundle theorist', while firmly believing that the mind is based in the brain (Parfit 1984: Part 3).

that we can't know how things are in reality. We can't even rule out the possibility that we're Berkeleian minds—and something even stranger may be true. It's intelligible (R-intelligible) to suppose that these unknowable (partly or wholly E-unintelligible) possibilities are actual; and it is of course also intelligible (to put it mildly) to suppose that we are in fact situated in a physical world in something like the way we ordinarily suppose.[18] The question whether there are realist objects is a 'question of fact' (153/12.12), and it's intelligible (to say the least) to suppose that if there are totally mind-independent external objects of some sort, affecting us roughly as we think they do and giving rise to our experience, then we do in fact refer to them when we talk about tables and chairs; even if we are in some sense limited—both as regards knowledge of reality, and as regards positively or descriptively contentful (E-intelligible) conceptions of it—to the contents of our own impressions and ideas.[19]

A clear parallel offers itself in the case of Causation. If there are such external objects, then it's intelligible (not to say overwhelmingly natural) to suppose that our regular-succession experience is experience (relationally) of Causation in those objects, and, hence, that we do in fact refer to Causation in those objects, in talking of causation—to 'the powers, by which bodies operate' (652/Abs§15), 'the principle, on which their mutual influence depends' (400/2.3.1.4), 'power, as it is in itself' (77 n./7.29 n.)—even if it is again true that we are in some sense limited by our epistemic situation, both as regards knowledge of reality and as regards positively contentful (E-intelligible) conceptions of it, to the contents of our impressions and ideas, and are therefore limited, so far as our experience of Causation is concerned, to experience of regularity.

Thus the E-intelligible meaning of the term 'causation' can only encompass certain aspects of the experience Causation *gives rise to*—its regular-succession content, on the one hand, and the feeling of determination that the experience of regular succession gives rise to in us, on the other hand. But the term may yet reach out referentially (if purely 'suppositionally', in Hume's terms) to the 'ultimate cause' of that experience, to what one might call the 'real essence' of causation—i.e. to Causation in the objects.

It may be noted, finally, that a large part of the point of Hume's seemingly unenthusiastic comments about putatively referring terms that lack any content-bestowing impression-source is that such terms are of no use to science or natural philosophy, contrary to the beliefs of certain philosophers of the time. Such terms can have no role to play in the explanation or understanding of particular phenomena.

---

[18] 'Something like' is designed to capture the sense in which it's true to say that nothing in science's view of the physical world undermines the ordinary view of it; both views count as realist views in the present sense.

[19] Compare the situation of the 'brain in a vat', who in talking about tables and chairs simply fails to be talking ('talking') about what it thinks it's talking about in the way that we succeed in doing, given that we are indeed in a world more or less as we think we are.

The notion of Causation or power is of no use to physics. But to say that the notion of Causation is of no (explanatory) use to physics is not to say that it is not (R-)intelligible. It simply doesn't follow—nor is it true—that it doesn't make any sense. Nor does it follow that the notion of Causation, explicitly conceived of as something whose nature is in some sense unknowable, doesn't have an indispensable role to play in any remotely plausible general philosophical account of things that takes epistemological problems seriously and at the same time takes reality (and its regularity) seriously. Granting, in line with R-intelligibility, that 'there may be several qualities both in material and immaterial objects, with which we are utterly unacquainted' (there is nothing ironic about this remark), Hume says that 'If we please to call these *power* or *efficacy*,'twill be of little consequence to the world' (168/ 1.3.14.27). And this is right, in the sense in which he intends it (it isn't flippant). Such terms are of no explanatory use to science; nor, crucially, do they express any understanding of the nature of nature in the way that the philosophers who believe in 'intelligible causes' think they do. Similarly, the idea that 'the perceptions of the mind...arise...from some...cause...unknown to us' (153/12.12) is R-intelligible although useless to science. If we speak of matter, and suppose that we have no positively contentful conception of it (not even as having primary qualities), then we leave it as a 'certain unknown, inexplicable *something*,...a notion so imperfect that no sceptic will think it worth while to contend against it' (155/12.16), a notion that is in a clear sense useless. But it is still R-intelligible, and may in its way express the truth.

To hold that putatively referring terms that lack any content-bestowing impression-source (Causation terms, expressions like 'the real nature' of bodies) do have such a role is fully compatible with holding, as Hume does, that thoughtless and over-confident use of such terms (use of them as if we could after all associate some theory-of-ideas-warranted, positively contentful conception with them) is disastrous, because it encourages the philosophically pernicious belief that the pseudo-subject of positive dogmatic metaphysics—'nothing but sophistry and illusion' (165/12.34)—is in fact a worthwhile field of enquiry where definite answers can be had and substantive progress made. Referring uses of Causation terms, although perfectly legitimate, must always be closely accompanied, as they always are in Hume, by clear protestations of our entire ignorance of the nature of Causation or power. For they strongly encourage the false belief that we do after all have some positive conception of the nature of Causation or power.

At this point the reader may skip to Part 2 or indeed Part 3—to the detailed argument that Hume not only grants a proper use to Causation terms as applied to objects, despite the fact that they are E-unintelligible, so applied, but also takes it that there actually is such a thing as Causation. First, though, I will briefly develop the parallel suggested above between Hume's use of (and explicit discussion of) the term 'external object' and his attitude to Causation terms, returning to some of the questions raised in 6.4–6.5.

13

'External objects' and Causation

13.1 The parallel

Some may still think that Hume would have rejected the (Meaning-Tension-involving) view that words may properly be used in such a way that we may refer to something that we take to exist, but of which we have (by the theory of ideas) no positively contentful conception. It may help to consider the suggestion that Hume's use of the word 'objects' (objects of whose 'secret' or 'unknown' 'real nature' or 'structure' or 'essence' he often speaks) generates the Meaning Tension independently of all his apparently referring uses of Causation terms (which have still to be considered in detail). If this is right, the Meaning Tension is not postulated just to account for the apparently referring uses of Causation terms. It has to be postulated in any case.

I've argued that Hume standardly 'writes as a realist', or at least as some sort of basic-realist (6.6), when talking about 'external objects'. At the very least, he holds that the realist (or basic-realist) use is intelligible: 'it is a question of fact, whether the perceptions of the senses be produced by external objects, entirely different from them'.[1] But the (basic) realist use of 'object' already generates the Meaning Tension. For according to the *Treatise* the best we can do 'is to form a relative idea of... external objects', when we try to form a conception of them as things which are in any way '*specifically* different from our perceptions' (68/1.2.6.9; cf. 6.5). We can't

---

[1] 153/12.12. Given the word 'produced', it should perhaps be noted that the present argument (to the effect that the Meaning Tension has to be postulated in Hume given only his use of external-object language, and so quite independently of his use of Causation terms) makes no particular use of the fact that part of the story about external objects is that they (causally) affect us and produce our perceptions. As far as possible, the argument considers Hume's use of and acceptance of the intelligibility of the notion of an external object independently of this feature. That said, it's not only 'a question of fact' whether objects exist, on Hume's view—and hence possibly true that they exist. It's also a question of fact whether they stand in causal relation to our perceptions—and hence possibly true that they do. (Hume takes it that they do.)

As remarked, Hume's use of an apparently non-regularity-theory notion of 'producing causation' in his account of the origin (the 'ultimate cause'—84/1.3.5.2) of our perceptions is paralleled by Kant's inclination to apply a notion of cause (the 'unschematized' notion of cause, in his terms) beyond what he believes to be the bounds of its proper or rather verifiable employment, and to postulate transcendental causes of our representations, and indeed of our physical actions in the 'empirically real' world—those which we perform *qua* spatio-temporal, embodied beings (see e.g. *Critique* A494/B522, A496/B524, A537–9/B565–7, A553/B581, A556/B584; see also B67 for a reference to 'what it is that is operative in the things themselves'). Would Kant have allowed that the order we experience is somehow grounded in a somehow corresponding (albeit non-temporal) order in the noumenal affecting thing? I think it is clear that he would.

suppose that we 'comprehend' their nature in any manner, insofar as they're specifically different from perceptions; in which case they're E-unintelligible, even though R-intelligible. So the Meaning Tension arises.

Before noting an important qualification to this claim, consider how natural it is for someone who takes up this position about objects to take up a similar position about Causation, as follows. The best we can do is to 'form a relative idea of... external objects' and *'their real nature and operations'* (63/1.2.5.25, 64, 638–9/1.2.5.26), i.e. their Causal operations, 'without pretending to comprehend' them or *'their real nature and operations'*, i.e. their Causal operations. If one supposes, in a (basic) realist way, that there are external objects specifically different from perceptions that affect us and give rise to our perceptions and are the reason why our perceptions are as they are (leaving aside any contribution our constancy-and-coherence-affected Imagination may make to their character), one may equally well suppose that R-intelligible but E-unintelligible Causation is a feature of those external objects that affect us and give rise to our perceptions and are the reason why our perceptions are as they are (the Causation = their 'real... operations'). So too, one may suppose that the Causation is the reason why our perceptions have the regular-succession-involving character they do.

13.2 A possible disanalogy

Having proposed a parallel or analogy between the (Meaning-Tension-creating) commitments implicit in Hume's use of 'external object' and his use of Causation terms, a possible disanalogy—clearer in the *Enquiry* than in the *Treatise*—should now be noted.

1. When Hume claims that it is a 'question of fact, whether the perceptions of the senses be produced by external objects, resembling them' (153/12.12), he's thinking of external objects as things of whose nature we may after all have some sort of positively descriptively contentful (E-intelligible) conception *even though* they're 'entirely different' (ibid.) from our perceptions. For he is at this point supposing that, although objects may be entirely ontically different from our perceptions (being entirely non-mental things), they may nonetheless 'resemble' our perceptions, and therefore not be entirely 'specifically' different from them in the sense discussed in 6.5 (pp. 44–9). That is, he's supposing that the nature of the real, 'primary qualities' of objects may after all be to some degree genuinely or contentfully captured by our ideas of primary qualities, as on Locke's theory, according to which our ideas of primary qualities 'resemble' primary qualities as they are in the objects. On this view, then, our idea of external objects is at least *partly* E-intelligible, for we have some genuine (properly sense-impression-based) conception of their qualities. When it comes to Causation in the objects, however, it seems that Hume

holds that we have no sort of positively contentful conception of it at all. So there's a disanalogy.

2. To this may be added his remark, two pages later in the *Enquiry*, that it's only when theorizing philosophers 'bereave matter of *all* its [E-]intelligible qualities', both secondary *and primary*, and so suppose that they have no positively or descriptively contentful conception of it at all, that they finish up with the—presumably unwelcome—result that they 'leave only a certain unknown, inexplicable *something*, as the cause of our perceptions; a notion so imperfect, that no sceptic will think it worth while to contend against it' (155/12.16). When they bereave it only of secondary qualities, by contrast, and, with Locke, grant it primary qualities which are 'intelligible' because our ideas of primary qualities are resembling representations of them, this doesn't happen.[2] But (it may be argued), given that he already holds that we have no positively contentful conception of Causation in the objects at all, it seems that Causation in the objects must equally be a 'certain unknown, inexplicable *something*', etc.

I'll take these points in reverse order.

The simplest reply to (2) simply grants what it says. On Hume's principles, Causation is indeed an 'unknown, inexplicable *something*', insofar it's something more than regular succession, as it is by definition. Unlike an external object considered within the framework of Locke's resemblance theory, Causation is completely E-unintelligible.

Actually, this reply seems too concessive. All that need be granted is that it's completely E-unintelligible *to precisely the extent to which it involves more than regular succession*. There's no reason not to treat regular succession as a genuine aspect of Causation itself, a fully E-intelligible aspect of it, so that Causation can be said to be partly E-intelligible. For present purposes, however, we can allow that Causation is completely E-unintelligible. For even if it is (to precisely the extent to which it involves more than regular succession), it doesn't follow that Hume therefore thinks that (or thinks that therefore) it doesn't exist. Parts 2 and 3 will try to show directly that he doesn't think this, but the general point—that (E-)'unintelligibility' and 'perfect inexplicability' don't entail non-existence, and that Hume doesn't think they do—is already clear.

The reply to (1) is that there may indeed be a disanalogy between the idea of Causation and the idea of an external object, if the idea of an external object is granted to be at least *partly* E-intelligible on Lockean resemblance-theory grounds (and if it's also denied that regular succession should be counted as a genuine and E-intelligible feature of Causation itself). But, first, Hume was dubious about the

---

[2] Even if there are then other problems to be faced.

viability of Locke's resemblance claim even in the *Enquiry* (153/12.11; see p. 45 n. 19 above). Secondly, the main claim of this chapter—the claim that Hume's notion of an external object produces the Meaning Tension—still holds so long as external objects are held to be partly E-unintelligible. If they're only partly E-unintelligible, the strong claim that we can't 'comprehend' external objects in any way gives way to the weaker claim that we can't 'comprehend' them fully. But the weaker claim still produces the essential feature of the Meaning Tension: it remains true that the notion of an external object is held to be R-intelligible although it has a completely E-unintelligible element.

In fact, Hume was sure that the notion of an external object would have an E-unintelligible element even if the Lockean claim could be largely made out. For he was sure that our impression-based idea of *solidity*—for example—couldn't possibly be supposed to resemble (and thus make E-intelligible) the primary quality of solidity as it is in itself in the external object (see 230–1/1.4.4.14, discussed in 19.2).

It remains only to repeat the point that Hume was in any case dubious about whether Locke's resemblance claim could be taken in the literal way in which he thought it would have to be taken in order to establish even the partial E-intelligibility of external objects.

13.3 An objection

Objection: Hume's introduction of the notion of a merely 'relative' idea, when discussing external objects, looks like an explicit attempt to deal with the Meaning Tension as it arises for the word 'object'. And Hume returns to this issue several times in the *Treatise* (as reported in 6.5). So why doesn't he (in the *Treatise*) face the problem of the Meaning Tension at least equally explicitly in the case of Causation terms—if he really does accept that the notion of Causation is R-intelligible although E-unintelligible in the same way as the notion of external objects?

This is a good question.[3] But the reply seems simple. When Hume was writing, the question of whether there were external objects 'specifically different' from perceptions was seen to be genuinely up for discussion. (Perhaps the irrefutable but unconvincing Berkeley—see 155/12.15 n.—was on the right lines.) Someone who accepted a Humean epistemology had good reason—especially after Berkeley, and Berkeleian doubts about Lockean resemblance claims and the coherence of materialism—to assert explicitly the intelligibility of the supposition that there might be objects specifically different from perceptions, even though we could form no positively contentful conception of their nature. The question whether there was Causation, by contrast, was not up for discussion. The true *nature* of Causation was thought to be up for discussion. (Was it all God's doing? Was it necessarily volitional in nature? Was it just

---

[3] I am grateful to Martha Klein for encouraging me to expand my initial reply to it.

some 'original, inherent Principle of Order ... in Matter' (*Dialogues* 125/174)?) That it *existed* was not. Hume insisted that the discussion of the nature of Causation was fruitless and forever undecidable, and that we could never know anything for sure about its nature; but he didn't doubt that it existed. Thus his whole argument for the unknowability of the nature of Causation or power is in effect an argument to the conclusion that we can at best form a 'relative' idea of it.[4]

The objection may now shift backwards. Can the view that the notion of an external object (specifically different from perceptions) is in some sense intelligible really be Hume's view in the *Treatise*? It seems to ignore the principles of his theory of ideas: there is no appropriate impression-source for the idea or expression 'external object'. All there is is a certain kind of complex 'constancy and coherence' among impressions of sensation. Hume is surely clear about this. He is surely clear that the idea of an external object is an impression-source-transcendent 'fiction', given his theory of ideas, and that the only legitimate meaning that his theory of ideas can really allow to the word 'object'—putatively conceived of as a word for a truly external, non-mental object—is a purely idealist meaning according to which objects are perception-(content)-constituted objects (p. 32 above).

This reaction is understandable.[5] But if it were right then it seems that those who reject the claim that the Meaning Tension is to be found in Hume, and accordingly seek to dissolve the appearance of Meaning Tension in the discussion of causation by saying that all Hume's (yet to be examined) apparently straightforwardly referring uses of Causation expressions are really just ironic, would have to say the same about all his apparent talk of realist external objects. They would have to claim that all his apparent talk of realist objects was really just ironic, because he thinks of the notion of realist objects as not only E-unintelligible but as completely 'unintelligible' or 'meaningless' in our strong senses of these words. If this is unacceptable—as it is—we need to acknowledge the Meaning Tension in Hume independently of considering his views on causation, because it's already there in his use of 'object'. We can no more 'manage to mean' an external object (insofar as it's specifically different from our perceptions) than we can 'manage to mean' Causation insofar as it involves anything more (powers and forces) than regular succession. Causation terms like 'power' and 'force' are not somehow radically worse off than the term 'external object' (although it's true that Causation also has the AP property). If anything, they're better off—as will be argued in 22.2.

---

[4] In the *Enquiry* Hume explicitly says that we have only a 'relative ... idea of *power*' in the objects (77 n./ 7.29 n.), having no 'idea of power, as it is in itself', and being able to get at it in thought only via its relation to 'the effect [which] is the measure of the power'. But nothing here rests on this.

[5] Clearly, and importantly, Hume does think that objects *as we encounter them in our direct experience of them* are *in a sense* creatures of our Imagination, and 'only in the mind' (cf. e.g. 152/12.9, discussed in ch. 6n. 43). At the same time, he never renounces the (basic) realist thought that what we are then interacting with are indeed external, wholly nonmental objects which are 'specifically different' from our perceptions, and are also the producing cause of our perceptions (see the quotations at the top of p. 129, and the discussion of 'weak basic realism' in 6.6).

It may finally be objected that these apparent references to external objects and Causation are not exactly ironic or tongue-in-cheek, but are rather employed simply for reasons of expository smoothness, and would be re-expressed in a fully explicit statement of Hume's position. The trouble with this is that it's hopelessly implausible to read Hume in this way. Once again the point is double. It's not only that his actual use of 'object' and Causation terms makes it unbelievable; it's also that it's too implausible to suppose that a clear-headed sceptic, who makes as few outright knowledge claims about existence *or non-existence* as possible, is positively asserting that there are quite definitely no external objects of any sort (no basic-realist objects of any sort), or that there is definitely no such thing as Causation.

Even in the *Treatise* Hume explicitly endorses the supposition that there is an external world of objects distinct from the internal world of his perceptions (218/1.4.2.57; see also 187/1.4.2.1). His commitment to belief in (basic) realist objects which are more than just perceptions is revealed in his remarks to the effect that 'the perceptions of the mind are perfectly known', while 'the essence and composition of external bodies are...obscure' (366/2.2.6.2). It's not possible to maintain that in all cases in which he seems to be writing as a realist about 'external objects' or 'bodies' he either has his tongue in his cheek, or has adopted a realist idiom simply for the sake of smoothness of exposition, or as a concession to the force of 'natural belief' in his readers (and in himself), while holding that any such realism is actually definitely false, strictly speaking, or actually unintelligible, or—incoherently—both together.

In sum, Hume accepts (1) that the term '(external) object' may have a proper and genuinely referring 'impression-source-transcendent' use and force, and he firmly believes that it does. Anyone who accepts (1) has powerful reasons for accepting (2) that Causation terms also have a proper and genuinely impression-source-transcendent use and force; and Hume assumes that they do.[6] Such a belief is wholly compatible with the theory of ideas, properly understood (properly integrated with Hume's distinction between supposing and conceiving, and with strictly non-committal scepticism with regard to knowledge claims about the nature of reality). I hope that the quotations in the next nine chapters will convince even the most passionate positivists that Hume generally takes this for granted, and also believes that there actually is something like Causation in the objects. Such positivists will only lose a hero, not a creed.

I'll base the main case for this claim on the *Enquiry*, in accordance with Hume's explicitly stated wishes (pp. 10–11 above), which are often ignored precisely by those who claim to be his true defenders. First, though, I'll argue that Hume already clearly holds this view in the *Treatise*. Those who are principally interested in the *Enquiry* should skip to 16.

---

[6] Even if one denies (1) one still has powerful reasons for asserting (2). See 22.2.

PART 2

Causation in the *Treatise*

14

Causation in the *Treatise*: 1

14.1 Introduction

Whether one considers the *Treatise* or the *Enquiry*, one's attitude to the question of whether Hume believes that there is such a thing as Causation (i.e. causal power or natural necessity) 'in the objects' (166/1.3.14.24) will depend partly on one's attitude to his use of referring expressions which appear to refer to Causation. Although they are obvious when they occur, I'll often signal these referring expressions by '[REF]', and by italicizing them. Similarly, I will sometimes signal Hume's epistemological remarks about causation by '[EP]'. On the present view these are merely epistemological remarks, i.e. they have no negative ontological implications. They claim only that we can know nothing about the nature of Causation in the objects, and neither claim nor imply that there is no such thing. Finally, I'll sometimes use '[NI]' to signal certain comments which—I suggest—form part of the most natural interpretation of what Hume says.

The claim that Hume acknowledges the existence of Causation in the objects is at the moment conditional. It's subject to a qualifying condition: Hume acknowledges the existence of Causation insofar as he 'writes as a realist' about external objects. But it can be more generally and more strongly stated in terms of *basic* realism (6.6) rather than in terms of realism: Hume believes in Causation (it never really occurs to him to doubt it) insofar as he ever adopts *any* basic-realist position with respect to objects: any interpretation of 'the objects' according to which their existence involves the existence of something other than our perceptions, something which affects us and gives rise to our perceptions and is the reason why they are as they are (leaving aside any contribution we ourselves make to their character).[1]

I've argued at some length that the qualifying condition is fulfilled: Hume does indeed adopt a (basic) realist position with respect to objects. In 22 it will be argued that the qualifying condition can be dropped completely. Hume believes in Causation, full stop. His belief isn't even conditional on the belief that some version of

---

[1] In the terminology of 6, any interpretation of 'the objects' according to which they are something more than strict-idealist objects. If solipsism is counted as a minimalist basic-realist option (ch. 6 n. 54), then the words 'affects us and' may be omitted.

basic realism might be true. Even if all that exist are perceptions, there must still be Causation.

14.2 Referring uses of Causation terms

The principal claim of Part 2 is that the standard account of Hume on causation is incorrect even as regards the *Treatise*. A key part of the argument for this claim (in 15.3) doesn't appeal to Hume's use of referring expressions that apparently refer to Causation. It concentrates instead on quotations that appear to *support* the standard view, in order to argue that they don't really do so. Hume does nevertheless make a considerable number of apparently straightforward references to Causation in the *Treatise*, and I will now briefly consider some of them, here and in 15.2, without expecting them to carry the main weight of the argument.

At the beginning of 1.3 Hume speaks without irony, and in an apparently straightforwardly referring way, of

(1) [REF] *the power,* by which one object produces another,

commenting that it is [EP] 'never discoverable merely from [the] idea' of the objects in question (69/1.3.1.1)

It may be said that it would be unwise to rest much on this quotation. A better example occurs in 1.3.6, where he says that when we are faced with two objects (i.e. two types of occurrence) that have always been conjoined,

(2) we [EP] cannot penetrate into [REF] *the reason* of the conjunction (93/1.3.6.15).

There is, certainly, [NI] a reason for the regular conjunction, but we cannot know anything about its intrinsic nature. For all we can ever detect in the objects is precedency, contiguity, and constant conjunction.

It is not only when we think of reality in the ordinary realist way that we see that this is so. It is equally so if we think of reality, so far as it exists beyond our perceptions and their content, in Berkeley's way. This is important to Hume. Indeed his belief that we cannot even rule out Berkeley's theory of the true nature of reality (see e.g. 84/1.3.5.2) is perhaps his second main reason (after his belief that Causation has the AP property, discussed in 11) for being so sure that we can never know anything of the nature of Causation or power as it is in reality.

At the heart of his discussion of our idea of causation in 1.3.14, Hume remarks that almost all philosophers agree that

(3) [REF] *the ultimate force and efficacy of nature* is [EP] perfectly unknown to us, and that 'tis in vain that we search for it in all the known qualities of matter. (159/1.3.14.8)

But [NI] it exists, for there must be some reason, in nature, why things are regular in the way they are. It's just that we can't know anything about it. If we did know about it, Hume thinks, we would have to be able to make a priori certain inferences about causal matters (see 11), and we know we could never do this. We 'have no adequate idea of power or efficacy in any object' (160/1.3.4.10).

Another reason why we can't know anything for sure about it (the point bears repetition) is that we can't even rule out Berkeley's hypothesis about the nature of the world and the power (the volition of a divine, immaterial, active substance) that gives it its order. As the Humean Philo says in the *Dialogues,*

our experience, so imperfect in itself, and so limited both in extent and duration, can afford us no probable conjecture concerning the whole of things (133/178).

But if we know so little about the world as a whole and the power that informs or governs it that we can't even decide between a more or less Lockean account of it and a Berkeleian account of it (let alone a Malebranchean account of it), and (further-more) can't even conceive of what sort of humanly accessible evidence could ever give us grounds for making a definite choice between these hypotheses, then it's very clear indeed that we don't really know anything for sure about its ultimate nature.[2]

For this reason alone, even if for no other, the seventeenth-century belief in 'intelligible causes'—in the possibility of knowledge of the true or ultimate nature of nature—can be seen to be a delusion. And this belief is one of Hume's main targets.[3]

Still in 1.3.14, Hume speaks of our never having any

(4) [EP] insight into [REF] *the internal structure or operating principle* of objects,

having just remarked that

(5) [REF] *the uniting principle* among our internal perceptions is as [EP] unin-telligible as that [*the uniting principle*] among external objects,

which nonetheless certainly exists, and is real, although we can never know anything about its ultimate nature.[4] Clearly he can't here mean the 'principles of association of ideas' by 'the uniting principle among our internal perceptions', for the principles of

---

[2] The respectability of the notion of the ultimate nature of reality was defended in 7.

[3] More particularly, many philosophers thought that they had some a priori insight into the nature of causation of a sort that allowed them to conclude with certainty that all causation or 'active power' must be mental or spiritual in nature; see Wright 1983: 163, and ch. 20 n. 6 below.

[4] 169/1.3.14.29. It seems clear that these external objects must be construed in a straightforwardly realist way, or at the very least in a basic-realist way—as must 'nature' in quotation (3). For if objects are just pc objects or pcc objects (cf. 6.2), then they don't really have any concealed, internal structure. (In fact, even if one gives the words 'external object' a non-basic-realist construal, here, interpreting them as pc objects or pcc objects, it seems that one is still left with a referring expression referring to Causation—to the completely unknown 'operating principle' of objects *whatever their ultimate ontic nature*; i.e. whether they are purely mental or not.)

association of ideas are fully intelligible. He explicitly states what they are (resemblance, contiguity, and causation), and what they amount to. So 'the uniting principle among our internal perceptions' must mean, roughly, 'whatever in-itself-unknown power or principle of operation makes our minds operate observably as they do'—the way in which our minds operate *observably* being fully captured by the description of the principles of association of ideas. In an exactly similar fashion, Newton's laws capture observable aspects of the theory-of-ideas unintelligible (E-unintelligible) 'uniting principle' among external objects (see 20 below).[5]

To these examples we may add one from the 'Abstract', where Hume says that

(6)   [REF] *the powers, by which bodies operate,* are [EP] entirely unknown. (652/Abs§15)

I think I can imagine how commitment to the standard view of Hume's account of causation may make it possible for some readers to read passages like these automatically as confirmation of the standard view. For such readers, Hume's epistemological, sceptical point about the complete undetectability of Causation still immediately generates the profoundly un-Humean ontological claim about the definite nonexistence of any sort of Causation. But one can no longer react like this once one has understood Hume's strictly non-committal scepticism with regard to knowledge claims about what does or doesn't exist, and his commitment to the idea that it's intelligible to suppose that there are things that are completely unintelligible to us, and of which we can only have a 'relative' idea; not to mention his realist or basic-realist *beliefs,* which are fully compatible with his scepticism, since his scepticism emphatically allows that these beliefs are R-intelligible (12.2), intelligible in the broad sense, and may in fact be true, insisting only that we can never know for sure whether they are or not.

Objection. Hume is only saying that 'the reason of the conjunction' of any two objects, the 'ultimate force and efficacy of nature', 'the powers, by which bodies

---

[5]   Insofar as we are able to work out the principles of association of ideas we are able to 'discover, *at least in some degree,* the secret springs and principles, by which the human mind is actuated in its operations' (14/1.15), although we cannot ever grasp the nature of the 'ultimate principle' which governs the mind. In fact, though, Hume thought that we could go a little further. His discussion of the principles of association of ideas in 1.2.5 is of particular interest. He begins by referring to 13/1.1.4.6, where he says that the causes of the mind's operating according to the principles of association of ideas 'are mostly unknown, and must be resolv'd into *original* qualities of human nature, which I pretend not to explain'. But he then (following Malebranche and Mandeville) goes on to offer as his own a fully fledged if very general *neurological* explanation of why the mind operates as it does: 'the mind is endow'd with a power of exciting any idea it pleases; whenever it despatches the spirits into that region of the brain, in which the idea is plac'd; these spirits always excite the idea, when they run precisely into the proper traces, and rummage that cell, which belongs to the idea. But as their motion is seldom direct, and naturally turns a little to the one side or the other—for this reason the animal spirits, falling into contiguous traces, present other related ideas in lieu of that which the mind desir'd at first to survey' (60–1/1.2.5.20). The nature of the 'ultimate principle' by which the brain thus operates is still entirely unknown and unintelligible, on this view, as is the nature of all causal power. Nevertheless we can give some kind of real explanation of why the principles of association of ideas govern our thought as they do, by reference to the nature of the brain.

operate', and so on, are perfectly *unknown,* and not in fact *unknowable.* Reply: since Hume holds that all that could ever become known to us, so far as causation in the objects is concerned, are regularities of succession, this objection must suppose that all Hume means by speaking of the 'perfectly unknown...ultimate force and efficacy of nature' (etc.) are other as yet undetected (presumably because much smaller) regularities of succession. The idea is then presumably that, given knowledge of minute regularities of succession between Cs and Ds, Es and Fs, say, we might come to see why there is some larger-scale regularity of succession—between As and Bs, say.

Three points may be made in reply to this suggestion; two have been made already. First, it's highly unnatural to read such phrases in this way.[6] Second, one of Hume's explicit reasons why we can't know the true nature of power is that if we did then we would be able to make a priori certain inferences about causal matters of a sort we know we cannot make. Learning about minute regularities of succession couldn't help with this. Third, since we can't even decide between Lockean and Berkeleian accounts of the true nature of reality, we can't possibly suppose that we could ever know the nature of 'the ultimate force and efficacy of nature'.

It's true that Hume does sometimes think of causes as being unknown in the sense that there are regularities of succession which are unknown but potentially discoverable. But this doesn't alter the fact that he thinks of the 'ultimate force and efficacy of nature' as something totally inaccessible to us. This issue is discussed further in 18.

---

[6] The reading is offered in support of the 'standard' view; but only a prior presumption that the 'standard' view is true can give one reason to favour it.

15

Causation in the *Treatise*: 2

15.1 Three stratagems

In this chapter I consider some further passages that contain referring uses of Causation terms. I also consider some passages that are typical of the sort that appear to provide direct support for the standard view. There are plenty of such passages, and they demand a response.

I'll try to undermine their apparent support for the standard view in three connected ways. First, by consideration of the details of some individual passages. Second, by developing the general and fundamental point that whenever Hume makes an apparently firm and unqualified ontological or metaphysical claim of the form 'X *is really nothing but* Y' (causation is nothing but constant conjunction, or observed uniformity; the mind is nothing but a series of perceptions)—a claim of a sort that seems flagrantly inconsistent with his basic sceptical principles—he is really always making a properly sceptical epistemological claim to the effect that X is nothing more than Y so *far as we have any notion or conception of X.*[1] If this point is correct (I think that after due consideration it emerges as obvious) then it immediately undercuts the standard view of Hume, according to which he is making the profoundly un-Humean claim that causation in objects is definitely nothing but regular succession.

There is one important (and by now familiar) qualification to this: the standard view is undercut except insofar as Hume sometimes means 'immediate' objects of mental attention by 'the objects' ('ontologically moderate pure-content-idealist' objects, in the terms of 6.2–6.3). If this is ever what he means by 'the objects' when discussing causation, then there's no reason to deny that he is adopting a regularity theory of causation in the objects, for there's a clear and important sense in which a regularity account of causation is actually correct, so far as such 'objects' are concerned.[2]

Certainly Hume doesn't always seem clear on this question in the *Treatise*. He does sometimes seem tempted to go beyond the properly sceptical, negative

---

[1] Here I'm indebted to Craig, who makes the point forcefully (1987: 110) and illustrates it (ch. 2 sect. 5) with special reference to Hume's discussion of the 'bundle' theory of mind.
[2] Cf. 6, §3 and Appendix. There can only be 'cartoon-film-world' causal relations between objects so conceived.

epistemological claim to make the anti-sceptical ontological claim that there is no such thing as Causation. Perhaps one good explanation of this is the one just proposed: when he does this he's thinking of 'the objects' as the things which are the 'immediate objects of experience' or mental attention. But this suggestion is in tension with the fact that Hume standardly writes of objects in an ostensibly realist (or basic-realist) style (referring, for example, to their secret natures).

This tension may be a simple fact about Hume's text, in which case the explanation just given may be correct (see n. 15). But a preferable suggestion is this: all that Hume means, when he says that causation in the objects is just regular succession, is that this is all it is so far as we can contentfully conceive of it: indeed, sometimes he simply *means* 'causation-so-far-as-we-can-contentfully-conceive-of-it' by 'caus-ation'; and when he does he certainly holds that causation in the objects is nothing but regular succession; but holding *this* view certainly doesn't involve denying the existence of Causation. (This suggestion will be discussed further in 15.5, and is very strongly supported by what Hume says about his two definitions of cause, which are discussed in 21.)

This connects with a further possible response to Hume's apparently anti-sceptical and profoundly un-Humean claims about the non-existence of Causation. This is the third undermining move mentioned above, which closely matches the allegations of irony and tongue-in-cheekery that form part of the standard view, insofar as it attributes a certain sort of rhetorical effect to Hume. It consists in saying that any apparently ontological or metaphysical claim that Hume may make—e.g. to the effect that causation in the objects is nothing but regular succession, or to the effect that the mind is nothing but a series of perceptions—is a kind of neat *dramatic exaggeration* of the corresponding, properly sceptical, negative epistemological claim: i.e. that all we can know of causation is regular succession (and all we can know of mind is a series of perceptions). The claim that causation in the objects is nothing but regular succession (first definition) of a sort that gives rise to certain feelings or beliefs or habits of inference in human beings (second definition) is thus always accompanied, implicitly or explicitly, by the epistemological qualification 'so far as we have any notion of it'.

This is (as always) too simple, because part of what the 'dramatic exaggeration' expresses is the semantical thought that regular succession is, in a sense, all we can 'manage to mean' when we talk about causation in the objects. And this is Hume's official-theory-of-ideas view. But in fact—as I have not yet finished insisting—he takes it for granted that there may be, and indeed that there is, something more to causation in the objects, unknown though it may be, and whatever we can be supposed to manage to mean on the terms of the theory of ideas; and to grant this is to grant that we can in some sense mean Causation—mean more than regular succession—when we talk about causation in the objects. We can mean it because we can refer to it, and we can refer to it because, assuming it to exist, as Hume does, we can pick it out with phrases that make no claim to convey any sort of positively

contentful conception of its nature: phrases such as 'the "perfectly unknown...
ultimate force and efficacy of nature"' (159/1.3.14.8), 'the "reason of the conjunction" of any two objects' (93/1.3.6.15), 'that on which the "regular course and
succession of objects totally depends"' (55/5.22).

The see-saw movements of the following argument may seem like the outcome of
an ill-judged attempt to impose a shaky interpretation on a recalcitrant text. But
the tensions they express match the tensions in the text. It should also be noted that
there are two main strategies open to a challenger of the standard view. One is to
make the strong claim that Hume is entirely consistent in his expression of his belief
in the existence of Causation, and that the standard view is completely wrong in its
overall view of Hume, despite apparent textual support for it. The other is to make
the weaker but still important claim that Hume is simply not completely consistent
on the question at issue. On this view he is at certain points definitely granting both
that the notion of Causation in the objects is an intelligible one (in our sense), and
that there actually is such a thing as Causation; while the standard view of what he is
saying is at other points substantially correct.

This concession does not go very far, however. For even if one felt obliged to stick
to the weaker claim when discussing the (perhaps essentially contestable) *Treatise*—
as I do not—one could advance to the stronger claim when discussing the *Enquiry*. So
it will be argued.[3]

15.2 Ignorance, irony, and reality

In section 1.2.5 of the *Treatise*, Hume considers the objection that his approach leads
him to

(7) explain only the manner in which objects affect the senses, without endeav-
     ouring to account for *their real nature and operations* (63/1.2.5.25)

To this he replies, in a passage with an ironic ring which requires comment,

(8) I answer this objection, by pleading guilty, and by confessing that my
     intention never was to penetrate into *the nature of bodies,* or explain [REF]

---

[3] I will make almost no appeal to the 'dramatic exaggeration' thesis, although it's widely agreed upon,
not only by commentators but also by Hume, who profoundly regretted 'the positive Air' he adopted in the
Treatise, inflamed as he then was with the 'Ardor of Youth' (letter to Stewart, 1754, quoted by Kemp Smith,
1941: 413); it should nonetheless be noted. Note also that if there is fundamental disagreement about some
aspect of an author's views, and both sides impute rhetorical devices like irony or dramatic exaggeration in
order to support their reading, then the relevant portions of the text—in this case all Hume's explicit
writings about causation—may be declared neutral ground, and the disputants may go to arbitration by
consulting other general features of the author's view. If this happens in the present case the result is I think
clear. Supporters of the standard view will appeal to a certain strict positivistic interpretation of Hume's
theory of ideas or meaning. Supporters of the present view will appeal to such things as his admiration for
Newton, his strictly non-committal scepticism with respect to knowledge claims about the nature of reality,
and his doctrine of the nature and content of 'natural belief'. The latter will win.

the secret causes of their operations. For besides that this belongs not to my present purpose, I am afraid that such an enterprize is beyond the reach of human understanding, and that [EP] *we can never pretend to know body otherwise than by those external properties, which discover themselves to the senses.* As to those who attempt any thing farther, I cannot approve of their ambition, till I see, in some one instance at least, that they have met with success. (64/1.2.5.26)

The irony is conveyed mainly by the use of 'guilty', 'confess', and 'afraid', and there's also irony in his saying that penetrating into the nature of bodies is not his present purpose, since he goes on to say that he thinks any such thing is impossible, at least for human beings (cf. 11). For the same reason, there's irony in his courtesy of expression when he talks of those who attempt such penetration, and says that his approval of their efforts must wait upon their success. Nevertheless he means what he says in this passage. He reiterates the point very strongly indeed in the passage in the Appendix marked for inclusion directly after this paragraph (638/1.2.5.26 n.), and it simply doesn't follow, from the presence of elements of irony, that his use of the referring expressions italicized in the quotations is ironic or tongue-in-cheek. The overall tenor of his discussion makes it impossible to maintain that such uses are ironic, in spite of the fact that the Meaning Tension arises with respect to them. Here as so often Hume is taking an explicitly Newtonian line, and his use of these expressions is no more ironic than Newton's use of similar expressions.[4] The stress of his irony is wholly epistemological; it insists on our irremediable ignorance of the nature of matter and causation, and teases those who believe we can surmount this ignorance.

Bodies *have* a nature (of course); and there is (of course) some reason in the nature of things why they are regular in their operations. But such things are utterly beyond our reach. They are inexplicable—like human understanding itself.[5] People who think otherwise deserve an ironic response because they're subject to a truly royal self-delusion. In fact they know so little about the true nature of reality that (once more) they can't even show that Descartes's or Locke's account of it, rather than (say) Berkeley's radically different account of it, is true. That is, they really know *nothing at all* for sure about its real nature. (And there is of course a sense in which this will always be so.)

The central, simple point remains. To say that the nature and causal powers of bodies are ungraspable by us is not to say that there are no such things, any more than to say that the nature and principles of operation of human understanding are perfectly inexplicable is to say that there are no such things. Hume may be right that 'we can never pretend to know body otherwise than by those external properties,

---

[4] Cf. the quotations from Newton on p. 186 below.

[5] Hume takes the term 'the understanding' to refer to 'the general and more establish'd properties of the imagination' (267/1.4.7.7), which is itself 'a kind of magical faculty in the soul ... inexplicable by the utmost efforts of human understanding (24/1.1.7.15)

which discover themselves to the senses', but in saying this he assumes—without irony—that bodies are in fact (or at the very least could be, so that the idea is intelligible) something more than their discoverable or perceptible properties.[6]

Whatever one thinks about this passage, it's worth comparing it with a similar one where Hume writes without irony (one must be very prejudiced in favour of the standard view to think otherwise):

(9)   It has been observ'd already, that in no single instance [REF] *the ultimate connexion* of any objects is discoverable, either by our senses or reason, and that we can never penetrate so far into the essence and construction of bodies, as to perceive [REF] *the principle, on which their mutual influence depends.* 'Tis their constant union alone, with which we are acquainted... (400/2.3.1.4; note that paragraph 32 of the Abstract is almost identical (660/ Abs§32))

This passage seems very clear. It is in no way ironic. It claims that there is certainly something more than constant union, something governing the operation of bodies; but that it is constant union alone with which we are acquainted.

But (it will be objected) the way in which the passage continues immediately provides strong support for the standard view:

(10)   'Tis their constant union alone, with which we are acquainted; and 'tis from the constant union the necessity arises.

That is, there is no necessity in objects.

But this may be fully granted, for (10) continues

'tis from the constant union the necessity arises, when the mind is determined to pass from one object to its usual attendant, and infer the existence of one from that of the other (400/2.3.1.4; 660–1/Abs§32)

Here 'necessity' refers either to the 'determination of the mind to pass from one object to its usual attendant', or to the positively contentful *idea* of necessity which we derive from this (this becomes clear when one considers the word 'arise', discussed further in 15.4, p. 150). And this passage—(9) plus (10)—is of interest precisely because it so clearly aims to distinguish, in a way that must always be put in question by the rigid interpretation of the theory of ideas, between

(A)   the necessity we take ourselves to be attributing to objects,

the necessity expressed or referred to by the genuinely positively contentful *idea* of necessity we actually manage to have, on the one hand, and, on the other hand,

---

[6] Recall again Hume's extremely demanding condition (see 11) on what would count as a genuine grasp of the nature or causal power of bodies: such a grasp has to bring with it the ability to make a priori certain inferences about causal matters.

(B)   the actual 'ultimate connexion' between objects, the actual 'principle, on which their mutual influence depends'

—something that is not any sort of idea, and of which we have in fact no properly contentful idea, although it exists, and although it is intelligible to suppose that we can refer to it. Our mistake—our deep and profoundly natural mistake, and Hume's principal target—is to think that (A) is an idea of (B), of Causation or necessary connection in the objects.[7] Hume doesn't think we ever have any experience of (B), the nature of causal power, but he does allow a sense in which we have experience of the nature of necessity.

15.3   Hume's global subjectivism about necessity

How can this be, given that Hume at one point definitionally equates 'necessity' with 'power, force, energy' (157/1.3.14.4)? The answer is striking.[8] In the middle of his main discussion of causation, Hume writes as follows:

(11)   the necessity, which makes two times two equal to four, or three angles of a triangle equal to two right ones, *lies only in the act of the understanding*, by which we consider and compare these ideas; *in like manner* the necessity or power, which unites causes and effects, lies in the determination of the mind to pass from the one to the other (166/1.3.14.23).

Here he explicitly states that the source of *all* necessity is human mental reactions, *as much in the case of mathematics and geometry as in the case of causation*. He takes a strictly subjectivist line: all necessity lies only in the mind. Even in the case of mathematical and geometrical relations there's no objective necessity of relation of a sort which can be supposed to exist independently of our mental reactions to them

---

[7] I discuss the passage quoted from 400/2.3.1.4 further in 15.4 One line of argument for the view that Hume believes in Causation may here focus on the fact that he seems committed to a notion of genuine Causation or determination in his account of the operations of the *mind* whatever his view about Causation in the *objects*. I'm going to bypass this (correct) point as far as possible, concentrating on the claim that Hume is committed to belief in the existence of Causation in the objects considered as quite independent of the mind. Note, though, Hume's uses of verbs like *influence* and *impel* not only when talking about the workings of nature conceived of as something existing independently of the human mind, but also and in particular when talking about the nature and workings of the human mind: e.g. *convey; carry; enliven*; one idea *introduces* another; naturally *produces*; *renders* more lively; an idea *strikes* more strongly; the presence of an object *excites* the idea of another; one idea or impression *determines* the mind to form another. Some may say that all such expressions must be given a pure regularity-theory reading in a fully tightened up statement of Hume's position; such a view is fantastically implausible given the manner of use of these expressions (i.e. independently of the fact that Hume isn't a regularity theorist about external objects). To insist on a pure regularity-theory account of the mind's operations is to hold that there is definitely no reason for their regularity. This is absurd in exactly the way in which the regularity-theory account of what goes on in the external world is absurd (amounting as it does to the claim that matter has no nature; see 5 and 8, and 22 below), and Hume's famous worries about his account of the mind in the Appendix to the *Treatise* further confirm the point.

[8] Beebee misunderstands the argument of this section (Beebee 2006: ch. 7) and I have tried to express it better in this revised edition.

when we consider and compare the ideas they involve. The claim is not just that 'experience only teaches us that a thing is so and so, but not that it cannot be otherwise' (Kant *Critique*: B3). Unlike Kant, Hume states here that all necessities whatever are definitely only in the mind. Necessity is just a feeling we have about certain things—about $7 + 5 = 12$, or about what this billiard ball does to that one, or about the sum of the angles of a triangle.[9]

Hume's famous supposed conclusion about causation appears to follow immediately: since any supposed causal power in objects has already been taken to be a kind of necessity, it too must lie 'only in the mind', and definitely not in objects—not in any sense—because all necessity is only in the mind. But even while he advances this unconditional, globally subjectivist claim about necessity in general Hume continues to differentiate the two things—necessity understood in the way just outlined, on the one hand, and power or force, on the other hand—that he has definitionally equated in his discussion of causation, in accordance with the philosophical usage of his time. He continues to differentiate necessity understood in the strong subjectivist way as something that is *inevitably* 'only in the mind' (i.e. (A)), from what he calls 'the principle, on which [the] mutual influence of bodies depends', the 'ultimate connexion' between objects—i.e. from Causation or causal power (i.e. (B)).[10] He continues to distinguish necessity understood in this way from causal power—he continues to distinguish 'necessity$_2$' from 'necessity$_1$', in J. L. Mackie's terms (1974: 12)—in order to continue to make the key epistemological and sceptical point he keeps making, e.g. in the quotations in (1)–(9) in 14 and 15.1: the point that our very best and most vivid idea of necessity cannot in any way manage to denote that thing X in the objects whose nature is unknown to us, which one can call causal power or Causation, and which is the reason why things are regular in their behaviour in the way that they are: 'the reason of the conjunction' (93/1.3.6.15) of constantly conjoined objects, whose nature we do not know, although many philosophers think they do. If one calls this something 'necessity', and then thinks of all necessity in the extreme subjectivist way, one risks losing one's grip on this point. This is why so many have thought that Hume is going further than he is.

The complex of ideas is dense here. The equation of necessity with causation is built into the idea that Causation has the AP property (see 11)—so that knowledge of it would have to make possible inferences which had the same certainty or *necessity* as mathematical or geometrical inferences. No less important, the equation of

---

[9] Hume doesn't take this line about all relations of ideas, only about mathematics and geometry, and it's plausible to suppose that he is responding to the considerations that led Kant to judge that the truths of mathematics and geometry are synthetic a priori. It's a pity Kant doesn't remark on this in the *Prolegomena* when he considers Hume's approach to mathematics (1783: §2, Ak4.272-3). In the *Enquiry*, however, Hume groups the truths of geometry and arithmetic together with truths about relations of ideas (25/4.1), and it's not likely that Kant would in 1783 have known about this passage from the *Treatise*.

[10] I'll use 'Causation and 'causal power' interchangeably for the rest of this section.

necessity with causation is theoretically and linguistically standard in the eighteenth century (and before), as already remarked: it's built into the 'necessitarian' conception of causation Hume found in circulation when he was writing and undertook to criticize in his discussion of free will.[11] For all this, Hume continues to recognize and appeal to the distinction between causal power and necessity (the necessity represented by our idea of necessity) just outlined.[12]

The extreme subjectivism about necessity, so strikingly stated by Hume (quotation (11)), probably plays an important part in his appearing at times so very confident and unequivocal in his famous claim that there is definitely no necessity in objects.[13] *Of course* there's no necessity in objects, on this view; after all, there isn't even any objective necessity in mathematical or geometrical relations. There's no necessity— no necessity-as-we-attribute-or-conceive-it—in anything at all, considered independently of our mental reactions. But once attention has been drawn to this deep subjectivist motivation for Hume's famous claim that necessary connection lies 'only in the mind', it only becomes clearer, given the overall structure of his position (as revealed both in his clear commitment to scepticism and e.g. in quotations (1)–(9) in 14 and 15.2) that the claim is most seriously misinterpreted when it's taken to be an ontological claim that there is definitely nothing in objects of the sort we (today) would think of as causal power (i.e. as Causation or natural necessity). Hume's principal point is again merely epistemological: *all* necessity (all *necessity-we-attribute-or-conceive-of*) is a human mental product, a feeling-derived, mental-reaction-derived idea. It *can't* be a property of anything considered independently of human mental reactions. But to say this is not to say that there isn't and can't be any such thing as *Causation*—some really existing 'principle, on which [the] mutual influence [of bodies] depends'. It's just to say that if there is such a thing as Causation, as there surely is, then we can't suppose that our feeling-of-determination-derived idea of necessity amounts to some—any—sort of genuine idea of its nature. Certainly we have no E-intelligible conception (p. 122) of its nature. But Hume explicitly allows that having no contentful idea of something doesn't entail its non-existence, in a passage (168/1.3.14.28) I'll discuss in 15.5.

Hume provides all the grounds for the misinterpretation, with his definitional equation of 'necessity' with 'causal power'.[14] It is nevertheless a misinterpretation.

---

[11] However 'curious' Hume's 'curious belief that "efficacy" or "power" means much the same thing as "necessary connexion"!' (Anscombe, 1971: 138), it's routine in his time. See ch. 11 n. 5; see also Harris 2005a for a discussion of the 'necessitarian' conception of cause as it featured in the free will debate.

[12] For a doubt about this way of putting it, see the reference to Beauchamp and Rosenberg in 8 above and 15.5 below.

[13] Even if this statement of global subjectivism about necessity could be shown to be at odds with Hume's views elsewhere, the significance of its occurrence at the heart of his discussion of the idea of necessary connection would remain undiminished: Hume states his famous conclusion that there is no necessity in objects no fewer than ten times in the passage in which it occurs (165–7/1.3.14.20–25).

[14] This is maintained in the *Enquiry* in repeated use of the phrase 'power or necessary connexion', but the global subjectivism about necessity is not repeated.

Passages like (1)–(6) and (9) above reveal his clear belief that there's some sort of causal power or Causation in objects, even though there couldn't possibly be any *necessity* in objects, *given* the subjectivist understanding of the notion of necessity. I don't think it's possible to understand Hume's discussion of causation in the *Treatise* without seeing how he distinguishes between (A), the (necessarily mental or 'subjective') necessity we 'project' onto objects, and then suppose ourselves to discern in them, and (B), the actual, objective 'uniting principle' between objects.

There's a nice illustration of this when Hume is discussing Causation between perceptions, and moves from a reference to (A) to a reference to (B). When two things are associated in our mind as cause and effect, and an impression of the former gives rise to an idea of the latter, Hume says,

> (12)   the *necessary connexion* is [the] determination, which we feel to pass from the idea of the one to that of the other. The [REF] *uniting principle* among [them] is as [EP] unintelligible as that among external objects (169/1.3.14.29).

The *necessary connection* is a feeling whose nature we know in having it. The *uniting principle* is something else, entirely unknown and so unintelligible.[15]

It may be protested that the passage asserting global subjectivism about necessity (quotation (11)) continues in a way which provides very strong support for the standard view. This continuation will be quoted and commented on shortly. Before that I want to return to 400/2.3.1.3.

15.4 The 'necessity, which we ascribe'; the 'necessity, which we conceive'

The extreme 'global subjectivist' motivation for Hume's claim that there is no necessity in objects can be distinguished from the standard theory-of-ideas

---

[15] There's an important further point here, but I think it will seem too complicated to convince many, so I'll state it briefly in a note. When Hume speaks of 'objects' in 1.3.14, it's arguable that he's thinking of them as immediate objects of mental attention, much of the time, as 'ontically moderate pure-content-idealist objects' or 'pcc objects', in the terms of 6.3; and that when he wants to switch to talking of external objects he signals this explicitly by using a word like 'external' or 'material' or 'bodies'. On this view, when he says 'When any object is presented to us, it immediately conveys to the mind a lively idea of that object, which is usually found to attend it; and this determination of the mind forms the necessary connection of these objects' (169/1.3.14.29), what he says is true without qualification. For here he means pcc objects, and there are no necessary connections between pcc objects considered in themselves, any more than there are between objects or events as they occur in a cartoon film (in which 'one thing just happens after another'): it's just that we project necessary connection onto them. This being so, there's no clash or confusion at all when, later in the same paragraph, Hume switches to talking explicitly of *external* objects, and makes an apparently straightforwardly referring use of a Causation expression, saying that 'the uniting principle among... external objects... is unintelligible'. For there's no tension in supposing (1) that there's no causal power in objects insofar as they're conceived of as pcc objects, on the one hand, and (2) that there is some real but to us unintelligible 'uniting principle' between objects insofar as they're conceived of as genuinely external objects.

motivation for saying that necessity (the necessity-we-attribute) can't be in objects, although the two are obviously closely connected. According to the theory of ideas, (A), the *necessity-we-attribute*, can't be in objects given that its impression-source is in the mind, even though there is (may be) (B), unknowable Causation in objects.

But it is indeed *only* (A) that is 'only in the mind', given its feeling-of-determination impression-source. And in spite of his definitional equation of causal power and necessity, Hume is (as a sceptic and (basic) realist about objects) vividly aware that it just doesn't follow that there's no such thing as (B) Causation, no such thing as 'the ultimate connexion' between objects, or 'the principle, on which their mutual influence depends', i.e. no such thing as what we call natural necessity, which is so vividly compared with mathematical necessity by Philo in the *Dialogues* (see pp. 110–11 above). It's true of (A) that

(13)   the actions of matter, have no necessity, but what is deriv'd from ... [their] constant *union* and the *inference* of the mind (400/2.3.1.4),

but before one takes this to be decisive support for the standard view one needs to consider the word 'derived', which is revealing, like the word 'arise' in quotation (10). The necessity in question here is indeed just in the mind, for the necessity in question is, quite simply, the feeling (impression or idea) of necessity produced by, and so deriving or arising from, the experience of uniformity and the inference it naturally prompts. In this passage Hume has explicitly set himself to 'consider ... on what the idea of a necessity in [the] operations' of matter is founded (400/2.3.1.3), i.e. from what it derives, and he's giving his standard answer in terms of a feeling of determination in the mind: *all* necessity-*we-attribute* is mental, even mathematical necessity, and so can't be in objects, or even in real geometrical or mathematical relations. But to say this is not to say that there is no such thing as (B) Causation—no such thing as 'the principle, on which [the] mutual influence [of objects] depends', no such thing as 'the reason [for their] conjunction' (93/1.3.6.15), no such thing as 'the power, by which one ... produces another' (69/1.3.1.1). It's just to say that (A), our idea of necessity, can't be supposed to be any sort of clear idea of (B), given its mental feeling-of-determination impression-source, and the way it arises.[16]

The 'Meaning Tension' is obviously present here, because the expressions just quoted ('the ultimate connexion', 'the principle, on which their mutual influence depends' etc.) can't really manage to (positively-contentfully) mean anything, given the theory of ideas. But these expressions aren't ironic or tongue-in-cheek. Their

---

[16] Those who are particularly struck by the way Hume appears to rely on the notion of Causation in his account of the operation of the mind (e.g. in the second definition of cause (170/1.3.14.31, 172/1.3.14.35) should note that even if (even though) Hume believes that Causation governs the operations of the mind, and even if (even though) he implicitly or explicitly appeals to this fact precisely in his account of the occurrence in us of the feeling of determination which is the source of our idea of necessity, he still doesn't think (and it doesn't follow) that our idea of necessity is thereby a genuine, positively contentful conception of the Causation that governs the operations of the mind.

function is to refer to Causation without purporting to express any positive conception or description of its nature. The Meaning Tension is not a problem when one has
'mastered the idea of the whole'.[17]

The same response is appropriate for the passage first quoted in Chapter 10, in
which Hume, having granted that the expression 'necessary connexion' isn't actually
meaningless, says that the idea of necessity doesn't 'represent... any thing, that does
or can belong to the objects' (164/1.3.14.19). This may again be thought to support
the standard view. It may seem like an ontological claim of a sort Hume can't
legitimately make, given his sceptical principles, to the effect that causation in the
objects definitely doesn't and can't involve any sort of Causation. In fact, though, it
means exactly what it says: it's a comment on the true *representational force or reach*
of our actual (positively contentful) idea of necessity (power, efficacy, etc.). It needs to
be read both in the light of his theory of ideas and in the light of his subjectivism
about necessity.

Read in the light of his theory of ideas, the point is just (once again) that the
necessity-we-attribute isn't in fact and can't in fact be in objects, given that the source
of our idea of necessity is an impression of reflexion or feeling of determination in the
mind. To say this is obviously not to exclude the possibility that there is some sort of
Causation in the objects of which we can have no impression or E-intelligible idea—
i.e. something about objects in virtue of which they're regular in the way they are.
Read in the light of the subjectivism about necessity, the point is that absolutely all
necessity-we-attribute, even mathematical or geometrical necessity, lies only in the
mind, and is just a feeling which is a product or aspect of an act of the mind, and so
doesn't and can't belong in external objects. But this, as Hume knows, is no warrant
for asserting in a dogmatic, anti-sceptical, un-Humean way that there not only isn't
but can't be any real 'principle, on which [the] mutual influence [of objects]
depends'—something about them in virtue of which they are regular in their
behaviour, something which is therefore not itself just regularity.

Another passage where Hume doesn't speak explicitly of necessity may be cited
against the present view. In 1.4.5 he's arguing that matter and motion may be causes
of thought, since 'thought and motion... are constantly united' (248/1.4.5.30), and
such union is sufficient for assuming a causal connection. He then says that

(14)   as the constant conjunction of objects constitutes the very essence of cause
        and effect, matter and motion may often be regarded as the causes of
        thought, *as far as we have any notion of that relation* (250/1.4.5.33)

—a claim that needs to be read with care, because the way the sentence is arranged
obscures the fact that the last of the three principal clauses, which I've italicized,

---

[17] 'If we take single passages, torn from their context, and compare them with one another, contradictions are not likely to be lacking, especially in a work that is written with any freedom of expression...; but
they are easily resolved by those who have mastered the idea of the whole' (Kant, *Critique* Bxliv).

qualifies 'causes'. The clause is about the relation of cause and effect, and the sentence can be rearranged as follows:

matter and motion may often be regarded as the causes of thought, as far as we have any notion of [the] relation [of cause and effect. This is because] the constant conjunction of objects constitutes the very essence of [the relation of] cause and effect, . . . *as far as we have any notion of that relation.*[18]

Here the second sentence makes it clear that Hume's claim about causation is his usual and fundamental epistemological claim. To say that 'the constant conjunction of objects constitutes the very essence of the relation of cause and effect, as far as we have any notion of that relation', is not to say, in the allegedly canonically 'Humean' way, that constant conjunction is actually all there is to causation in the objects. On the contrary: it's to make explicit the idea that the relation of cause and effect does in fact (or at the very least may) involve something more, of which we are ignorant.

15.5 'So far as we have any notion of it'

The last quoted passage introduces the general point mentioned at the beginning of 15.1: if Hume makes what looks like a dogmatic ontological claim that causation is nothing but regular succession,[19] so that there is in fact nothing like Causation in the objects, one will best understand his claim if one adds the qualification 'so far as we have any notion of it', or 'so far as it is anything to us', or some such phrase. This qualification may for example be applied to the passage which immediately follows the 'global subjectivism about necessity' passage, which may at first seem like conclusive support for the standard view.[20] Having equated power and energy and efficacy with necessity (157/1.3.14.4), and having just argued in high subjectivist fashion that all necessity lies only in the mind, Hume continues as follows:

(15)   The efficacy or energy [or necessity or power] of causes is neither plac'd in the causes themselves, nor in the deity, nor in the concurrence of these two principles; but belongs entirely to the soul. . . . *'Tis here that the real power of causes is plac'd*, along with their connexion and necessity. (166/1.3.14.23)

And of course this must be so, if power (so far as we have any notion of it) is the same as necessity, and all necessity whatever is only in the mind. Thus Hume's global subjectivism about necessity—and also, no doubt, a certain pleasure in creating a

---

[18]   And what we find, in fact, is that matter and motion are constantly conjoined with thought just as billiard ball movements of type A are constantly conjoined with billiard ball movements of type B.

[19]   More fully: causation is nothing but regular succession (1st definition) which has a certain effect on human minds (specified in the 2nd definition).

[20]   It may also be taken as support for the Causation-only-in-the-mind view noted and put aside in nn. 7 and 16.

dramatic effect—leads him to make what looks like the outright, dogmatic, meta-physical claim that there is quite definitely no sort of Causation in objects.[21]

It is, however, central to Hume's overall position that the passage may be expanded as follows:

So far as the efficacy or energy or necessity or power of causes is something of which we have any positively or descriptively contentful (E-intelligible) idea at all, and can positively-contentfully talk about at all, it is neither placed in the causes themselves, nor in the deity, nor in the concurrence of these two principles; but belongs entirely to the soul.... It is here that the real power of causes is placed—so far as we have any positively contentful (impression-grounded, E-intelligible) notion of power, that is; it is here that the connexion and necessity of causes is placed—so far as we have any notion of necessity, that is.

Two pages later, after a further dramatic passage, he makes this point explicit, in a remark already quoted. He says that he is

(16)   indeed, ready to allow, that there may be several qualities both in material and immaterial objects, with which we are utterly unacquainted; (168/ 1.3.14.27)

and he adds that we may if we wish 'call these *power* or *efficacy*'. But when we use 'power' and 'efficacy' in this way, 'meaning these unknown qualities...with which we are utterly unacquainted', ''twill be of little consequence to the world'; and we must be quite clear what we are doing. Above all, we must not suppose, as so many misguided philosophers (believers in 'intelligible causes') have done, that the terms 'power' and 'efficacy' 'signify something, of which we have a clear idea'.

That's all; there is no irony here. In the very next paragraph he refers three times to this utterly unknown power, in passages already quoted: the 'uniting principle among our internal perceptions' and the 'uniting principle...among external objects' are utterly (E-)unintelligible to us, for 'experience...never gives us any insight into *the internal structure or operating principle of objects*'. That is, it never gives us any insight into the nature of Causation or power:

(17)   we have [EP] *no other notion* of cause and effect, but that of certain objects, which have been *always conjoin'd* together.... We cannot penetrate into [REF] *the reason of the conjunction*.[22]

---

[21]   Elsewhere his inclination to sound as if he is making such a claim is (as noted in 15.1) perhaps to be explained principally by his inclination to think of 'the objects' as nothing but immediate mental objects of experience, perception-constituted objects or content-constituted objects for which a regularity theory of causation is in a sense correct (6.3 and Appendix A).

[22]   93/1.3.6.15. The device of adding some variety of the phrase 'insofar as we have any idea (or notion or conception) of it' applies to all other passages that seem to support the standard view, e.g. 165/ 1.3.14.20,169/1.3.14.29, 171/1.3.14.33, 173/1.3.15.5. They come particularly thick and fast in the text immediately before and after Hume's explicit statement of global subjectivism about necessity.

As remarked, Hume states his dramatic conclusion ten times at the climax of 1.3.14 (165–7/1.3.14.20–25): the necessity we take ourselves to be acquainted with in objects is not in fact in objects; it's nothing but a determination of the mind, an impression of reflexion, a feeling we have when we experience or think about certain things; 'the necessary connexion betwixt causes and effects' with which we take ourselves to be acquainted '*is* the transition [of our thought] ... from one to the other ... arising from the accustomed union' (165/1.3.14.21). And for present purposes we can grant that his argument for the conclusion that we neither do nor can have any experience of necessity or causal power in the objects is entirely successful.[23] We can grant that it's defensible even in its modern form, which makes no use of Hume's premiss that true experience of Causation would have to confer the capacity for a priori certain inference about causal matters (it simply stresses the idea that all we can ever come upon, e.g. in scientific investigation, are regularities of succession). For the point that matters here is that it has no positive ontological implication. Hume isn't saying that there's definitely no such thing as Causation, only that we have no experience of it of a sort that could give us any insight into its nature (contrary to the rationalist philosophers he was arguing against).

Immediately after quotation (15) he goes on to say that this is a violently paradoxical claim. And so it is, both for ordinary people who are convinced that they have direct experience of causal force, and for philosophers who are convinced that they have some genuine understanding of the nature of causal power in the world, and that 'the universe [is] in principle intellectually transparent'.[24] But the violent paradox lies in the epistemological claim that we have no idea of Causation at all, and that the necessary connection we suppose ourselves to discern in objects lies only in the mind. It really is quite extraordinary that it should upon reflection turn out that we have absolutely no idea of the ultimate nature of Causation, given that we are ourselves genuinely Causally efficacious agents, and live in a world governed by Causation, by some inflexible 'operating principle', a world in which 'everything is surely governed by steady, inviolable laws' (Philo, *Dialogues* 125/174). It is, however, a complete mistake to think that the 'violent paradox' consists in the claim that there is definitely no such thing as Causation in reality—no reason at all why reality, whatever its ultimate unknown nature, is regular in the way that it is. Poor old Hume—lumbered with such a claim.[25]

There's a another decisive passage in 1.4.2, which again requires care. Hume writes that

[23] For doubts, see Anscombe op. cit. and 23 below. For an important qualification to the claim that this is Hume's view, see 19.2.
[24] Craig 1987: 38.
[25] This reading is further confirmed by the comparable passage in the *Enquiry*, discussed on pp. 189–90 below.

(18)   the only conclusion we can draw from the existence of one thing to that of
       another, is by means of [1] the relation of cause and effect, which *shews*, that
       there is [2] a connexion betwixt them, and that *the existence of one is*
       dependent on that of the other. [3] The idea of this relation is deriv'd from
       past experience [of constant conjunction] ... (212/1.4.2.47).

[3] is the *idea* of the relation of cause and effect which we derive from experience of
constant conjunction. [1] is the relation of cause and effect itself, as defined in the
first definition of cause. It's the relation of cause and effect insofar as it's something of
which we have some positively contentful conception, something which we can
detect in things, something which can thereby 'shew' us something, something
which we can make use of in drawing conclusions.[26] What is of principal importance
is the distinction Hume makes between [1] and [2]. For [1]—the relation of cause and
effect in the sense of something which we can detect, and which can thereby 'shew' us
something—is explicitly distinguished from [2], i.e. the actual Causal connection, the
relation of *real existential dependence* between objects. If [1] is detected as holding
between two (types of) objects A and B, Hume says, that *shows* that something *other*
than [1], i.e. [2], is present. So [1] and [2] can't possibly be identified. Hume's claim,
to restate it, is that when the conditions laid down in the regularity-theory definition
of cause look to be fulfilled by A and B, we can *conclude* from that that there is a real
causal (Causal) connection between them, real existential dependence (whose intrinsic nature we cannot however know). *Observed constant conjunction* between A and
B shows us that, or is evidence that, there is *real causal connection* between A and B;
conjunction is *evidence* for connection. Clearly, then, constant conjunction and real
causal connection aren't the same thing, and Hume is not a 'Humean'.

(19)   Constant conjunction ... *proves a dependence* (4–5/1.1.1.8).

It doesn't constitute one.

(20)   Constant conjunction [between two things] *sufficiently proves*, that the
       one ... is the cause of the other (174/1.3.15.9).

Constant conjunction is *evidence*—good evidence, a sufficient proof—of causal
connection. It's not the same thing. If constant conjunction of A and B were the
same thing as causal connection between A and B, it couldn't do anything as weak as
'sufficiently prove' causal connection between them.

(21)   We are never sensible of any connection between causes and effects, and ...
       'tis only by our experience of their constant conjunction, [that] we can
       arrive at any knowledge of this relation (247/1.4.5.30).

---

[26] See 21 for the point that the two definitions of cause are only held to capture what causation is so far
as it's something of which we have some positively contentful conception, some more than merely 'relative'
idea. Hume explicitly states that they fail to capture the nature of causation as it is in itself, in reality.

There's more to causal connection than constant conjunction, but this is all the knowledge we can have of it. We are ignorant of the nature of things, as any sceptic knows. We fall short.

That's one very clear implication of these passages. Another is that there's something importantly right about a point made by Rosenberg and Beauchamp discussed in 8. This is the point that Hume sometimes distinguishes—in a way that seems very odd to us—between [1] causal relations ('the relation of cause and effect'), on the one hand, and [2] the operations of nature, or the actual connection between objects whereby 'the existence of one is dependent on that of the other', on the other hand. He makes just such a distinction in passage (18).

The explanation of this fact has been provided. When Hume makes such a distinction, by [1], the 'relation of cause and effect', he means the relation of cause and effect so far as it is anything to us, positively-contentfully speaking, and accordingly distinguishes it from [2], the actual connection between objects in virtue of which 'the existence of one is dependent on that of the other'.

The reason why it's important to note his tendency to make such a distinction is that it makes the following way of putting things seem possible. 'Yes, Hume does indeed hold a regularity theory of causation. He does indeed hold that "the relation of cause and effect" is (first definition) just a matter of regular succession between objects, of a sort (second definition) which affects the mind in a certain way. But he *also*, and fully compatibly with this, believes in Causation—in something in the objects which is not just this regularity, given which they are regular in the way they are. He just doesn't *call* this "the relation of cause and effect", for he uses this expression in the theory-of-ideas-sanctioned way. He calls it "the ultimate connexion" between them ("the uniting principle", the "reason of the conjunction" of objects, etc.) He doesn't call it "the relation of cause and effect" because by "the relation of cause and effect" he means the relation of cause and effect so far as it's something of which we have a positively contentful conception.'

I think this is an important part of the truth about Hume's text. It solves many difficulties. One reason why it can't be the whole truth is that Hume later makes such claims as that experience and observation can give us no 'acquaintance with the nature of cause and effect' (68/7.18). Here, by 'cause and effect', he means the actual unknown 'ultimate connexion'—since experience and observation do give us acquaintance with regular succession, and also with the feeling of determination in the mind. This matter will be discussed in Part 3.

The complexity of Hume's text produces many complications in commentary, but the basic point is simple. The 'necessity-we-attribute' is only in the mind. The relation of cause and effect *so far as we have any positive conception of it* is fully captured by the two definitions of cause. There is (of course) such a thing as Causation, the 'ultimate force and efficacy of nature' (159/1.3.14.8). There is natural necessity, in that sense. But its nature is perfectly unknown to us insofar as it's something more than regular succession.

Those who are feeling the force of the adage *exemplum docet, exempla obscurant* should skip to Part 3 (they may soon feel it again). Those who are still unconvinced may consider this: we should perhaps grant that Hume's explicit discussion of causation in the *Treatise* is essentially contestable. It may be very hard to see—to feel—the force of the present account of Hume until one has seen that it's unavoidable, given (a) the nature of his strictly non-committal scepticism with regard to questions about what may or may not exist, (b) his connected remarks about what we may intelligibly *suppose* to exist, as opposed to what we may contentfully *conceive* of, (c) his natural pre-philosophical—but *also fully philosophically endorsed*—realism or at least basic realism with respect to external objects,[27] (d) his entirely unquestioned belief that there must be something about the nature of reality in virtue of which it is regular in the way that it is—i.e. Causation, and (e) his constant use of referring expressions referring to Causation. To these must be added (f) his careful rephrasal of his position in the *Enquiry* in response to misunderstanding of the *Treatise*.[28] For this rephrasal contains no support for the 'standard' view at all (as I'll shortly try to show). It's not seen by Hume as a significant revision of his earlier views, and he endorsed it as a final statement of his 'philosophical statements and principles' in his plea to future readers—his 'Advertisement', his warning or notice—at the beginning of the *Enquiry*.

This said, I realize that it may not be thought possible to win the argument decisively on the ground of Hume's explicit discussion of causation in the *Treatise*. For although there is a great deal of direct evidence for the present view (e.g. (e)), and massive—decisive—indirect evidence (e.g. (a), (b), (c), (f)), and although the apparent counter-evidence can be fully accounted for, it is arguable that the standard view is also compatible with the evidence of the explicit discussion of causation.

15.6 Conclusion

In sum: Hume doesn't hold anything like the strong, realist (ontological), regularity theory of causation in the *Treatise*. He believes there is such a thing as Causation (natural necessity) in reality, but that we can't know anything about its nature. This claim is of course, and as always, in some tension with his view that the notion of Causation or power in the objects is 'unintelligible' (E-unintelligible). But the appearance of tension is superficial, because to say that the notion of Causation is unintelligible is simply to say that we have (given his theory of ideas) no positive, descriptively contentful conception of the nature of Causation (apart from regular succession), and to say this is not to say that it doesn't exist, or that we can know that

[27] See again (e.g.) 187/1.4.2.1, 218/1.4.2.57, and also 222–4/1.4.3.9.–10. To say that Hume naturally believes in external objects is not to say that the belief somehow doesn't really count for him, philosophically speaking. It's to say that he really does believe in the existence of external objects.
[28] On the issue of the priority of the *Enquiry* see further Appendix C, §2.

it doesn't exist, or that we can't achieve any reference to 'it' at all. It's not to say that we can't intelligibly *suppose* that it exists (6.5), or that we can't possess a 'relative' idea of it. We do possess a 'relative' idea of it: it is that in reality—the 'ultimate force and efficacy of nature' (159/1.3.14.8)—in virtue of which reality is regular in the way that it is.

On balance, it's best to represent Hume as claiming only that causation *so far as we know about it in the objects* is nothing but regular succession, while assuming (with Newton and others) that there is something more to it in fact. He says that

(i)   this multiplicity of resembling instances... constitutes the very essence of power or connexion (163/1.3.14.16);

that

(ii)   necessity... is nothing but an internal impression of the mind (165/1.3.14.20);

that this necessary

(iii)   connexion, tie, or energy lies merely in ourselves (266/1.4.7.5);

that it is

(iv)   the constant conjunction of objects, along with the determination of the mind, which constitutes a physical necessity (171/1.3.14.33).

All these claims are remarks about the true and highly surprising origin (the impression-source) of our supposedly genuinely contentful *idea* of Causation or power or necessity. They all require the addition 'so far as we have any notion of it, so far as it is (positively-contentfully) anything to us'. They're all entirely compatible with the view that there is power or Causation in objects. The point is the same: even though there is or may be such a thing, that's not what our supposed idea of power or Causation is really an idea of, contrary to the convictions of those rationalist philosophers who believe in intelligible causes. Our idea of necessity simply can't mean or reach out to Causation in the way we think, given its origins. It's

(v)   not possible for us ever to form the most distant idea of... necessity... consider'd as a quality in bodies (165–6/1.3.14.22);
(vi)   if we pretend... to have any *just idea* of this efficacy, we must produce some instance, wherein the efficacy is plainly discoverable to the mind, and its operations obvious to our consciousness or sensation. By the refusal of this, we acknowledge, that the idea is impossible and imaginary (157–8/1.3.14.6).

It's impossible to form a just—i.e. accurate and empirically warranted idea—of real causal efficacy; the idea we think we have is in fact a product of the Imagination.

What about the following three passages?

(vii)   the constant conjunction of objects determines their causation (173/1.3.15.1)

(viii)   constant conjunction [is that] on which the relation of cause and effect totally depends (173/1.3.15.1)

(ix)   there must be a constant union betwixt the cause and effect. 'Tis chiefly this quality, that constitutes the relation (173/1.3.15.5)

In (vii) the use of 'determine' is epistemological, like the other two uses in the paragraph from which it's taken. 'Determines their causation' means 'establishes their causal relatedness'. Hume's claim is his standard claim that we determine that (and which) objects are causally (Causally) connected by establishing that they're constantly conjoined. (viii) and (ix) are summary abbreviations that are as such particularly likely to mislead, but the underlying idea is the same.[29] Note that the claim in (viii) is not that there is nothing but constant conjunction 'in the objects'; to think that would be to ignore the force of the word 'depends'. It's the relation of cause and effect *qua* positively contentful human concept that totally depends on constant conjunction—the relation of cause and effect as defined in the two definitions of cause. The phrase 'the relation of cause and effect' is used in the same way in the passage discussed on p. 156 above ('the only conclusion we can draw from the existence of one thing to that of another, is by means of the relation of cause and effect, which *shews*, that there is a connexion betwixt them' 212/1.4.2.46). Constant conjunction *shows* that there is a causal connection between them; it doesn't constitute the causal connection as it is in itself in the objects. When two (types of) objects qualify for being counted as standing in the relation of cause and effect, by being constantly conjoined, that shows that there is a connection between them. (viii) states that constant conjunction is that on which the relation of cause and effect totally depends, so far as we have any idea or conception of it.

The force of (ix) is similar: it's chiefly constant union, that constitutes the relation of cause and effect, so far as we have any idea of it—so far as it is anything to us, and capturable in a definition which is contentful on the terms of the theory of ideas.

Back come the defenders of the standard view. 'If the idea we have can't mean the thing in question, then it seems we can't talk about it at all. In particular, it seems that we can't say, *of* something that we can't mean, *that* we can't mean it.' But Hume grants, precisely and soundly, that we can.[30] This is the 'Meaning Tension'. We can suppose that a certain something exists, believe it exists, have reason to believe it does (in our looser sense of 'have reason'),[31] successfully refer to it if it does, and hence 'mean' it, even while failing to mean it in the sense of having any *empirically contentful* positive conception of its nature. There's no inconsistency here (nor any real tension). Hume, Locke, Newton, and Kant all agree on this (along with many

---

[29] They may be read in the light of the point brought out by Rosenberg and Beauchamp and discussed on p. 88 above.

[30] See also the discussion of *Enquiry* 77/7.29 on p. 191 below.

[31] Note, though, Hume's own use on 28/1.2.1.4–5, quoted on pp. 50–1 above.

others). Their understanding of this issue is superior to that of large numbers of philosophers in the meaning-empiricism-befuddled twentieth century.

Those who are still suspicious of the Meaning Tension should bear in mind that one has to posit it in any case, independently of one's account of Hume's view of causation, for it arises at a very general level from the tension between his scepticism and his theory of ideas. But there is—finally—a dramatic illustration of it in the context of discussion of causation. Hume claims that the causal 'connexion, tie, or energy lies merely in ourselves' (266/1.4.7.5), and goes on to say that

(22)   it appears, that when we say we desire to know *the ultimate and operating principle*, as something, which resides in the external object, we either contradict ourselves, or talk without a meaning (267/1.4.7.5).[32]

Then, five lines later, he makes another entirely non-ironic, straightforwardly referring use of a Causation expression, of exactly the sort his strict theory of ideas has to rule out as contradictory or meaningless. He makes the purely epistemological claim that

(23)   in the most usual conjunctions of cause and effect we are as ignorant of *the ultimate principle, which binds them together*, as in the most unusual [conjunctions]. (267/1.4.7.6)

This is the statement of someone who takes it as obvious that there must be some such 'ultimate principle', and merely wishes to insist, over and over again, that we're entirely ignorant of its nature and can't make any positively or descriptively contentful claim about its nature—despite the highly paradoxical nature of this claim and the convictions of many previous philosophers.

It may finally be said that this whole discussion overlooks the large scale dialectical movement of the *Treatise*. On this view, when Hume discusses causation in 1.3, he makes use of the assumption that there are objects in the realist (or basic-realist) sense, in order to make the point that even if we suppose that there are such objects we can't suppose that we can understand or refer to anything like Causation, conceived of as a quality of such objects. But (the objection continues) this discussion

---

[32] This is very precise. We're involved in *contradiction* if we take the term to have clear meaning *as applied to the external object*, because, however unwittingly, we're using a term that, given its impression-source, essentially means something *non*-external in the mind. So we're treating something entirely internal and mental as external and non-mental: contradiction. So too, if we take it that we manage to 'hit' the external object—that we succeed in talking about the external object in using the term—then we *ipso facto talk without a meaning*, because the term we use corresponds to no empirically or positively descriptively contentful conception of anything in the object. Compare the claim that we '*necessarily* involve ourselves in *contradictions* and *absurdities*' when we conjecture about 'the essence and composition of external bodies' (2.2.6.2/366). These terms aren't expostulatory flourishes. The sense in which there is contradiction has just been noted, and 'absurdity' corresponds to 'talking without a theory-of-ideas-warranted meaning' (note that the bodies here must be realist or basic-realist bodies; they can't be pc objects or pcc objects).

is in a sense superseded *(aufgehoben)* by the discussion in 1.4.2, where objects themselves suffer the same fate as Causation (already prefigured at the end of 1.2). Thus the apparently referring uses of Causation terms are temporarily permitted, along with the apparently realist (or basic-realist) use of 'object', but only as part of an overall argument that says 'Even if there are realist (or basic-realist) objects, you can't know or even conceive of any causal power in them; but in fact you can't even know or *even conceive* of such objects either, so the problem doesn't really arise after all.'

The trouble with this view is that this account ignores Hume's scepticism. It has the consequence that Hume turns out to be some kind of dogmatic or committed (strict) idealist after all, although his non-committal scepticism forbids this. This can be shown as follows: (1) he certainly holds that 'the objects' exist in some sense. (2) On the present view, he holds that the *only possible meaning* of the word 'objects' is objects understood in some idealist sense. (3) Hence 'the objects' definitely are just idealist objects. It is a sufficient objection to this view that it fails to take account of Hume's scepticism with respect to knowledge claims about the ultimate nature of reality; it may be added that it is in any case magnificently at odds with the spirit of the text considered independently of those passages which are explicitly to do with the ontologically non-committal nature of scepticism.

There are many more apparently referring uses of Causation terms in the *Treatise*, but I'll now consider the *Enquiry*. Given that the central points of the present interpretation are now in place—the Meaning Tension, the nature of Hume's scepticism, the nature of his realist or basic-realist assumptions—the rest of the discussion is mostly straightforward, and consists principally in the application of these points to a series of quotations. 20 and 21 suffice to make the point. But there are a number of other interesting quotations in 16–19. Many of the points made in Part 2 recur in Part 3, because the two parts are designed to be independent of each other.

PART 3

Causation in the *Enquiry*

16

Enquiry Section 4: the question of irony

According to the standard view, Hume holds that there is no such thing as Causation in the objects. The first question that arises, when one turns to the *Enquiry*, and puts aside the point that his scepticism rules out this view, is whether one may or should take at face value the repeated and apparently straightforwardly referring use of expressions that purport to refer to Causation in the objects—expressions like 'power', 'force', 'ultimate springs or principles', 'ultimate cause', 'energy', 'tie', 'ultimate principle', 'operating principle', 'principle which binds', 'principles productive of natural phenomena', and so on. In what follows I'll consider some of Hume's apparently referring uses of these expressions, in the hope that it will become clear that there's no good reason not to take them at face value.[1] As in Part 2, I'll sometimes use '[REF]' to flag such referring expressions, '[EP]' to signal epistemological remarks, and '[NI]' to signal comments which (I claim) are part of the most natural interpretation of what Hume says.

In Section 4 Part 1 Hume writes that

(1) no philosopher, who is rational and modest, has ever pretended to assign [REF] *the ultimate cause* of any natural operation, or to show distinctly the action of [REF] *that power, which produces* any single effect in the universe (30/4.12)

Agreeing here with Newton (cf. p. 186), he goes on to say that we can indeed greatly simplify our account of the workings of nature, reducing it to 'a few general causes',

(2) but as to [REF] *the causes of these general causes*, we should [EP] in vain attempt their discovery...These [REF] *ultimate springs and principles* are [EP] totally shut up from human curiosity and enquiry.[2]

---

[1] The claim is not that any use of these expressions commits one to the view that they're meaningful in a way Hume denies. One can talk of 'alleged or supposed powers in objects' without committing oneself either to the existence of such powers or to the idea that such expressions are truly meaningful in such contexts. The argument is concerned with the apparently straightforwardly referring uses.

[2] 30/4.12. One can argue that the reference to 'a few general causes' is to be understood in a merely regularity-theory way, but then it simply becomes clearer that the reference to 'the causes of these causes' is a reference to causes understood in a non-regularity-theory way as those features of nature (those 'ultimate

But [NI] they certainly exist. Theorists who detect irony may demur, but they ignore Hume's admiration for Newton, and the fact that Hume wrote the first *Enquiry* specifically to clear up he misunderstanding of the *Treatise* (see pp. 10–11 above). Four paragraphs later Hume writes that nature

(3) [EP] conceals from us those [REF] *powers and principles on which the influence of... objects entirely depends....* It is allowed on all hands that there is [EP] no known connexion between the sensible qualities and [REF] *the secret powers* [of bodies] (33/4.16)

This seems like a very clear referring use of Causation terms: Causation exists [NI], but we can know nothing of its ultimate nature.

There is a mildly ironic tone to the passage from which this quotation is taken, and its import may be thought unclear for this reason. In fact the force of the irony is entirely epistemological. It's directed against those who think that we might be able to *know* the nature of Causation in the objects—know the nature of those powers and principles on which the influence of objects entirely depends—not against the idea that there is (must be) such a thing. This can, however, be disputed, because Hume's claim that the notion of power is actually 'unintelligible' (at least when the power is thought of as something in objects) is also in play. And since statements like the one just quoted are arguably a kind of nonsense, given this claim, the irony may be thought to be directed not only against those who believe that we can know something about the nature of power, but also against the very use of any term purporting to refer to any such putative power.

This interpretation fails to take account of the 'Meaning Tension' (12.1): Causation terms may manage to *refer* to something which we can intelligibly *suppose* to exist, and which Hume firmly believes to exist, even if we can form no positive *conception* of the nature of this something on the terms of the theory of ideas. Certainly this can be said to give rise to a 'Meaning Tension': Hume claims that Causation terms are 'unintelligible' or 'meaningless', as applied to objects, and yet he applies them to objects (so too Locke says that the word 'gold' 'comes to have no signification at all', when used to refer to the real essence of gold). And it is perhaps not surprising that many commentators have thought that the best way to deal with this apparent inconsistency is to deny that it really exists, and so to take all the apparently referring uses of Causation terms as provisional or tongue-in-cheek or uses 'in a loose and popular sense' (33/4.16n.) that is later renounced. But, first, here Hume follows Locke, who used 'gold' to refer to gold while claiming that the word 'comes to have no signification at all' when used to refer to the real essence of gold (see pp. 46–7 above). Secondly, the Meaning Tension threatens his use of the words 'object' and 'body' as much as his use of Causation terms (see 13). Thirdly, once one grants the point that to say that X is unintelligible or inconceivable or

springs and principles') *in virtue of which* it is regular in its behaviour. Cf. the quotations from Newton in 20.

incomprehensible is simply to say that although X surely exists (or at the very least may exist), it's something of whose nature we can form no positively contentful conception on the terms of the theory of ideas, it becomes clear that the Meaning Tension is really no tension at all. It merits the description 'tension' only because of our tendency to assimilate Hume's use of 'unintelligible' to our own stronger philosophical use, according to which to say that the idea of something is unintelligible is to suggest that it's incoherent in some way, and that the thing it purports to be an idea of doesn't and can't really exist.

There are present-day positivists and anti-realists who would approve of this assimilation. They go further than Hume, who had too much good sense to do what they do. I don't think all the blame for the positivistic misinterpretation of Hume should be pinned on Mach (see p. 13 above), because Hume provides grounds for it in the *Treatise*. It is nevertheless odd, when discussing the *Enquiry*, to find oneself in the position of attacking an interpretation of its content for which there doesn't appear to be any serious textual support at all.

One objection may be this: 'Hume talks *as if* Causation (powers and forces) exists for ease of exposition, granting its existence to his opponents simply for the sake of argument, so that he can then hammer home his epistemological point that even if it does exist we can know nothing about its nature. But he doesn't really believe in it at all.' This view is probably irrefutable, because it denies simply the relevance and force of all the direct evidence against it. The trouble is that there's no good reason to believe it. There's no good reason to claim that Hume (the admirer of Newton) either believes that there is in fact definitely nothing at all about the nature of reality in virtue of which it is regular in the way that it is, so that its regularity is an objective fluke from moment to moment, or even that there *may* be nothing about the nature of reality in virtue of which it is regular in the way that it is, so that the regularity *may* be an objective fluke from moment to moment. He is, certainly, prepared to grant, and concerned to insist, that we can't know whether the 'original, inherent principle of order [lies] in thought or in matter', but he's very clear on the point that there is some such principle of order: 'chance has no place, on any hypothesis, sceptical or religious.'[3]

It may be worth adding the following point. When Hume speaks of inertial force, 'that wonderful force or power, which would carry on a moving body for ever in a continued change of place' (33/4.16) his use of 'wonderful' may be thought to involve irony about the Causation term 'force or power'. But, first, he speaks without irony when he says in the *Treatise* that 'reason is nothing but a wonderful and unintelligible instinct' (179/1.3.16.9); there's no reason at all to think his use of the word 'wonderful' is ironic. Secondly, he may have had particular reservations about the notion of

---

[3] Philo in the *Dialogues* (125/174). This quotation provides an opportunity to vary a point made in 9: it would be an elementary error to think that there is an incompatibility between 'Any thing may produce any thing', as Hume intends it, and 'chance has no place on any ... sceptical ... hypothesis'.

inertial force as a real force in nature, as opposed to other forces (cf. Wright 1983: §16). Against this, however, we must set the straightforward reference in Section 7, where he takes the same line about *vis inertiae* as about the 'active power...of gravity': when we speak of 'a *vis inertiae*, we only mark [certain observed]...facts, without pretending to have any idea of *the inert power*' (73/7.25n.).

Thirdly, the irony in this passage is complex; it doesn't have the ontological implication it's sometimes supposed to have. I think it's worth trying to set out this point in some detail, for even those who find it implausibly complicated may be persuaded that unanalysed attributions of irony establish very little. I suggest that the force of the irony is entirely epistemological. Insofar as irony is directed against the Causation term itself, it's directed against it simply because Causation is something of which [EP] (i) 'we cannot form the most distant [positively or descriptively contentful] conception (33/4.16). Now, given the theory of ideas, (i) entails (ii) that *the thing we (or certain philosophers) think we positively-content-fully mean* by 'power' *can't exist at all*. Why? Because (iii) given the way we intend the expression 'power', no real power in the objects could possibly correctly count as *the thing we think we mean* by 'power' unless it had the following property: the property of being *something such that we were **right** in thinking that we had some sort of positive conception of it*. But (iv) there *is* no power in the objects that has the property specified in (iii), because we have no positive conception at all of power or Causation in the objects, as remarked in (i); the (contentful) meaning we put into the word 'power' derives wholly from an impression of reflexion in the mind.

Ostensibly ontological claim (ii) follows: *the thing we think we positively-content-fully mean* when we use the term 'power' can't exist at all; irony about our misapprehension is accordingly in place. However, (ii) is entirely compatible with the view (Hume's view) that there is in fact something the term is reaching out to referentially, something which certainly exists, but of which we cannot 'form the most distant conception'. So the thing we in our presumptuous ignorance think we *positively-contentfully* mean cannot exist; but there is of course causal power in the objects, of which we have no positive conception. What provokes Hume's irony is the failure of so many to see that true philosophical modesty requires us to acknowledge that we can at best only have a 'relative' and therefore (according to the theory of ideas) positive-descriptive-content-lacking idea of the power.

17

Enquiry Section 4: Causation and inductive scepticism

After speaking of

(4) our natural state of ignorance with regard to *the power and influence* of all objects (37/4.21)

Hume goes on to give an argument against the appeal to past experience in justifying induction that makes essential use of the idea that Causation ('power', etc.) exists. He argues as follows. Although particular experiences of objects at particular times show us

(5) that those particular objects, at that particular time, were endowed with... [REF] *powers and forces* (38/4.21)

we can never be sure that they will continue to have just those same powers in the future. The reason why induction cannot be justified by appeal to past experience, therefore, is that [REF]

(6) *the secret nature* [of bodies], and consequently all their effects and influence, may change (38/4.21)

between now and the next time we observe them. That is, the reason why induction is not rationally justifiable by appeal to past experience is *not* that bodies have no secret nature governing their effects and influence, so that anything might happen. On the contrary. Bodies do have a secret nature which determines their effects and influence. The trouble with appeals to past experience is that past experience can never provide a guarantee that *the secret nature* will not change, bringing change in the effects and influence of bodies.

In full, Hume's claim is that the 'secret nature [of bodies], and consequently all their effects and influence, may change, *without any change in their sensible qualities*' (38/4.21). One might wonder how *all* their effects and influence could change without any change in their sensible qualities—without any change in the way they appear. But the idea is clear: a body could go on looking and feeling the same to us when not involved in any obvious causal interaction with some other body, while its unobservable nature (its 'secret nature') had changed. The bread may still look the same even if it is no longer nourishing, but poisonous.

Even a stone lying motionless on the ground is involved in all sorts of causal interactions, and the ways it looks and feels are among its effects and influences. To this extent, Hume hasn't put the point very well. But the idea is quite clear, and the illustrative point of the quotation is unaffected. In this passage Hume is appealing to the Causation notion of the power-and-force-grounding-or-involving secret nature of bodies, and to the idea that this secret nature could conceivably change from one moment to the next without our realizing it, in order to make the point that induction can't be rationally justified by appeals to past experience.

Clearly, then, there is no necessary connection between inductive scepticism, as expounded here, and a regularity theory of causation. This argument for inductive scepticism appeals essentially to Causation—to an essentially non-regularity-theory notion of causation.

In so doing it constitutes another proof that Hume is committed to Causation. Causation deniers can't allow any sense in which things have a *nature* at all, a nature given which they behave in one way rather than another. Hume says that 'our senses inform us of the colour, weight, and consistence of bread; but neither sense nor reason can ever inform us of *those qualities which fit it* for the nourishment and support of a human body' (33/4.16). Causation deniers, by contrast, can't allow that things have qualities which fit them for anything at all.

18

Enquiry Sections 5–6: undiscovered and undiscoverable

In Section 5 Hume says that

(7) [REF] *the particular powers, by which all natural operations are performed*, [EP] never appear to the senses (42/5.3)

And yet [NI] they exist. He goes on to say that experience can [EP] never give any idea or knowledge of

(8) [REF] *the secret power*, by which the one object produces the other (42/5.4)

And yet [NI] it exists.

Some may still take the epistemological claim about our ignorance to amount to (or entail) an ontological claim about the definite nonexistence of any such secret power. This interpretative reflex may die hard, and it will always be arguable that it finds some support in Hume's theory of ideas. But only on the false assumption that 'X is unintelligible' in Hume's (entirely Lockean) sense entails 'There is really no such thing as X, despite the apparently referring expression "X". The trouble is that the assumption that there can be nothing unintelligible by us is directly at odds with Hume's strictly sceptical position on what we can know to exist or know not to exist, other than perceptions, and the manner and context of his apparent (or patent) referring uses of Causation terms make such a reading untenable even when one considers the question independently of any appeal to the principles of his scepticism.

If it's now objected—again—that Hume the sceptic can no more claim that Causation definitely does exist than that it doesn't, this may be enthusiastically conceded. The present claim is only that Hume firmly *believes* in the existence of Causation. His natural conviction sits comfortably with his formal scepticism about *knowledge* claims.[1] The standard view of Hume has it that he claims to prove and hence to know that there's no such thing as Causation. This is not compatible with his scepticism.[2]

---

[1] *Why* is he so convinced? Presumably for the sorts of reasons given in 5 and 8 above and 22 below.

[2] Quine is arguably a true Humean, on the present view: '*That* there have been regularities, for whatever reason, is an established fact of science ... *Why* there have been regularities is an obscure question, for it is hard to see what would count as an answer' (1969: 126). Indeed. But to be an outright regularity theorist is to claim that there is a clear answer to the question, which is that there is, definitely, no reason at all why there is regularity.

Later in Section 5, Hume writes that

(9) [REF] *the powers and forces*, by which the [course of nature] is governed, [are] [EP] wholly unknown to us (54/5.21)

But [NI] they exist. (How could they have the property of being unknown to us if they didn't exist?) It's just that we know nothing about their ultimate nature. So far as 'external objects' are concerned,

(10) we are [EP] ignorant of [REF] *those powers and forces*, on which [the] regular course and succession of objects *totally depends.* (55/5.22)

This passage, which has already been quoted several times, seems decisive. It follows from (10) that regular succession is not all there is to causation in the external objects: for regular succession in the external objects 'totally depends' on the existence of certain powers or forces which are distinct from it and which give rise to it.[3]

Here again Hume's confidence that we can know nothing of these powers and forces derives partly from his awareness that while our experiences *may* be produced by something like physical objects ordinarily understood, e.g. something like Lockean objects, things may be much stranger than that; we can't even rule out Berkeley's hypothesis that the powers and forces are ultimately entirely mental in character.[4]

It should perhaps be noted that this use of the word 'depends' is presumably not meant to indicate any sort of causal dependence. Perhaps the way in which regular succession depends on powers and forces may be supposed to be something like the way the properties of a substance like mercury are held to 'depend' on its 'essential' property of having a certain atomic structure (having atomic number 80). However that may be, the essential point Hume is making is simply that there is something in the nature of things—Causation—in virtue of which things are regular in the way they are, something which is therefore not just the fact of the regularity. One could express this by saying that regular succession is a *manifestation* or even an *aspect* of Causation, and 'depends' on it in that sense.[5]

In Section 7, Hume considers

(11) how soon nature [EP] throws a bar to all our enquiries concerning causes, and reduces us to an acknowledgement of our ignorance (61/7.2)

There's no irony here, even if old interpretative reflexes may make it seem that there is. Hume thinks we can learn a lot about causes, in the sense of learning about

---

[3] Recall that to suppose the contrary—to suppose as a realist that causation in the objects is just regular succession—is to fall into the absurdity of strong regularity realism (see 5). In 22 the argument of 5 is taken further: the absurdity charge does not just affect the realist view; it affects any view at all that accepts that there is real regularity—whatever the nature of reality.

[4] Cf. 84/1.3.5.2, 153/12.11, and pp. 99–100 above.

[5] Cf. 13.2. Compare McGinn's discussion of the relations between a substance's essential property and its 'secondary properties' (McGinn 1974–5).

regularities of succession, but we can never get beyond experienced regular succession, so far as our knowledge of causal power is concerned. But of course [NI] such causal power really exists, as something over and above regular succession. It's that feature of the world *given which* it is regular in its behaviour, on which its regularity 'totally depends'. If causes were just a matter of regular succession, there'd be no bar at all, nor any ignorance.

This last claim may be disputed, because it's true, and important, that when Hume talks of our ignorance of causes, he isn't always making the point that these are forever unknowable,

(12)   [EP] *totally* shut up from human curiosity and enquiry. (30/4.12)

Sometimes (and it's arguable that quotation (11) is an example of this) he's only making the point that there are particular *causal connections*—between A and B, say—which we cannot know of simply because A-type and B-type events are too minute or too far away for us to observe *constant-conjunction* relations between them. Such *causal connections* are accordingly unestablishable, because it's only by detecting *constant-conjunction* relations that we can have any knowledge of the existence of real causal connections. Such causal-connection-indicating constant conjunctions—and hence such causal connections themselves—are hidden 'simply by reason of their minuteness or remoteness' (87/8.13, 132/1.3.12.5), but are not in principle undiscoverable.[6]

This is certainly part of what Hume is saying. At the same time, however, he holds that there's a fundamental sense in which the *nature* of real causal connection or causal power is always and forever undiscoverable by us, for true detection of it would have to make us capable of something of which we know we will always be incapable: a priori certain inferences about causal matters (see 11). So the sense in which we may be able to gain knowledge of real causal connections which are at present concealed from us because they're too minute or too remote is a limited one. All we will be able to acquire, by coming to detect constant-conjunction relations between things at present too minute or too remote for us to detect, is knowledge of the *existence* of certain real causal connections (and of what particular things, e.g. As and Bs, Cs and Ds, they hold between). This won't amount to any sort of knowledge of the *nature* of real causal connections.

The two uses of 'causes'—as things which may be only contingently unknown (and perhaps contingently unknowable) and as things which are necessarily unknown—are arguably well-illustrated in the *Enquiry* (30–1/4.12; see quotation (2) above). The

---

[6] For this distinction between real causal connection and constant conjunction, and Hume's use of it, see the discussion of 212/1.4.2.47 on p. 156 above, and e.g. 174/1.3.15.9 and 247/1.4.5.30. Causal connection is not the same as constant conjunction. Rather, a constant conjunction between two things (two types of thing) indicates that there is a (real) causal connection between them. Familiarity with the 'standard' view is likely to hinder a proper grasp of this simple and fundamental point.

essential point to retain is simple and familiar. Hume allows that there's a sense in which 'secret causes' can be discovered (given their constant-conjunction manifestations) even if they're at present unknown. But he also holds, as remarked, that there is a sense in which the nature of Causation—causal power—is forever undiscoverable, although it's something real. At certain points he appears to suggest that 'causes' may be unknown simply because of their minuteness or remoteness—in which case they are in principle discoverable. It would, however, be a great mistake to argue from this fact to the conclusion that he can only ever mean constant-conjunction relations by 'powers', 'forces', and so on. The two main reasons why these will remain forever unknowable by us remain untouched.[7]

Suppose one concedes, for the sake of argument, that Hume is really—and always—talking only of unknown but not unknowable constant conjunctions, when he talks in plural terms of 'secret powers', 'ultimate springs and principles', 'wholly unknown…powers and forces, by which the course of nature is govern'd', and so on. This won't help the standard view of Hume much, because a survey of the quotations in Chapters 17–20 that contain the clearest apparently referring uses of Causation terms finds five plural uses, and sixteen singular uses, and whatever the case with respect to the plural uses, it's hopelessly implausibe to suppose that Hume is only talking about merely unknown constant conjunctions, unknown because too small or too remote, where the singular uses are concerned. See, for example, quotation (13), which follows in the next paragraph.[8]

I hope any remaining doubts on this issue will be removed by Hume's comments on his two definitions of cause, discussed in 21. I'll end this chapter with a passage which occurs at the beginning of Hume's search (63–73/7.5–7.25) for the impression from which the idea of Causation (necessary connection, power, etc.) is derived. This is another passage which appears to suffice on its own to establish the present view. Hume remarks that

(13)   the scenes of the universe are continually shifting, and one object follows another in an uninterrupted succession; but [REF] *the power or force, which actuates the whole machine*, is [EP] entirely concealed from us, and never discovers itself in any of the sensible qualities of body. (63–4/7.8)

Although Causation 'actuates' the world or universe, we can't 'comprehend' or *representationally encompass* its nature in any way at all, in our idea. We can refer

---

[7]   (1) They have the 'AP' property, and (2) we can't even decide between the realist and the idealist accounts of the nature of the world, let alone any others there might be. It's true that Hume sometimes says that certain things are 'unintelligible' simply because too minute to observe, and that unintelligibility therefore doesn't necessarily entail irreducible inaccessibility. But the two main reasons for holding that the true nature of causal power must be forever unknowable remain.

[8]   Or (1), (15), (17), (20), (23), (24), (26)–(28), and (30). This is not how one talks if one's fundamental thesis is that really there are only constant conjunctions, all the way down, and no real relations of causal production or influence.

to it, but we can't form any sort of positive conception of its nature, insofar as this goes beyond its manifestation in the phenomena of regular succession. We can have a 'relative' idea of power or Causation; it is after all that thing, whatever its inmost nature, on which the observable regularity of nature 'totally depends' (55/5.22). But we can't have any positively contentful idea of it 'as it is in itself' (77/7.29 n.).

One of Locke's mistakes on this subject, according to Hume, was to think that the purely abstract argument to the effect 'that there must somewhere be a power capable of producing...new productions in matter' (64/7.8 n.) could be the origin of some sort of genuine idea of power 'as it is in itself'. In fact such an argument can only support a 'relative' idea of power.[9]

The next chapter consists mainly of more detailed illustrations of the point. Those who omit it should perhaps note the last paragraph of 19.1, and the short section 19.2.

---

[9] As remarked in 9, the question of what reason or experience can reveal about the source of order and regularity in the universe is the central question of the *Dialogues*; the idea that there might be no source or ground of order and regularity is never considered. The principal question is whether matter itself, rather than God, might contain the principle of order, and Philo's remark (quoted in 9) seems worth repeating: 'For aught we can know a priori, Matter may contain *the Source or Spring of Order originally*, within itself...; and there is no more Difficulty in conceiving, that the several Elements, from an internal unknown Cause, may fall into the most exquisite Arrangement, than to conceive that their Ideas, in the great, universal Mind, from a like internal, unknown Cause, may fall into that Arrangement' (55-6/46).

19

Enquiry Section 7: Causation and human beings

19.1 Will and force: a last look at irony

We have, Hume says, no knowledge of

(14) [REF] *the power or force*, by which [the will] operates

in controlling the body (65/7.12). To say this is of course to imply [NI] that there is such a force. Hume invariably talks in a thoroughgoing realist fashion about the mind as something which cannot but react as it does to exposure to impressions, given its nature. We are *determined* to respond in certain ways, given (ultimately inexplicable) *instincts* implanted in us by *nature* (cf. e.g. 55/5.22).[1] Everything he says about the mind is saturated with the presumption that there is something about the mind which is the reason why mental causation involves the particular regularities it does, something which is therefore not just the regularities themselves. Those who still think that Hume adopts a purely regularity theory of causation with respect to *non-mental* and *non-human* objects realistically conceived must certainly find it hard to be so sure that he adopts a purely regularity theory when he talks about the operation of human beings (mind, imagination, will, organs, limbs, and all). And then they're open to the objection that if one accepts some sort of non-regularity-theory view about the workings of human beings, it's bizarre not to adopt it about other physical objects; since if one is being some sort of realist about physical objects in general then one must surely grant that human beings are themselves (at least partly) physical objects, whatever else they may also be.[2] It's an entirely general point that

---

[1] See 12.3 for the point that he never accepted a bundle theory of mind (expanded in Strawson 2011: Part 2). See 14.2 for the point that he distinguishes, in a Newtonian way, between the 'principles of the association of ideas', which are fully statable, and the unknown 'ultimate' principles of operation of the mind.

[2] In quotation (17) below Hume explicitly compares the case of human beings and other objects. On 248–50/1.4.5.31–2 he argues that materialism is at least no worse off than dualism, and implies that it's better off. See also, again, the *Dialogues*: 'How could things have been as they are, were there not an original, inherent principle of order somewhere, in thought or in matter? And it is very indifferent to which of these we give the preference' (125/174): given our epistemic situation, we can have no decisive grounds for preferring the one to the other. See also Hume's neurological explanation of the principles of the association of ideas on 60–1/1.2.5.20, quoted on p. 140 above.

(15)   [EP] experience only *teaches* us, how one event constantly follows another; without instructing us in [REF] *the secret connexion, which binds them together*, and *renders them inseparable*.

The immediate context is a discussion of the influence of the will over the body; but the remark is worded to have quite general application.

It may possibly be thought to be open to ironic interpretation. And since defenders of the standard view will always find it easy to imagine irony in Hume's apparently straightforwardly referring use of Causation terms, in spite of the fact that he wrote the *Enquiry* to correct misunderstanding of the *Treatise*, it seems worthwhile to address the issue one more time.

Consider how easy it would have been for Hume, if his intentions had been generally ironic—or even if he had simply wished to record doubt about the reality of causal power—to write 'any' instead of 'the' (or 'this', 'that', 'those', etc.) in front of nearly all the apparently straightforwardly referring uses of Causation terms. Writing 'any' instead of 'the' immediately makes an ironic or ontologically non-committal reading far more natural and effective. In quotation (15) the implied ironic reading is: 'experience never instructs us in any (supposed, alleged, putative, piously-and-foolishly-hoped-for, in-fact-(ho-ho)-non-existent) secret connection, which binds them together, and renders them inseparable'. Substituting 'any' for 'the' ('that', etc.) greatly facilitates ironic interpretation, and immediately cancels any appearance of commitment to the existence of such a 'secret connexion'. Hume writes that 'when we reason a priori, and consider merely any object or cause, as it appears to the mind, independent of all observation, it never could suggest to us the notion of any distinct object, such as its effect; much less, show us the inseparable and inviolable connexion between them' (31/4.13). Why write 'the inseparable and inviolable connexion between them' when you could just as well write 'an inseparable and inviolable connexion between them'?

An equally effective alternative is to add the word 'supposed': to say, for example, that experience never instructs us in 'the supposed secret connexion, which binds [events] together, and renders them inseparable'. Again the suggestion of irony is greatly strengthened; again the existence implication is cancelled. The same treatment can be applied to nearly all the apparently referring uses of Causation terms quoted in Parts 2 and 3. Suitably modified, quotation (3) becomes: nature 'conceals from us those supposed powers and principles on which the influence of... objects entirely depends... there is no known connexion between the sensible qualities and any secret powers [of bodies]'. And so on.[3]

---

[3] (1) 'Any' for 'the', and for 'that' (or 'that supposed' for 'that'); (2) 'the supposed' for 'the'; (4) 'the supposed' for 'the'. In (5) it isn't possible; Hume's commitment to the existence of Causation is not easily weakened here, and the same goes for (6). (7) 'the supposed' for 'the'; (8) 'any' for 'the'; (9) 'the supposed' for 'the'; (10) very difficult to cancel the existence commitment, given 'totally depends'; (11) 'the supposed real cause' for 'the real cause'; and so on.

This seems to be yet another point that suffices to establish the present interpretation. Perhaps only the effects of custom on the Imagination (long exposure to a regular succession of understandable but incorrect accounts of Hume) can induce anyone to fail to see this. At the very least, Hume would have had to use 'any' instead of 'the'—or to add a word like 'supposed'—far more often than he does, for the irony view to be plausible. He isn't perverse. He is dismayed by being misunderstood, and is trying to make his position as clear as possible in the *Enquiry*, as remarked in 1. He means what he says.

He does sometimes use 'any'—see e.g. 73–4/7.26. But this use of 'any' is simply part of the standard epistemological insistence that there isn't any force or power in objects *of which we could have any knowledge*. It's followed in the next sentence by two of his usual apparently straightforwardly referring uses of Causation terms.[4]

To continue. Still talking about the way the will governs bodily motion, Hume remarks that 'we learn from anatomy, that the immediate object of power in voluntary motion, is not the member itself which is moved, but certain muscles, and nerves, and animal spirits, and, perhaps, something still more minute and more unknown'. This, he holds, furnishes

(16)   a...certain proof, that [REF] *the power, by which this whole operation is performed*..., is to the last degree [EP] mysterious and unintelligible. (66/7.14)

Again the point is merely epistemological. The power by which the operation is performed certainly exists, but it's entirely unknown, for we have no impression of it. Hence we have no positively contentful conception of its nature, hence it's 'unintelligible' (E-unintelligible); we know it only by its observable manifestations. We may grant that something may be held to be unintelligible simply because too minute, but this actually strengthens the point that unintelligibility doesn't entail non-existence. It doesn't threaten the fundamental sense in which Hume believed that the nature of power is forever unknowable by us.

Pursuing the question of the source of our *idea* of power, and still speaking of the causation involved in human action, Hume writes that

----

Note that this suggestion, phrased as it is, relies on our strongly dubitative sense of 'supposed', which is not Hume's (cf. the discussion of the distinction between supposing and conceiving in 6.5). At one point Hume does speak of 'the supposed tie or connection' (29/4.10), but here he's criticizing the view that there might be a connection of such a sort that we could hope for a priori *knowledge about what follows from what in nature*. He isn't questioning the idea that there is Causation, as quotations (1)–(3) above from the immediately following paragraphs sufficiently show.

[4] The same response applies to 63/7.6, first full paragraph, and 66/7.13. Even if Hume had consistently used 'any' instead of 'the', this would not have provided much support for the 'standard' view. The plausibility of the claim that Hume was (as a sceptic) committed to not ruling out the possible existence (R-intelligibility) of Causation—of something about reality in virtue of which it is regular in the way that it is— would have been undiminished.

(17)   [REF] *the power or energy,* by *which* [animal motion] is effected, like that in
       other natural events, is [EP] unknown and inconceivable.

So it can't be the source of our idea of power. We do in fact have a contentful idea
of power of some sort. But the content of this idea is derived from a feeling or
impression of determination in the mind, and so we can't suppose that it correctly
and descriptively-contentfully represents the power that is actually involved in
natural events. The nature of the power that is actually involved in natural events
remains unknown to us.

Hume makes the point over and over again. He is still discussing mental goings on
when he varies the particular point made in quotation (17), remarking that when we
call some thought or idea to mind

(18)   the manner, in which this operation is *performed,* [REF] *the power by which
       it is produced,* is [EP] entirely beyond our comprehension. (68/7.17)

There is such a power [NI]. For although we can have no access to it—we can only
have access to perceptions, and can't therefore have access to those workings of the
mind which are not themselves perceptions and in virtue of which perceptions arise
as they do—still there must (obviously) be *something* about the mind in virtue of
which it behaves as it does.[5] Clearly, we have no knowledge of the power by which the
mind operates, for such knowledge would have to involve a grasp of how it is that the
causes produce the effects they do—knowledge of a sort that would make a priori
certain inference about such matters possible.[6]

In the next paragraph, remarking again that the command of the mind both over
itself and over body is limited, Hume writes that

(19)   these limits are not known by *reason, or any acquaintance with the nature
       of cause and effect,* but only by experience and observation.

The natural reading is as follows: we have no acquaintance with the *nature of cause
and effect*; experience and observation give us no knowledge of it. It follows that the
nature of cause and effect cannot be just a matter of regular succession (Hume's first

---

[5] *viz.* the 'unintelligible ... [but nonetheless real] uniting principle among our perceptions' (169/
1.3.14.29).
[6] Cf. 11. There is arguably a certain degree of irony in this passage. Hume says that calling up some idea
appears to be '[1] a production of something out of nothing: Which implies a power so great, that it may
seem, at first sight, beyond the reach of any being, less than infinite. At least it must be owned, [2] that such
a power is not felt, nor known, nor even conceivable by the mind'; and some will take the irony in the first
part of this quotation to imply ironic questioning of the idea that the power referred to in the quotation in
the main text could even exist. But according to the most natural reading of this passage, the irony in (1) is
designed entirely to compel assent to (2)—to drive home the usual epistemological claim (of great
importance for Hume, since he has Locke among others to contend with on this point) that we can
know absolutely nothing about the true nature of the power governing *mental* operations; so that our
experience of thinking and willing cannot be supposed to provide us with any sort of genuinely contentful
idea of the power that is involved 'in ... natural events'.

definition of cause), of a kind that gives rise to certain feelings of determination or habits of inference in the mind (Hume's second definition). For experience and observation *do* give us acquaintance with these things. Regular succession (consisting of priority±contiguity relations and constant conjunction relations) is, precisely, observed; feelings of determination are, precisely, things which feature in our experience.

19.2 Resemblance, solidity, and force

It's arguable that a further important thought about the unknowability of power is influencing Hume, here and elsewhere. It can be brought out by means of a comparison of what he says about the idea of power with what he says about the idea of solidity in the *Treatise*, where he argues as follows: given the nature of the feelings or impressions that give rise to our idea of solidity, we cannot suppose that our idea of solidity in any way copyingly 'resembles' and thus descriptively-contentfully represents solidity as it is in itself in external objects. For, as he plausibly argues,

'Tis easy to observe, that tho' bodies are felt by means of their solidity, yet the feeling is a quite different thing from the solidity; and that they have not the least resemblance to each other.[7]

Exactly similarly, we can't suppose that any impression-based idea of power that we may have really 'resembles' power as it is in itself in the objects. And this is so even when we simply put to one side Hume's claim that this is because the impression from which the idea of power is derived is just a feeling of determination in the mind, as well as all the other main arguments for the claim that power (or necessary connection) in the objects must be unknowable.[8] For (here is the new point) suppose we claim that we *do* have some sort of impression of power deriving from the objects, given that

(20)   no animal [human or otherwise] can put external bodies in motion without the sentiment of a *nisus* or endeavour; and every animal has a sentiment or feeling from the stroke or blow of an external object, that is in motion . . . (78/7.29 n.)

Even if we grant this—even if we grant that there is some sense in which we can receive some sort of impression of power or force from our experience of action, or of the action on us of external objects, and grant, as Hume does, that it does indeed form part of our ordinary idea of power (which is accordingly 'confused')—we *still* can't suppose that this sentiment or feeling in any way *copyingly resembles* power as it is in the objects, in such a way as to give us a genuine positively contentful idea of its

---

[7] 230/1.4.4.13. He continues with a further argument on 231/1.4.4.14. Reid is very good on this point (see e.g. Reid 1764: §5.2, §5.4). See also Evans 1980: 268–71, discussed on pp. 233–4 below.

[8] i.e. because it has the 'AP property' (cf. 11); because we can't even decide between the Lockean or Berkeleian accounts of its nature (84/1.3.5.2, 152–3/12.11); and because all necessity is in any case merely subjective, a product or aspect of human mental reactions (cf. 15.3).

nature. We can't suppose this in the case of the impression or idea of power any more than we can suppose it in the case of the impression or idea of solidity.

Hume follows this passage with his standard AP-property-based argument for the conclusion that the nature of causal power is unknowable. Real though it is, this feeling of power derived from pushing or being struck by objects can't be the source of a genuine idea of power in objects, because 'we can *à priori* draw no inference' from it, as we would have to be able to do if it were the source of a genuine idea of power (cf. 11). He makes the same point earlier: the 'sentiment of an endeavour to overcome resistance' cannot give us true knowledge of power—although it is part of our ordinary idea of power, 'it can afford no *accurate precise* idea of power'—since it cannot equip us with any capacity to make a priori inferences about causal matters.[9]

19.3 A rhetorical question

I'll end this discussion of Causation and human beings with a detailed point which may be omitted. One reason for considering it is to show how apparent support for the standard view may simply dissolve on closer examination.

After the passage quoted in (18), Hume goes on to note that we learn about *variation* in the mental power that is involved in the command we have over mind and body (i.e. its variation in sickness and health, in the morning and the evening) only by experience. But (he has claimed) genuine acquaintance with the nature of this power would enable us to know about such variation prior to actual experience of it (cf. 11). So we cannot have any such acquaintance with this power. Accordingly, he asks a rhetorical question:

(21)   Where then is the power, of which we *pretend* to be conscious? (68/7.19)

This may at first be thought (in line with the standard view) to be a rhetorical question implying that there's no power at all. But Hume isn't suggesting that there's no power at all. He's simply saying that there's no power-of-which-we-are-conscious. Of course there's a power involved, but we aren't and can't be conscious of it, i.e. we can't know it. Its nature is 'secret'. So it can't be a source of our idea of power in the way that so many (including especially Locke) think that it is. But this doesn't mean that it doesn't exist.

The interpretation is confirmed by the continuation of the passage, another rhetorical question which provides another reason why we cannot be conscious of

---

[9] 67/7.17 n. A general *objection* to Hume's argument here will be developed in 23, roughly as follows: of course no sense-content-copying idea of power in the objects can be a true idea of power. But such sensory experience of power or force can still contribute crucially to the development of our essentially partly *intellectual* idea of power (it is essentially partly 'intellectual' in the sense of being irreducible to sense-contents); and this essentially partly intellectual idea of power may indeed be said to be, in its essentially partly abstract way, a true idea of power as it is in the objects.

the power in question, and which some may (once again) read as providing support for the standard view:

(22)   [Where then is the power, of which we pretend to be conscious?] Is there not here, either in a spiritual or material substance, or both, some secret mechanism or structure of parts, upon which the effect depends, and which, being entirely unknown to us, renders the power or energy of the will equally unknown and incomprehensible? (68–9/7.19)

(22) may at first be thought to be a rhetorical question expecting the answer 'No', and therefore in line with the standard view: 'No, there isn't some secret mechanism or structure of parts.' But it doesn't expect the answer 'No', it expects the answer 'Yes', according to the normal conventions of rhetorical questions. If it expected the answer 'No', it wouldn't contain the word 'not' as its third word.[10] The question needs to be read with the stress on 'secret'. The gist of the first part of it is, 'Since it's already been shown that there is no power operating of which we are *conscious*, and since there must (of course) be *some* explanation of the undeniably real power or energy of the will, we have to suppose that there is some secret or unknown mechanism operating, of which we're *not* conscious.'

The rhetorical force of the question is not to the ontological effect that there is no power or secret mechanism at all. The point is as usual entirely epistemological, but it is, like the sentence, rather convoluted. It involves a distinction between X, the undeniably real 'power or energy of the mind or will', and Y, the basis of this power, some secret mechanism or structure of parts in the spiritual and/or material and/or still-more-unknown (153/12.12) substance of the mind, and can be restated as follows: '(1) you have to grant that Y (the secret structure or mechanism of mental power) is unknown, because you learn about the variability and extent of X (mental power) only by experience, whereas if you really knew the nature of Y (its mechanism) you could know *prior* to such experience how X would vary. So (2) you have to grant that the true nature of X, "the power or energy of the will" that depends on this structure or mechanism Y, is also completely unknown, and that our experience of mental power—of willing and mental command—can't provide us with a true idea of the nature of power—contrary to what so many people believe. For (3) if the true nature of X were really known, then Y, its essential mechanism, would have to be known too; for knowing the "mechanism" of a power is just part of what it is to know its true nature.'

---

[10]   Although the 'not' is decisive here, it's not always decisive in such cases. Although the basic force of the rhetorical-question construction 'Is it not the case that *p*?' is undoubtedly that it expects the answer 'Yes', this fact, like any other, can itself be ironically (or sarcastically) exploited, in particular in the context in which one implicitly attributes the 'Is it not the case that *p*?' question to one's opponent. There are, however, no grounds at all for thinking that this is what Hume is doing here.

20

Enquiry Section 7: the Occasionalists

When things go normally, ordinary people ordinarily suppose that they perceive

(23)   [REF] *the very force or energy* of the cause, by which it is connected with its effect. (69/7.21)

They only feel the need to invoke some invisible, unperceived power when something happens which they think of as extraordinary. But some philosophers realize that

(24)   even in the most familiar events, [REF] *the energy of the cause* is... [EP] unintelligible. (70/7.21)

They realize, that is, that we have no genuine, positive conception of its ultimate nature in any case at all. (But [NI] it certainly exists, as much in the normal case as in the abnormal.) Going on to talk of the Occasionalists, or Cartesians, Hume sets out their view

(25)   that the true and direct principle of every effect is not any power or force in nature, but a volition of the Supreme Being.[1]

He strongly implies that he finds their view absurd (insofar as they are realists about physical objects, which they are), and ill-motivated even on religious grounds.[2] More important for present purposes, however, is the methodological argument he

---

[1] 70/7.21. Note that as soon as he is concerned with people who, unlike himself, positively deny the existence of any sort of Causation in nature, he naturally puts into their mouths the distancing, existence-commitment-cancelling 'any'.

[2] 'They rob nature, and all created beings, of every power, in order to render their dependence on the Deity still more sensible and immediate.' But they're foolish to do so, because they thereby diminish his attributes: 'it argues surely more power in the Deity to delegate a certain degree of power to inferior creatures' than to be 'obliged every moment to adjust' all the parts of nature himself (71/7.22). Independently of this point, it's clear here that Hume doesn't think much of philosophers who are realists about objects and yet deny that there is any sort of Causation in objects. But this is thought by some to be precisely his own view. There's worse, for at least the Cartesians have God as the reason why there is regularity in nature; their view is not simply crazy. The standard modern 'Humean' view, by contrast, has *nothing at all* as the reason why there is regularity in nature. So it is that some positivists and 'Humeans', congratulating themselves on purging the excesses of the bad old metaphysics, finish up with the most rococo, most magical, metaphysics ever proposed.

presents against them, which goes as follows. First, he observes that it is precisely their acknowledgement of our *ignorance* of power or energy in objects that leads the Occasionalists to 'rob nature . . . of every power', and attribute all power to God. Next, he observes that it is awareness of 'the same ignorance' that then leads them to rob the human mind too of power, and to 'assert that the Deity is [also] the immediate cause of the union between soul and body', e.g. when we act.

He then grants that they are right about our ignorance in these departments: we are indeed

(26)   [EP] totally ignorant of [REF] *the power on which depends the mutual operation of bodies* (70/7.21)

(although of course there must be such a thing); just as

(27)   we are [EP] no less ignorant of [REF] *that power on which depends the operation of mind on body, or of body on mind* (70/7.21)

(although of course there must be some such thing). But if it's acknowledgement of our *ignorance* that is leading the Occasionalists to attribute all power to God, then they should realize that our ignorance of any power that might be attributed to God is equally complete:

(28)   we are [EP] ignorant, it is true, of [REF] *the manner in which bodies operate on each other*: Their [REF] *force or energy* is [EP] entirely incomprehensible: But are we not equally ignorant of the manner or force by which . . . even the supreme mind, operates either on itself or on body?[3]

Yes, he answers—continuing with another remark that appears to suffice to refute the standard view of Hume, according to which his repeated remarks about our total ignorance and lack of comprehension of the nature of Causation are supposed to amount to or in effect entail the claim that there actually is no such thing as Causation:

(29)   *were our ignorance, therefore, a good reason for rejecting any thing*, we should be led into that principle of denying all energy in the Supreme Being as much as in the grossest matter. We surely comprehend as little the operations of one as of the other. (72–3/7.25)

Here things seem very clear. Our ignorance is not a good reason for rejecting the possible existence of *anything*. This gives Hume a powerful argument against the

---

[3] 72/7.25. Note that even uses of verbs like 'operate' may be counted as referring uses of Causation terms, since nothing ever strictly speaking *operates* on anything else according to the regularity theory ('in nature one thing just happens after another'). Regularity theorists can say that talk of such operation is just a *façon de parler* that can be given a regularity-theory interpretation. Of course. But there is no reason to think that this is Hume's intention here or anywhere else.

Occasionalists as he presents them: given their use of the appeal to ignorance, they have no good reason at all for denying power to objects, and attributing it only to God.[4] But it also refutes the view that Hume can be supposed to be positively denying the existence of Causation in the objects, in going on at such length about how we are utterly ignorant of it, and cannot in any way comprehend it.[5]

The long footnote to the argument against the Occasionalists (73/7.25 n.) also appears to contain a clear realist protest about the need to acknowledge the reality of Causation or causal powers in the objects, and a distinction between what we *mean* and what there *is* which illustrates how unproblematic the Meaning Tension is for Hume. He says that

(30)   when we talk of gravity, we *mean* certain effects, without [EP] ever comprehending [REF] *that active power* [of gravity].

That is, the observable effects, or, better, manifestations, of the force of gravity are (given the theory of ideas) all we can mean by the word. This is all the meaning we can put into the word, because we can't 'comprehend' the active power in question in the sense of encompassing it in thought, by forming some positive conception of its nature apart from its observable manifestations. But—once again—to say this is to talk about it. It's to refer to it. So we can 'mean' it after all, in some way; we can form a 'relative' idea of it and refer to it. Certainly Hume usually uses the word 'mean' to mean theory-of-ideas-accredited meaning, i.e. impression-copy content (although see ch. 12 n. 6). The referring expression 'that active power' is then 'meaningless', on his view. But it's still an unproblematically genuinely referring expression, on his

---

[4] For denying 'second causes', and leaving only a 'first cause', in the terminology of the time. Many held that the notion of power was only really intelligibly attributed to mental beings, but the Occasionalists Hume presents can't support this claim by arguing that we do have some genuine knowledge or experience of power in the case of our own mental activity, because they've already argued that we're entirely ignorant of mental power in our own case.

[5] Here Hume assumes the existence of God for the purpose of argument against his opponents, for it's central to their position (the suggestion that this is what he is doing in the case of causal power was considered in 16). Some may take the use of referring expressions purportedly referring to God as grounds for the following argument: Hume uses such referring expressions; but doesn't believe in God; so too he uses expressions purportedly referring to Causation, but doesn't believe in Causation. In reply: (1) even if the parallel were strong, Hume wouldn't wish to claim that there is definitely and knowably no sort of supernatural being or divine mental power, even if there can't (given, say, the problem of evil) be anything like the Christian God. (See Philo's wonderfully two-edged concession that there is some kind of deity in Part 12 of the *Dialogues*; and, in support of the identification of Hume with Philo despite this, his remark that 'In every Dialogue, no more than one person can be supposed to represent the author', *Letters* 1.173). (2) In fact the parallel is not strong. Hume in his time had good reasons for not advertising his belief that there was no God, reasons which led him to delay publication of the *Dialogues* until after his death. If he had believed that there was no such thing as Causation, he would have had no such reasons for not declaring this belief. Some may doubt (2) on the grounds that Hume might have feared that even the denial of Causation would be taken to be atheistic. Reasons for supposing that this would not have deterred him from expressing his views on causation may be derived from the way in which he responds to the claim that a denial of the 'principle, *That whatever begins to exist must have a cause of existence* ... leads to Atheism' in his *Letter from a gentleman to his friend in Edinburgh*, pp. 22–3.

view, which refers to something whose existence is simply assumed and not questioned. Newton agrees: 'the cause of Gravity...I do not pretend to know' (letter to
Bentley, January 1693 *Correspondence* 3.240). But there is some such cause, to which
we can refer.

Hume's note goes on to say that 'It was never the meaning of Sir Isaac Newton to
rob second causes of all force or energy'. Newton, he suggests, was not so foolish: he
was a realist about Causation (or force or power or energy) in the objects. Newton
himself, commenting on his account of forces in *Principia*, Definition VIII, says that
he intends

only to give a mathematical notion of those forces, without considering *their physical causes
and seats*

and that he considers certain

forces not physically, but mathematically: wherefore the reader is not to imagine that by those
words [attraction, impulse, or propensity towards a centre] I anywhere take upon me to define
the kind, or the manner of any action, *the causes or the physical reason thereof*, or that
I attribute *forces, in a true and physical sense*, to certain centres.

Newton is clear that we have a merely 'relative' idea of such forces. We can have no
knowledge of their essence, beyond the knowledge we have of their observable
manifestations.[6]

What has been said about gravity can be said about causal power generally. When
we talk about causal power as it is in the objects, we can (given the theory of ideas)
only really manage to mean certain observable aspects of its existence—the observable, regular-succession aspects. But causal power, understood in some essentially
non-regularity-theory way as something whose existence is *the reason why* there is
observable regularity in the world (or: something of whose existence observable
regularity is a manifestation), exists nevertheless. It is just that we can only have a
'relative' idea of it.

---

[6] Newton's views changed over time; there are complexities which extend beyond the scope of this book.
Some of them have theological imbrications, and relate to the notion of 'active power' mentioned in
quotation (30). Here it's enough to note that Hume's rejection of the *theologically* motivated aspects of the
Newtonian notion of 'active power'—more generally, his rejection of the idea (widely endorsed by his
contemporaries) that only a mental being can ever properly speaking be said to be possessed of 'active
power'—doesn't put in question the point that he conceives of gravity itself as being or involving power in
some essentially non-regularity-theory, Causation sense. As for Newton—whatever his later difficulties
with the idea that there might be physical Causation operating independently of God's power—he insists
on a positivist interpretation of his laws precisely because he believes we can't claim to know the nature of
Causation. 'Gravity must be caused by an agent acting constantly according to certain laws, but whether
this agent be material or immaterial is a question I have left to ye consideration of my readers' (op. cit.
3.253–4). On this issue see Kemp Smith 1941: 53–61, Wright 1983: §16 (for his discussion of Hume on the
Occasionalists, see pp. 136–47), McMullin 1985: 10–12. Reid gives a very clear account of the notion of
active power (1785: 1.5 and 1.6).

This may be said to make causal power or gravity 'a certain unknown, inexplicable *something*,...a notion so imperfect, that no sceptic will think it worth while to contend against it'—to adapt what Hume says about a certain notion of matter to the case of the notion of causation (155/12.16). But this is no objection to the present account of Hume, according to which his view is precisely that Causation is completely 'unknown' and 'inexplicable' in being something more than regularity. As he says, we do not have 'any acquaintance with the nature of cause and effect' (68/7.18). Our idea of Causation is accordingly a merely 'relative' idea, and is therefore very 'imperfect', in lacking any positive descriptive content. But, precisely because it lacks any positive descriptive content, to endorse it is not to make any claims of the kind that sceptics must always contend against, claims to express some sort of positively descriptively contentful metaphysical knowledge of the true *nature* of Causation (considered apart from its observable manifestations).[7]

Some today still think that sceptics should not only challenge metaphysical claims to know the *nature* of Causation, but also the assumption that it exists at all. Whatever the merits of such a view, the present point is merely that it is not Hume's view. He never questions the idea that there is Causation—something about the nature of reality in virtue of which it is regular in the way that it is—although he is passionate and brilliant in his attack on the view that we know anything about its nature.[8]

---

[7] In full the passage runs '[t]he command of the mind over itself is limited, as well as its command over the body; and these limits are not known by reason, or by any acquaintance with the nature of cause and effect, but only by experience and observation...' (68/7.18). It is natural to take the passage as I have here—as expressing the general claim that experience and observation don't give us any acquaintance with the fundamental nature of the relation of cause and effect. But it should be noted that Hume could mean, rather, that experience and observation do not give us any acquaintance with the nature of the things which stand in the relation of cause and effect. (Those I have asked have preferred the former interpretation, but I think the latter is at least equally plausible.)

[8] Perhaps the closest he ever gets to questioning the existence of Causation is in his use of the word 'may' instead of the word 'are' when he writes, with Causation in mind, 'I am indeed, ready to allow, that there may be several qualities...in...objects, with which we are utterly unacquainted' (168/1.3.14.27). But this is not very close. The dubitative use of 'may' is polemical in a polemical passage, and all his energy is going into the point that although there are (no doubt/of course) such qualities, we can't 'manage to positively-contentfully mean' them *in any way whatever*, and have no understanding whatever of their nature. The passage is discussed in 15.5.

21

Enquiry Section 7: the two definitions of cause

21.1 Extraordinary ignorance

Towards the end of Section 7 there is a famous passage which may at first seem to support the standard view. Hume claims that when we step back from our ordinary, uncritical belief that we observe power or necessary connection in the objects, and adopt a properly philosophical perspective, we realize that the belief is incorrect. We realize that the truth of our epistemic situation, critically assessed, is as follows:

(31)   All events [EP] seem entirely loose and separate. One event follows another; but [EP] *we never can observe* any tie between them. They [EP] *seem conjoined*, but never *connected*. And as [EP] *we can have no idea* of any thing which never appeared to our outward sense or inward sentiment, the necessary conclusion *seems* to be that [EP] *we have no idea* of connexion or power at all, and that these words are absolutely without any meaning (74/7.26)

—i.e. without any theory-of-ideas-accredited, impression-derived content. But Hume goes straight on to say that the Causation terms 'power' and 'connexion' are not in fact without any such impression-derived meaning, giving the well-known account of the source of their meaning discussed in 10. We form the idea of power or connection from an impression or feeling of connection or determination in the mind, a 'sentiment or impression' which arises in us because of our innate mental disposition upon exposure to regularities of succession (75/7.28).

It follows, according to him, that

(32)   when we say ... that one object is connected with another, *we mean only* that they have acquired a connexion in our thought ...: A conclusion which is somewhat extraordinary, but which seems founded on sufficient evidence. (76/7.28)

We try to talk about causation in the objects, about the real force or energy in the world, but these words, in our use, only reach as far as—only manage to (positively-contentfully) mean—their impression-source: a feeling of determination in the mind. Or, as he sometimes puts it, they only manage to mean regular succession in the *objects* (priority ± contiguity and constant conjunction), on the one hand, and the feeling of determination in the *mind*, on the other hand, which the regular succession in the objects gives rise to.[1]

But—Hume doesn't say that regular succession is all that causation *is*, in the objects. As always, the point is that this is all we can *know* of causation in the objects. To say that regular succession is all we really mean when we talk about causation in the objects is to say that regular succession is all we can *positively-contentfully* mean when we talk about causation in the objects. It's not to say that it's all that causation in the objects is, or that it's all we ever really refer to when we talk about causation.

The epistemological nature of the point is immediately confirmed in the text. Hume admits that it seems 'somewhat extraordinary' that when we talk of causal connection between two objects we don't really mean the real causal connection between them (which of course exists), but (given the theory of ideas) mean only that they have acquired a connection in our thought on account of having been observed to be constantly conjoined. He doesn't, however, take this conclusion as grounds for any sort of ontological assertion that this is all that causation (really) is or involves, but rather as an occasion for an epistemological remark about the *profound limitations on the human capacity to grasp the nature of reality*:

(33)   what stronger instance can be produced of the surprising ignorance and weakness of the understanding than the present [one]? (76/7.29)

In our unreflective moments (or alternatively our excessively exalted philosophical moments) we're pretty sure we know about causal power in the objects if we know about anything. It is after all supremely important to us in all the affairs of common life. 'If there be any relation among objects which it imports us to know perfectly, it is that of cause and effect' (76/7.29). In fact, however, human understanding is so restricted that it can't even 'comprehend' the nature of causal power. It can't representationally encompass the nature of causal power in any way, insofar as causal power involves more than observable regular succession. We don't have 'any acquaintance with the nature of cause and effect' (68/7.18).

The 'somewhat extraordinary' conclusion, then, is not that there's really no such thing as Causation, as some have thought. This (the so-called 'Humean' view of causation) would certainly be an extraordinary conclusion, but I don't think it ever crossed Hume's mind (see 20, n. 8). His point is this: it's truly extraordinary that despite the fact that there is (of course) such a thing as Causation or causal power, and despite the fact that it is all around us, all-pervasive, governing our thoughts and actions and our world in all respects,[2] still human understanding is utterly incapable

---

[1] Cf. 10. This duality is expressed by the two definitions of cause.
[2] As the Humean Philo says 'Every thing is surely governed by steady, inviolable laws' (*Dialogues* 125/174).

of grasping its true nature *in any way*. It is 'perfectly incomprehensible'. That's how limited we are:

(34)   Our thoughts and enquiries are..., every moment, employed about this relation. Yet so imperfect are the ideas which we form concerning it, that it is impossible to give any just definition of cause, *except what is drawn from something extraneous and foreign to it*. (76/7.29)

It concerns us at every moment, but we can't grasp its true nature at all. This truly extraordinary but purely epistemological point is what the rationalist philosophers Hume was arguing against couldn't believe—and naturally enough. Quotation (33) provides particularly powerful support for the view that Hume does believe in Causation in the objects, for if he were really saying that there is no such thing as Causation, or that causation in the objects is really just regular succession, *there would be no ignorance or weakness of understanding at all*! There'd be no fundamental failure to encompass the actual nature of things.[3]

21.2 The two definitions

This view is resoundingly confirmed by what he goes on to say about his two famous definitions of cause. Having just said that we're ignorant of the true nature of causation, and that our ideas can't encompass it, he continues with the passage just quoted:

(34)   so imperfect are the ideas which we form concerning it, that it is impossible to give any just definition of cause, *except what is drawn from something extraneous and foreign to it*.[4]

This is yet another quotation which effectively suffices to establish the present view of Hume as a believer in Causation, because it refers to, and is immediately followed by, the famous two 'definitions' of cause: 'we may define a cause to be'

---

[3] Except insofar as some things are just too small to detect; but this is not what Hume has in mind here. Remember that the nature of causal power is unknowable by us, not just unknown. It not only has the AP property; we can't even know whether it is ultimately mental or physical in nature, or something 'still more unknown' (153/12.12).

A desperate defender of the standard view might now argue that the weakness of our understanding in question is revealed not in our failing to know anything about the nature of something as important and all-pervasive as causal power, but rather in our being so misguided as to suppose that causation is something more than regular succession. This view cannot survive a moderately careful reading of the surrounding text; and see quotation (29).

[4] 76/7.29. Compare the *Treatise*, in which Hume similarly considers the objection that both the definitions might be held to be defective 'because drawn from something foreign to the cause' (170/1.3.14.31), and goes on to challenge anyone to do better. (The irony in the challenge may be misinterpreted: Hume's confidence about our ignorance of the true nature of causation (which is thus to be understood as Causation) may be mistaken for an assertion of belief in its non-existence.)

[i] *an object, followed by another, and where all the objects, similar to the first, are followed by objects similar to the second* (76/7.29)

or

[ii] *an object followed by another, and whose appearance always conveys the thought to that other* (77/7.29)

The two definitions are held to be imperfect (as is our idea of causation, which they in effect capture) because they can't representationally encompass causation or power 'as it is in itself' (77/7.29 n.), but can define it only by reference to what is 'extraneous and foreign' to it. Immediately after giving the definitions, Hume reiterates the point:

(35)   though both these definitions of cause be drawn from something foreign to *the cause*, we cannot remedy this inconvenience, or attain any more perfect definition, which may point out *that circumstance in the cause*, which *gives it a connexion* with its effect. (77/7.29)

There's an enormous exegetical literature on the two definitions, but I'll say little about it. This is because I'm principally concerned with Hume's view of the *status* of the two definitions—his view that it's actually impossible for us to give anything other than an 'imperfect' definition of cause—rather than with the details of their content. Roughly speaking, the two definitions of cause give an account of the content of the *idea* of cause we actually possess, given the idea's impression-sources. They give information about what we actually positively-contentfully mean, and indeed about all we can really (positively-contentfully) mean, according to the theory of ideas, when we talk about causes. The problem, according to Hume, is that they're seriously imperfect as definitions (whatever exactly Hume thought the purpose of definitions was) because they're drawn from something 'foreign to the cause' itself. So they can't really capture the true nature of causation at all. We can't fix this imperfection, Hume says: both these definitions are in fact drawn from something foreign to *the cause*, but, again,

we cannot remedy this inconvenience, or attain any more perfect definition, which may point out *that circumstance in the cause*, which *gives it a connexion* with its effect. (77/7.29)

Which is to say that although there is (of course) something about the individual cause-event in virtue of which it is causally connected with its effect (contrary to the regularity theory of causation)—'that [actual] circumstance in the cause, which gives it a connexion with its effect'—we don't and can't know its nature, or what it actually is.

Clearly, if causation in the objects were just regular succession, there would be no inconvenience or imperfection of any sort in the first definition.[5] And, in giving the

---

[5] Or the second: if causation in the objects were just regular succession of a sort which gave rise to a feeling of determination (or habit of inference) in the mind, the two definitions would be perfect.

first definition, we could hardly be said to be in the position of finding it 'impossible to give any just definition of cause, except what is drawn from something extraneous and foreign to it'.[6]

It may be objected that all that Hume means when he says that one has to refer to circumstances 'foreign to' the cause is that one has to go beyond the individual cause-event considered on its own, and mention the effect-event (not to mention types of cause-event and effect-event), or indeed the human mind. But although this may be part of what he meant, it doesn't put the present point in doubt. For he holds that the definitions are imperfect specifically because they can't 'point out [REF] *that circumstance in the cause*, which [actually] *gives it a connexion* with its effect'. That is, they're imperfect because they can't state the nature of the power involved in the causation. Hume has already said that to know the 'circumstance in the cause, which gives it a connexion with its effect' would be to know the power involved in the causation: to 'know a power [would be to]...know *that very circumstance in the cause*, by which it is enabled to produce the effect' (67–8/7.17).

So the reason why the definition has to 'be drawn from something foreign to the cause' itself, and is thus 'imperfect' as a definition, is that there's something about the cause itself which it can't capture or represent. The imperfection in question is the imperfection that definitions have when they don't fully capture the nature of the thing they're meant to be definitions of. We can't give a perfect definition of causation because of our ignorance of its nature. All we can encompass in our definition is its observable manifestations—the observable regular-succession manifestations in the objects, and the observable feelings of necessity or determination (or habits of inference) in the mind to which these give rise. That is, all we can do is to say what it is to us, so far as we have any positively contentful grasp or experience of it.

Burke's 1757 comments on the eighteenth-century conception of definition are very telling in this connection: 'A definition may be very exact', he says,

> and yet go but a very little way towards informing us of the nature of the thing defined.... When we define, we seem in danger of circumscribing nature within the bounds of our own notions, which we often ... form out of a limited and partial consideration of the object before us, instead of extending our ideas to take in all that nature comprehends, according to her manner of combining...' (1757: 12)

Here, I propose, Burke uses 'definition' in exactly the same way as Hume. So too Priestley in 1778:

> A *definition* of any particular thing... cannot be anything more than an enumeration of its known properties. (1778: 34)

---

[6] Should I also appeal to the fact that Hume's restatement of the first definition of cause—'*if the first object had not been, the second never had existed*' (76/7.29)—is strongly counterfactual in form? It's not clear how much weight to put on this, especially since the restatement involves a logical slip. It may certainly be argued that the counterfactual form further confirms Hume's commitment to a non-regularity-theory notion of cause, but the present argument has no need of such support.

A definition of a natural phenomenon, as opposed to a definition of a geometrical figure, records human understanding's best take on that phenomenon. As such, it may be very 'exact' and 'precise' (169/1.3.14.30) while also being very 'imperfect', 'limited and partial' in its representation of the nature of the phenomenon defined.[7]

Hume restates the point with very great clarity in the next section of the *Enquiry*:

(36) If we examine the operations of body, and the productions of effects from their causes, we shall find that all our faculties can never carry us farther in our knowledge of this relation than *barely* to observe that particular objects are **constantly conjoin'd** together [first definition], and that the mind is carried, by a **customary transition**, from the appearance of one to the belief of the other [second definition]. (92/8.21)

That is, all we can get to know of causation is the content of the two definitions. That is, we can't get very far. We can barely (i.e. merely) observe this much. So these two definitions *do not say what causation*—('the operations of body, and the productions of effects from their causes')—*actually is*; they just express all we know of it.

So we have to admit that we are ignorant of the nature of causation. And

(37) this conclusion concerning human ignorance [is] the result of the strictest scrutiny of this subject... [W]e know nothing farther of causation... than *merely* the **constant conjunction** of objects [first definition], and the consequent *inference* of the mind from one to another [second definition]. (92/8.21)

There is (of course) more to causation, but we are ignorant of it.

The core argument of section 8 of the *Enquiry* turns on this ignorance, and runs as follows. (1) Exceptionless causal order—causal necessity—holds in the case of all the operations of matter; this is universally acknowledged. (2) Exceptionless causal order—causal necessity—also holds in the case of human actions; but this is not universally acknowledged. (3) This difference of attitude is entirely unjustified— although it can be psychologically explained (94n./8.22n.). (4) For when we reflect, we see that we have exactly the same reasons for supposing that there is exceptionless causal order (necessity) in both cases. Put otherwise: we have exactly the same conception of what causal necessity is in both cases. We don't know anything more about causal necessity in the case of the operations of matter than we do in the case of human action, and we have no reason whatever to think that there is some special necessary force in the case of matter that isn't present in the case of human actions.

---

[7] The practice isn't restricted to the eighteenth century. Russell uses 'define' in the Hume/Burke/ Priestley sense when discussing the nature of matter: 'all that we ought to assume is series of groups of events, connected by discoverable laws. These series we may *define* as "matter". Whether there *is* matter in any other sense, no one can tell' (1927: 93). Russell makes it very clear that to give a definition is not to make an ontological declaration. Compare also Eddington's remark that 'we know nothing about the intrinsic nature of space, and so it is quite easy to conceive it satisfactorily' (1928: 51); it is in this sense that Hume's definitions of cause are exact and satisfactory.

This is because there is no more content to our conception of necessity ('the necessity, which we conceive in matter' 93/8.22) than the content specified in the two definitions of cause (the 'constant conjunction of objects, and subsequent inference of the mind from one to another' ibid). We 'know nothing farther of causation' than this, and we apply exactly the same conception of causal necessity in both cases.[8]

In sum: the trouble is that we have [EP] no

> (38)   idea of [REF] *power, as it is in itself.* (77/7.29 n.)

We're ignorant of

> (39)   [REF] *the **unknown** circumstance of an object, by which the degree or quantity of its effect is fixed and determined,* (ibid.)

although we 'call that [i.e. the unknown circumstance] its power'. (In saying this last thing Hume clearly allows, in his use of the word 'call', that the Causation term 'power' does manage to reach out referentially to Causation or power in the object after all, although we have no positive conception of it.)

Again:

> (40)   [T]he frequent use of the words, Force, Power, Energy, &c...., is no proof, that we are [EP] acquainted, in any instance, with [REF] *the connecting principle between cause and effect* (ibid.)

which [NI] nonetheless exists

> (41)   or can account ultimately for the production of one thing by another. (ibid.)

The 'Meaning Tension' is strong here, because when Hume talks of 'defining' a 'cause' he takes it that he is at best stating all that we can positively-contentfully (or positively-descriptively) mean by our use of the word or idea 'cause' on the terms of the theory of ideas. But his very statement of the point relies essentially on referring uses of Causation terms which count as 'unintelligible' or 'meaningless' on the terms of the theory of ideas: he makes essential (R-intelligible) use of Causation terms in order to state the point that our idea of causation, and, hence, the correct account or 'definition' of our idea of causation, is imperfect.[9]

---

[8] Compare Harris's somewhat different account (Harris 2005*a*).

[9] Note that this point about how Hume uses Causation terms in order to state why our definition of causation is imperfect is distinct from the familiar point that he seems to use Causation terms in the very process of stating the second definition. This second point is also correct, however: the second time Hume states the second definition of a cause in the *Treatise*, for example, he talks of how the idea or impression of one thing '*determines the mind*' to form the idea of another (172/), and comments that 'such an influence on the mind is in itself *perfectly extraordinary and incomprehensible*' (i.e. E-unintelligible). This is just the sort of remark he usually makes about Causation: such an influence is indubitably real; it's just that it's E-unintelligible, incomprehensible on the terms of the theory of ideas. But regularity-theory causation is not incomprehensible in this sense. On the contrary, it's entirely

Consider finally, and again decisively, Hume's restatement of his second 'definition' of cause in the *Treatise*:

An object precedent and contiguous to another, and so united with it in the imagination, that the idea of the one determines the mind to form the idea of the other, and the impression of the one to form a more lively idea of the other (172/1.3.14.35).

In the following sentence he comments:

Such an influence on the mind is in itself perfectly extraordinary and incomprehensible; nor can we be certain of its reality, but from experience and observation (172/1.3.14.35).

Here Hume says that this 'influence on the mind', which is of course a causal influence, is 'perfectly...incomprehensible'—perfectly unintelligible. And this, of course, is what he always says about causal power, causation conceived of in some essentially non-regularity-theory way. But he goes on to say that we can none the less be 'certain of its reality'. *We can be certain of its reality in spite of the fact that it is incomprehensible.*

The Meaning Tension is not a fault in Hume. It doesn't detract from the validity of his intended argument. He knows exactly what he means by 'meaning', 'intelligible', 'incomprehensible', 'inconceivable', and so on, even if others don't, because they no longer mean the same thing by these words. After remarking that we can't 'point out that circumstance in the cause, which gives it a connexion with its effect', Hume continues, 'We have no idea of this connexion, nor even any distinct notion what it is we desire to know, when we endeavour at a conception of it' (77/7.29). And this last clause is worth noting because in it Hume seems to pick up Berkeley's terminological device for attempting to deal with the Meaning Tension—his distinction between an *idea*, which must have an impression-source in order to have content, and a *notion*, which may be thought of as essentially more purely cognitive in nature than an idea, and as capable of some sort of contentfulness despite lacking any impression-source which it can call its own.[10] Hume's thought seems to be that even when we concede (contrary to the strict theory of ideas) that we may have a notion of something that is in *some* sense contentful or *semantically non-null*, despite the fact that it lacks an impression-source, still we don't really know what we are getting at, in the case of Causation—even though we may be sure that there is such a thing.

As has been noted several times, Hume's principal targets are those optimistic philosophers who think that they mean or know something more than the most he

comprehensible—its nature is fully captured in the first definition. It can't therefore be right to suppose that one can give a regularity-theory account of the 'incomprehensible...determin[ing]...influence on the mind' referred to in the second definition. So Hume definitely does appeal to a non-regularity-theory notion of causation (i.e. a notion of Causation) in giving his account of the notion of causation that we actually and E-intelligibly have.

[10] The root of *idea* being *εἴδω, I see, as opposed to *nosco* (γιγνώσκω), I know, the root of *notion*; Kant continues the tradition with his distinction between phenomena and noumena.

says it is possible to mean or know—those who think that the intrinsic nature of causation as it is in the objects is (fully) 'intelligible', and indeed that they have some sort of genuine understanding of its ultimate nature (see p. 109 above, n. 5). They don't. It's dangerous to use words like 'power', 'force', and 'energy' without continual stress on our ignorance, in philosophy, because the use of these terms soon tempts us into thinking that we do after all have some true grasp of the nature of causal power. We don't. Human understanding is very narrowly bounded. We are utterly ignorant of the nature of causation, insofar as it involves something more than regular succession (and the feelings of determination or habits of inference to which it gives rise in human beings). This *ignorance* is what has to be shown and argued for from all sides, in Hume's view; it's very hard to see, for philosophers and non-philosophers alike.[11]

Awareness that it is such philosophers who are Hume's principal target should remove any remaining inclination to suppose that his epistemological remarks have ontological implications. It should also allow Hume's theory of ideas to appear in a truer light—as (above all) a powerful device employed in the service of scepticism. It's designed to puncture the pretensions—the 'sophistry and illusion' (165/12.34)—of philosophers who claim to have contentful conceptions and indeed knowledge of aspects of reality of which they have had no genuinely content-furnishing experience, and to foster a proper appreciation of the limitation of human understanding.[12] We are far less rational, and far more ignorant, than we think.[13,14]

---

[11] Recall that Hume's claim about the hiddenness of Causation is tied to his idea that it has the AP property (so that genuine acquaintance with it would have to make us capable of making a priori certain inferences about causal matters, of a sort we know we could never make). Clearly, one who has this picture of what acquaintance with Causation would be like will think Anscombe's observation about the sense in which we do have direct experience of forces (in lifting things, being pushed, and so on) to be completely beside the point (cf. 19.2).

[12] Compare Wright 1983: 125: 'Hume's principle that every idea is derived from a corresponding impression plays an essentially sceptical role in his philosophy; it shows us the limitations of the beliefs which we can found upon our ideas.' See also Craig 1987: ch. 2.

[13] A final note about the definitions. Craig (1987: §2.4) also doubts whether Hume means what we mean by 'definition', and his doubt acquires force once one puts aside Hume's (important) insistence that the two definitions are imperfect, and considers instead the fact that he does nevertheless offer them as his two 'definitions' of cause. What sort of definitions, then? Craig argues that they're best seen as (i) 'presenting two descriptions of the circumstances under which belief in causal connection arises, one concentrating on the outward situation, the other on the state of the believer's mind that those outward facts induce' (1987: 108). This seems clearly correct, and is wholly compatible with the present suggestion that (ii) the definitions simply express the empirically warranted, human concept of cause, cause-so-far-as-it-is-anything-to-us. (i) and (ii) are closely linked, for according to Hume the right way to establish the content of our concept of cause (as in (ii)) is precisely to look at the circumstances in which the concept is thought to apply (as in (i)).

[14] Die-hard opponents of the present view may quote passages like the following: (1) 'Necessity [or cause] may be defined two ways ... It consists either in the constant conjunction of like objects, or in the inference of the understanding from one object to another', these two senses being 'at bottom the same' (97/8.27); (2) we can [EP] form no 'idea of causation and necessity, except that of a constant conjunction of objects, and subsequent inference of the mind from one to another ..., these circumstances form[ing] ... the whole of that necessity, which [EP] we conceive in matter' (93/8.22). For a detailed rebuttal of the appeal to

21.3 Conclusion

That's what Hume said. He said it over and over again in section 7 of the *Enquiry*. At no point does he even hint at the thesis that there is (or even might be) no such thing as Causation; i.e. at the thesis that there might be nothing in the nature of things in virtue of which they are regular in the way that they are. Certainly he stresses the point that *reason* can give no reason why any one particular thing in nature should (or should not) produce any other particular thing in nature. So far as reason is concerned, 'any thing may produce any thing' (173/1.3.15.1); 'if we reason a priori, anything may appear able to produce anything' (164/12.29; a milder statement). Reason can't give any reason why gold is soluble in a mixture of one part nitric acid to four parts hydrochloric acid (*aqua regia*), for example. A priori (by means of reason alone) we can't work out anything about what will produce what. We can't in examining a single object determine anything a priori about what effects it may have. We have to wait for experience to show us.

But to make this point is *not* to say that there might be no such thing as Causation. It is not even to *imagine* (even implicitly) that there might be no such thing as Causation (although one could of course go on to imagine this). When Hume makes the point that reason has nothing to say on the question of what actually goes with what, or what actually produces what, in nature, he isn't considering the possibility that there might be nothing at all about the nature of things which is in fact the reason why things produce each other in the way they do. He takes it for granted that there's some reason for regularity: some reason why As produce Bs rather than Cs, and why Cs produce Ds rather than Es, something about the *nature* of reality, something about the *nature* of As, Bs, Cs, Ds, and Es. His point—one more time—is just that *reason* has nothing to say on the question of what actually goes with what.[15]

such passages, see 15.3–15.5 above. Here it may be said, first, that (2) strongly supports (ii) (in n. 13 above) as an account of the point of the two definitions; secondly, that given the parallel between (1) and (2) and their shared surrounding context, it seems clear that (1) is just a dramatic version of (2); thirdly, that the key words in (1) and (2) are 'define' (give a positively contentful account of) and 'conceive' (form a positively contentful conception of). Hume's claim, then, is his familiar claim is that constant conjunction and the inference of the mind are all we can know of necessity or causation in objects.

[15] To express the point in another Humean idiom: for any two objects, one can imagine the one producing the other without involving oneself in any logical contradiction—and whatever is thus imaginable is *logically* possible. But to say this is not to say or even to suppose that there might be no real *causal-production* (Causal) relations. It's just to say that we can know nothing of them a priori. Again: 'all events seem entirely loose and separate' (74/7.26) is just another way of putting the claim that all we ever strictly speaking observe are their priority ± contiguity relations and (as types) constant-conjunction relations; we don't observe causal power as such. It's a merely epistemological remark about the senses which carries no hint of the thought that there might not be any causal power. On the contrary, it derives its force as a comment on the profound limitations of our understanding precisely from the unquestioned supposition that there is causal power, of whose intrinsic nature we know nothing.

This point applies equally to Hume's stress on the claim that *reason* can't rule out a priori the idea that an event might occur without a cause (see pp. 6–7). Someone who makes such a claim certainly doesn't have to be thinking or even imagining either that there is or that there may be no such thing as Causation. He doesn't have to be thinking or even imagining that there is or may be nothing about the nature of reality in virtue of which things are regular in the way that they are.

The—apparently—'standard' view of Hume is incorrect. Any *prima facie* textual evidence in favour of it is massively outweighed by the evidence against it. No doubt he has always had readers who have understood what he was saying, but he has been massively misunderstood by a large number of people (perhaps this can justify some of the repetition in this book). It would have been a miracle if so intelligent and sceptical a man had ever dogmatically maintained such a fantastic thesis as the thesis that there is definitely and indeed provably nothing at all about reality given which it is (and cannot but be) regular in the way that it is. And, while Hume did not think that miracles were actually impossible, he did doubt that we would ever have good reason to believe that one had occurred.

PART 4

Reason, Reality, and Regularity

22

Reason, Reality, and Regularity

22.1 A summary of Hume's position

I'll end with some more general reflections about causation, returning to questions already raised in 5 and 8. Before that, a final summary statement of Hume's position.

The overall dialectical situation is as follows. Hume is certainly making the negative sceptical epistemological claim that

(1)   we cannot know anything about the nature of Causation in the objects.

He's certainly not making the non-sceptical, dogmatic, ontological-metaphysical claim that

(2)   there is no such thing as Causation in the objects, and that Causation does not exist.

On the contrary. Although he's a strictly non-committal sceptic with respect to *knowledge* claims about the ultimate nature of reality, he firmly *believes* that there is an external reality of realist or at least basic-realist objects, and he takes it for granted that

(3)   Causation does exist in reality, although we are entirely ignorant of its ultimate nature.

He takes it for granted that there is something about reality in virtue of which it is regular in its behaviour, something which is not just the regularity itself.

There's certainly real regularity. There's real regularity even if perceptions are, somehow, all that exist. There's real regularity (a certain sort of constancy and coherence) even if there's no genuinely external reality at all, only perception-constituted objects or perception-content-constituted objects (6.2). And there is in the end exactly as much reason to suppose that there is a reason for *this* real regularity—something which is therefore not just the regularity itself—as there is in the case of any other real regularity. There'd be something badly wrong with an account of Hume's views according to which he took it for granted that there must be supposed to be a reason for regularity given a realist or basic-realist account of reality, and failed to see that there must equally be supposed to be a reason for regularity given an account of reality according to which all that exist are perceptions.

Accordingly, and as promised in 6 and 14, I will shortly argue that Hume's belief in Causation is completely unconditional: it is not conditional on his writing as a realist or even as a 'basic realist' (p. 52ff.).

First, though, it must be noted that things are somewhat more complicated than (1)–(3) above suggest. For although Hume isn't making claim (2), he is making a claim that sounds like (2). On the terms of the meaning of 'meaning' delivered by his theory of ideas, he is claiming that

(4)   there is definitely (and fully ontologically speaking) nothing in the objects corresponding to what we actually (positively-contentfully) mean when we use Causation terms to speak of the objects.[1]

(4) comes in two versions, depending on whether one insists (a) that the Causation terms must be supposed to have some (theory-of-ideas-accredited, positively-contentful) *meaning* or other, or (b) that the Causation terms must be seen as having application or *reference to the objects*, whatever they manage to say or fail to say about them. Thus suppose we insist that

(4a)   we do manage to (positively-contentfully) *mean* something by Causation terms.

In this case it turns out that what we really mean is only a feeling of determination in the mind (for this is the meaning-conferring impression-source of causation terms). So what we mean is definitely not 'in the objects'.

Alternatively, suppose we grant that

(4b)   Causation terms do travel right out to refer to something in the objects, and don't carry us only to an impression-source only in the mind.

In this case we have to say that the Causation terms (positively-contentfully) mean nothing, for there is no content-bestowing impression-source for them in the objects.[2]

Hume is making claim (4), then. But he isn't making claim (2). Even if it were true that he ought to make claim (2), given some strict interpretation of his theory of ideas or meaning, it would be as clear as ever that he ought not to make claim (2) given his strictly non-committal scepticism, which is correctly open on the question of what may conceivably exist, and insists only that we should not presume to rule dogmatically on the nature of reality.

---

[1] This makes it easy to see how the standard view of Hume arose.
[2] Here as in 10 it is natural to read (4a) and (4b) as applying to objects taken as realist physical objects, but it's important to see they apply equally well (suitably modified) to objects understood as strict-idealist objects (perception-constituted objects or perception-content-constituted objects), and therefore as themselves 'only in the mind'. See ch. 10 nn. 7 and 8.

Is there some sort of stand-off between his theory of ideas and his scepticism? By no means. The scepticism that forbids (2) overrides any strict interpretation of the theory of ideas that seems to require (2). Properly understood, Hume's theory of ideas or meaning is not in conflict with his strictly non-committal scepticism with regard to knowledge claims about the nature of reality. Properly understood, it crucially incorporates the acknowledgement (essential both for scepticism and for realism) that we may intelligibly *suppose* that there exist things of which we can form no positively or descriptively contentful or 'meaningful' *conception* (6.5). Hume's theory of ideas or meaning is (as remarked in the last chapter) an argumentative instrument wholly in the service of scepticism, a weapon in the fight to expose human beings' inflated pretensions to knowledge of the unknowable. Obviously one can't know the unknowable; but by applying the theory of ideas one can perhaps hope to know what's unknowable—one can hope to know where (possible) knowledge stops. It's here that the theory of ideas may serve one well.[3]

Given his strictly non-committal scepticism, Hume is committed to accepting

(5) there may be something like Causation in reality;

for we may suppose the existence of things we can't contentfully conceive of on the terms of the theory of ideas—things of which we can only form a 'relative' idea (6.5). In fact he goes further and makes claim (3) above. He puts forward (3) as something he firmly believes, just as he firmly believes that there's an external (realist or at least basic-realist) world, completely compatibly with his strictly non-committal scepticism with regard to claims about what we can know.

22.2 The general form of the argument for Causation

I'll now argue that Hume believes (3) without qualification. He believes in the existence of Causation without qualification, and not only insofar as he writes as a realist (or basic-realist) about objects. This isn't surprising, because the general argument for accepting (3) doesn't depend on adopting any realist or basic-realist view of the nature of reality according to which there is something other than our perceptions, something which affects us and gives rise to our perceptions and is the reason why they are as they are (leaving aside any contribution which we may make to their character).[4] No doubt Hume would have been quick, as a consummate sceptic, to acknowledge the logical possibility of the pure regularity view of causation

---

[3] Kant's approach is close to Hume's in this respect, despite Kant's very different view about the origins of our ideas or concepts. On the relation between Hume and the later positivists, and its elements of farce, see Craig 1987: §2.6. See also Livingston 1984: ch. 6, Wright 1983: 124–7.

[4] I say 'our perceptions' and 'us'. Someone more cautious might wish to say 'one's own perceptions' and 'one'. (See ch. 6 n. 32.)

as a theory about the nature of reality considered as a whole. But I can see no evidence that he ever considered this possibility.[5]

The general form of the argument for (3) expands on the argument against the specifically realist version of the regularity theory of causation given in 5.

(i) You must be a realist of some sort. You must accept that

(I)   something exists.

You may be a realist of a fairly minimal sort—a Berkeleian immaterialist, or even an atheistic 'bundle' theory solipsist, for example. But to deny that there is anything at all is pragmatically self-defeating. Your act of denial is already something real.

(ii) If you accept (I), as you must, then you need only accept one other thing in order to have compelling (if not logically conclusive) reason to postulate Causation. The only other thing you need accept is something nobody denies:

(II)   there is some sense in which the reality whose existence you admit is highly regular in character.[6]

(iii) For as soon as you accept this, you have reason to suppose that

(III)   there is some reason why reality is regular in character—*however exactly reality is conceived.*

That is, you have reason to suppose that there is something about reality in virtue of which it's regular in the particular way that it is, something which is therefore not simply the fact of regularity itself. That is, you have reason to accept that there is such a thing as Causation in reality.[7]

To accept the contrary view—to assert that there is simply nothing about reality in virtue of which it is regular, and that there is just the fact of the regularity—is to assert that the regularity is (ontically, metaphysically, ultimately) a completely chance matter from instant to instant. It's true (we may grant it many times over) that this possibility can't be logically ruled out. But there's good reason to reject it. This is not because one is rationally obliged to 'infer to the best explanation' of the world's

---

[5] Remember that his claim that 'any thing may produce any thing' (173/1.3.15.1), moderated in the *Enquiry* to 'anything may appear able to produce anything' (164/12.29), doesn't constitute any sort of acknowledgement of this possibility. Nor does his argument that we can't provide a rational foundation for our reliance on induction.

[6] Certain realists about possible worlds may deny this: for if reality consists in the plenum of all possible worlds, there is in a clear sense no regularity in it, considered as a whole. There can be no *pattern* at all (hence no regularity) displayed by the Totality of Possibility taken as a whole. (There can be no pattern displayed within a grid of squares if all the squares are filled in.)

[7] I take it that the actual world is the only world, and that it is an objective fact that it is regular in character. But I will consider an objection to this, of the sort raised in 5, in n. 13 below.

regularity. No substantive explanation of regularity is being offered here. All that is being claimed is

(A)   it is reasonable to suppose, *completely unspecifically*, that there is something about the nature of the world given which it is (cannot but be) regular in the way that it is, something which is therefore not just the regularity itself

and

(B)   it is in any case unreasonable to deny dogmatically that there is anything about the world given which it is regular.

Some philosophers may object that the argument establishes only (B), and not (A). They may agree that one shouldn't positively assert that there is nothing about the nature of the world in virtue of which it is regular—nothing about the world in virtue of which, given its nature, it can't but be regular in the way it is. They may agree that it's positively *un*reasonable to do this. But they will then argue that it doesn't follow that it is intrinsically reasonable to assert that there *is* something about the nature of the world in virtue of which it is regular. They'll question the credentials of this appeal to some fundamental (not-further-justifiable) notion of what is intrinsically reasonable, especially in such a cosmic context as this. They'll recommend, instead, a perfect agnosticism. Faced with (universe-sized) regularity of the sort we are faced with, they'll say, it is in no way intrinsically more reasonable to suppose that there is a reason in the nature of things for the regularity than it is to suppose that there is no reason in the nature of things for the regularity. Who are we to try to rule on what it is objectively, ultimately, intrinsically reasonable to suppose, when considering the universe as a whole?

The objection may seem attractive. Still, in reply, one may point out that we're talking about reality, no less, and that, reality being what it is, either there is, in fact, or there isn't, in fact, something about the nature of reality in virtue of which it is (can't but be) regular in the way it is; and that if one had to choose one of the two hypotheses over the other, for some reason or another, it would surely be reasonable to choose the hypothesis that there is something about the nature of reality given which it is not a complete fluke that the world is, from moment to moment and from aeon to aeon, regular in the way that it is. The objectors, however, may simply refuse to contemplate this choice, and there is no conclusive argument against their agnostic position.

I suggest, nevertheless, that (A) as well as (B) is true. Given the regularity of the world, it is (B) not reasonable to suppose that the regularity is definitely a complete coincidence from moment to moment, aeon after aeon, in the sense that there is definitely nothing about the nature of reality in virtue of which it is regular in the way it is. It is also (A) reasonable to suppose that there is something about the nature of the world in virtue of which it is regular in the way that it is.

—What is it? Why is the world regular (in the particular way that it is)?

'Because of the nature of matter.'

—Why is the nature of matter the particular way it is?

'That's just the way things are.'[8]

This is the exchange considered in 8. The second question may reasonably be held to have no answer, other than 'That's just the way things are', in the same way as the question 'Why is there something rather than nothing?'[9] The crucial point is that it remains true, given these answers, that there's a fundamental difference between the present position and a regularity account of things. For according to the outright regularity theory of causation it's a metaphysical fact that the regularity of the world is a complete fluke from moment to moment. According to the present view, by contrast, it's a metaphysical fact that the regularity of the world is not a complete fluke from moment to moment, and that it is in the nature of things to be regular as they are.

At the risk (worthwhile, I think) of seeming to move confusingly close to the regularity-theory position, one could express the present position as follows. According to the present position, reality is *constitutionally* regular. In particular, it's 'R-regular', where this denotes the particular form of regularity exhibited by our universe. To say that reality is *constitutionally* R-regular is not just to say that it *just is* R-regular, for it's true of an objectively utterly random world which is flukishly identical to our world in respect of its R-regularity properties that it *just is* R-regular.[10] To assert that reality is constitutionally regular is to reject the regularity theory of causation utterly, for it's to assert that there is Causation, something about the nature of reality in virtue of which it is regular in the way that it is: *so that the mere fact of its regularity isn't the only relevant fact there is, so far as the question of what causation is is concerned.*

The point may seem fine to some, as remarked in 8. But the phrase just italicized expresses a denial of the heart of the regularity theory of causation. However fine the

---

[8]   As Philo says, it may well be that '*such* is the nature of material Objects, ... that they are all originally possessed of a *faculty* of order and proportion' (*Dialogues* 97/163).

[9]   As Philo says, 'Why not stop at the material world?', when seeking for an ultimate explanation of the order of things. If everything needs an explanation, 'How can we satisfy ourselves without going on *in infinitum?* And 'what satisfaction is there in that ...? Let us remember the story of the INDIAN philosopher and his elephant' (*Dialogues* 94/161; see also Locke, *Essay* 2.23.19).

[10]   The difference between the claim that the world just is regular and the claim that the world is constitutionally regular is like the difference between the sequence 0, 1, 2, 3, 4, 5 ..., as produced by a true random number generator, and the same sequence as produced by a device programmed to produce it. But the contrast needn't be just between an unlimitedly random world and a genuinely causally ordered world. Imagine a world W whose laws are such that each of its n ultimate constituents has an equal likelihood in being in any one of ten states at any instant, over and above its spatiotemporal location state. (Thus, leaving aside changes of spatial position, there are at any instant 10^n different possible state-configurations at the next instant.) Imagine that W is in fact indistinguishable from our world by our best (but still merely regularity-detecting) science. It is in fact R-regular—just like our world in respect of regularity—although it could develop in many ways utterly incompatible with R-regularity. In this case it is an objective fluke that W is R-regular.

point, it is philosophically—metaphysically—momentous. If the mere fact of the regularity of the world were the only relevant fact there was, so far as the question of what causation is was concerned, then the objectively utterly random world, in which it was *ex hypothesi* a fluke that it was R-regular in the way our world is, would be a causally ordered world in every sense in which our world is.[11]

The argument set out in (i)–(iii) shows that belief in Causation doesn't depend in any way on basic realism, for even if one abandons basic realism, and attempts to suppose that all that exists is a string of experiences or perceptions, one still has complex regularity features[12] about which the same old question arises: is there or is there not a reason in reality for the real regularity manifested in or by these real existences, these perceptions? And one still has the two possible answers, Yes or No. And there is as much reason as ever to reject the No answer. There is, in the end, exactly as much reason to reject the No answer in this case as there is in the case when one supposes that some solidly materialistically realist account of the world is true.

In sum, then, and to repeat, it doesn't matter what one's conception of reality is—it needn't be realist or even basic-realist—so long as one continues to think of reality as regular in character. Whatever one's particular conception of reality (or indeed one's scepticism about claims to know the nature of reality), one has reason to suppose that there is something about reality in virtue of which it is regular in the way it is, something which is therefore not just the regularity itself—some entirely objective feature of its nature given which it is in fact the case that it cannot but be regular in the way that it is. And so one has reason to reject the regularity theory of causation; or, at the very least, reason not to assert it.

The only way to avoid this conclusion, which flows from the twin suppositions (1) that something is real and (2) that it is (objectively) regular in character, is to reject (2), since one cannot reject (1). But if one rejects (2) one has no reason to accept the regularity theory of causation—for one has rejected the very thing it was a theory about. Hence there is no case in which one can reasonably adopt the regularity theory of causation, even though it is apparently logically possible that it is true.[13]

---

[11] Having put the point in these general terms one can go on to try to characterize Causation in various further ways: in terms of one thing *producing* or *bringing about* or genuinely *affecting* or *modifying* another, in terms of the *existential derivativeness* of one thing from another, and so on. See 8 and 23 below.

[12] Those features which the experiences have insofar as they have (for someone somehow constituted out of them) the character of being experiences of a highly regular world. They have this character even if they're interrupted and highly changeable, like our own experiences in daily life.

[13] Unless, perhaps, one is (unreasonably) a certain sort of realist about possible worlds. As remarked in 5, it may be said that regularity is in the eye of the beholder: that every possible sequence of events can in principle be seen as instantiating a regularity, so that the supposed distinction between a reality which is objectively regular in character and one which is not is spurious: regularity is not in fact an objective property of things. This suggestion has a certain attraction, but I think the correct response to it is to dismiss it—along with the realism about possible worlds mentioned in n. 6. That leaves our world, the actual world, about which it is an objective fact that it's regular. There is however a further response, considered in 8, which deserves variation in a note. Assume, then, that every world has a beginning. Then it is indeed formally correct to say that every world can in principle be seen as instantiating a regularity (up to

That Hume was generally aware of such issues as these is certain, not only given the nature of the problems that preoccupied some of the philosophers he studied, but also given the arguments he considers in his *Dialogues Concerning Natural Religion*. As observed in 8 and again in 21, the question regarding the source of order and regularity in the world is the principal question in the *Dialogues*. Hume argues that we can't know the nature of the source of order. We can't, for example, know that it is divine, rather than 'an *original, inherent principle of order... in matter*'. At the same time, he never doubts that there must be some reason in reality for the order and regularity: Philo's assertion that 'chance has no place, on any Hypothesis' goes unchallenged.[14] Hume could of course have grasped the total fluke hypothesis—neither reason nor the senses can rule it out. As far as strictly non-committal scepticism goes, the only thing that is certain is the existence of perceptions (unless it can be shown that their existence entails the existence of something irreducible to them). But (once again) Hume never considers the fluke hypothesis—the outright regularity theory of causation. Indeed, and as remarked in 9, Causation (a source or principle of order) is, along with the existence of perceptions, the only thing whose existence he never seriously questioned, when it came to considering the nature of reality. An external world of physical objects: that

the present moment). So too one can take any (finite) sequence S of numbers which is in fact generated by a random number generator, and, at any stage k of S specify an algorism—say A—which would produce that sequence S_k. And one can then say that S_k is regular relative to A. But suppose A is offered as an algorism which not only fits but also generated S_k. Then A will tell us what the next number should be, and the next number after that, and so on. And of course (logically possible miracles aside) it will soon turn out that A is not in fact generating S. One can at each stage revise one's hypothesis about the algorism generating S, but each hypothesis will be defeated.

With this in mind, one can define a notion of a *grounded* regularity or *G-regularity* of sequence given which not all (finite) sequences are regular, even though all (finite) sequences are formally regular or *F-regular* in the sense that they could have been the result of the application of a possible algorism or rule of generation. A sequence is G-regular if (and only if) it is in fact being generated in accordance with a particular algorism. It is then not merely F-regular, for there is a reason for the particular regularity instantiated (and the future progress of the sequence can be reliably predicted). The regularity is grounded—objectively grounded—in something: in the fact that the number generator is executing a particular algorism.

The relevance of this analogy to the case of sequences of events is obvious enough. We may grant that all worlds are F-regular. But a world is G-regular if (and only if) there is something about the nature of the world in virtue of which it's regular in the way that it is. So while a fluke world may be qualitatively identical to ours in respect of surface regularity (F-regularity, observable regularity), it won't be G-regular. The present claim can then be stated as follows: suppose one grants that regularity is, in a sense, in the eye of the beholder (S_1 may look random to X but not to Y, because Y discerns a complicated pattern X cannot discern; similarly for S_2, Y and Z; and so on). Even so, if one does think that the world is regular in a certain kind of way—if one takes oneself to discern a certain deep and constant pattern in things, as we do—then (here is the claim) it's reasonable for one to suppose that that regularity is a G-regularity, not just an F-regularity. It's reasonable for one to suppose that it is objectively grounded in some way: that there is something about the nature of reality in virtue of which it has the (observable) regularity properties it does have.

[14] *Dialogues* 125/174. 'Original' here particularly suggests underived from (any) God.

he was genuinely prepared to be 'extravagantly sceptical' about, at least temporarily and for the sake of argument; but not Causation.

Hume, then, is not a 'Humean'. He standardly takes it for granted that if there is real regularity in the objects, as there is, then there must be something about the objects in virtue of which they are regular—something which is therefore not itself just the fact of regularity. He takes this for granted and insists only that we can know nothing about this something.[15]

There is one rather complicated and etiolated sense in which he may be said to be a regularity theorist, which it is worth recalling from 6.3. He may be said to be a regularity theorist about causation in 'the objects' just insofar as by 'objects' he means the 'immediate' mental objects of mental attention—'ontologically moderate pure-content-idealist objects' (strict-idealist, perception-content-constituted, *pcc* objects—p. 37). But insofar as he ever intends anything more by 'the objects' (as he standardly does) his claim is only that causation *so far as we know about it* in the objects is nothing but regular succession; not that all there is to causation is regular succession.

Even if it is right to say that Hume does at certain points conceive of 'the objects' as *pcc* objects, objects for which a regularity theory of causation is appropriate, he's *still* not a regularity theorist through and through. For he takes it for granted that (1) there must be something about reality in virtue of which it is regular. It follows that the claim that causation in the (*pcc*) objects is really nothing but regular succession is defensible only on the supposition that (2) the *pcc* objects are *not in fact all there is to reality*. If causation ('causation') in the *pcc* objects is really nothing but regular succession, then, given (1), reality considered as a whole must have some further aspect—since there must be something in reality which is that in virtue of which the *pcc* objects are regular in the way they are. Thus the *pcc* objects must have some further ontic nature or backing (God, in Berkeley's view), material or immaterial, as ground or as cause, over and above their existence as contents.

Once supposition (2) has been made, one can perfectly well suppose that there *is* something about reality considered as a whole which is the reason for the *pcc* objects' regularity—something which lies in the nature of their content-transcending ontic backing—while continuing to insist that when one considers the objects *just as contents* (as 'immediate' mental objects of mental attention), and in complete independence from their unknowable ontic backing,[16] then it is correct to say that causation, *in those objects so considered*, is just regular succession (ch. 15 n. 15).

If, on the other hand, one opts for the *ontologically outright* version of pure-content idealism (6.3), and supposes that the *pcc* objects do not have any further ontic backing at all—if one supposes that there is absolutely nothing more to reality

---

[15] Wouldn't 'a nothing…serve just as well as a something about which nothing could be said' or known? (Wittgenstein 1953: §304). No (see e.g. Strawson 2011: 31–2).

[16] As one may have good sceptical reasons for doing—cf. 6.7.

than *pcc* objects, and that they, pure contents, are themselves the ultimate *realia*—then one[17] can immediately no longer think of causation in the objects as just regular succession. For now one has only the *pcc* objects themselves in which to locate that in virtue of which reality is regular in the way that it is. So one has to suppose that causation in the *pcc* objects is more than regular succession after all: one has to suppose, however obscurely, that there is something about the nature of the *pcc* objects themselves, *qua* pure contents, in virtue of which they are regular in their behaviour in the way they are, something which is therefore not just their regularity.

So Hume can be a real regularity theorist about causation in the objects only insofar as he understands 'the objects' in such a way that there is some further aspect of reality which is over and above 'the objects', and which contains the reason for their regularity. He can't be a regularity theorist *tout court* in any case at all (he never wished to be any such thing). The only viable regularity theory of causation in the objects is one that supposes that 'the objects' are not in fact all there is to reality.

These last few paragraphs may seem fairly arcane, but Hume in his time would have found the line of thought they pursue natural, and, I submit, obvious. His only difficulty, I think, would have been with the suggestion that anyone could take the out-and-out regularity theory of causation seriously, as a theory about reality considered as a whole.

Hume is a great philosopher. He is not a 'Humean'. He takes it for granted that there is something about the nature of reality in virtue of which reality is regular in the particular inflexible way that it is, something of which we can form no positively contentful conception on the terms of the theory of ideas. He takes it for granted that there is Causation, some 'power or force, which actuates the whole machine . . . of the universe', and 'on which [the] regular . . . succession of objects totally depends' (55/5.22).

Appendix The Contingent Reality of Natural Necessity

1 In his paper 'Strawson on Laws and Regularities' (1991) Nicholas Everitt objects to my discussion of the regularity theory of causation in this book. I think the objection misses the point, but the point it misses is in a way a delicate one, and hard to express, and the general worry he expresses is a natural one. For that reason it is important, and its importance is reflected in the fact that it is very difficult to find a satisfyingly substantive way of stating the difference between regularity theories of causation and non-regularity theories of causation. I have had no new ideas about how to do this since I wrote 'Realism and Causation' and *The Secret Connexion*, but I will restate some of the ideas in the former, and in chapters 8 and 22 of the latter, in order to try to answer Everitt, who considers only chapter 5.

2 My principal doubt about Everitt's type of objection is this. Is it going to have the consequence that the regularity theory of causation is an a priori truth? I assume that most

---

[17] 'What is one?', one wonders.

philosophers would agree that the regularity theory of causation is not an a priori truth, and that any objection to an attempt to state a non-regularity theory of causation which had the consequence that the regularity theory of causation was an a priori truth would be unsatisfactory. I may be wrong in making this assumption: it may be that some defenders of the regularity theory of causation would not mind if their account of things had the consequence that the regularity theory was an a priori truth. But it would be very good to get this fact out into the open, if it is a fact.

Everitt's objection divides into two parts, which he calls (a) and (b) (Everitt 1991: 206). He is right that (a) is beside the point, and I will concentrate on (b), or rather on the general objection of which (b) is one particular expression. In talking of explanation he sets up the issue in terms I tried to avoid, but the basic point is nevertheless usefully summarized, again in terms of explanation, in the entry on the cosmological argument in Flew's *A Dictionary of Philosophy*, where it is observed that any attempt

to explain why things are as they are must always ultimately be made in terms of general facts that are not, and cannot be, further explained. So why should the existence of the Universe, and perhaps the fact that it has whatever fundamental regularities it does have, not be accepted as the fundamentals, requiring no further explanation? (1979: 74)

3 Going into a little more detail, I think one can state Everitt's final argument against my position as follows. (1) Either there is no ultimate explanation (or reason) for how things are, or there is. (2) To suppose that there is an ultimate explanation (or reason) for how things are is to suppose that some sort of 'ontological argument' can be used to show that what exists necessarily exists (perhaps by showing that there is something which necessarily existed in the past, whose existence necessitated, and explains, the existence of what now exists). (3) All such ontological arguments are hopeless. (4) So we have to accept that there is no ultimate explanation or reason for how things are.

But I am prepared to accept that ontological arguments are hopeless, and that there can be no ultimate explanation for how things are. So why is it thought that this undermines my objection to the regularity theory of causation?

Perhaps the idea that it does comes to this:

—You (G. S.) accuse the regularity theory of causation of being grossly implausible in claiming that the regularity of the behaviour of the universe has been, for fifteen billion years, a fluke, a matter of complete chance. And yet you are prepared to grant that there can be no ultimate explanation for anything. But to grant that there can be no ultimate explanation for anything is presumably to grant that everything is ultimately a fluke or a matter of complete chance— including, presumably, the regularity of the universe.

Most of us don't want to say that there is a reason for everything. We don't want to invoke the Principle of Sufficient Reason (according to which there is a reason for everything), and we know explanations come to an end. Nor do we want to employ ontological arguments to the effect that something that exists in the world necessarily exists. Most of us don't want to say that about anything. And so we seem obliged to hold that, ultimately, there is no reason for anything, and a fortiori, no ultimate reason why the world is regular in the particular way that it is.

You propose *the nature of matter* as the reason why the world is regular in the particular way that it is (see pp. 205–6). But those who do this face the question why the nature of matter is constant or regular in the way that it is. And if they give a reason R1 why the nature of matter is constant and regular in the way that it is, they will be asked why whatever is invoked in R1 is constant and regular in its underwriting of the constancy and regularity of the nature of matter. And if they give a reason R2 why whatever is invoked in R1 is constant and regular in its underwriting of the constancy and regularity of the nature of matter, they will be asked why whatever is invoked in R2 is constant and regular in its underwriting of the constancy and regularity of whatever is invoked in R1. The only way to stop this regress, short of an ontological argument, is to answer, at some point, 'That's just the way things are.'

In reply: I'm happy to say 'That's just the way things are' at some point. If someone asks why the nature of matter is as it is, I will say 'That's just the way things are', agreeing with Hume's spokesman Philo in his *Dialogues Concerning Natural Religion*. Philo asks the fundamental question: 'How could things have been as they are, were there not an original, inherent Principle of Order somewhere...?' (125/174). He knows explanations come to an end, and accordingly says 'Why not stop at the material World?' (94/161), when seeking to stop the regress of demands for explanation. For as he says, it may well be that 'such is the Nature of material Objects...that they are all originally possessed of a *Faculty* of Order and Proportion' (97/163). He suggests that 'were the inmost Essence of things laid open to us, we should then discover a Scene, of which, at present, we can have no Idea'. For 'we should clearly see, that it was absolutely impossible for them, in the smallest article, ever to admit of any other Disposition.' (125–6/174–5)

It may yet be asked how I can say 'That's just the way things are.' It may be said that to give this answer is to concede that regularity is an ultimate fact, not further explicable in terms of something which is a reason for it. And since the 'That's just the way things are' answer must be given at some point, it seems regularity must be an ultimate fact, not only not further explicable in any way, but also something for which there is, objectively, no reason. But to say this is to say that the regularity theory of causation must be true. And we reach this conclusion from our armchairs. So the regularity theory of causation is after all an a priori truth.

It is, however, a trivial point that all explanations come to an end. It would be very odd if it followed from this that the regularity theory of causation must be true. Ultimately we must stop giving reasons and say 'This is just how things are.' But this does not commit us to the necessary truth of the regularity theory of causation. It does not commit us to the view that there is, objectively, *in the nature of things as they currently exist*, no reason why they are regular in the way that they are—so that their regularity of behaviour from moment to moment to moment is, in some inescapable sense, a continuous fluke. For the matter which is 'just how things are' is: matter with a nature given which it cannot but behave as it does; matter whose nature is such that there is, as an ultimately *contingent* matter of fact, such a thing as 'natural necessity'.

And this, of course, is how things are. And so I am entirely happy to accept that there may be a sense in which it is, in Everitt's terms, 'flukish that the universe should contain precisely [the] set of basic substances' that it does (1991: 208). This is meant to be his final objection to my position, but I simply accept it, insofar as I accept the story of the Big Bang, and the coherence of the (admittedly difficult) idea that the Big Bang is itself something for which there was no reason at all! For, plainly, what banged into existence in the Big Bang was matter with a nature given which it cannot but behave as it does.

4 In the end, the whole thing comes down to the old question of whether one is prepared to accept the idea that there is or could be such a thing as natural necessity. Many empiricists and positivists cannot bear the idea of natural necessity. Even this late in the century [the date is 1991], they are tempted to say that the idea of natural necessity is 'unintelligible', meaning not just that we cannot fully understand it even if it exists, but that it is incoherent in some way, so that it cannot exist. They think that we cannot genuinely suppose that something exists unless we can say what would count as observing it, or at least as having good evidence for its existence. And they think that the regularity of the world does not count as (good but, of course, logically inconclusive) evidence for the existence of natural necessity, but only as (conclusive) evidence for the existence of regularity. In fact, they turn the regularity theory of causation into an a priori truth in their own inimitable way, by endorsing a theory of meaning according to which no attempt to state a rival theory of causation, that is, a non-regularity theory of causation, can count as properly meaningful. But I am still assuming that any account of things that turns the regularity theory of causation into an a priori truth is *ipso facto* vitiated.

Let me restate the point. Suppose there is not only no humanly attainable *explanation* of the existence of the universe, but also no *reason* for the existence of the universe. It just does not follow that everything that happens is ultimately a matter of chance, any more than it follows that a man is a bastard if his parents are. For what could possibly come into existence, by chance, is, precisely, some inherently non-chancy stuff—matter—something whose nature is such that it cannot but be regular in its behaviour—something that is, by its nature, *constitutionally* regular in its behaviour. And that, of course, is what we've got in this universe, however it came to exist.

At the risk of seeming to move confusingly close to the regularity view, one might express this position as follows. Reality is constitutionally regular. To say that reality is *constitutionally* regular is *not* to say that it *just is* regular. For it is true of an objectively utterly random (and therefore not constitutionally regular) world which is flukishly identical to our world in respect of its regularity properties that it *just is* regular. So to assert that regularity is constitutionally regular is to reject the regularity theory utterly. For it is to assert that there is something about the nature of reality in virtue of which it is regular in the way that it is: *so that the mere fact of its regularity isn't the only fact there is, when it comes to the question of what causation is.* The point may seem fine to some, but the italicized phrase denies the heart of the regularity theory.

5 Explanations come to an end, philosophical arguments go on for ever. I sympathize with Quine when he says

That there have been regularities, for whatever reason, is an established fact of science... *Why* there have been regularities is an obscure question, for it is hard to see what would count as an answer.[18]

---

[18] 1969: 126. In fact one can think that 'natural necessity' is a very good answer, while respecting the positivism that finds it hard to know what such an answer amounts to.

In these terms, the present position can be expressed as follows. We may grant for the sake of argument that the universe came into existence with the Big Bang, and that the Big Bang was not merely something of which we can give no explanation, but something for which there was, objectively, no reason. Now, however, the universe is in existence, and it has (we may assume) been running in a regular way ever since it came into existence. Let's suppose that Quine is right to say that it is hard to see what could count as an answer to the question of why there have been regularities. It is nevertheless a real question. And if the right answer to it is not 'There is some reason why, *given the nature of what came into existence in the Big Bang*', then the right answer to it is 'There is no reason why, *given the nature of what came into existence in the Big Bang*.' Perhaps my adherence to the non-regularity view of causation amounts to this: I cannot accept the second answer, and so I accept the first.

23

The meaning of 'cause'

23.1 Content: experience and concepts

One thing, perhaps, is undisputed. Hume claims that we have no sort of positively contentful experience or conception or understanding of the nature of power or causation as it is in the objects, insofar as it's more than regular succession. So far I've allowed that there's an important sense in which Hume is right about this. I wish now to question this. How far is he right in his claims about the nature and content of our *experience* of causation, and in his closely connected (too closely connected) claims about the nature and content of our *concept* of causation? How far is he right to say that regular succession is all we ever actually experience of causation, whatever causation may or may not be in itself? And how far is he right to say that the idea of power or necessary connection, which he holds to be part of the concept of causation, can only be an idea of a certain sort of feeling in the mind, insofar as it has any positive descriptive content? I'll argue that he is wrong in at least one important respect: our ordinary, essentially non-regularity-theory concept of causation is, despite its imprecision, fundamentally correct. It's fundamentally correct in its representation of the nature of causation in the world, and it is indeed a concept of the nature of causation *in the world*—contrary to Hume's view that its non-regularity-theory element (its power or necessary connection element) can only be an idea of a feeling in the mind.

I'll proceed loosely, and consider a number of different positions. One way to compare these positions is to assess their different attitudes to the four following claims.

(A) Causation is capital-C Causation. There is such a thing as causal power. There's something about the nature of the world in virtue of which it is regular in the way that it is, something which is therefore not just the regularity itself. The order and regularity of the world are not a coincidence from moment to moment to moment.

(B) The basic causation-relevant content of our directly object-derived experience of causation is just *regular succession* (our experience is experience of precedency ± contiguity-involving regular conjunction of types of object or event, made up of experience of precedency ± contiguity relations between particular objects/events).[1]

(C) Genuine Causation relations are not the same as, but entail, regular-succession relations. That is, if one particular event is truly said to be the cause of another particular event, then all events of the first type are succeeded by events of the second type; i.e. there is some description of the two events, say 'F' and 'G', under which they instantiate the universal generalization 'All Fs are succeeded by Gs'.[2]

(D) The *concept* of Causation, properly understood, essentially involves the concept of regular succession.

(D) is, as it were, the conceptual or epistemological correlate of (C). No doubt many people who can reasonably be said to have the concept of Causation don't think much about regular succession, but the concept of Causation may nonetheless be said to 'involve' the concept of regular succession, when properly understood. It may for example be said that it involves the idea of regular succession *a fortiori* just insofar as it involves the idea of necessity—or alternatively just insofar as it involves the thought that if a particular A-type event really is the true and sufficient cause of a particular B-type event, then it must be the case that if another A were to occur, it would bring about another B (or, more neutrally, another B would occur).[3] I take it that Hume accepts all of (A)–(D), although I will in what follows allow that the attribution of (A) to him can be disputed. Anscombe is an interesting example of someone who challenges (B), (C), and (D).

When setting out a position I will record its attitude to these four claims in square brackets, by writing [+A] if it accepts (A), [−A] if it rejects (A), [?A] if it positively asserts uncertainty about A, and ±A when it is compatible both with the assertion and the denial of A. When the position's attitude to one of these claims is

---

[1]   Obviously experience of precedency ± contiguity relations between particular objects/events isn't itself regular-succession experience, but it is the foundation of all regular-succession experience.

[2]   The regular-succession relation can be more strongly stated by adding the requirement that all events of the second type are preceded by events of the first type to the requirement that all events of the first type are succeeded by events of the second type. (Roughly, one adds 'If B then A' to 'If A then B'.) As Mackie has observed (1974: 62), the sort of thing we pick out as 'the' cause of something is, typically, neither necessary nor sufficient on its own for the thing we pick out as the effect. It is, rather, in his terms, an 'inus' condition (an insufficient but non-redundant part of an unnecessary but sufficient condition) of it. This, however, is no grounds for an objection to the idea that Causal relations entail regular-succession relations—the idea that, if circumstances exactly similar to the cause circumstances were to be realized again, then circumstances exactly similar to the effect circumstances would ensue.

[3]   The regularity-theory concept of causation obviously involves the concept of regular succession essentially, and many take the ordinary strong concept of Causation to include everything that is in the regularity-theory concept of causation while adding something more.

unimportant given the context of discussion, I will bracket the reference to the claim, or omit it altogether. Thus a position might be characterized as follows:

$[+A, +B, (\pm C), \pm D]$,

which could equally well be written as

$[+A, +B, \pm D]$.

The first position I wish to consider accepts (A). To accept (A) is to accept that our experience of causation in the objects is in fact experience of Causation. It's to accept that our experience of causation is experience *relationally* of Causation: that Causation is the phenomenon in the world that is actually being experienced.

The first position also agrees with Hume on (B). That is, it accepts that in spite of the truth of (A) there's a clear sense in which it's true to say that all we ever actually experience of causation in the objects is regular succession. The basic (causation-relevant) experiential content of our experience of causation in the world is just regular succession, even though that experience is in fact experience relationally of Causation. Regular succession is all the causation-relevant content that our experience of Causation has in itself, as it were, prior to the point at which the custom-influenced 'Imagination' (in Hume's special sense of the term—see p. 47 above) gets to work on it and makes it seem like something more.

I'll express this by saying that our directly object-derived experience of causation is *experientially* of Causation, but *relationally* only of regular succession. It may be objected that a full specification of the experiential content of an experience E will standardly involve reference to what E is relationally of. Perhaps so, but the above distinction—between what an experience is relationally of and what it is experientially of in the present sense—is clear enough, and useful. As the two terms are understood here, an experience may be relationally of a tree stump (seen in a mist, perhaps) and experientially not of a tree stump at all, but rather of a man.[4]

So far, then the first position accepts both (A) and (B). It may also be supposed to accept (C)—that Causation relations entail regular-succession relations; and, hence, to accept that if experience is relationally of Causation it is necessarily also relationally of something which involves regular succession.

We may summarize this position in Fig. (E1)

Fig. (E1). $[+ A, + B (+ C)]$. Our (overall) experience of causation in the objects is

	regular succession		Causation	
Relationally of	1	Yes	3	Yes
Experientially of	2	Yes	4	No

---

[4] I use 'experiential' in apposition to 'relational', rather than Quine's term 'notional' (Quine 1955), because 'notional' is more appropriate in the case of concepts and beliefs than in the case of experiences, and will be used in connection with concepts later on.

It's arguable that Hume holds this position. I think he does, for, as remarked, it seems clear that he accepts (C) as well as (B) (and (A)). And it seems equally clear that he accepts (D).[5]

The main alternative to this view is of course the view that Hume is a 'heroic' regularity theorist after all, and so rejects (A), holding the position shown in Fig. (e1).

Fig. (e1). [−A, + B, + C]. Our (overall) experience of causation in the objects is

		regular succession		Causation
Relationally of	1	Yes	3	No
Experientially of	2	Yes	4	No

This is of course a possible position. But Hume is not a 'heroic' regularity theorist in this sense.[6]

It may be suggested that the best thing to say is that Hume was perfectly agnostic on the question of whether or not (A) was true, so that the diagram should be as in Fig. (e2).

Fig. (e2). [?A, + B (+ C, + D)]. Our (overall) experience of causation in the objects is

		regular succession		Causation
Relationally of	1	Yes	3	?
Experientially of	2	Yes	4	No

Again, I simply note this position. I've argued that it is not Hume's position, and that he held the existence of Causation to be as certain as the existence of perceptions, hence that he accepted (A).

Although the box diagrams are rough, they may be useful. One complication in their interpretation will be of some importance later on, and is worth mentioning now. It concerns box 1. Does box 1 state that our experience of causation in the objects is relationally of something which involves *exceptionless* regular succession? Or does it just state that it is relationally of something that *involves* regularity of succession—no doubt a great deal of it—but does not in fact involve *exceptionless* regular succession? Both attitudes to box 1 are possible. For the moment no decision on the question is necessary.

Now for another objection to (E1) as an account of Hume's position: although he holds that our *experience* of causation in the objects is, in respect of its true or basic content, just experience of regular succession, he also and nevertheless holds that our

---

[5] At this stage the truth or falsity of (C) and (D) are unimportant.

[6] Clearly, if one holds that causation is just regular succession, one needn't take up a position on (C) and (D). One may hold that they're untenable, or that they're true but irrelevant.

ordinary *concept* of causation is a concept of Causation: he holds that it's an essentially non-regularity-theory concept of causation, because he holds that it essentially involves the notion of necessary connection (162/1.3.14.14, 74–5/7.27). It seems, then, that we may need to add a separate diagram of our *concept* of causation to the diagram of our *experience* of causation. And the present suggestion is that Hume's overall view is best represented by Fig. (E1), as before, and also by a concept diagram (c1).

Fig. (c1). [+ A, + B, (+ C, + D)]. Our concept of causation in the objects is

		regular succession		Causation
Relationally of	1	Yes	3	Yes
Notionally of	2	?/Yes	4	Yes

(c1) won't do, however, for a simple reason—the words 'in the objects'.[7] Although Hume grants that our concept of causation is a concept of something which essentially involves necessary connection or power, he also holds that the notion of necessary connection or power in question is essentially derived from something— a feeling—that exists only in the mind, and that cannot therefore be said to be a notion of—or to be notionally of—some property *in the objects*. (It will be argued later that this is, in a sense, his central classical empiricist mistake, and that in one passage he comes very close to seeing this.) So he would certainly have rejected (c1) as an account of the nature of our concept of causation in the objects. For the essential principle of Hume's empiricism is that all concepts derive directly from experience in such a way that the notional content of a concept cannot exceed the content of the experience from which it is derived. So the diagram of our concept of causation as it is in the objects mustn't ascribe more genuine content to the concept than there is to be found in the basic content of experience of causation in the objects. So although Hume may grant that there is some real sense in which our concept of causation is indeed a concept of Causation—i.e. an essentially non-regularity-theory concept of causation—he will nevertheless insist that it isn't a concept of Causation as it is *in the objects*: we can't attain to such a notion at all, given our experience. We're 'perfectly ignorant' of the nature of Causation as it is in the objects. We're deluded when we think that our admittedly non-regularity-theory concept of causation really is a true concept of causation-in-the-objects. Our actual admittedly non-regularity-theory concept of causation is a curious hybrid, deriving its non-regularity-theory element from a feeling in the mind. So the concept-diagram (c1) is incorrect: a 'No' must be entered in box 4. If (E1) is the correct diagram of Hume's position with

---

[7] The question-mark occurs in box 2 because Hume doesn't have to claim that the ordinary person, who thinks of causation as involving necessary connection, has to think explicitly of it as involving precedency ±contiguity and constant conjunction.

respect to the nature of our *experience* of causation in the objects, then the matching diagram (C1) is the correct diagram of his position on the nature of our *concept* of causation in the objects:

Fig. (C1). [+ A, + B (+ C, + D)]. Our concept of causation in the objects is

		regular succession		Causation
Relationally of	1	Yes	3	Yes
Notionally of	2	?/Yes	4	No

The Imagination has many devices, according to Hume, and can 'feign' all sorts of things. But the 'true' content of our concept of causation in the objects cannot really come apart from the 'true' content of our experience of causation. The content of the concept of causation in the objects can't *exceed* the content of the experience of causation in the objects, even if it can fall short of it in some way (as with the '?' in box 2 of C1—cf. n. 7).

It's worth noting that some today are inclined to agree with Hume that the content of our experience of causation and the content of our concept of causation can't come apart. But they reverse the direction of argument, holding that this is because experience is essentially concept-structured and concept-driven in such a way that the nature of our experience of causation is essentially determined by our concept of causation.

23.2 The 'Anscombean' approach

I wish now to consider a different approach to this question. I'll call it the 'Anscombean' approach, after one of its main proponents, although the following account of it may not be true to her intentions in all respects. It questions (B), (C), and (D), but not (A). With regard to (B), it takes on Hume directly, when he 'confidently challenges us to "produce some instance, wherein... [causal] efficacy is plainly discoverable to the mind, and its operations obvious to our consciousness or sensation"'.[8] It suggests that we may indeed be said to have directly object-derived experience of the nature of Causation (or force) in our everyday, active and passive (and essentially conceptually informed) experience of things like cutting, drinking, scraping, pushing, carrying, burning, bumping, squashing, and so on.[9] Our experience of causation in the objects may be not only relationally but also experientially of Causation, contrary to the Humean view, according to which it's experientially only of regular succession even if it's relationally of Causation.

[8] Anscombe 1971: 137, quoting Hume 157–8/1.3.14.6. Others have also argued that we have direct experience of causal power, and I'll only consider certain aspects of Anscombe's position.
[9] Ibid. See also P. F. Strawson 1985: 123–5.

There's a simple version and a more complex version of the view that we have directly object-derived experience of Causation. According to the simpler view, the merely sensory quality of our experience (e.g. of resistance and bodily interaction) is crucial. Independently of what concepts we may or may not bring to bear, we have direct experience of causal power or force. Thus a baby who has yet to acquire any concepts has such experience. I will call this 'simple direct realism'. According to the more complex view (which is perhaps closer to Anscombe's position) the fact that our experience of things is constitutively informed by a certain non-regularity-theory *conception* of causation (mastery of which is presupposed in mastery of words like 'scrape', 'push', 'carry') is equally important. Or more important: some who hold this view may claim that the way in which our experience is constitutively informed by our ordinary non-regularity-theory conception of causation is sufficient for it to count as directly object-derived experience of Causation even if the simple direct realist view of our experience of Causation is rejected. I'll call this 'complex (or concept-assisted) direct realism', and will consider the difference between the two versions further below.

How does the Anscombean view relate to the Humean view as summarized in (E1) and (C1)? Taking (E1) as a basis, the immediate challenge is to box 4. The suggestion is that the 'No' in box 4 should be changed to 'Yes', to give (e3). And the same should be done in (C1).

Fig. (e3). [+ A, −B]. Our (overall) experience of causation in the objects is

		regular succession		Causation
Relationally of	1	Yes	3	Yes
Experientially of	2	Yes	4	Yes

The Anscombean challenge goes further, however. It also challenges (C), the claim that Causation relations entail regular-succession relations, and in particular (C)'s conceptual correlate (D), the claim that the concept of causation properly understood necessarily involves the concept of regular succession. As regards (C), Anscombe suggests that a particular sequence of events F–G may be causal without it being true that if an F-type event (an event just like F in all respects) were to occur again then a G-type event would have to occur again. So, as far as (D) is concerned, properly to conceive of F as the cause (even as the individually sufficient, or total cause) of G is not *ipso facto* to conceive of Fs and Gs as being so related that any F is (necessarily) followed by a G.

It is in fact the rejection of (D) that is primary here. The fundamental idea is that the concept of causation does not essentially involve the idea that two things that stand in the relation of cause to effect *ipso facto* stand in the relation of being instances of types of event that stand in a regular-succession or constant-conjunction relation. Someone who rejects (D) can apparently leave open the question of the truth or falsity of (C), granting that it may in fact be the case that all Causation relations necessarily involve regular-succession relations, while denying that this is a necessary part either of our existing concept of causation, or of any improved version of it which we may feel moved to propose as philosophers.[10]

This suggests (E2) as an 'Anscombean' diagram of our experience of causation.

Fig. (E2). [+ A, −B, ?C]. Our (overall) experience of causation in the objects is

	regular succession		Causation	
Relationally of	1	?	3	Yes
Experientially of	2	?	4	Yes

There is, however, a problem about how exactly box 1 is to be interpreted. It may be said that, although Anscombeans hold that a particular sequence of events F–G may be causal without it being true that if an event exactly like F were to occur again then an event exactly like G would have to occur again (in which case our experience of causation in the world is not experience of an *exceptionless* regular succession world),[11] they don't wish to claim that our *overall* experience of causation might not be of regularities of succession at all. In which case the '?' in box 1 is unwarranted, and should be replaced by 'Yes'. Anscombeans will surely grant that there is a great deal of regularity in the world, and that our experience of causation is to a large extent of real—even if not exceptionless—regularities.

At this point, however, one may take up the option of understanding regular succession as 'exceptionless regular succession' when considering box 1. I shall do this from now on; it seems a good course to adopt when considering the Anscombean position. The question is then 'Is our experience of that which constitutes causation in the world in fact relationally of exceptionless regular succession?'[12] And the Anscombean suggestion is that it may not be: that there may be event sequences (F–G, H–J, K–L, etc.) which are in fact causal sequences although the types of event of which F and G, H and J, K and L are instances do not stand in the constant-conjunction or regular-succession relation, considered as pairs. In which case our *general, overall* experience of causation may be relationally of Causation and yet not relationally of something which involves (exceptionless) regular succession. One doesn't have to deny (1) that any extended experience of causation is bound to involve

---

[10] As regards the concept: it may be, as remarked, that many (perhaps most) who can reasonably be said to have a concept of causation, and indeed an essentially non-regularity-theory concept of causation, wouldn't find (D) compelling when presented with it, even if it were fully explained to them, and even if they appeared to take it for granted in practice. As regards the fact: it may be argued that a possible world in which (C) is false may nonetheless be a world in which there is Causation.

[11] In an exceptionless regular-succession world, if F–G is causal, then if an event identical to F occurs, an event identical to G must (will certainly) occur.

[12] Perhaps it's worth pointing out that even a 'Yes' answer to this question in no way rules out the possibility of indeterministic occurrences, for such occurrences will, precisely, not involve causation.

a certain amount (indeed a great deal) of regular-succession experience in order to deny (2) that experience of causation must be experience of what is in fact an exceptionless regular succession world.[13]

If one adopts an Anscombean view of causation, then, one can claim that experience may be (relationally) of Causation without being (relationally) of *exceptionless* regular succession. Thus one can put a '?' (or even a 'No', if one thinks one has good grounds for it) in box 1 of the diagram. Again, someone can hold that the 'true' or basic experiential content of one's experience of causation is as Hume supposed (involving precedency±contiguity constant-conjunction experience) even if the world it is relationally speaking an experience of is not in fact an *exceptionless* regular-succession world. So a 'Yes' can be entered in box 2 even if a '?' or a 'No' is entered in box 1.

The interpretation of the diagram is accordingly a little more complex than it appears. For a 'Yes' in box 1 means that one's experience of causation in the objects is relationally of exceptionless regular succession; whereas a 'Yes' in box 2 (together with a 'No' in box 4) means simply that one's experience of causation in the objects is experientially as Hume supposed,[14] and doesn't mean that it is experientially of *exceptionless* regular succession.

(E2), then, gives the 'Anscombean' account of our *experience* of causation. The correct account of the *concept* of causation closely matches the account of the experience, as shown in C2.

Fig. (C2). [+ A, −B, −C, −D]. Our concept of causation in the objects is

	regular succession		Causation	
Relationally of	1	?	3	Yes
Notionally of	2	?/No	4	Yes

This diagram explicitly incorporates the objection to (D), with '?/No' in box 2. On this view, to have a correct conception of what it is for one thing to cause another is not necessarily to conceive of them as so related that anything just like the first thing is always (or necessarily) followed by a thing just like the second thing.

23.3 The wisdom of nature

Two main positions have emerged: the (real) Humean position (E1)/(C1), and the 'Anscombean' position (E2)/(C2). I'll now state a third position which combines

---

[13] Someone might conceivably deny (1)—the question is whether it is coherent to suppose that there could be a world (an apparently chaotic world) in which everything was in fact governed by Causation although this Causation never involved any regularity of succession (not because event-types never occurred more than once, but because, although F caused G one time, the next time it caused H or J).

[14] Ignoring for now his important concession (78/7.29n) discussed in 19.2 above.

elements of both, and in so doing I'll try to give, in an informal and impressionistic way, a general account of our concept of causation. This will mix elements of empiricism and rationalism into a kind of theory-of-evolution-assisted, 'intellectua-listic direct-realist' account of our relation to and apprehension and understanding of Causation—the essentially non-regularity-theory causation which (I take it) actually exists in the world. I'll suggest that our acquaintance with Causation may be, in one sense, experientially speaking indirect while being intellectually or conceptually speaking direct.

This third position accepts that there is such a thing as Causation (+A). Next, in order to make its principal point, it simply concedes to Hume and the Humeans (and the 'Humeans') that there's an important sense in which the basic (causation-relevant) experiential content of our *experience* of causation in the objects is just regular succession, even though it's experience that is relationally of Causation (+B). That is, it puts aside—if only for the sake of argument—the suggestion that there's a sense in which we have direct experience of causal power.[15] But it then claims—crucially—that it simply doesn't follow that our *concept* of causation in the objects isn't a genuine concept of Causation in the objects. Thus it simply rejects the essential principle of empiricism of the Humean kind. It suggests that the content of our ordinary, strong conception of causation (in the objects) naturally and unproblem-atically extends beyond the regular-succession experience that figures as the basic content of our experience of causation, in such a way as to be a true or genuine concept of Causation. The concept goes beyond the regular-succession experiential basis as a result of a process of essentially cognitive or intellectual elaboration (if the Humean framework is suitably stretched, this can be seen as a process of elaboration by the Imagination, resulting from the effect of custom on the Imagination). It thereby manages to genuinely contentfully latch on to, and in some important sense correctly represent, the nature of causation in the world.

On this view, our ordinary, everyday, intuitive idea of causation as something essentially more than regular succession is essentially correct (or at least may be—this is all one has to grant, in order to see the present point). Contrary to Hume's official theory of ideas (cf. 10), the content of an idea or concept isn't a strict function of its impression-source. If it's said to be a product of the 'Imagination' working on the basic experiential content delivered by the senses and elaborating a richer notion of causation out of this basic content, so much the better for the Imagination. The Imagination is then not a source of error, or of fiction in some pejorative sense. It's a source of truth. (It's just that we cannot know that it is.)

---

[15] Again it's worth recalling Hume's argument (78/7.29n, see p. 180) that such experience, even if (or rather even though) real, can't be supposed to yield any sort of genuine grasp of the nature of Causation. Hume puts the point unsatisfactorily from the present point of view, because he's so concerned to stress the fact that experience can't give us a capacity for a priori certain causal inference, but there's an extremely important and valid point in what he says, discussed further in 23.4.

Thus there is Causation (+A). But we experience it through the *evidential bottle-neck* of our experience of regular succession (+B). Regular-succession experience is, in a fundamental sense, all that is delivered by sense experience alone. Despite this, our essentially partly cognitive or intellectual or Imagination-enhanced (and in any case not merely sense-based) concept of causation can be said to capture—to capture correctly—something about the nature of reality which is simply not given in sense experience. Certainly we can't know for sure that it does. (−A) may be true. But it may, and it very probably does. (Of course it does.)[16]

The diagram of our experience is thus as in Fig. (E3). Recall that the answer in box 1 is now to the question whether our experience of causation is in fact of *exceptionless* regular succession.[17] The answers in boxes 2 and 4 are to the question whether the basic content of our experience of causation is just regular-succession content. Boxes 2 and 4 correspond to (+B), the fundamental Humean claim about the content of our experience of causation in the world.

Fig. (E3). [+ A, + B (±C, ±D)]. Our (overall) experience of causation in the objects is

	regular succession		Causation	
Relationally of	1	?/Yes	3	Yes
Experientially of	2	Yes	4	No

The diagram of our *concept* of causation is as in (C3). And this closely corresponds to the Anscombean diagram of the concept.[18]

Fig. (C3). [+ A, + B (±C, ±D)]. Our concept of causation in the objects is

	regular succession		Causation	
Relationally of	1	?/Yes	3	Yes
Notionally of	2	?	4	Yes

It is worth noting that a matching of 'Yes's or 'No's across a horizontal line indicates *representational success* on the part of the experience or concept. It indicates

[16] Hume can't put things like this, of course. Given the strict theory of ideas, the contribution of the effect of custom on the Imagination to our idea of causation can only be to produce another impression (of power or force) whose source is in the mind; and we will be mistaken if we think that this impression can contribute to a correct idea of causation in the objects. It's only when one starts operating with the richer and looser notion of the Imagination mentioned in 23.1, according to which 'the Imagination' is taken as a general name for certain very basic structuring features of our cognitive apparatus, that one can say that the Imagination can be a source of truth about the world.

[17] The '?' corresponds to the Anscombean (±C); the 'Yes' corresponds to (+C). Recall (n. 12) that (+C) is compatible with the denial of determinism: it says only that *causal* relations involve regular-succession relations, not that everything is caused.

[18] It's equally compatible with Mackie's causally temperamental chocolate machines (1974: ch. 2), and his observation that what we pick out as 'the' cause of something is, typically, an 'inus' condition of it (cf. n. 2).

that the experience or concept is in some way or genuinely 'notionally' capturing the nature of the thing it is relationally a concept of. In the diagram pair (E3)/(C3) the concept is held to improve on the experience: it achieves a representation of an aspect of reality—Causation—that isn't achieved by the basic experiential content of our experience of causation. Thus the natural, fully fledged, intellectually or cognitively elaborated concept of causation which most people ordinarily possess, elaborated on the basis of regular-succession experience, is not merely some kind of 'fictional' (in Hume's sense) product of the 'Imagination', a sort of 'post-modern' (in the archi-tectural sense of 'functionally or practically useless') extension of the basic, strict empiricist, fully sensory-experience-grounded, positivistically vetted, regular-succession concept of causation. For while it is indeed an extension of the purely sense-experience-grounded concept of causation (given (+B)), it also gets closer to reality, as a reality-representer, than the positivistically vetted concept (as repre-sented in (C1)). Thus the Imagination (arising as a result of evolution by natural selection) has a role in helping us to achieve a truer representation of reality. It is not just a source of error. Since it is (in Humean phrase) something implanted in us by nature in its wisdom, it's not surprising that it helps us to get things right, even if we can (for familiar sceptical reasons) never actually prove that it gets things right.

In the (E3)/(C3) diagram pair, then, the concept is held to improve on the experience in a certain key respect. But this difference between experience and concept emerges only given the use of (a) a notion of the 'basic' experiential content of experience which considers our experience independently of the way in which it is informed by our concepts, and the adoption for the sake of argument of (b) an essentially Humean view of what this basic content of our experience of causation is. Clearly, one can drop (b), and return to a more Anscombean position, by replacing the 'No' in box 4 of (E3) by a 'Yes'. But it needs to be borne in mind that there are two versions of the Anscombean position: the 'simple' direct realist version and the 'complex (concept-assisted)' direct realist version. The simple direct realist suggests that direct experience of Causation—causal force—is part of the basic content of our experience even when our experience is considered independently of our automatic deployment of concepts of causal power or force. Thus a baby has such experience prior to any acquisition of concepts. The complex direct realist holds that it is only when and insofar as we consider our experience as something constitutively informed by our concepts that we can reasonably be said to have direct experience of causal power or force, in experiencing the world as we do in our everyday life. The two views can be reconciled, for one can endorse the first while agreeing that it is also important to acknowledge the way in which our concepts inform and affect the phenomenal character of our experience.

In the next section I'll say something more about the process of intellectual or Imaginative 'elaboration' that equips us with a true concept of Causation. First, though, it may help to relate the present position a bit more closely to Hume's views.

The first thing to note is that it can be represented within the Humean framework by means of a simple extension of the diagram used (in 10, p. 103) to illustrate the

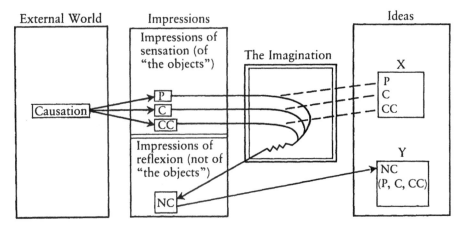

Figure 2 The experience of cause and the concept of cause

application of Hume's theory of ideas to the idea or concept of causation. All one has to do is to add the 'External World' to the diagram, as something distinct from impressions of sensation, and as something in which there is Causation, which gives rise to our experience of causation. Given this addition it can be said that there's a clear sense in which it is Y, the Imagination-enhanced concept of causation in the objects, not X, the empiricistically pure concept of causation in the objects, which gets the world right, although the process by which it does so is complicated, as shown by the line(s) from Causation in the world, on the left, to the NC-incorporating idea of Causation on the right. Departing further from Hume, one can have the lines from P, C, and CC converging in the Imagination—'the Imagination' being in effect a name for our evolved innate cognitive equipment—and heading straight for Y.)

Speaking of the Imagination, Hume says that it is 'a magical faculty in the soul, which... is inexplicable by the utmost efforts of human understanding' (24/1.1.7.15). It's arguable, however, that it isn't inexplicable at all. It's a product of evolution by natural selection, and is vital to survival.[19] And in fact this is a possibility which Hume arguably comes very close to acknowledging at one point, although his emphasis, in the passages I will quote, is principally on the fact of our natural reliance on inductive processes (which we share with non-concept-possessing animals),

---

[19] On the question of inexplicability, note that there is no inconsistency in holding both (1) that the principles of operation of the Imagination are, so far as their ultimate nature is concerned, completely mysterious and inexplicable, but also (2) that its existence in us and its nature is explicable in a *general* way by reference to the fact that it is 'necessary to the subsistence of our species' (55/5.21). (The general explanation goes simply as follows: if we exist, something like the Imagination has to exist and work something like this—whether God or evolution brings this about.)

rather than on the correlative fact that we, as fully fledged concept-exercising creatures, possess and believe in the validity of an explicit concept of Causation.

I offer these quotations because I think they're suggestive. I do not claim to prove that Hume is thinking along the lines I have in mind. There is, he says,

a kind of *pre-established harmony* between the course of nature and the succession of our ideas; and though *the powers and forces, by which the former is governed,* be wholly unknown to us; yet our thoughts and conceptions have still, we find, gone on in the same train with the other works of nature. (54–5/5.21)

That is, in their way our thoughts and conceptions match and accurately represent the actual power-and-force-governed character of nature, involving as they do our deep commitment to belief in the existence of necessary connection in nature (this being the conceptually explicit expression of our natural reliance on inductive processes).

Hume continues as follows:

Custom is that principle, by which this *correspondence* has been effected; so *necessary to the subsistence of our species*...Those who delight in the discovery and contemplation of *final causes*, have here ample subject to employ their wonder and admiration (55/5.21)

when they consider the question of how this fundamental principle of the human mind came to be established (by God, or by some natural process such as evolution).

[T]his operation of the mind, by which we infer like effects from like causes, and *vice versa*, is so essential to the subsistence of all human creatures, [that] it is not probable, that it could be trusted to the fallacious deductions of our reason, which is slow in its operations...and... extremely liable to error and mistake. It is more conformable to the ordinary wisdom of nature to secure so necessary an act of the mind, by some *instinct or mechanical tendency*...[N]ature has...implanted in us an instinct, *which carries forward the thought in a correspondent course to that which she has established among external objects*; though we are ignorant of those powers and forces, on which this regular course and succession of objects totally depends. (55/5.22)

In making causal inferences as we do, and with the beliefs that accompany those inferences, we are in effect deploying a concept of Causation.[20] And we're *right* to do so. What happens is that the Imagination works the merely regular-succession notion of causation in the objects into a truer notion of causation in the objects, a notion of Causation.

Hume obviously can't put things in this way, because he's committed to his strict empiricist account of the positive descriptive content of concepts. He can, certainly, say that it's part of the wisdom of nature to make us rely implicitly on inductive procedures, and reason about matters of fact as if we knew that the world was

---

[20] This is the right thing to say given that we're language-endowed, concept-exercising creatures, but it's important to note the sense in which dogs and other animals may also be said to make such inferences (see 176–9/1.3.16).

governed by necessary causal laws. But he can't say that our power-or-necessary-connection-involving *concept* of causation in the objects is a truer or more complete concept of causation in the objects, because the power-or-necessary-connection element in our actual concept of causation doesn't derive from the objects in the way it must, according to the theory of ideas, if it is genuinely to apply to, or be about, the objects. The devious route from Causation (or NC) in the world to the concept Y (or NC) in the mind isn't an acceptable one, according to the theory of ideas.

The present suggestion is that it is an acceptable route. Y can count as a true idea of causation in the objects, given such an aetiology. Consider, after all, the route by which we acquire the notion of a genuinely external physical object, according to Hume. It is in effect the same as the route by which we acquire our strong notion of causation as Causation: the Imagination works mere 'constancy and coherence' (194–5/1.4.2.18–20) among impressions into ideas of genuinely external objects. These ideas are simply the result of the effect of a certain kind of experience—constancy-and-coherence experience—on the Imagination.

This comparison between our idea of objects and our idea of causation is worth bearing in mind. For many today who think that we can form a genuine notion of an external object endorse Hume's reasons for rejecting the claim that we can form any genuine notion of causation in the objects as being something more than regular succession. It seems, however, that the reasons for rejecting the claim that we can form a genuine notion of Causation in the objects threaten to count as much against the claim that we can form a genuine notion of external objects. For all their faults, the phenomenalists were at least vividly aware of this.

I'll end this section by suggesting that there is an important sense in which Hume is a *nativist* with respect to the concept of causation—and, in particular, with respect to the necessary-connection-involving, non-regularity-theory concept of Causation that (as he rightly observes) we all ordinarily possess. This suggestion may at first seem preposterous, but I think it is both harmless and true, even if Hume would not have wished to put things this way.

The argument for it is simple, and implicit in the foregoing. It can be given in question-and-answer form. Why is it that we, as concept-exercising creatures, invariably respond to our experience of regularities by forming and deploying the (concept-of-Causation-involving) belief that there is Causation in the world? We could in theory have responded quite differently (if it had not been for the wisdom of nature). It might have been the case that regularity-experience made us laugh or cry, or think of frogs or the colour pink. So why is it that the basic effect of custom on the Imagination is always the same, and so very specific, so far as regularity-experience is concerned?

The ultimate answer is: because of the wisdom of nature, or the operation of evolution by natural selection. This answer contains as a part the more specific answer which is relevant at present: the reason why this, among all possible effects, is the particular and invariable effect of custom on the Imagination, so far as regularity-experience is concerned, is that we are *innately disposed* in such a way that we respond to this sort of experience by developing and deploying this concept. And in that sense the concept of Causation is innate in us. Certainly the concept must be *activated* by experience. But this is no objection to the claim that it is innate, for sophisticated nativists like Leibniz have always acknowledged that innate concepts may need to be activated by experience (compare Kant, *Critique* B1). The crucial point is simply this: Hume is clear that it is always this particular imaginative-cum-cognitive reaction that is forthcoming in response to regularity-experience; it is this particular concept or idea that is duly activated and deployed. How can this be so, unless it's innate in us in the moderate sense of the word 'innate' just mentioned? It's innate in us in just the sense in which all the characteristic principles of operation of the mind (and passions) are, on Hume's (essentially correct if necessarily rather unspecific) view of the matter.

A similar argument can be given for the view that he's a nativist with respect to the concept of an object: an essentially concepts-of-objects-involving view of the world is what we invariably come up with, when exposed to constancy-and-coherence experience. The process is 'natural and necessary in the human mind' (266/1.4.7.4), and our concepts of an object and of causation doubtless evolve together. They're inextricably intertwined, and to deal with them separately is somewhat artificial even if it's not misleading.[21, 22]

23.4 Causation: a non-sensory property

To conclude. The present position acknowledges the force of direct realism (both simple and complex) about experience of Causation, but grants for the sake of argument the Humean view of the 'true' basic content of our experience of causation in the objects (nothing but regular succession). Accordingly it holds that our experience of Causation is filtered through a kind of evidential bottleneck which delivers only regular-succession experience, and is then 'intellect-enhanced' (as in a computer-enhanced image), in fully fledged concept-exercising creatures like ourselves, and in a way laid down by the 'wisdom of nature', or in other words by evolution,

---

[21] It's worth considering the idea that Kant could have included the concept of an object among the categories, along with the concept of causation (it seems that he once did, in the *Duisburg Nachlass*—see Walker 1978: 107). Hume's clearly correct idea that these two concepts are innate in us, in the sense that they're an essential part of the innate cognitive response-structure of the human mind, is importantly akin to Kant's conception of innate, fundamental experience-structuring categories.

[22] Note added in 2012. When I published *The Secret Connexion* I didn't know about work in developmental psychology on the innateness of the concepts OBJECT and CAUSE (see e.g. Spelke 1990, Baillargeon 2004). One natural picture of the innateness of these concepts dispenses with the idea of the Imagination (our innate cognitive disposition) 'working' the material delivered by sense into fully fledged concepts of objects, in favour of the idea of some simpler 'triggering' of the innate concept by appropriate sensory inputs.

into a genuine concept of Causation which genuinely applies to and in its own inexplicit way correctly represents something essential to the actual nature of causation in reality. That is, it represents the fact that causation is Causation, and essentially involves something more than regular succession, however exactly one proposes to characterize this something more: in terms of causal power, or of the 'fundamental forces', or in terms of one thing bringing about or producing another, or in terms of the *existential derivativeness* or *existential dependence* (212/1.4.2.47) of one thing on another, or—superneutrally and perhaps preferably—simply in terms of something about reality given which it is and can't but be regular in the way that it is.[23] This genuine concept of Causation—our ordinary pre-philosophical concept, with all the indeterminacy that the words 'our' and 'ordinary' bring with them—is perhaps essentially vague. Nevertheless it captures something true and fundamental about reality in going essentially beyond a merely regular-succession conception of causation in the way that it does.

Humeans ('Humeans') will say that this is a classic case of the mind 'projecting' onto objects features of its own devising that aren't really there in the objects—or at least aren't to be found in what they're prepared to count as the true content of our experience of objects.[24] But the present position can grant that it may be reasonable to talk of some sort of projection taking place. For, instead of seeing this process as a source of error, it sees it as a source of truth and understanding. If we 'project', why do we project as we do, in the case in which we apply a concept of Causation to reality? Because nature (evolution by natural selection) has formed us in this way. But nature has formed us in this way because of the fundamental respect in which truth is generally useful; we're designed to form true beliefs on many matters, especially on matters of vital importance. This is one such matter.

There's a predictable objection to this, which is formally correct but hardly damaging: 'Evolution by natural selection would have formed us in exactly the same way in an outrageous-run-of-luck universe which was just like ours except that there was in fact nothing but regular succession.' This point can simply be granted here (although one may reasonably protest that the notion of evolution by natural selection is itself an entirely non-regularity-theory notion).[25] For the claim is not that we can *prove* that there is Causation by reference to the fact that evolution has designed us to believe in it. We can't *prove* it by any means. The idea is rather that evolution may very well bring us to formulate a certain idea about the nature of reality (the idea that there is Causation in reality) because the idea is in fact a usefully

---

[23] Hume and Anscombe are arguably close to agreement here: where Hume says that in the case of causal connection between two things 'the existence of one is dependent on that of the other' (212/ 1.4.2.47), Anscombe (1971: 136) suggests that 'causality consists in the derivativeness of an effect from its causes. This is the core, the common feature, of causality in its various kinds.'

[24] They'll see 'complex' ('concept-assisted') direct realism (p. 221) as incorporating a kind of projection.

[25] In a fluke universe there would be something that looked just like evolution by natural selection, but it wouldn't really be any such thing.

correct idea about the nature of reality, although the aspect of the nature of reality which it is a correct idea about is (contrary to simple direct realism) not directly accessible in the basic content of our experience of nature.

One could say this: when thinking about concept-formation, empiricism goes wrong in limiting itself to the *ontogenetic* perspective, the case of the *individual's* elaboration of concepts on the basis of experience. It ought to think also in *phylo-genetic* terms, in terms of the evolution over millions of years of the unvarying predisposition of animals like ourselves (who have now come to be concept-exercis-ing creatures in the strongest possible sense) to form certain specific concepts in response to their experience. We, products of evolution, are all disposed to come to believe that there is Causation in reality on the basis of our experience.[26] So even if we do in some sense just 'project' our idea of Causation onto the world, in spite of the fact that we don't really find Causation in the 'true' or basic experiential content of our experience of the world (it's very questionable whether this is in the end a helpful thing to say), this is because experience of Causation *is* in effect to be found in the millions-of-years-long history of the race.[27]

So we 'project', if you like. But what we project really is out there in reality, and its presence out there in reality is in fact the true explanation of why we are so inflexibly disposed to project in the way we do. If we project a concept of Causation onto reality, it's because the presence of Causation in reality has caused us, over millions of years, to become such as to project in this way, i.e. to get things right in this way. And exactly the same is true of objects—one can substitute 'objects' for 'Causation' in the preceding sentence. So understood, projectivism about X is compatible with fully fledged realism about X. The aeonic process of the formation of our intellect (which includes the Humean Imagination) is part of the process whereby we, as we are, are able to come at truth, and represent the world, in certain respects, and to a certain extent, as it really is.[28]

This, then, is one way of bringing the theory of evolution into the discussion: by suggesting that empiricism should take account of the phylogenetic dimension and time-scale in giving its account of the nature of concept-formation on the basis of experience. One could put the point by saying that there is a sense in which the theory of evolution comes strongly to the support of rationalism—but there need be no conflict between empiricism and rationalism, as currently conceived. For the present suggestion is that the theory of evolution comes strongly to the support of

---

[26] We would certainly be right to trace the origins of this disposition back to a non-concept-exercise-based reactive tendency in our remote ancestors which is still to be found everywhere in the rest of animal creation, but this doesn't affect the present point.

[27] Similar but lesser things can be said about animals that don't have language or concepts in the way we do.

[28] Again it may be asked why so many philosophers are ready to be realists about objects, holding that there's a fundamental sense in which we get things right with our concepts of objects, while continuing to insist that we don't get anything right with our concept of causation.

rationalism only via the fundamental empiricist premiss, to which a phylogenetic interpretation has been given: that all concepts are derived from experience.

Simple direct realists may again object that we do have direct experience of Causation, that the concession to Hume in box 4 of (E3) is excessive, and that position 2—(E2) + (C2)—is closer to the truth. And, with one major qualification, the objection may be allowed, because the currently central claim—the claim that our ordinary concept of causation is fundamentally correct in its representation of the nature of causation in reality—doesn't depend on rejecting it.

The qualification is very important, however. It would be a great mistake to think that direct experience of force or efficacy of the sort envisaged by the simple direct realists can be supposed to be the sole and sufficient source of the regularity-theory-transcending component of our notion of causation as Causation. The point was in effect made by Hume, and discussed in 19.2: mere sensory experience of knocks and scrapes, etc. can't be supposed to provide any sort of adequate foundation of our actual concept of Causation, because our actual concept of Causation has essentially sensory-experience-transcending content. In the same way, experiences of the solidity of objects—experiences like the experience of one's arm resting on a table—cannot, *qua* sensory experiences, be supposed to convey the nature of solidity, or provide an adequate foundation of our actual concept of it. And the same goes, more generally, for our overall conception of a physical object and its properties. All these concepts are in essential respects *non-sensory concepts*, concepts of *non-sensory properties*, properties which have the following characteristic: it's an essential feature of our conception of them that they—their nature—can't possibly be fully revealed in sensory experience. Perhaps Hume's greatest failure is that he can't allow for this idea on the official terms of his theory of ideas.[29]

Evans puts the point very well in the passage quoted on p. 83, which I'll repeat here. He restricts his discussion to considering our concepts of those fundamental, non-sensory properties which are traditionally known as the primary properties (or qualities) of objects, but I doubt whether he would have quarrelled with the present suggestion, which is, in effect, that causation should be included in the class of fundamental, non-sensory properties of reality, although causation is not a member of the traditional class of primary qualities of objects.

After remarking that the class of non-sensory properties is extremely heterogeneous, Evans goes on to point out that it includes those properties 'constitutive of the idea of material substance as *space-occupying stuff*':

These include properties of bodies immediately consequential upon the idea of space-occupation—position, shape, size, motion; properties applicable to a body in virtue of the primary

---

[29] No more can Berkeley, or Locke, given his official 'imagist' conception of ideas—although there's a fruitful vagueness about some of Locke's formulations which can make him seem less far from the truth on this question than Berkeley or Hume. It is to Reid's great credit that he can allow for it.

properties of its spatial parts; and properties definable when these properties are combined with the idea of force (e.g. mass, weight, hardness).[30]

Clearly the notion of force—or, as I would wish to say, the notion of Causation—forms part of the interconnected system of non-sensory properties which we attribute to objects and which are essentially constitutive of our fundamental (pre-scientific) conception of their nature.

The way these [non-sensory] properties relate to experience is quite different from the way sensory properties relate to it. To grasp these primary [or non-sensory] properties, one must master a set of interconnected principles which make up an elementary theory—of primitive mechanics—into which these properties fit, and which alone gives them sense. One must grasp [implicitly, more or less explicitly] the idea of a unitary spatial framework in which both oneself and the bodies of which one has experience have a place, and through which they move continuously. One must learn of the conservation of matter in different shapes, of the identity of matter perceived from different points of view and through different modalities, and of the persistence of matter through gaps in observation. One must learn how bodies compete for the occupancy of positions in space, and the resistance one body may afford to another. And so on.

To say that these primary properties of matter are theoretical is not to explain or to mystify, but to highlight an analogy between the way our grasp of them rests upon implicit knowledge of a set of interconnected principles in which they are employed, and the way our understanding of such a property as electric charge rests upon explicit knowledge of a set of propositions more familiarly regarded as a theory. Certainly [and nb], to deny that these primary properties are *sensory* is not at all to deny that they are *sensible* or *observable*, for we are obviously able, after the appropriate training, to perceive the shape, motion, and hardness of things. The point is rather *that it is not possible to distil the concept of hardness solely out of the experiences produced by deformation of the skin which is brought into contact with a hard object, for it is not possible to distil out of such an experience the theory into which the concept fits.* It is no more possible to have a purely sensory concept of hardness than it is possible to...master the concept of electricity solely by learning to recognize electric shocks. And, though this is less obvious, it does not appear to be possible to regard the concept of the shape of a material thing—with all the propositions about its characteristic behaviour and interaction with other bodies which that implies—as the same as whatever shape concepts might be grounded in the colour mosaic thought to be given in immediate visual experience.[31]

Similarly, it is not possible to distil our ordinary concept of causation out of regular-succession experience, nor even out of regular-succession experience together with the direct experience of force in our everyday active and passive interaction with objects insisted on by the simple direct realists. It is no more possible to have a purely sensory concept of causation in the objects—of causation as it really is, Causation—than it is possible to master the concept of electricity solely by learning to recognize

---

[30] Evans 1980: 269; obviously only such fundamental, non-sensory properties of reality are of concern here. (There are many other non-sensory properties, such as this watch's property of belonging to Emilie.)

[31] Ibid. 269–70. Evans borrows the phrase 'primitive mechanics' from Daniels (1974: xiv).

electric shocks. And Hume was well aware of this. But, contrary to Hume, to say this is not to say that we can't have any genuine conception of it at all so far as it is more than regular succession. Here Hume was wrong. We can, and we do.

The world can't be fully intelligible to us given our limitations. We can leave room for the idea that there'll always be a sense in which the nature of causal interaction is unintelligible to us. But this creates no obstacle to supposing that there is a crucial sense in which our ordinary concept of causation is fundamentally correct.

References

Anscombe, G. E. M. (1971/1981) 'Causality and Determination' in *Metaphysics and the Philosophy of Mind* (Oxford: Blackwell).

Armstrong, D. M. (1983) *What is a Law of Nature?* (Cambridge: Cambridge University Press).

Ayer, A. J. (1973) *The Central Questions of Philosophy* (Harmondsworth: Penguin).

Baillargeon, R. (2004) 'Infants' reasoning about hidden objects: evidence for event-general and event-specific expectations' in *Developmental Science* 7.

Bayne, T. and Montague, M. (2011) 'Introduction' in *Cognitive Phenomenology*, ed. T. Bayne and M. Montague (Oxford: Oxford University Press).

Beauchamp, T. L. and Rosenberg, A. (1981) *Hume and the Problem of Causation* (New York: Oxford University Press).

Beebee, H. (2006) *Hume on Causation* (London: Routledge).

Berkeley, G. (1710/1975) *A Treatise Concerning the Principles of Human Knowledge* in *Philosophical Works*, ed. M. R. Ayers (London: Dent).

—— (1713/1998) *Three Dialogues between Hylas and Philonous*, ed. J. Dancy (Oxford: Oxford University Press).

—— (1721/1975) *De motu* in *Philosophical Works*, ed. M. R. Ayers (London: Dent).

Blackburn, S. (1984) *Spreading the Word* (Oxford: Clarendon Press).

—— (1990/1993) 'Hume and Thick Connexions', in *Essays in Quasi-Realism* (New York: Oxford University Press).

Boyle, R. (1681/1979) 'A Discourse of Things Above Reason, Enquiring whether a Philosopher should Admit there are Any such' in *Selected Philosophical Writings of Robert Boyle*, ed. M. A. Stewart (Manchester: Manchester University Press).

Brown, T. (1818) *Inquiry into the Relation of Cause and Effect*, third edn (London: Henry Bohn).

Buckle, S. (2001) *Hume's Enlightenment Tract: The Unity and Purpose of* An Enquiry concerning Human Understanding (Oxford: Oxford University Press).

Burke, E. (1757/1990) *A Philosophical Enquiry into the Origin of our Ideas of the Sublime and Beautiful*, ed. A. Phillips (Oxford: Oxford University Press).

Carnap, R. (1928/1967) *The Logical Structure of the World and Pseudoproblems in Philosophy* (London: Routledge and Kegan Paul).

Craig, E. J. (1987) *The Mind of God and the Works of Man* (Oxford: Clarendon Press).

Daniels, N. (1974) *Thomas Reid's Enquiry* (New York: Burt Franklin).

Descartes, R. (1644/1985) *The Principles of Philosophy*, in Descartes (1985), vol. 1.

—— (1985) *The Philosophical Writings of Descartes*, vols. 1 and 2, trans. J. Cottingham et al. (Cambridge: Cambridge University Press).

Dixon, T. (2010) 'Introduction' in *Thomas Brown: Selected Philosophical Writings* (Thorverton: Imprint Academic).

Evans, G. (1980/1985) *Collected Papers* (Oxford: Clarendon Press).

—— (1982) *The Varieties of Reference* (Oxford: Clarendon Press).

Everitt, N. (1991) 'Strawson on Laws and Regularities' *Analysis* 51.

Flew, A. (1961) *Hume's Philosophy of Belief* (London: Routledge and Kegan Paul).

Foster, J. (1982) *The Case for Idealism* (London: Routledge and Kegan Paul).

——(1982–3) 'Induction, Explanation, and Natural Necessity' *Proceedings of the Aristotelian Society* 83.

——(1985) 'Berkeley on the Physical World' in *Essays on Berkeley*, ed. J. Foster and H. Robinson (Oxford: Clarendon Press).

——(1985) and Robinson, H. eds. *Essays on Berkeley* (Oxford: Clarendon Press).

Garrett, D. (2009) 'Hume's Theory of Causation: Realist, Reductionist, or Projectivist?' in *The Oxford Handbook of Causation*, eds. H. Beebee, P. Menzies, C. Hitchcock (Oxford University Press).

Hamlyn, D. W. (1987) *A History of Western Philosophy* (London: Penguin).

Hardy, G. H. and Wright, E. M. (1960) *Theory of Numbers*, 4th edn (Oxford: Oxford University Press).

Harré, R. and Madden, E. H. (1975) *Causal Powers* (Oxford: Blackwell).

Harris, J. (2005a) *Of Liberty and Necessity: The Free Will Debate in 18th-Century British Philosophy* (Oxford: Oxford University Press).

——(2005b) 'The Reception of David Hume in Nineteenth-Century British Philosophy' *The Reception of David Hume in Europe* (London: Thoemmes Continuum).

Hill, J. (2012) 'How Hume became the "new" Hume: A developmental approach' *The Journal of Scottish Philosophy* 10.2.

Hume, D. (1727–76/1932) *The Letters of David Hume*, vols 1 and 2, ed. J. Y. T. Greig (Oxford: Clarendon Press).

——(1737–76/1978) *New Letters of David Hume*, ed. R. Klibansky and E. C. Mossner (Oxford: Oxford University Press).

——(1739–40/1978) *A Treatise of Human Nature*, ed. L. A. Selby-Bigge and P. H. Nidditch (Oxford: Oxford University Press).

——(1739–40/2000) *A Treatise of Human Nature*, ed. D. F. Norton and M. Norton (Oxford: Clarendon Press).

——(1741–2/1985) *Essays, Moral, Political, and Literary* (Indianapolis: Liberty Classics).

——(1742/1985) 'The Sceptic' in *Essays, Moral, Political, and Literary* (Indianapolis: Liberty Classics).

——(1745/1967) *Letter from a gentleman to his friend in Edinburgh*, ed. E. C. Mossner and J. V. Price (Edinburgh: Edinburgh University Press).

——(1748–51/1975) *Enquiries Concerning Human Understanding*, ed. L. A. Selby-Bigge (Oxford: Oxford University Press).

——(1748/2000) *An Enquiry concerning Human Understanding*, ed. T. Beauchamp (Oxford: Clarendon Press).

——(1751/1932) Letter to Sir Gilbert Elliot (10 March) in *The Letters of David Hume*, vol. 1.

Hume, D. (1754/1932) Letter to John Stewart (February) in *The Letters of David Hume*, vol. 1.

——(1779) *Dialogues Concerning Natural Religion*, 2nd edition (London).

——(1779/1947) *Dialogues Concerning Natural Religion*, ed. N. Kemp Smith (Edinburgh: Nelson).

Jackson, F. (1977) 'A Causal Theory of Counterfactuals' *Australasian Journal of Philosophy* 55.

Kail, P. (2007a) 'How to Understand Hume's Realism' in *The New Hume Debate* (London: Routledge).

—— (2007b) *Projection and Realism in Hume's Philosophy* (Oxford: Clarendon Press).

Kant, I. (1781–7/1933) *Critique of Pure Reason*, trans. N. Kemp Smith (London: Macmillan).

——(1783/1953) *Prolegomena*, trans. P. G. Lucas, Manchester: Manchester University Press).

Kemp Smith, N. (1941) *The Philosophy of David Hume* (London: Macmillan).

Kneale, W. (1949) *Probability and Induction* (Oxford: Clarendon Press).

Kripke, S. A. (1982) *Wittgenstein on Rules and Private Language: An Elementary Exposition* (Oxford: Blackwell).

Levine, M. (1986–7) 'Mackie's Account of Necessity in Causation', *Proceedings of the Aristotelian Society* 87.

Lewis, D. (1986a) 'Introduction' in *Philosophical Papers* (New York: Oxford University Press).

——(1986b) *On the Plurality of Worlds* (Oxford: Blackwell).

——(1972) 'Psychophysical and Theoretical Identifications', *Australasian Journal of Philosophy* 50.

Livingston, D. W. (1984) *Hume's Philosophy of Common Life* (Chicago: University of Chicago Press).

Locke, J. (1689–1700/1975) *An Essay Concerning Human Understanding*, ed. P. H. Nidditch (Oxford: Clarendon Press).

Mackie, J. L. (1974) *The Cement of the Universe: A Study of Causation* (Oxford: Clarendon Press).

Madden, E. H. *see* Harré, R.

Malebranche, N. (1674–5/1980) *The Search after Truth*, trans. T. M. Lennon and P. J. Olscamp (Columbus, OH: Ohio State University Press).

McCracken, C. J. (1983) *Malebranche and British Philosophy* (Oxford: Clarendon Press).

McGinn, C. (1974–5) 'A Note on the Essence of Natural Kinds' *Analysis* 35.

——(1983) *The Subjective View* (Oxford: Clarendon Press).

—— (1989) 'Can We Solve the Mind–Body Problem?' *Mind* 98.

——(1996) *The Character of Mind*, second edn (Oxford: Oxford University Press).

McMullin, E. (1985) 'A Case for Scientific Realism' in J. Leplin, ed. *Scientific Realism* (Berkeley: University of California Press).

Mill, J. S. (1865/1969) 'Auguste Comte and Positivism' in *Essays on Ethics, Religion and Society*, ed. J. Robson (Toronto: University of Toronto Press).

Molnar, G. (1969) 'Kneale's Argument Revisited', *Philosophical Review* 78.

Montague, M. *see* Bayne, T.

Nagel, T. (1979) 'Panpsychism' in *Mortal Questions* (Cambridge: Cambridge University Press).

——(1986) *The View from Nowhere* (New York: Oxford University Press).

Newton, I. (1661–1727/1959–77) *Correspondence*, ed. H. W. Turnball and others (Cambridge: Cambridge University Press).

——(1687–1726/1934) *Principia*, trans. A. Motte and F. Cajori (Berkeley: University of California Press).

O'Hear, A. (1985) *What Philosophy is: An Introduction to Contemporary Philosophy* (Harmondsworth: Penguin).

Parfit, D. (1984) *Reasons and Persons* (Oxford: Oxford University Press).

Peacocke, C. (1988) 'The Limits of Intelligibility: A Post-Verificationist Proposal' *Philosophical Review* 97/4.

Psillos, S. (2009) 'Regularity Theories' in *The Oxford Handbook of Causation*, ed. H. Beebee, P. Menzies & C. Hitchcock (Oxford: Oxford University Press).

——(2011) 'Regularities all the way down: Thomas Brown's Philosophy of Causation' in K. Allen and T. Stoneham eds. *Causation and Modern Philosophy* (London: Routledge).

Putnam, H. (1981) *Reason, Truth, and History* (Cambridge: Cambridge University Press).

Quine, W. V. (1955/1966) 'Posits and Reality' in *The Ways of Paradox* (New York: Random House).

——(1956/1966) 'Quantifiers and Propositional Attitudes' in *The Ways of Paradox* (New York: Random House).

——(1969) 'Natural Kinds' in *Ontological Relativity and Other Essays* (New York: Columbia).

Ramsey, F. (1929/1990) 'Theories' in *Philosophical Papers*, ed. H. Mellor (Cambridge: Cambridge University Press).

Reid, T. (1764/1997) *An Inquiry into the Human Mind*, ed. D. Brookes (Edinburgh: Edinburgh University Press).

——(1785/2010) *Essays on the Active Powers of the Human Mind*, ed. K. Haakonssen and James A. Harris (Edinburgh: Edinburgh University Press).

Rosenberg, A. *see* Beauchamp, T. L.

Russell, B. (1927/1992) *An Outline of Philosophy* (London: Routledge).

Schacht, R. (1984) *Classical Modern Philosophers: Descartes to Kant* (London: Routledge and Kegan Paul).

Shepherd, M. (1824) *An Essay upon the Relation of Cause and Effect, controverting the doctrine of Mr. Hume, concerning the nature of that relation; with Observations upon the opinions of Dr. Brown and Mr. Lawrence connected with the same subject* (London: Hookham).

Shoemaker, S. (1984) 'The Inverted Spectrum' in *Identity, Cause, and Mind* (Cambridge: Cambridge University Press).

Skrbina, D. (2005) *Panpsychism in the West* (Cambridge, MA: MIT Press).

Spelke, E. (1990) 'Principles of Object Perception' *Cognitive Science* 14.

Strawson, G. (1987/2008) 'Realism and Causation' in G. Strawson *Real Materialism and Other Essays* (Oxford: Oxford University Press).

——(1989/2008) '"Red" and Red' in G. Strawson *Real Materialism and Other Essays* (Oxford: Oxford University Press).

Strawson, G. (1991) 'The Contingent Reality of Natural Necessity', *Analysis* 51/4.

——(2000a/2008) 'Epistemology, semantics, ontology, and David Hume' in G. Strawson *Real Materialism and Other Essays* (Oxford: Oxford University Press).

——(2000b/2008) 'David Hume: Objects and Power' in G. Strawson *Real Materialism and Other Essays* (Oxford: Oxford University Press).

——(2002/2008) 'Knowledge of the World' (revised as 'Can we know the nature of reality as it is in itself?') in G. Strawson, *Real Materialism and Other Essays* (Oxford: Oxford University Press).

——(2011) *The Evident Connexion: Hume on Personal Identity* (Oxford University Press).

——(2013) 'On "Humean": a note' http://www.academia.edu/4942420/.

Strawson, P. F. (1966) *The Bounds of Sense* (London: Methuen).

——(1985) 'Causation and Explanation' in B. Vermazen and M. B. Hintikka, eds. *Essays on Davidson: Action and Events* (Oxford: Clarendon Press).

Stroud, B. (1977) *Hume* (London: Routledge and Kegan Paul).

Tooley, M. (1987) *Causation: A Realist Account* (Oxford: Clarendon Press).

van Fraassen, B. (1980) *The Scientific Image* (Oxford: Clarendon Press).

Walker, R. (1978) *Kant* (London: Routledge and Kegan Paul).

Weissmann, D. (1965) *Dispositional Properties* (Carbondale, IL: Southern Illinois University Press).

Wittgenstein, L. (1953) *Philosophical Investigations* (Oxford: Blackwell).

Woolhouse, R. (1988) *The Empiricists* (Oxford: Oxford University Press).

Wright, J. P. (1983) *The sceptical realism of David Hume* (Manchester: Manchester University Press).

——(1995) 'Critical Review of *Hume's Theory of Consciousness*, by Wayne Waxman' *Hume Studies* 21.

——(2000) 'Hume's Causal Realism: Recovering a Traditional Interpretation' in *The New Hume: for and against realist readings of Hume on causation*, ed. R. Read and K. Richman (London: Routledge).

——(2005) 'The Scientific Reception of Hume's Theory of Causation: establishing the Positivist Interpretation in Early Nineteenth-Century Scotland' in P. Jones ed. *The Reception of David Hume in Europe* (London: Thoemmes Continuum).

Index

This index does not cite every occurrence of every listed term or topic. Page numbers in bold type indicate the place at which a term is introduced or defined or the main discussion of a topic.

Index of Passages from Hume